# John Donne

## SELECTED PROSE

# John Donne
# SELECTED PROSE

CHOSEN BY
EVELYN SIMPSON

EDITED BY HELEN GARDNER
AND TIMOTHY HEALY

OXFORD
AT THE CLARENDON PRESS
1967

*Oxford University Press, Ely House, London W. 1*

GLASGOW NEW YORK TORONTO MELBOURNE WELLINGTON
CAPE TOWN SALISBURY IBADAN NAIROBI LUSAKA ADDIS ABABA
BOMBAY CALCUTTA MADRAS KARACHI LAHORE DACCA
KUALA LUMPUR HONG KONG TOKYO

PRINTED IN GREAT BRITAIN

# PREFACE

WHEN Evelyn Simpson died in 1963, at the age of seventy-eight, she was engaged in preparing an anthology of Donne's prose. She had projected making a selection many years before, but had laid her notes for it aside. With the completion in 1962 of the California edition of the *Sermons*, the moment seemed ripe for an anthology to be published, and the Clarendon Press suggested to her that she should provide one. She took up the work in the last year of her life, and, at her death, notes for it were found among her papers. It seemed to me that it would be a fitting memorial to her life and work to complete the anthology, and I was fortunate in that the Revd. Timothy Healy, S.J., who was in Oxford preparing an edition of *Ignatius His Conclave*, very generously agreed to assist me in the task of editing.

In this selection from Donne's prose, every passage that Evelyn Simpson had marked for inclusion is included. In one section, the Letters, she had plainly made no more than a beginning in selecting passages; and, most unfortunately, in the Sermons it was obvious that two or more pages of her notes were missing. The selection from the Letters is, therefore, almost wholly ours. For the Sermons, we have had to supplement what was found in the papers. We have included all the passages that Evelyn Simpson had marked; but in some cases we have expanded the passage she chose. We have supplemented her imperfect list of passages by noting which sermons and which passages she singled out for special praise in the introductions to the ten volumes of the California edition. We have tried to cover the range of Donne's style as a preacher, and to represent his thought. In addition to striking short passages, we have included a number of longer extracts in which the reader can see Donne deploying an argument, and we have also printed two sermons in full. In selecting from the Sermons and the Letters we have kept particularly in mind what will interest students of Donne's poetry and have deliberately included many passages for the parallels they provide with the poems.

There was little indication in the notes that she left of how much annotation Evelyn Simpson had intended to provide. The introductions to the sections and the annotations are ours; but they are mainly based on information provided by her in *The Prose Works of John Donne* (second edition, 1948) and in the masterly introductions to the separate volumes of the California edition of the Sermons. Where her exact words are used, they are given in quotation marks; and, unless square brackets are employed, the information given is taken from her work. She had obviously intended to provide headings for passages selected from the minor works where the text did not provide one. We have carried out her intention here, thinking the provision of headings will assist readers to find passages they are looking for.

Although, as editors, Fr. Healy and I must take final responsibility for the selection of passages and for the introductory material and annotations in this volume, it is so entirely based on Evelyn Simpson's work that it is proper that it should appear under her name. It is our hope that it will make more widely available the fruits of her lifelong, devoted study of Donne's prose, the first results of which appeared in the original edition of her *A Study of the Prose Works of John Donne* in 1924, and which culminated in the completion of the ten noble volumes of the edition of the Sermons in 1962.

We are greatly indebted to the University of California Press for allowing us to excerpt so fully from the California edition of *The Sermons of John Donne*, edited by G. R. Potter and Evelyn M. Simpson, 10 vols., 1953–62. We have to thank Miss Elizabeth Wade White, who assisted Evelyn Simpson in her work on the *Sermons*, for her care and patience in reading the proofs.

HELEN GARDNER

*Oxford*

# CONTENTS

# CONTENTS

# CONTENTS

# NOTE ON THE TEXTS

A LIST of references will be found on pp. 393–7. Where no modern editions exist and we have printed from the original editions, or from transcripts of manuscripts, or from editions that follow the typography of the original editions, we have modernized the use of i/j and u/v. We have throughout adopted the modern distinction between *than* and *then*, *their* and *there*, *to* and *too*, and *of* and *off*, and in a few cases, where retention of the spelling of the original might mislead, we have altered it; e.g. we print *coarse* for Donne's habitual spelling *course*. We have silently corrected misprints and patent scribal errors, and occasionally emended punctuation.

# CHRONOLOGY OF IMPORTANT DATES

Dean of St. Paul's: moved to Deanery                    19 November 1621
Seriously ill: composed *Devotions* (published 1624)             Winter 1623
Appointed Vicar of St. Dunstan's in the West                  March 1624
Died at Deanery                                       31 March 1631
*Poems*                                                       1633
*LXXX Sermons*, with first version of Walton's *Life of Donne*
    prefixed                                                  1640
*Biathanatos*                                               [1646]
*Fifty Sermons*                                              1649
*Letters*                                                    1651
*Essays in Divinity*                                         1651
*XXVI Sermons*                                               1661

————

Edmund Gosse, *The Life and Letters of John Donne*, 2 vols.        1899
H. J. C. Grierson, *Poems of John Donne*, 2 vols.                   1912

# PARADOXES AND PROBLEMS

B

THE *Paradoxes and Problems* were first printed, under the title *Juvenilia: or certaine Paradoxes, and Problemes, written by J. Donne*, for Henry Seyle in 1633, and reprinted in the same year. These first two editions contained only eleven Paradoxes and ten Problems. A third, enlarged edition, containing twelve Paradoxes and seventeen Problems, was published by John Donne the Younger in 1652. In 1923 the Nonesuch Press issued an edition, with a preface by Sir Geoffrey Keynes; its text followed the second edition, amplified from the edition of 1652, and by the addition of an eighteenth Problem from manuscript.

Many of the manuscript collections of Donne's poems include the *Paradoxes and Problems*, which are also extant in manuscript independently of the poems. The manuscript that Seyle used was a poor one, and the printed text is in many places obviously corrupt. It also omits clauses and passages preserved in the manuscripts that are plainly authentic. Evelyn Simpson was at work for many years on an edition of the *Juvenilia*, but was forced to abandon it in order to concentrate on her edition of the Sermons. An edition, making use of her work, is announced as forthcoming by the Renaissance English Text Society, but we are unfortunately unable to use its text. We have, therefore, printed from the Nonesuch edition of 1923; but we have adopted into it from the manuscripts the readings that Evelyn Simpson recorded with approval in her two articles on the manuscripts of the *Paradoxes and Problems* (*R.E.S.* iii, April 1927, and x, July and October 1934). We have not included any of the additional passages found in manuscript, or attempted the very complicated task of editing the *Juvenilia*, but have contented ourselves with correcting the obvious errors of the printed text. Conjectural emendations are printed in square brackets. We are regretfully aware that the text we present is unsatisfactory.

The *Paradoxes* are probably Donne's earliest prose works, and belong mainly to his time as a student at Lincoln's Inn. Latin Paradoxes had been written for centuries, but the English 'paradox' as a literary form was derived from Italy. The *Paradossi* of Ortensio Lando were first published in 1543. They were translated into French by Charles Estienne [Stephanus], and twelve of them were translated into English by Anthony Munday, who published them in 1593 as *The Defence of Contraries*. It is likely that most of the Paradoxes are early, but some may be later in date, and some of the Problems certainly are. A reference to Kepler dates one Problem after the publication of *De Stella Nova in Cygno* at Prague in 1606, and the Problem about Raleigh must have been written after his trial in 1603. There are references to 'problems' in Donne's letters to Goodyer during his Mitcham period; see, for instance, Letter 15 (p. 126) and also Letter 11 (p. 122). Donne was apparently willing to amuse himself and his friends by composing these squibs and trifles during most of the time that he was writing his poetry.

# PARADOXES AND PROBLEMS

## 1. A Defence of Womens Inconstancy

THAT Women are *Inconstant*, I with any man confesse, but that *Inconstancy* is a bad quality, I against any man will maintaine: For every thing as it is one better than another, so is it fuller of *change*; The *Heavens* themselves continually turne, the *Starres* move, the *Moone* changeth; *Fire* whirleth, *Ayre* flyeth, *Water* ebbs and flowes, the face of the *Earth* altereth her lookes, *time* stayes not; the Colour that is most light, will take most dyes: so in Men, they that have the most reason are the most alterable in their designes, and the darkest or most ignorant, do seldomest change; therefore Women changing more than Men, have also more *Reason*. They cannot be immutable like stockes, like stones, like the Earths dull Center; Gold that lyeth still, rusteth; Water, corrupteth; Aire that moveth not, poysoneth; then why should that which is the perfection of other things, be imputed to Women as greatest imperfection? Because thereby they deceive men. Are not your wits pleased with those jests, which coozen your expectation? You can call it Pleasure to be beguil'd in troubles, and in the most excellent toy in the world, you call it Treachery: I would you had your *Mistresses* so constant, that they would never change, no not so much as their *smocks*, then should you see what sluttish vertue, *Constancy* were. *Inconstancy* is a most commendable and cleanly quality, and Women in this quality are farre more absolute than the Heavens, than the Starres, Moone, or any thing beneath it; for long observation hath pickt certainety out of their mutability. The Learned are so well acquainted with the Starres, Signes and Planets, that they make them but Characters, to read the meaning of the Heaven in his owne forehead. Every simple Fellow can bespeake the change of the *Moone* a great while beforehand: but I would faine have the learnedst

man so skilfull, as to tell when the simplest Woman meaneth to
varie. Learning affords no rules to know, much lesse knowledge to
rule the minde of a Woman: For as *Philosophy* teacheth us, that *Light
things doe alwayes tend upwards*, and *heavy things decline downeward*;
Experience teacheth us otherwise, that the disposition of a *Light*
Woman, is to fall downe, the nature of Women being contrary to
all Art and Nature. Women are like *Flies*, which feed among us at
our Table, or *Fleas* sucking our very blood, who leave not our most
retired places free from their familiarity, yet for all their fellowship
will they never bee tamed nor commanded by us. Women are like
the *Sunne*, which is violently carryed one way, yet hath a proper
course contrary: so though they, by the mastery of some over-
ruling churlish Husbands, are forced to his Byas, yet have they a
motion of their owne, which their Husbands never know of. It is
the nature of nice and fastidious mindes to know things onely to
bee weary of them: Women by their slye *changeablenesse*, and
pleasing doublenesse, prevent even the mislike of those, for they
can never be so well knowne, but that there is still more unknowne.
Every Woman is a *Science*; for hee that plods upon a Woman all his
life long, shall at length find himselfe short of the knowledge of her:
they are borne to take downe the pride of wit, and ambition of
wisedome, making *fooles* wise in the adventuring to winne them,
*wisemen* fooles in conceit of losing their labours; witty men starke
mad, being confounded with their uncertaineties. *Philosophers* write
against them for spight, not desert, that having attained to some
knowledge in all other things, in them onely they know nothing,
but are meerely ignorant: *Active* and *Experienced* men raile against
them, because they love in their livelesse and decrepit age, when all
goodnesse leaves them. These envious *Libellers* ballad against them,
because having nothing in themselves able to deserve their love, they
maliciously discommend all they cannot obtaine, thinking to make
men beleeve they know much, because they are able to dispraise
much, and rage against *Inconstancy*, when they were never admitted
into so much favour as to be forsaken. In mine Opinion such men
are happy that Women are *Inconstant*, for so may they chance to bee
beloved of some excellent Women (when it comes to their turne)
out of their *Inconstancy* and mutability, though not out of their owne

desert. And what reason is there to clog any Woman with one Man, bee hee never so singular? Women had rather, and it is farre better and more Judiciall to enjoy all the vertues in severall Men, than but some of them in one, for otherwise they lose their taste, like divers sorts of meat minced together in one dish: and to have all excellencies in one Man (if it were possible) is *Confusion* and *Diversity*. Now who can deny, but such as are obstinately bent to undervalue their worth, are those that have not soule enough to comprehend their excellency, Women being the most excellentest Creatures, in that Man is able to subject all things else, and to grow wise in every thing, but still persists a foole in Woman? The greatest *Scholler*, if hee once take a Wife, is found so unlearned, that he must begin his *Horne-Booke*, and all is by *Inconstancy*. To conclude therefore; this name of *Inconstancy*, which hath so much beene poysoned with slaunders, ought to bee changed into *variety*, for the which the world is so delightfull, *and a Woman for that the most delightfull thing in this world.*

## 2. That Women ought to paint

*Foulenesse* is *Lothsome*: can that be so which helpes it? who forbids his Beloved to gird in her waste? to mend by shooing her uneven lamenesse? to burnish her teeth? or to perfume her breath? yet that the *Face* bee more precisely regarded, it concernes more: For as open confessing sinners are alwaies punished, but the wary and concealing offenders without witnesse doe it also without punishment; so the secret parts needs the lesse respect; but of the *Face*, discovered to all Examinations and survayes, there is not too nice a Jealousie. Nor doth it onely draw the busie eyes, but it is subject to the divinest touch of all, to *kissing*, the strange and mysticall union of soules. If shee should prostitute her selfe to a more unworthy Man than thy selfe, how earnestly and justly wouldst thou exclaime? [Then] for want of this easier and ready way of repairing, to betray her body to ruine and deformity (the tyrannous *Ravishers*, and sodaine *Deflourers* of all Women) what a heynous Adultery is it? What thou lovest in her *face* is *colour*, and *painting* gives that, but thou hatest it, not because it is, but because thou knowest it. Foole, whom ignorance makes happy; the Starres, the Sunne, the Skye whom thou admirest, alas, have no *colour*, but are faire, because they seeme to bee coloured: If this seeming will not satisfie thee in her, thou hast good assurance of her *colour*, when thou seest her *lay* it on. If her *face* bee *painted* on a Boord or Wall, thou wilt love it, and the Boord, and the Wall: Canst thou loath it then when it speakes, smiles, and kisses, because it is *painted*? Are wee not more delighted with seeing Birds, Fruites, and Beasts *painted* than wee are with Naturalls? And doe wee not with pleasure behold the *painted* shape of Monsters and Divels, whom true, wee durst not regard? Wee repaire the ruines of our houses, but first cold tempests warnes us of it, and bytes us through it; wee mend the wracke and staines of our Apparell, but first our eyes, and other bodies are offended; but by this providence of Women, this is prevented. If in *kissing* or *breathing* upon her, the *painting* fall off, thou art angry. Wilt thou be so, if it sticke on? Thou didst love her; if thou beginnest to hate her, then 'tis because shee is not *painted*. If thou wilt say now, thou didst hate her before, thou didst hate her and love her together. Bee constant in something, and love her who shewes her great *love* to thee, in taking this paines to seeme *lovely* to thee.

## 3. That by Discord things increase

*Nullos esse Deos, inane Cælum*
*Affirmat Cælius, probatque quod se*
*Factum vidit, dum negat haec, beatum.*

So I assevere this the more boldly, because while I maintaine it, and feele the *Contrary repugnancies* and *adverse fightings* of the *Elements* in my Body, my Body increaseth; and whilst I differ from common opinions by this *Discord*, the number of my *Paradoxes* increaseth. All the rich benefits we can frame to our selves in *Concord*, is but an *Even* conservation of things; in which *Evennesse* wee can expect no *change*, no *motion*; therefore no *increase* or *augmentation*, which is a *member of motion*. And if this *unity* and *peace* can give *increase* to things, how mightily is *discord* and *war* to that purpose, which are indeed the onely ordinary *Parents* of *peace*. *Discord* is never so barren that it affords no fruit; for the *fall* of one *estate* is at the worst the *increaser* of another, because it is as impossible to finde a *discommodity* without *advantage*, as to finde *Corruption* without *Generation*: But it is the *Nature* and *Office* of *Concord* to *preserve* onely, which property when it leaves, it differs from it selfe, which is the greatest *discord* of all. All *Victories* and *Emperies* gained by *warre*, and all *Judiciall* decidings of doubts in *peace*, I doe claime children of *Discord*. And who can deny but *Controversies* in *Religion* are growne greater by *discord*, and not the *Controversie*, but *Religion* it selfe: For in a *troubled misery* Men are alwaies more *Religious* than in a *secure peace*. The number of *good* men, the onely charitable nourishers of *Concord*, wee see is thinne, and daily melts and waines; but of *bad discording* it is infinite, and growes hourely. Wee are ascertained of all *Disputable* doubts, onely by *arguing* and differing in *Opinion*, and if formall *disputation* (which is but a painted, counterfeit, and dissembled *discord*) can worke us this benefit, what shall not a full and maine *discord* accomplish? Truely me thinkes I owe a *devotion*, yea a *sacrifice* to *discord*, for casting that *Ball* upon *Ida*, and for all that businesse of Troy, whom ruin'd I admire more than *Babylon*, *Rome*, or *Quinzay*. Nor are removed *Corners* fulfilled onely with her *fame*, but with *Cities* and *Thrones* planted by her *Fugitives*. Lastly, between *Cowardice* and *despaire*, *Valour* is gendred; and so the *Discord* of *Extreames* begets all vertues, but of the *like things* there is no issue without a miracle:

> *Uxor pessima, pessimus maritus*
> *Miror tam male convenire.*

Hee wonders that betweene two so *like*, there could be any *discord*, yet perchance for all this *discord* there was nere the lesse *increase*.

## 4. That good is more common than evill

I HAVE not been so pittifully tired with any *vanity*, as with silly *Old Mens* exclaiming against these times, and extolling their owne: Alas! they betray themselves, for if the *times* be *changed*, their manners have changed them. But their senses are to *pleasures*, as *sick Mens* tastes are to *Liquors*; for indeed no *new thing* is done in the *world*, all things are what, and as they were, and *Good* is as ever it was, more plenteous, and must of necessity be *more common than evill*, because it hath this for *nature* and *perfection* to bee *common*. It makes *Love* to all *Natures*, all, all affect it. So that in the *Worlds* early *Infancy*, there was a time when nothing was *evill*, but if this *World* shall suffer *dotage* in the extreamest *crookednesse* thereof, there shall be no time when nothing shal be *good*. It dares appeare and spread, and glister in the *World*, but *evill* buries it selfe in night and dark-nesse, and is chastised and suppressed when *good* is cherished and rewarded. And as *Imbroderers*, *Lapidaries*, and other *Artisans*, can by all things adorne their workes; and by adding better things, better their shew, *Lustre* and *Eminency*; so *good* doth not onely prostitute her *amiablenesse* to all, but refuses no ayd, no not of her utter con-trary *evill*, that shee may bee the more *common* to us. For *evill manners* are *parents* of *good Lawes*; and in every *evill* there is an *excellency*, which (in common speech) we call *good*. For the fashions of *habits*, for our moving in *gestures*, for phrases in our *speech*, we say they were *good* as long as they were used, that is, as long as they were *common*; and wee eate, wee walke, onely when it is, or seemes *good* to doe so. All *faire*, all *profitable*, all *vertuous*, is *good*, and these three things I thinke embrace all things, but their utter *contraries*; of which also [*foule*] may be *rich* and *vertuous*; *poore* may bee *vertuous* and *faire*; *vitious* may be *faire* and *rich*; so that *good* hath this good meanes to be *common*, that some subjects she can possesse intirely; and in subjects poysoned with *evill*, she can humbly stoop to accom-pany the *evill*. And of *indifferent* things many things are become perfectly good by being *common*, as *customes* by use are made binding *Lawes*. But I remember nothing that is therefore *ill*, because it is *common*, but *Women*, of whom also; *They that are most common, are the best of that Occupation they professe.*

## 5. That all things kill themselves

To affect, yea to effect their owne *death* all *living* things are im-portuned, not by *Nature* only which perfects them, but by *Art* and *Education*, which perfects her. *Plants* quickened and inhabited by the most unworthy *soule*, which therefore neither *will* nor *worke*, affect an *end*, a *perfection*, a *death*; this they spend their *spirits* to attaine, this attained, they languish and wither. And by how much more they are by mans *Industry* warmed, cherished, and pampered; so much the more early they climbe to this *perfection*, this *death*. And if amongst *Men* not to *defend* be to *kill*, what a hainous *selfe-murther* is it, not to *defend it selfe*. This *defence* because *Beasts* neglect, they kill themselves, because they exceed us in *number*, *strength*, and a *lawlesse liberty*: yea, of *Horses* and other beasts, they that inherit *most courage* by being bred of *gallantest parents*, and by *Artificial nursing* are bettered, will runne to their owne *deaths*, neither sollicited by *spurres* which they need not, nor by *honour* which they apprehend not. If then the *valiant* kill himselfe, who can excuse the *coward*? Or how shall *Man* bee free from this, since the *first Man* taught us this, except we cannot kill our selves, because he kill'd us all. Yet lest something should repaire this *Common ruine*, we daily kill our *bodies* with *surfeits*, and our mindes with *anguishes*. Of our *powers*, *remembring* kils our *memory*; Of *Affections*, *Lusting* our *lust*; Of *vertues*, *Giving* kils *liberality*. And if these kill themselves, they do it in their best & supreme *perfection*: for after *perfection* immediately follows *excesse*, which changeth the natures and the names, and makes them not the same things. If then the best things kill themselves soonest, (for no *affection* endures, and all things labour to this *perfection*) all travell to their owne *death*, yea the frame of the whole *World*, if it were possible for *God* to be *idle*, yet because it *began*, must *dye*. Then in this *idlenesse* imagined in *God*, what could kill the *world* but it selfe, since *out of it, nothing is*?

## 6. That it is possible to find some vertue in Some Women

I AM not of that feard *Impudence* that I dare defend *Women*, or pronounce them good; yet we see *Physitians* allow some *vertue* in every *poyson*. Alas! why should we except *Women*? since certainely, they are good for *Physicke* at least, so as some *wine* is good for a *feaver*. And though they be the *Occasioners* of many sinnes, they are also the

*Punishers* and *Revengers* of the same sinnes: For I have seldome seene one which consumes his *substance* and *body* upon them, escape *diseases*, or *beggery*; and this is their *Justice*. And if *suum cuique dare*, bee the fulfilling of all *Civill Justice*, they are *most just*; for they deny that which is theirs to no man.

*Tanquam non liceat nulla puella negat.*

And who may doubt of great wisdome in them, that doth but observe with how much labour and cunning our *Justicers* and other *dispensers* of the *Lawes* study to imbrace them: and how zealously our *Preachers* dehort men from them, onely by urging their *subtilties*, and *policies*, and *wisedome*, which are in them? Or who can deny them a good measure of *Fortitude*, if hee consider how *valiant men* they have overthrowne, and being themselves overthrowne, how much and how patiently they *beare*? And though they bee most *intemperate*, I care not, for I undertooke to furnish them with *some vertue*, not with *all*. *Necessity*, which makes even bad things good, prevailes also for them, for wee must say of them, as of some sharpe pinching *Lawes*; If men were free from *infirmities*, they were needlesse. These or none must serve for *reasons*, and it is my great happinesse that *Examples* prove not *Rules*, for to confirme this *Opinion*, the World yeelds not *one Example*.

## 7. That Old men are more fantastike than Young

WHO reads this *Paradox* but thinks mee more *fantastike* now, than I was yesterday, when I did not think thus: And if one day make this sensible change in mee what will the burthen of many yeeres? To bee *fantastike* in *young men* is *conceiptfull distemperature*, and a *witty madnesse*; but in *old men*, whose senses are withered, it becomes *naturall*, therefore more full and perfect. For as when wee *sleepe* our *fancy* is most strong; so it is in *age*, which is a *slumber* of the *deepe sleepe of death*. They taxe us of *Inconstancy*, which in themselves *young* they allowed; so that reprooving that which they did approove, their *Inconstancy* exceedeth ours, because they have changed *once more* than wee. Yea, they are more idlely busied in *conceited apparell* than wee; for we, when we are *melancholy*, weare *blacke*; when *lusty*, *greene*; when *forsaken*, *tawney*; pleasing our owne *inward* affections, leaving them to others indifferent; but they prescribe *lawes*, and constraine the *Noble*, the *Scholer*, the *Merchant*, and all *Estates* to a certaine *habit*. The *old men* of our time have changed with patience their owne *bodies*, much of their *lawes*, much of their *languages*; yea their *Religion*, yet they accuse us. To be *Amorous* is proper and *naturall* in a *young man*, but in an *old man* most *fantastike*. And that *ridling humour* of *Jealousie*, which seekes and would not finde, which requires and repents his knowledge, is in them most common, yet most *fantastike*. Yea, that which falls never in *young men*, is in them most *fantastike* and *naturall*, that is, *Covetousnesse*; even at their *journeyes end* to make great provision. Is any *habit* of *young men* so *fantastike*, as in the hottest seasons to be *double-gowned* or *hooded* like our *Elders*? Or seemes it so *ridiculous* to weare long haire, as to weare *none*. Truely, as among the *Philosophers*, the *Skeptike*, which *doubts all*, was more contentious, than either the *Dogmatike* which *affirmes*, or *Academike* which *denyes all*; so are these uncertaine *Elders*, which both [call] them *fantastike* which follow others *inventions*, and them also which are led by their owne humorous suggestion, more *fantastike* than other.

# 8. That Nature is our worst Guide

SHAL she be *guide* to all *Creatures*, which is her selfe one? Or if she also have a *guide*, shall any *Creature* have a better guide than wee? The affections of *lust* and *anger*, yea even to *erre* is *naturall*; shall we follow these? Can shee be a good *guide* to us, which hath corrupted not us onely but her selfe? Was not the *first man*, by the desire of *knowledge*, corrupted even in the *whitest integrity* of *Nature*? And did not *Nature* (if *Nature* did any thing) infuse into him this desire of *knowledge*, and so this *corruption* in him, into us? If by *Nature* wee shall understand our *essence*, our *definition*, our *Reasonablenesse*, then this being alike common to all (the *Idiot* and the *Wizard* being equally *reasonable*) why should not all men having equally all one *nature*, follow one course? Or if we shall understand our *inclinations*; alas! how unable a guide is that which followes the *temperature* of our slimie *bodies*? for we cannot say that we derive our *inclinations*, our *mindes*, or *soules* from our *Parents* by any way: to say that it is *all from all*, is *error* in *reason*, for then with the first nothing remaines; or is a *part from all*, is *errour* in *experience*, for then this *part* equally imparted to many children, would like *Gavel-kind lands*, in few generations become nothing; or to say it by *communication*, is *errour* in *Divinity*, for to communicate the *ability* of communicating *whole essence* with any but God, is utter *blasphemy*. And if thou hast thy *Fathers nature* and *inclination*, he also had his *Fathers*, and so climbing up, all come of one man, and have one *nature*, all shall imbrace one course; but that cannot bee, therefore our *complexions* and whole *bodies*, wee inherit from *Parents*; our *inclinations* and minds follow that: For our minde is heavy in our *bodies afflictions*, and rejoyceth in our *bodies pleasure*: how then shall this *nature* governe us, that is governed by the worst part of us? *Nature though oft chased away, it will returne*; 'tis true, but those *good motions* and *inspirations* which be our guides must bee *wooed*, *courted*, and *welcomed*, or else they abandon us. And that old *Axiome*, *nihil invita dices faciesve Minerva* must not be said thou *shalt*, but thou *wilt* doe nothing against *Nature*; so *unwilling* he notes us to curbe our *naturall appetites*. Wee call our *bastards* alwayes our *naturall issue*, and we define a *Foole* by nothing so ordinary, as by the name of *naturall*. And that poore knowledge whereby we conceive what *raine* is, what *wind*, what *thunder*, wee call *Metaphysicke*, *supernaturall*; such *small* things, such *no* things doe we allow to our pliant *Natures* apprehension. Lastly, by following her, we lose the pleasant, and lawfull commodities of this life, for wee shall drinke water and eate rootes, and those not sweet and delicate, as now by Mans *art* and *industry* they are made: we shall lose all the necessities of *societies*, *lawes*, *arts* and *sciences*, which are all the workemanship of *Man*: yea we shall lack the last *best refuge* of misery, *death*; because *no death is naturall*: for if yee will not dare to call all *death violent* (though I see not why *sicknesses* be not *violences*) yet *causes* of all *deaths* proceed of the *defect* of that which *nature* made perfect, and would preserve, and [are] therefore all against *nature*.

## 9. That only Cowards dare dye

*Extreames* are equally removed from the *meane*; so that headlong *desperatenesse* as much offends true *valour*, as backward *Cowardice*: of which sort I reckon justly all *un-inforced deaths*. When will your *valiant* man dye of necessity? so *Cowards* suffer what cannot be avoided: and to runne into *death unimportun'd*, is to runne into the first condemned desperatenesse. Will he dye when he is *rich* and *happy*? then by living he may doe more good: and in *afflictions* and *miseries, death* is the chosen refuge of *Cowards*.

*Fortiter ille facit, qui miser esse potest.*

But it is taught and practised among our *Galants*, that rather than our reputations suffer any *maime*, or we any *misery*, wee shall offer our *brests* to the *Cannons* mouth, yea to our *swords* points: And this seemes a very *brave* and a very *climbing* (which is a *Cowardly*, earthly, and indeed a very *groveling*) spirit. Why doe they *chaine* these slaves to the *Gallyes*, but that they thirst their *deaths*, and would at every loose leape into the *sea*? Why doe they take weapons from *condemned* men, but to barre them of that ease which *Cowards* affect, *a speedy death*. Truely this *life* is a *tempest*, and a *warfare*, and he which *dares dye*, to escape the *anguish* of it, seems to mee, but so *valiant*, as hee which dares *hang* himselfe, lest hee be *prest* to the *warres*. I have seene one in that extremity of *melancholy*, which was then become *madnesse*, to make his owne *breath* an *Instrument* to stay his breath, and labour to choake himselfe, but alas! he was *mad*. And we knew another that languished under the *oppression* of a poore *disgrace* so much, that hee tooke more *paines to dye*, than would have served to have nourished *life* and *spirit* enough to have outlived his *disgrace*. What *Foole* will call this *Cowardlinesse, Valour*? or this *Basenesse, Humility*? And lastly, of these men which dye the *Allegoricall death* of entring into *Religion*, how few are found fit for any shew of *valiancy*? but onely a *soft* and *supple metall*, made onely for *Cowardly* solitarinesse.

## 10. That a Wise Man is knowne by much laughing

*Ride, si sapis, ô puella ride*; If thou beest *wise*, *laugh*: for since the *powers* of *discourse*, *reason*, and *laughter*, bee equally *proper* unto Man onely, why shall not hee be onely most *wise*, which hath most use of *laughing*, as well as he which hath most of *reasoning* and *discoursing*? I alwaies did, and shall understand that *Adage*;

*Per risum multum possis cognoscere stultum*,

That by much *laughing* thou maist know there is a *foole*, not, that the *laughers* are *fooles*, but that among them there is some *foole*, at whome *wisemen* laugh: which moved *Erasmus* to put this as his first *Argument* in the mouth of his *Folly*, that *shee made Beholders laugh*: for *fooles* are the most laughed at, and laugh the least themselves of any. And *Nature* saw this *faculty* to bee so necessary in man, that shee hath beene content that by *more causes* we should be importuned to *laugh*, than to the *exercise* of any other *power*; for things in themselves utterly *contrary*, beget this effect; for wee laugh both at *witty* and *absurd* things: At both which sorts I have seen Men *laugh so long*, and *so earnestly*, that at last they have *wept* that they could laugh no more. And therfore the *Poet* having described the quietnesse of a *wise retired man*, saith in one, what we have said before in many lines; *Quid facit Canius tuus? ridet*. We have received that even the *extremity* of *laughing*, yea of *weeping* also, hath beene accounted *wisedome*: And that *Democritus* and *Heraclitus*, the *lovers* of these *Extremes*, have been called *lovers of wisedome*. Now among our *wisemen* I doubt not, but many would be found who would laugh at *Heraclitus* weeping, none which weepe at *Democritus* laughing. At the hearing of *Comedies* or other witty reports, I have noted some, which not understanding *jests*, &c. have yet chosen this as the best meanes to seeme *wise* and *understanding*, to laugh when their *Companions laugh*; and I have presumed them *ignorant*, whom I have seene *unmoved*. A *foole* if he come into a *Princes Court*, and see a *gay* man leaning at the wall, so *glistering*, and so *painted* in many *colours* that he is hardly discerned from one of the *pictures* in the *Arras* hanging, his *body* like an *Iron-bound-chest*, girt in and thicke ribb'd with *broad gold laces*, may (and commonly doth) envy him. But alas!

shall a *wiseman*, which may not onely not *envy*, but not *pitty* this *monster*, do nothing? Yes, let him *laugh*. And if one of these *hot cholerike firebrands*, which nourish themselves by *quarrelling*, and kindling others, spit upon a *foole* one *sparke* of *disgrace*, he, like a *thatcht house* quickly burning, may bee *angry*; but the *wiseman*, as *cold* as the *Salamander*, may not onely not be *angry* with him, but not be *sorry* for him; therefore let him *laugh*: so he shall be knowne a Man, because he can *laugh*, a *wise Man* that hee knowes at *what* to laugh, and a *valiant Man* that he *dares* laugh: for he that *laughs* is justly reputed more *wise*, than at whom it is *laughed*. And hence I thinke proceeds that which in these later *formall* times I have much noted; that now when our *superstitious civility* of *manners* is become a mutuall *tickling flattery* of one another, almost every man affecteth an *humour* of *jesting*, and is content to be *deject*, and to *deforme* himselfe, yea become *foole* to no other *end* that I can spie, but to give his *wise Companion* occasion to *laugh*: and to shew themselves in *promptnesse* of *laughing* is so great in *wisemen*, that I thinke all *wisemen*, if any *wiseman* do reade this *Paradox*, will *laugh* both at it and me.

## 11. That the gifts of the Body are better than those of the Minde

I SAY againe, that the *body* makes the *minde*, not that it created it a *minde*, but *formes* it a *good* or a *bad mind*; and this *minde* may be confounded with *soule* without any violence or injustice to *Reason* or *Philosophy*: then the *soule* it seemes is enabled by our *body*, not this by it. My *Body* licenseth my *soule* to *see* the Worlds *beauties* through mine *eyes*; to *heare* pleasant things through mine *eares*; and affords it apt *Organs* for the conveiance of all perceivable *delight*. But alas! my *soule* cannot make any *part*, that is not of it selfe disposed, to *see* or *heare*, though without doubt she be as able and as willing to see *behind* as *before*. Now if my *soule* would say, that shee enables any part to taste these pleasures, but is her selfe onely delighted with those rich *sweetnesses* which her *inward eyes* and *senses* apprehend, shee should dissemble; for I see her often solaced with *beauties*, which shee sees through mine *eyes*, and with *musicke* which through mine *eares* she heares. This *perfection* then my *body* hath, that it can impart to my *minde* all her *pleasures*; and my *minde* hath this maime, that she can neither teach my *indisposed* part her *faculties*, nor to the best *disposed* parts shew that *beauty* of *Angels*, or *Musicke* of *Spheres*, whereof she boasts the *contemplation*. Are *chastity*, *temperance*, and *fortitude* gifts of the *mind*? I appeale to *Physitians* whether the *cause* of these be not in the *body*; *health* is the gift of the *body*, and *patience* in sickenesse the gift of the *minde*: then who will say that *patience* is as good a happinesse, as *health*, when wee must be extremely *miserable* to purchase this *happinesse*. And for nourishing of *civill societies* and *mutuall love* amongst men, which is our *chiefe end* while wee are men; I say, this *beauty*, *presence*, and *proportion* of the *body*, hath a more *masculine* force in begetting this *love*, than the *vertues* of the *minde*: for it strikes us *suddenly*, and possesseth us *immoderately*; when to know those *vertues* requires some *Judgement* in him which shall discerne, a *long time* and *conversation* betweene them. And even at *last* how much of our *faith* and *beleefe* shall we be driven to bestow, to assure our selves that these *vertues* are not *counterfeited*: for it is the same to *be*, and *seeme vertuous*, because that he that hath *no vertue*, can *dissemble* none, but he which hath a *little*, may *gild* and *enamell*, yea and transforme much *vice* into *vertue*: For allow a man to be *discreet* and *flexible* to *companies*, which are great *vertues* and gifts of the *minde*, this *discretion* will be to him the *soule & Elixir* of all *vertues*, so that touched with this, even *pride* shal be made *humility*; and *Cowardice*, honourable and wise *valour*. But in things *seene* there is not this danger, for the *body* which thou lovest and esteemest *faire*, is *faire*; certainely if it bee not *faire* in *perfection*, yet it is *faire* in the same *degree* that thy *Judgement* is good. And in a *faire body*, I doe seldome suspect a *disproportioned minde*, and as seldome hope for a *good* in a *deformed*. When I see a *goodly house*, I assure my selfe of a *worthy possessour*, from a *ruinous weather-beaten building* I turn away, because it seems either stuffed with *varlets* as a *Prison*, or handled by an *unworthy* and *negligent tenant*, that so suffers the *waste* thereof. And truely the gifts of *Fortune*, which are *riches*, are onely *handmaids*, yea *Pandars* of the *bodies pleasure*; with their service we nourish *health*, and preserve *dainty*, and wee buy *delights*; so that *vertue* which must be loved for *it selfe*, and respects no further *end*, is indeed *nothing*: And *riches*, whose *end* is the *good* of the *body*, cannot be so *perfectly good*, as the *end* whereto it levels.

## PROBLEMS

### 1. Why Puritanes make long Sermons?

IT needs not *perspicuousnesse*, for God knowes they are plain enough: nor doe all of them use *Sem-briefe-Accents* for some of them have *crotchets* enough. It may bee they intend not to rise like *glorious Tapers* and *Torches*, but like *Thinne-wretched-sicke-watching-Candles*, which *languish* and are in a dimme *Consumption* from the first minute, yea in their *snuffe*, and *stink* when others are in their more profitable *glory*. I have thought sometimes, that out of *conscience*, they allow *long measure* to *coarse ware*. And sometimes, that *usurping* in that place a *liberty* to *speak freely* of *Kings*, they would *raigne* as long as they could. But now I thinke they doe it out of a *zealous* imagination, that, *It is their duty to preach on till their Auditory wake againe.*

### 2. Why is there more variety of Green than of other Colours?

IT is because it is the figure of *Youth* wherin *nature* wuld provide as many [*greens*], as *youth* hath *affections*; and so present a *Sea-green* for *profuse wasters* in *voyages*; a *Grasse-green* for sudden *new men enobled* from *Grasiers*; and a *Goose-greene* for such *Polititians* as pretend to preserve the *Capitol*. Or else *Prophetically* foreseeing an *age*, wherein they shall all *hunt*. And for such as *misdemeane* themselves a *Willow-greene*; For *Magistrates* must as well have *Fasces* born before them to *chastize* the *small* offences, as *Secures* to *cut off* the *great*.

### 3. Why hath the common Opinion afforded Women Soules?

IT is agreed that wee have not so much from them as any *part* of either our *mortall soules* of *sense*, or *growth*, and we deny *soules* to others equal to them in all but in *speech* for which they are beholding to their *bodily instruments*: For perchance an *Oxes* heart, or a *Goates*, or a *Foxes*, or a *Serpents* would speake just so, if it were in the *breast*, and could move that *tongue* and *jawes*. Have they so many *advantages* and *meanes* to hurt us (for, ever their *loving* destroyed us) that we dare not *displease* them, but give them what they will? And so when some call them *Angels*, some *Goddesses*, and the *Peputian*[1] *Heretikes* made them *Bishops*, wee descend so much with the streame, to allow them *soules*? Or doe we somewhat (in this dignifying of them) flatter *Princes* and *great Personages* that are so much governed by them? Or do we in that *easinesse* and *prodigality*, wherein we daily lose our owne *soules*, allowe *soules* to we care not whom, and so labour to perswade our selves, that sith a *woman* hath a *soule*, a *soule* is no great matter? Or doe wee lend them *soules* but for *use*, since they for our sakes, give their *soules* againe, and their *bodies* to boote? Or perchance because the *Devill* (who is all *soule*) doth most *mischiefe*, and for *convenience* and *proportion*, because they would come neerer him, wee allow them some soules; and so as the *Romanes* naturalized some *Provinces* in revenge, and made them *Romans*, onely for the *burthen* of the *Common-wealth*; so we have given *women* soules onely to make them capable of *damnation*?

### 4. Why do Women delight much in Feathers?

THEY think that Feathers imitate wings, and so shew their restlessness and instability. As they are in matter, so they would be in name, like *Embroiderers*, *Painters*, and such *Artificers* of curious *vanities*, which Varro and the vulgar edition call *Plumarios*. Or else they have feathers for the same reason, which moves them to love

---

[1] i.e. Montanist.

the unworthiest men, which is, that they may be thereby excusable
in their inconstancy and often changing.

## 5. Why doth not Gold soyl the fingers?

DOTH it direct all the venom to the heart? Or is it because bribing
should not be discovered? Or because that should pay purely, for
which pure things are given, as *Love*, *Honor*, *Justice* and Heaven? Or
doth it seldom come into innocent hands but into such as for former
foulness you cannot discern this?

## 6. Why are Courtiers sooner Atheists than men of other conditions?

I s it because as *Physitians* contemplating Nature, and finding many
abstruse things subject to the search of Reason, think therefore
that all is so; so they (seeing mens destinies made at Court, necks
put out and in joynt there, *War*, *Peace*, *Life* and *Death* derived from
thence) climb no higher? Or doth a familiarity with greatness, and
daily conversation and acquaintance with it breed a contempt of all
greatness? Or because that they see that opinion or need of one
another, and fear makes the degrees of servants, Lords and Kings,
do they think that God likewise for such Reason hath been mans
Creator? Perchance it is because they see Vice prosper best there,
and, burthened with sinne, doe they not, for their ease, endeavour
to put off the feare and Knowledge of God, as facinorous men deny
Magistracy? Or are the most Atheists in that place, because it is
the foole that said in his heart, There is no God?

## 7. Why was Sir Walter Raleigh thought the fittest Man, to write the Historie of these Times?

WAS it because that being told at his Arraignement, that a Witness
accusing himself had the strength of two; he may seem by Writing
the ills of his own Time to be believed? Or is it, because he might

reenjoy those Times by the Meditation of them? Or because if he should undertake higher Times, he doth not think, that he can come nearer to the Beginning of the World? Or because like a Bird in a Cage, he takes his Tunes from every passenger, that last whistled? Or because he thinks not that the best Echo which repeats most of the Sentence, but that which repeats Less more plainly?

# BIATHANATOS

*Biathanatos*, Donne's treatise on suicide, was not published in his lifetime. Evelyn Simpson dated it as most probably written around 1609. In 1619 Donne sent a manuscript copy to Sir Robert Ker, and some time before this he sent another manuscript copy, with annotations in his own hand, to Sir Edward Herbert; see Letters 32 and 23 (pp. 152 and 140). The work was published by John Donne the Younger in 1646, and again in 1648. The text here is from the first edition, with some correction of punctuation and with the marginal notes and references omitted.

The treatise is an extended exercise in casuistry, taking as its problem 'whether self-homicide is so naturally a sin that it may never be otherwise'. Donne divides his solution into three sections. Part I examines the question from the point of view of natural law; Part II explores positive law, both civil and ecclesiastical; Part III collects and comments on texts from the Scriptures and the Fathers condemning suicide. This threefold approach was classical and aimed at presenting a solution which was philosophically, legally, and theologically sound.

Throughout the work Donne's prose seldom rises to the eloquence of the Sermons. There are some striking passages, but they are brief. The sustained organization and rhythms so evident in the later prose are lacking here. As a long and careful piece of casuistry *Biathanatos* is, however, interesting. It reveals the legal precision of Donne's mind, and generously displays his wide and curious erudition. There are also several passages of biographical interest.

Perhaps the most important revelation *Biathanatos* makes is of Donne's capacity for understanding and sympathy even in one of the darker areas of Christian speculation. He shows this quite simply in the purpose he sets for himself in writing: 'that to those many learned and subtile men which have travelled in this point, some charitable and compassionate men might be added'.

# BIATHANATOS

## 1. Authors cited in this Booke[1]

In citing these authors, for those which I produce only for ornament and illustration, I have trusted my owne old notes; which though I have no reason to suspect, yet I confess here my lazines; and that I did not refresh them with going to the Originall. Of those few which I have not seene in the bookes themselves, (for there are some such, even of places cited for greatest strength,) besides the integrity of my purpose, I have this safe defence against any quarreller, that what place soever I cite from any Catholique Author, if I have not considered the Book it selfe, I cite him from another Catholique Writer. And the like course I hold in the Reformers. So that I shall hardly be condemned of any false citation, except to make me Accessorie, they pronounce one of their owne friends principall.

## 2. The Preface

### Declaring the Reasons, the Purpose, the way, and the end of the
#### Author

*Beza*, a man as eminent and illustrious, in the full glory and Noone of Learning, as others were in the dawning, and Morning, when any, the least sparkle was notorious, confesseth of himself, that only for the anguish of a Scurffe, which over-ranne his head, he had once drown'd himselfe from the Millers bridge in *Paris*, if his Uncle by chance had not then come that way; I have often such a sickely inclination. And, whether it be, because I had my first breeding and conversation with men of a suppressed and afflicted Religion, accustomed to the despite of death, and hungry of an imagin'd Martyrdome; Or that the common Enemie find that doore

---

[1] This note follows a list of over one hundred and seventy authors.

worst locked against him in mee; Or that there bee a perplexitie and flexibility in the doctrine it selfe; Or because my Conscience ever assures me, that no rebellious grudging at Gods gifts, nor other sinfull concurrence accompanies these thoughts in me, or that a brave scorn, or that a faint cowardlinesse beget it, whensoever any affliction assailes me, mee thinks I have the keyes of my prison in mine owne hand, and no remedy presents it selfe so soone to my heart, as mine own sword. Often Meditation of this hath wonne me to a charitable interpretation of their action, who dy so: and provoked me a little to watch and exagitate their reasons, which pronounce so peremptory judgements upon them.

A devout and godly man, hath guided us well, and rectified our uncharitablenesse in such cases, by this remembrance, *Scis lapsam*, &c. *Thou knowest this mans fall, but thou knowest not his wrastling; which perchance was such, that almost his very fall is justified and accepted of God.* For, to this end, saith one, *God hath appointed us tentations, that we might have some excuses for our sinnes, when he calles us to account.*

An uncharitable mis-interpreter unthriftily demolishes his owne house, and repaires not another. He loseth without any gaine or profit to any. And, as *Tertullian* comparing and making equall, him which provokes another, and him who will be provoked by another, says, *There is no difference, but that the provoker offended first, And that is nothing, because in evill there is no respect of Order or Prioritie.* So wee may soone become as ill as any offendor, if we offend in a severe increpation of the fact. For, *Climachus* in his *Ladder of Paradise*, places these two steps very neere one another, when hee sayes, *Though in the world it were possible for thee, to escape all defiling by actuall sinne, yet by judging and condemning those who are defiled, thou art defiled.* In this thou art defiled, as *Basil* notes, *That in comparing others sinnes, thou canst not avoid excusing thine owne.* Especially this is done, if thy zeale be too fervent in the reprehension of others: For, as in most other Accidents, so in this also, Sinne hath the nature of Poyson, that it *enters easiest, and works fastest upon cholerique constitutions.* It is good counsell of the Pharises stiled, *Ne judices proximum donec ad ejus locum pertingas.* Feele and wrastle with such tentations as he hath done, and thy zeale will be tamer. For, *Therefore* (saith the Apostle) *it became Christ to be like us, that he might be mercifull.*

If therefore after a Christian protestation of an innocent purpose herein, And after a submission of all which is said, not only to every Christian Church, but to every Christian man, and after an entreaty, that the Reader will follow this advise of *Tabæus*, *Qui litigant, sint ambo in conspectu tuo mali et rei*, and trust neither me, nor the adverse part, but the Reasons, there be any scandall in this enterprise of mine, it is Taken, not Given. And though I know, that the malitious prejudged man, and the lazy affectors of ignorance, will use the same calumnies and obtrectations toward me, (for the voyce and sound of the Snake and Goose is all one) yet because I thought, that as in the poole of *Bethsaida*, there was no health till the water was troubled, so the best way to finde the truth in this matter, was to debate and vexe it, (for *We must as well dispute* de veritate, *as* pro veritate,) I abstained not for feare of mis-interpretation from this undertaking. Our stomachs are not now so tender, and queasie, after so long feeding upon solid Divinity, nor we so umbragious and startling, having been so long enlightened in Gods path, that wee should thinke any truth strange to us, or relapse into that childish age, in which a Councell in *France* forbad *Aristotles Metaphysiques*, and punished with Excommunication the excribing, reading, or having that booke.

Contemplative and bookish men, must of necessitie be more quarrelsome than others, because they contend not about matter of fact, nor can determine their controversies by any certaine witnesses, nor judges. But as long as they goe towards peace, that is Truth, it is no matter which way. The tutelare Angels resisted one another in *Persia*, but neither resisted Gods revealed purpose. *Hierome* and *Gregorie* seem to be of opinion, that *Salomon* is damned; *Ambrose* and *Augustine*, that he is saved: All Fathers, all zealous of Gods glory. At the same time when the *Romane* Church canonized *Becket*, the Schooles of *Paris* disputed whether hee could be saved; both Catholique Judges, and of reverend authoritie. And after so many Ages of a devout and religious celebrating the memory of Saint *Hierome*, *Causæus* hath spoken so dangerously, that *Campian* saies, hee pronounces him to be as deepe in hell as the Devill. But in all such intricacies, where both opinions seem equally to conduce to the honor of God, his Justice being as much advanced in the one,

as his Mercie in the other, it seemes reasonable to me, that this
turne the scales, if on either side there appeare charity towards
the poore soule departed. The Church in her Hymnes and Anti-
phones, doth often salute the Nayles and Crosse, with Epithets of
sweetnesse, and thanks; But the Speare which pierced Christ when
he was dead, it ever calles, *dirum Mucronem.*

This pietie, I protest againe, urges me in this discourse; and what
infirmity soever my reasons may have, yet I have comfort in *Tres-
megistus* Axiome, *Qui pius est, summe Philosophatur.* And therefore
without any disguising, or curious and libellous concealing, I
present and object it, to all of candor, and indifferencie, to escape
that just taxation, *Novum malitiæ genus est, et intemperantis, scribere quod
occultes.* For as, when *Ladislaus* tooke occasion of the great schisme,
to corrupt the Nobility in *Rome*, and hoped thereby to possesse the
Towne, to their seven Governours whom they called *Sapientes*, they
added three more, whom they called *Bonos* and confided in them;
So doe I wish, and as much as I can, effect, that to those many
learned and subtile men which have travelled in this point, some
charitable and compassionate men might be added.

If therefore, of Readers, which *Gorionides* observes to be of foure
sorts, (Spunges which attract all without distinguishing; Howre-
glasses, which receive and powre out as fast; Bagges, which retaine
onely the dregges of the Spices, and let the Wine escape; And Sives,
which retaine the best onely,) I finde some of the last sort, I doubt
not but they may bee hereby enlightened. And as the eyes of *Eve*,
were opened by the taste of the Apple, though it bee said before
that shee saw the beauty of the tree, So the digesting of this may,
though not present faire objects, yet bring them to see the nakednesse and deformity of their owne reasons, founded upon a rigorous
suspition, and winne them to be of that temper, which *Chrisostome*
commends, *He which suspects benignly would faine be deceived, and bee
overcome, and is piously glad, when he findes it to be false, which he did
uncharitably suspect.* And it may have as much vigour (as one observes
of another Author) as the Sunne in *March*; it may stirre and dissolve
humors, though not expell them; for that must bee a worke of a
stronger power.

Every branch which is excerpted from other authors, and

engrafted here, is not written for the readers faith, but for illustration and comparison. Because I undertooke the declaration of such a proposition as was controverted by many, and therefore was drawne to the citation of many authorities, I was willing to goe all the way with company, and to take light from others, as well in the journey as at the journeys end. If therefore in multiplicity of not necessary citations there appeare vanity, or ostentation, or digression my honesty must make my excuse and compensation, who acknowledg as *Pliny* doth *That to chuse rather to be taken in a theft, than to give every man due, is* obnoxii animi, et infelicis ingenii. I did it the rather because scholastique and artificiall men use this way of instructing; and I made account that I was to deale with such, because I presume that naturall men are at least enough inclinable of themselves to this doctrine.

This my way; and my end is to remove scandall. For certainly God often punisheth a sinner much more severely, because others have taken occasion of sinning by his fact. If therefore wee did correct in our selves this easines of being scandalized, how much easier and lighter might we make the punishment of many transgressors? For God in his judgements hath almost made us his assistants, and counsellers, how far he shall punish; and our interpretation of anothers sinne doth often give the measure to Gods Justice or Mercy.

If therefore, since *disorderly long haire which was pride and wantonnesse in* Absolon, *and squallor and horridnes in* Nebuchodonozor, *was vertue and strength in* Samson, *and sanctification in* Samuel, these severe men will not allow to indifferent things the best construction they are capable of, nor pardon my inclination to do so, they shall pardon this opinion, that their severity proceeds from a self-guiltines, and give me leave to apply that of *Ennodius, That it is the nature of stiffe wickednesse, to think that of others, which themselves deserve and it is all the comfort which the guilty have, not to find any innocent.*

## 3. [The dispensing power of conscience]

No law is so primary and simple, but it fore-imagines a reason upon which it was founded: and scarce any reason is so constant, but that circumstances alter it. In which case a private man is Emperor of himselfe; for so a devout man interprets those words, *Faciamus hominem ad imaginem nostrum*, id est, *sui juris*. And he whose conscience well tempred and dispassion'd, assures him that the reason of selfe-preservation ceases in him, may also presume that the law ceases too, and may doe that then which otherwise were against that law.

And therefore if it be true that *it belongs to the Bishop of* Rome, *to declare, interpret, limit, distinguish the law of God*, as their Doctors teach, which is, to declare when the reason of the Law ceases: it may be as true which this Author, and the Canons affirme, that he may dispense with that Law: for hee doth no more than any man might doe of himselfe, if he could judge as infallibly. Let it be true that no man may at any time doe anything against the law of nature, yet, *As a dispensation workes not thus, that* I *may by it disobey a law, but that that law becomes to me no law, in that case wher the reason ceases*; So may any man be the Bishop & Magistrate to himselfe, and dispense with his conscience, where it can appeare that the reason which is the soule and forme of the law, is ceased. Because, as in Oathes and Vowes, so in the Law, the necessitie of dispensations proceedes from this, that a thing which universally considered in it selfe is profitable and honest, by reason of some particular event, becomes either dishonest or hurtfull; neither of which, can fall within the reach, or under the Commandement of any law; and in these exempt and priviledged cases, the priviledge is not *contra jus universale*, but contra *universalitem juris*. It doth onely succor a person, not wound, nor infirme a law; no more, than I take from the vertue of light, or dignitie of the Sunne, if to escape the scortching thereof, I allow my selfe the reliefe of a shadow.

## 4. [The disease of the desire for martyrdom]

So *Ignatius* stiles himselfe in his Epistles, Martyr. Yea more than the rest he brought down the value thereof, and the deare purchase, for he sayes *That as he which honors a Prophet in the name of a Prophet, shall have a Prophets reward; So hee shall have a Martyrs reward which honors vinctum Christi.* And so our most blessed Saviour, proceeding in his mercifull purpose of encreasing his Kingdome upon earth, yet permitting the Heathen Princes to continue theirs as yet, the Christian Religion was dilated and oppressed; and the professors thereof, so dejected and worne with confiscations and imprisonments, thought that as in the *Passeover* from *Egypt* every doore was sprinkled with blood; So Heaven had no doore from this world but by fires, crosses, and bloody persecutions: and presuming Heaven to be at the next step, they would often stubbornly or stupidly winke, and so make that one step.

God forbid any should be so malignant, so to mis-interpret mee, as though I thought not *the blood of Martyrs to be the seed of the Church,* or diminished the dignity thereof; yet it becomes any ingenuity to confesse, that those times were affected with a disease of this naturall desire of such a death; and that to such may fruitfully be applyed those words of the good B. *Paulinus, Athleta non vincit statim, quia ernitur: nec ideo transnatant, quia se spoliant.* Alas! we may fall and drown at the last stroke; for, to sayle to heaven it is not enough to cast away the burdenous superfluities which we have long carried about us, but we must also take in a good frayte. It is not lightnesse, but an even-reposed stedfastnesse, which carries us thither.

## 5. [Some metaphors re-interpreted]

THERE are many Metaphoricall and Similitudinarie Reasons, scattered amongst Authors, as in *Cicero* and *Macrobius*, made rather for illustration, than for argument or answer; which I will not stand to gleane amongst them, since they are almost all bound up in one sheafe, in that Oration of *Josephus* . . . *Josephus* then in that Oration hath one Reason drawen from the custome of an Enemy. We esteeme them enemies, who attempt our lives, and shall we bee enemies to our selves? But besides that, in this place, *Josephus* speakes to save his owne life, and may justly be thought to speak more *ex animo*, and dispassioned, where in the person of *Eleazar* hee perswades to kill themselves, there is neither certaine truth in the Assertion, nor in the Consequence. For do we esteeme God, or the Magistrate our enemy, when by them death is inflicted? And do not Martyrs, in whose death God is glorified, kisse the Executioners, and the Instruments of their death? Nor is it unlawfull, unnaturall, or unexpedient for us, in many cases, to be so much our owne Enemies, as to deny our selves many things agreeable to our sensitive nature, and to inflict upon our selves many things repugnant to it, as was abundantly shewed in the first part.

In the same Oration he hath another allusorie argument, *That a Servant which runnes away, is to be punished by the Law, though his Master bee severe; much more if we runne away from so indulgent a Master, as God is to us.* But not to give strength or delight to this reason, by affording it a long or diligent answer; wee say, In our case the Servant runnes not from his Master, but to him, and at his call obeys his voyce. Yet it is as truely, as devoutly sayd, *The devill is overcome by resisting, but the world, and the flesh by running away.* And the farther, the better.

His last, which is of any taste, is, *That in a tempest, it were the part of an idle and treacherous Pylot, to sinke the Ship.* But I say, if in a Tempest we must cast out the most precious ware aboard, to save the lives of the Passengers, and the Marchant who is damnified thereby, cannot impute this to any, nor remedie himselfe, how much more may I, when I am weather-beaten and in danger of betraying that precious soule which God hath embarqued in me, put off this burdenous flesh, till his pleasure be that I shall resume it? For this is not to sinck the ship but to retire it to safe Harbour, and assured Anchor.

## 6. [Virgin Martyrs]

THE Church whose dignity and constancy it becomes well, that
that Rule of her owne Law, be ever justly said of her self, *Quod
semel placuit amplius displicere non potest* where new reasons do not
interpose, celebrates upon the 9. of *February* the Birth, (that is the
death), of the Virgin and Martyr *Appollonia*; who, after the persecutors had beat out her teeth, and vexed her with many other
tortures, when she was presented to the fire, being inflamed with a
more burning fire of the Holy Ghost, broke from the Officers hands,
and leapt into the fire.

For this act of hers many Advocates rise up for her, and say, that
either the History is not certain, (yet the Authors, are *Beda*,
*Usuardus, Ado*, and as *Barronius* sayes *Latinorum cæteri*) Or else, says
*Sayr*, you must answer that she was brought very neer the fire,
and as good as thrown in: Or else that she was provoked to it by
divine inspiration. But, but that another divine inspiration, which
is true Charity, moved the beholders then to beleeve, and the
Church ever since to acknowledge, that she did therein a Noble and
Christian act, to the speciall glory of God, this act of hers, as well as
any other, might have been calumniated to have been done, out
of wearinesse of life, or fear of relapse, or hast to Heaven, or ambition of Martyrdome.

The memory of *Pelagia*, as of a virgin and Martyr, is celebrated
the ninth of *June*. And though the History of this woman suffer
some perplexity, and give occasion of doubting the truth thereof,
(for *Ambrose* says, That she and her Mother drownd themselves;
and *Chrysostome* that they flung themselves downe from a house top;
And *Baronius* saw this knot to be so hard to unentangle, that he says,
*Quid ad hoc dicamus, non habemus*) yet the Church, as I said, celebrates
the Act, as though it were glad to take any occasion, of approving
such a courage in such a cause, which was but preservation of
Chastity. *Their Martyrdome saith Saint* Augustine *was ever in the
Catholique Church frequented* Veneratione Celeberrima.

And Saint *Ambrose*, when his sister *Marcellina*, consulted him
directly upon the point, what might be thought of them who kill
themselves in such cases, (and then it is agreed by all that the

opinions of the Fathers are especially to be valued, when they speake of a matter, not incidently or casually, but directly and deliberately) answers thus, *We have an example of such a Martyrdome in* Pelagia. And then he presents her in this religious meditation, *Let us die, if we may have leave, or if we be denied leave, yet let us die. God cannot be offended with this, when we use it but for a remedy*; and our faith takes away all offence. Here is no difficulty: for who is willing to dye, & cannot, since there are so many waies to death? I will not trust my hand least it strike not home: nor my breast, least it withdraw it selfe: I will leave no escape to my flesh, for we can dye with our own weapons, and without the benefit of an Executioner.

And then having drest her selfe as a Bride, and going to the water, Here, sayes she, let us be baptized; this is the Baptisme where sinnes are forgiven, and where a kingdome is purchased: and this is the baptisme after which none sinnes. This water regenerates; this makes us virgines, this opens heaven, defends the feeble, delivers from death, and makes us Martyrs. Onely we pray to God, that this water scatter us not, but reserve us to one funerall. Then entred they as in a dance, hand in hand, where the torrent was deepest, and most violent. And thus dyed, (as their mother upon the bank called them) *These Prelates of virginitie, Captaines of Chastitie, and companions in Martyrdome.*

# 7. [Of the light of Nature, the light of Reason, and the light of Scripture]

THAT light which issues from the Moone, doth best represent and expresse that which in our selves we call the light of Nature; for as that in the Moone is permanent and ever there, and yet it is un-equall, various, pale, and languishing, So is our light of Nature changeable. For being at the first kindling at full, it wayned presently, and by departing further and further from God, declined by generall sinne, to almost a totall Eclipse: till God comming neerer to us, first by the Law, and then by Grace, enlightned and repayred it againe, conveniently to his ends, for further exercise of his Mercy and Justice. And then those Artificiall Lights, which our selves make for our use and service here, as Fires, Tapers, and such resemble the light of Reason, as wee have in our Second part accepted that Word. For though the light of these Fires and Tapers be not so naturall, as the Moone, yet because they are more domestique, and obedient to us, wee distinguish particular objects better by them, than by the Moone; So by the Arguments, and Deductions, and Conclusions, which our selves beget and produce, as being more serviceable and under us, because they are our creatures; particular cases are made more cleare and evident to us; for these we can be bold withall, and put them to any office, and examine, and prove their truth, or likeliehood, and make them answere as long as wee will aske; whereas the light of Nature, with a solemne and supercilious Majestie, will speake but once, and give no Reason, nor endure Examination.

But because of these two kindes of light, the first is too weake, and the other false, (for onely colour is the object of sight, and we not trust candlelight to discerne Colours) we have therefore the Sunne, which is the Fountaine and Treasure of all created light, for an Embleme of that third best light of our understanding, which is the Word of God. *Mandatum lucerna, et Lex lux*, sayes *Solomon*. But yet as weake credulous men, thinke sometimes they see two or three Sunnes, when they see none but Meteors, or other apparance; so are many transported with like facilitie or dazeling, that for some opinions which they maintaine, they think they have the light and authority of Scripture, when, God knowes, truth, which is the light of Scriptures, is [hidden] truely under them, and removed in the farthest distance that can bee. If any small place of Scripture, misappeare to them to bee of use for justifying any opinion of theirs; then (as the Word of God hath that precious nature of gold, that a little quantity thereof, by reason of a faithfull tenacity and ductilenesse, will be brought to cover 10000. times as much of any other Mettall,) they extend it so farre, and labour, and beat it, to such a thinnesse, as it is scarce any longer the Word of God, only to give their other reasons a little tincture and colour of gold, though they have lost all the waight and estimation.

But since the Scripture it self teaches, *That no Prophecie in the Scripture, is of private interpretation*, the whole Church may not be bound and concluded by the fancie of one, or of a few, who being content to enslumber themselves in an opinion, and lazy prejudice, dreame arguments to establish, and authorize that.

A professed interpreter of Dreames, tells us, *That no Dreame of a private man may be interpreted to signifie a publike businesse.* This I say, because of those places of Scriptures, which are aledged for the Doctrin which we now examine, scarce any one, (except the Precept, *Thou shalt not kill*) is offered by any two Authors. But to one, one place, to another, another seemes directly to governe in the point, and to me, (to allow Truth her naturall and comely boldnesse) no place, but that seemes to looke towards it.

And therefore in going over all those sentences, which I have gathered from many Authors, and presenting convenient answers and interpretations thereof, I will forbeare the names of those Authors, who produced them so impertinently, least I should seeme to discover their nakednesse, or insimulat them even of prevarication.

If any Divine shall thinke the cause, or persons injured herein, and esteeme me so much worth the reducing to the other opinion, as to apply an answer hereunto, with the same Charitie which provoked me, and which, I thanke God hath accompanied me from the beginning, I beseech him, to take thus much advantage from me and my instruction, that he will doe it without bitternesse. He shall see the way the better, and shew it the better, and saile through it the better, if he raise no stormes.

Such men, as they are *Fishers of men*, so may they also hunt us into their nets, for our good. But there is perchance, some mystique interpretation belonging to that Canon which allowes Clergy men to hunt; for they may doe it by Nets and Snares, but not by Dogges; for clamour and bitings are forbidden them.

## 8. [The presumed suicide of Judas][1]

AND it falls out very often, that some one Father, of strong reputation and authority in his time, doth snatch and swallow some

---

[1] Cf. the contradictory texts, Matt. xxvii. 5 and Acts i. 18.

probable interpretation of Scripture: and then digesting it into his
Homilies, and applying it in dehortations, and encouragements, as
the occasions and diseases of his Auditory, or his age require, and
imagining thereupon delightfull and figurative insinuations, and
setting it to the Musique of his stile, (as every man which is accustomed to these Meditations, shall often finde in himselfe such a
spirituall wantonnesse, and devout straying into such delicacies,)
that sense which was but probable, growes necessary, and those
who succeed, had rather enjoy his wit, than vexe their owne; as
often times we are loath to change or leave off a counterfeit stone,
by reason of the well setting thereof.

By this meanes, I thinke, it became so generally to be beleeved,
that the fruit which *Eve* eat, was an Apple; And that *Lots* wife was
turned to a pillar of Salt; And that *Absalon* was hanged by the haire
of the head; And that *Iephthe* killed his Daughter; And many other
such, which grew currant, not from an evidence in the Text, but
because such an acceptation, was most usefull, and applyable. Of
this number, *Iudas* case might be.

But if it were not, that act of killing himselfe, is not added to his
faults in any place of Scriptures; no not in those two Psalmes of
particular accusations, and bitter imprecations against him, as they
are ordinarily taken to be Prophetically purposed and directed.

And even of this man, whose sinne, if any can exceed mercy, was
such, *Origen* durst hope, not out of his erronious compassion, and
sinnefull charity, by which he thinks that even the Devill shall be
saved, but out of *Judas* repentance. He sayes, *The Devill led him to
the sinne, and then induced him to that sorrowfulnesse which swallowed him.*
But speaking of his repentance, he sayes, *Those words*, when *Judas*
saw that he was condemned, *belong to* Judas *himselfe, for Christ was not
then condemned.* And upon this conscience and consideration, began
his repentance. *For, it may be, saith* Origen, *that Satan which had
entred into him, staid with him till Christ was betray'd, and then left him,
and thereupon repentance followed.* And perchance, sayes he, he went
to prevent, and goe before his Master, who was to dye, and so to
meet him with his naked soule, that he might gaine Mercy by his
confession and prayers.

## 9. Conclusion

AND this is as farre as I allowed my discourse to progesse in this way: forbidding it earnestly all darke and dangerous Secessions and divertings into points of our Free-will, and of Gods Destiny: though allowing many ordinary contingencies, to be under our Election, it may yet seem reasonable, that our maine periods, of Birth, of Death, and of chief alterations in this life be more immediately wrought upon by Gods determination. It is usefully said, and appliable to good purpose (though by a wicked man, and with intention to crosse *Moses*,) *That man was made of shadow, and the Devil of fire.* For as shaddow is not darknes, but grosser light, so is mans understanding in these mysteries, not blind but clouded. And as fire doth not always give light (for that is accidentall, and it must have aire to work upon,) but it burneth naturally, so that desire of knowledge which the Devill kindles in us, (as he doth as willingly bring bellows to inflame a heart curious of knowledge, as he doth more ashes to stupifie and bury deeper, a slumbering understanding) doth not alwaies give us light, but it always burnes us, and imprints upon our judgment stigmaticall marks, and at last seares up our conscience.

If then reasons which differ from me, and my reasons be otherwise equall, yet theirs have this disadvantage, that they fight with themselves and suffer a Civill Warre of contradiction. For many of their reasons incline us to a love of this life, and a horror of death, and yet they say often, that wee are too much addicted to that naturally. But it is well noted by *Alcuinus*, (and I thinke from Saint *Augustine*) *That though there bee foure things which wee must love, yet there is no precept given upon any more than two, God and our neighbour.* So that the other which concerne our selves, may be pretermitted in some occasions.

But because of the benefits of death, enough hath beene occasionally interserted before, having presented *Cyprians* encouragement to it, who out of a contemplation that the whole frame of the world decayed and languished, cries to us, Nutant parietes, *The walls and the roofe shake, and would'st not thou goe out? Thou art tyred in a pilgrimage, and wouldst thou not goe home?* I will end with applying *Ausonius* thanks to the Emperour, to death, which deserveth it better, *Thou providest that thy benefits, and the good which thou bringest shall not be transitory; and that the ills from which thou deliverest us, shall never returne.*

# PSEUDO-MARTYR

*Pseudo-Martyr* is the longest and, without doubt, the least interesting of Donne's early works. It was the first of his works to be published and was printed only once, in 1610. Walton says that it was written at the request of King James, and in the space of six weeks. This cannot be true. It is clear from the preface that the work was not written at the King's instigation, and it was certainly not written without long and careful study and thought. It won the King's approval, and gained for Donne an honorary M.A. from the University of Oxford and a reputation as a serious controversialist. Donne read the text carefully and supplied a long list of *errata*, to which he draws the reader's attention in the Advertisement. There are copious marginal references, which we have omitted.

After the discovery of the Gunpowder Plot the Government attempted to impose an Oath of Allegiance on all recusants. This was resisted on the grounds that the Oath explicitly denied the Pope's power to depose a king and implicitly denied his authority to excommunicate one. The 'appellant' party among the Catholics blamed the Jesuits for provoking the recusant refusal to take the Oath: a charge which the Government were as willing to support as they had been to sponsor it. *Pseudo-Martyr* attacks the recusant position; but reserves its particular attention and vehemence for the Jesuits.

Amid the standard controversial barrages fired off by both sides, Donne's line of argument is novel. He attacks the recusant position as legally doubtful, and says that, since this is the case, any sufferings individuals undergo for refusing to take the Oath cannot properly be called martyrdom. For all its subtlety, the intricate argument has little interest for modern readers.

In its main lines the controversy was at least as much political as theological. Thus there is a certain interest in Donne's fulsome dedication of his work to James I. Our second selection illustrates the one quality which, generally, marks Donne as a controversialist, his reasonableness. He can hit hard; but the tone he prefers is irenic.

# PSEUDO-MARTYR

## 1. The Epistle Dedicatorie

*Most mightie and sacred Soveraigne.*

As Temporall armies consist of Press'd men, and voluntaries, so doe they also in this warfare, in which your Majestie hath appear'd by your Bookes. And not only your strong and full Garisons, which are your Cleargie, and your Universities, but also obscure Villages can minister Souldiours. For, the equall interest, which all your Subjects have in the cause (all being equally endanger'd in your dangers) gives every one of us a Title to the Dignitie of this warfare; And so makes those, whom the Civill Lawes made opposite, all one, Paganos, Milites. Besides, since in this Battaile, your Majestie, by your Bookes, is gone in Person out of the Kingdome, who can bee exempt from waiting upon you in such an expedition? For this Oath must worke upon us all; and as it must draw from the Papists a profession, so it must from us, a Confirmation of our Obedience; They must testifie an Alleageance by the Oath, we, an Alleageance to it. For, since in providing for your Majesties securitie, the Oath defends us, it is reason, that wee defend it. The strongest Castle that is, cannot defend the Inhabitants, if they sleepe, or neglect the defence of that, which defends them; No more can this Oath, though framed with all advantagious Christianly wisedome, secure your Majestie, and us in you, if by our negligence wee should open it, either to the adversaries Batteries, or to his underminings.

The influence of those your Majesties Bookes, as the Sunne, which penetrates all corners, hath wrought uppon me, and drawen up, and exhaled from my poore Meditations, these discourses: Which, with all reverence and devotion, I present to your Majestie, who in this also have the power and office of the Sunne, that those things which you exhale, you may at your pleasure dissipate, and annull; or suffer them to fall downe againe, as a wholesome and fruitfull dew, upon your Church & Commonwealth. Of my bold-nesse in this addresse, I most humbly beseech your Majestie, to admit this excuse, that having observed, how much your Majestie had vouchsafed to descend to a conversation with your Subjects, by way of your Bookes, I also conceiv'd an ambition, of ascending to your presence, by the same way, and of participating, by this meanes, their happinesse, of whome, that saying of the Queene of *Sheba*, may bee usurp'd: Happie are thy men, and happie are those thy Servants, which stand before thee alwayes, and heare thy wise-dome. For, in this, I make account, that I have performed a duetie, by expressing in an exterior, and (by your Majesties permission) a publicke Act, the same desire, which God heares in my daily prayers, That your Majestie may very long governe us in your Person, and ever, in your Race and Progenie.

## 2. An Advertisement to the Reader

THOUGH I purposed not to speake any thing to the Reader, otherwise than by way of Epilogue in the end of the Booke, both because I esteemed that to be the fittest place, to give my Reasons, why I respited the handling of the two last Chapters,[1] till another time, and also, because I thought not that any man might well and properly be called a Reader, till he were come to the end of the Booke: yet, because both he, and I, may suffer some disadvantages, if he should not be fore-possessed, and warned in some things, I have changed my purpose in that point.

For his owne good therefore (in which I am also interessed) I must first intreat him, that he will be pleased, before hee reade, to amend with his pen, some of the most important errors, which are hereafter noted to have passed in the printing. Because in the Reading, he will not perchance suspect nor spy them, and so he may runne a danger, of being either deceived, or scandalized.

And for my selfe, (because I have already received some light, that some of the Romane profession, having onely seene the Heads and

---

[1] The 'Table of Chapters' contains the headings for fourteen chapters, but only twelve of these are found in the book.

Grounds handled in this Booke, have traduced me, as an impious and profane under-valewer of Martyrdome,) I most humbly beseech him, (till the reading of the Booke, may guide his Reason) to beleeve, that I have a just and Christianly estimation, and reverence, of that devout and acceptable Sacrifice of our lifes, for the glory of our blessed Saviour. For, as my fortune hath never beene so flattering nor abundant, as should make this present life sweet and precious to me, as I am a Moral man: so, as I am a Christian, I have beene ever kept awake in a meditation of Martyrdome, by being derived from such a stocke and race, as, I beleeve, no family, (which is not of farre larger extent, and greater branches,) hath endured and suffered more in their persons and fortunes, for obeying the Teachers of Romane Doctrine, than it hath done. I did not therefore enter into this, as a carnall or over-indulgent favourer of this life, but out of such reasons, as may arise to his knowledge, who shall be pleased to read the whole worke.

In which, I have abstained from handling the two last Chapters upon divers reasons; whereof one is, that these Heads having beene caried about, many moneths, and thereby quarrelled by some, and desired by others, I was willing to give the Booke a hasty dispatch, that it might cost no man much time, either in expecting before it came, or in reading, when it was come.

But a more principall reason was, that since the two last Chapters depend upon one another, and have a mutual Relation, I was not willing to undertake one, till I might persevere through both. And from the last chapter it became me to abstaine, till I might understand their purposes, who were formerly engaged in the same businesse. For the first Discoverie gives some title to the place, and secludes others, without the Discoverers permission; And in men tender and jealous of their Honour, it is sometimes accounted as much injurie to assist, as to assault.

When therefore I considered, that the most Reverend and learned Sir *Edward Coke*, Lord chiefe Justice of the common Pleas (whom, they which are too narrow to comprehend him, may finde arguments enow to love, and admire, out of the measure and proportion of his malice who hath written against him, since wee ought to love him so much, as such men hate him) had in this point of Jurisdiction, laid so solid foundations, raised so strong walls, & perfited his house upon so sure a Rocke, as the lawes of this Kingdome are. And when I saw, that as the divell himselfe is busiest to attempt them, who abound in strength of Grace, (not forbearing our Saviour himselfe) so an ordinary Instrument of his, (whose continuall libels, and Incitatorie bookes, have occasioned more afflictions, and drawne more of that bloud, which they call Catholique, in this Kingdome than all our Acts of Parliament have done,) had oppugned his Lordships Booke, and iterated and inconculcated those his oppositions, I could not know whether his Lordship reserved any farther consideration of that matter to his owne leasures, or had honoured any other man, with his commandement, or allowance to pursue it. Till therefore I might know, whether any such were embarqued therein, as would either accept my Notes, and dignifie them with their stile, or submit their Notes to my method, and the poore apparell of my language, or undertake it entirely, or quit it absolutely, as a body perfit already, by that forme which his Lordship hath given it, I chose to forbeare the handling thereof at this time.

One thing more I was willing the Reader should be forewarned of; which is, that when he findes in the printing of this Booke oftentimes a change of the Character, hee must not thinke that all those words or sentences so distinguished, are cited from other Authors; for I have done it sometimes, onely to draw his eye, and understanding more intensly upon that place, and so make deeper impressions thereof.

And in those places which are cited from other Authors (which hee shall know by the Margine) I doe not alwayes precisely and superstitiously binde my selfe to the words of the Authors; which was impossible to me, both because sometimes I collect their sense, and expresse their Arguments or their opinions, and the Resultance of a whole leafe, in two or three lines, and some few times, I cite some of their Catholique Authors, out of their owne fellowes, who had used the same fashion of collecting their sense, without precise binding themselves to All, or onely their words. This is the comfort which my conscience hath, and the assurance which I can give the Reader, that I have no where made any Author, speake more or lesse, in sense, than hee intended, to that purpose, for which I cite him. If any of their owne fellowes from whom I cite them, have dealt otherwise, I cannot be wounded but through their sides. So that I hope either mine Innocence, or their own fellowes guiltinesse, shall defend me, from the curious malice of those men, who in this sickly decay, and declining of their cause, can spy out falsifyings in every citation: as in a jealous, and obnoxious state, a Decipherer can pick out Plots, and Treason, in any familiar letter which is intercepted.

And thus much it seemed necessary to mee, to let the Reader know, to whose charitable and favourable opinion I commit the booke, and my selfe to his Christianly and devout Prayers.

## 3. From the Preface[1]

### (i)

AND if they will be content to impute to me all humane infirmities, they shall neede to faine nothing: I am, I confesse, obnoxious enough. My naturall impatience not to digge painefully in deepe, and stony, and sullen learnings: My Indulgence to my freedome and libertie, as in all other indifferent things, so in my studies also, not to betroth or enthral my selfe, to any one science, which should possesse or denominate me: My easines, to affoord a sweete and gentle Interpretation, to all professors of Christian Religion, if they shake not the Foundation, wherein I have in my ordinary Communication and familiar writings, often expressed and declared my selfe: hath opened me enough to their malice, and put me into their danger, and given them advantage to impute to me, whatsoever such degrees of lazines, of liberty, of irresolution, can produce.

But if either they will transferre my personall weakenesses upon the cause, or extend the faults of my person to my minde, or to her purest part, my conscience: If they will calumniate this poore and innocent worke of mine, as if it were written, either for *Ostentation* of any ability or faculty in my selfe; or for *Provocation*, to draw

[1] The preface is addressed 'to the Priests, and Jesuits, and to their Disciples in this Kingdom.'

them to an aunswere, and so continue a Bookewarre; or for *Flattery* to the present State; which, thogh my services be by many just titles due to it, needs it not; or for *exasperation*, to draw out the civill sword in causes, which have some pretence and colour of being spirituall; or to get *Occasion* hereby to uncover the nakednes, and lay open the incommodious and undefensible sentences and opinions, of divers severall Authors in that Church; or to maintaine and further a scisme and division amongst you, in this point of the Popes pretence to temporall jurisdiction: I have no other shelter against these imputations, but an appeale to our blessed Saviour, and a protestation before his face, that my principall and direct scope and purpose herein, is the unity and peace of his Church. For as when the roofe of the Temple rent asunder, not long after followed the ruine of the foundation it selfe: So if these two principall beames and Toppe-rafters, *the Prince* and *the Priest*, rent asunder, the whole frame and Foundation of Christian Religion will be shaked. And if we distinguish not between Articles of faith & jurisdiction, but account all those super-edifications and furnitures, and ornaments which God hath affoorded to his Church, for exteriour government, to be equally the Foundation it selfe, there can bee no Church; as there could be no body of a man, if it were all eye.

They who have descended so lowe, as to take knowledge of me, and to admit me into their consideration, know well that I used no inordinate hast, nor precipitation in binding my conscience to any locall Religion. I had a longer worke to doe than many other men; for I was first to blot out, certaine impressions of the Romane religion, and to wrastle both against the examples and against the reasons, by which some hold was taken; and some anticipations early layde upon my conscience, both by Persons who by nature had a power and superiority over my will, and others who by their learning and good life, seem'd to me justly to claime an interest for the guiding, and rectifying of mine understanding in these matters. And although I apprehended well enough, that this irresolution not onely retarded my fortune, but also bred some scandall, and endangered my spirituall reputation, by laying me open to many mis-interpretations; yet all these respects did not transport me to any violent and sudden determination, till I had, to the measure of my poore wit and judgement, survayed and digested the whole body of Divinity, controverted betweene ours and the Romane Church. In which search and disquisition, that God, which awakened me then, and hath never forsaken me in that industry, as he is the Authour of that purpose, so is he a witnes of this protestation; that I behaved my selfe, and proceeded therin with humility, and diffidence in my selfe; and by that, which by his grace, I tooke to be the ordinary meanes, which is frequent praier, and equall and indifferent affections.

And this course held in rectifying and reducing mine understanding and judgment, might justifie & excuse my forwardnes; if I shold seeme to any to have intruded and usurped the office of others, in writing of Divinity and spirituall points, having no ordinary calling to that function. For, to have alwaies abstained from this declaration of my selfe, had beene to betray, and to abandon, and prostitute my good name to their misconceivings and imputations; who thinke presently, that hee hath no Religion, which dares not call his Religion by some newer name than *Christian*. And then, for my writing in Divinity, though no professed Divine; all Ages, all Nations, all Religions, even yours, which is the most covetous and lothest to divide, or communicate with the Layety, any of the honours reserved to the Clergie, affoord me abundantly examples, and authorities for such an undertaking.

## (ii)

To let blood in some diseases, saith the eloquentest Physitian, is no new thing; but that there should scarce be any disease, in which we should not let blood, is (saith he) a strange and new fashion: So to offer our lives for defence of the Catholique faith, hath ever beene a religious custome; but to cal every pretence of the Pope, Catholique faith, and to bleede to death for it, is a sickenesse and a medicine, which the Primitive Church never understood. For the implicite faith, and blinde assent, which you were used heretofore to give to the spirituall supremacy, was put upon you, as

*Annibal*, to entrappe and surprise his enemies, mingled their wine with *Mandrake*, whose operation is betwixt sleepe and poyson: for though it brought you into a drowsie and stupid adoration of the Pope, & some dull lethargies & forgetfulnesses of your temporall dueties, yet it was not so pestilent and contagious, but that a civill state might consist with it, though in a continual languishing and consumption. But this doctrine of temporall Jurisdiction is not onely a violent and dispatching poyson, but it is of the nature of those poysons, which destroy not by heat nor cold, nor corrosion, nor any other discerneable quality, but (as physitians say) out of the specifique forme, and secret malignity, and out of the whole substance. For as no Artist can finde out, how this malignant strength growes in that poyson, nor how it workes, So can none of your Writers tell, how this temporall Jurisdiction got into the Pope, or how he executes it, but are anguished and tortured, when they come to talke of it, as Physitians and Naturalists are, when they speake of these specifique poysons, or of the cause and origen thereof, which is, *Antipathie*.

And yet we finde it reported of one woman, that she had so long accustomed her body to these poysons, by making them her ordinary foode, that shee had brought herself, and her whole complexion and constitution, to be of the same power as the poyson was, and yet retaind so much beauty, as shee allurd Kings to her embracement, and kild and poisond them by that meanes: So hath the Romane faith beene for many yeares, so fedde and pampred with this venemous doctrine of temporall jurisdiction, that it is growne to some few of them to bee matter of faith it selfe; and shee is able to drawe and hold some Princes to her love, because for all this infection, she retaines some colour and probability of being the same shee was. And as that Fish which *Ælianus* speakes of, lies neere to the rocke, and because it is of the colour of the rocke, surprises many fishes which come to refresh themselves at the rocke: so doth the Romane doctrine, because it can pretend by a locall and personall succession (though both interrupted) that it is so much of the colour of the rocke, and so neare it, as *Petrus* and *Petra*, envegle and entrappe many credulous persons, who have a zealous desire to build upon the rocke it selfe.

(iii)

I call to witnesse against you, those whose testimonie God himselfe hath accepted. Speake then and testifie, O you glorious and
triumphant Army of Martyrs, who enjoy now a permanent triumph
in heaven, which knew the voice of your Shepheard, and staid till
he cald, and went then with all alacritie: Is there any man received
into your blessed Legion, by title of such a Death, as sedition,
scandall, or any humane respect occasioned? O no, for they which
are in possession of that Laurell, are such as have washed their
garments, not in their owne blood onely (for so they might still
remaine redde and staind) but in the *blood of the Lambe which changes
them to white*. . . .

Thus much I was willing to premit, to awaken you, if it please
you to heare it, to a just love of your owne safetie, of the peace of
your Countrey, of the honour and reputation of your Countreymen,
and of the integritie of that, which you call the Catholicke cause;
and to acquaint you so farre, with my disposition and temper, as
that you neede not be afraid to reade my poore writings, who joyne
you with mine owne Soule in my Prayers, that your Obedience
here, may prepare your admission into the heavenly *Hierusalem*, and
that by the same Obedience, *Your dayes may bee long in the land,
which the Lord your God hath given you*. Amen.

## 4. ['This rich *Carbuncle* our soule']

As a *Depositarie* to whose trust some pretious thing were committed,
is not onely encombred and anxious, to defend it from the vio-
lencies and subtleties of outward attempters, but feeles within
himselfe some interruptions of his peace, and some invasions upon
his honesty, by a corrupt desire, and temptation to possesse it,
and to employ upon his owne pleasure or profit, that of which he
is no *Proprietary*: and never returnes to his security, out of these
watchfulnesses against other, and reluctations with himselfe; till
he who delivered this Jewell resume it againe: So, till it please the
Lord, and owner of our life to take home into his treasurie, this rich

*Carbuncle* our soule, which gives us light in our night of ignorance, and our darke body of earth, we are still anguished and travelled, as well with a continuall defensive warre, to preserve our life from sickenesses, and other offensive violences; as with a divers and contrary covetousnes, sometimes to enlarge our State and terme therein, somtimes to make it so much our owne, that we may unthriftily spend it upon surfets, or licentiousnes, or reputation.

## 5. ['This matter of *Exemption*']

As Christ asked of the *Jewes, for which of his good workes they would stone him*: Princes may aske of the Romane Church, for which of their benefites they are so injurious to them? Is it for having established a Primacy upon that Bishoppe, above his fellow Patriarches, which was so long litigious? Or for withdrawing him from the jawes of the Barbarous devourers of *Italy*? Or for enriching him with a *Patrimony*, and *Priviledges* almost equall to their owne? Is it for any of these, that you say, *A Clergy man cannot be a traytor, though he rebell; because he is no subject?* By which you cut off so great and so good a part, as in your opinion the state without it, is but a meere Carcasse, for the Clergie is the soule.

And you extend those immunities, not onely to your boyes which light your Candles, and locke the Church doores, but to every sullen fellow, that will retire himselfe into a wood, without either assuming Orders, or subjecting himself to any Religious Rule, or despoiling himselfe of his temporall possessions, as you say of your *Ermits*: Yea to *Nunnes*, who though they be not of the Clergie, yet are *Ecclesiastique persons*, and yet they are so prophane, as *they may not be admitted to touch any thing which belongs to the Altar.* And not onely the Nunnes within profession, have these priviledges, but also their Novices, who are under no vow: yea they enjoy them, whom you call *Canonicas Saeculares*, which may travell, traffique, marry, and do any civill, or uncivil function: (for of the continency of *Regular Nunnes* I am of a better perswasion, for this reason especially; that the *Jesuites* by a Constitution, are forbid to have the care of them): and those secular women, which I mentioned, are *Ecclesiastici fori* (by a late *Decision* in the *Rota*) because though they be not *Ecclesiasticae*, yet they are *Personæ Miserabiles*, and *weare an uniforme habite*: and to raise the number, you say, *If an injury be done to any kinsman of an Ecclesiastique person, it is done to him.* And that if any *offence bee committed by divers persons, amongst whome there is one Clergie man, none of the offenders can bee subject to Temporall Jurisdiction.*

And not onely all these persons, but all which appertaines to them, becomes spirituall: and by a new *Alchimy*, they doe not onely extract spirit out of every thing, but transmute it all into spirit, and by their possessing them, *Houses*, *Horses*, and *Concubines* are spirituall. But as every thing returnes to his first state, and being; and so Rome which was at first built, and governed by *Shepheards*, is returned to the same forme after the decay of the Empire: and as the name of *Bishopp*, which was at first given to *Clerkes of the Market*, and Overseers of things to be bought and solde, agrees still with these Symoniaque Bishoppes of Rome: so many of these pretious Jewels, which are employed about the Images and Reliques, which were at first *temporall*, and then by this tincture growne to be *spirituall*, returne againe to their temporall nature, when any of the Popes take ocasion to serve their pleasure, or foment dissensions amongst other Princes, and schisme amongst themselves, by coyning the Images, as *Urbanus* did, in such a case.

But the greatest injury that is done to Princes in this matter of *Exemption*, is, that they will not be beholden to Princes for it: but plead their *Jus Divinum*, not onely the positive Divine Law, by which, they say, that the Popes if they had not found these men naturally exempted, and if Princes had not granted these exemptions, might by their Constitutions, have exempted them, without asking leave of Princes, but they pretend text of Scripture, though detorted and misus'd, to prove this Exemption. And for the Persons they pretend many; but with no more directnes, than that by which they prove exemption of their goods, from secular charges and burdens, which is, *Domini est terra, et plenitudo eius*, and since it is the Lords, it is theirs.

## 6. [The Pope's power over wind and sea]

ALL which they quarrell at in the oath, is that anything should be pronounced, or any limits set, to which the Popes power might not extend: but they might as well say that his *spirituall* power were limited or shortned, and so the Catholique faith impugned, if one should denie him to have power over the winde and sea; since to tame and commaund these, *in ordine ad spiritualia*, would advance the conversion of the *Indies*, and impaire the *Turks* greatnesse, and have furthered his fatherly and spirituall care of this Kingdome in 88.[1]

[1] Cf. the inscription on one of the Armada medals: 'God blew with his winds and they were scattered.'

# IGNATIUS HIS CONCLAVE

THE liveliest of Donne's early prose works is his satire on the Jesuits, *Ignatius His Conclave*. It was written in Latin between May and December 1610 and was almost immediately translated into English. Donne's name does not appear on any of the four printings before his death (two in Latin and two in English), although his authorship was known in court and university circles. He intended the satire as a layman's sardonic contribution to the learned theological controversy in which James I, Thomas Morton, and Lancelot Andrewes, as well as a host of lesser worthies, argued against the Jesuit Cardinal Robert Bellarmine. Like *Pseudo-Martyr*, but in a lesser way, it also served as part of the Government's campaign to divide the appellant and recusant groups among the Roman Catholics in England.

The satire, which is frequently wrongly called 'menippean', is a debate much in the manner of Seneca's *Pumpkinification of Claudius* or Erasmus's *Julius Exclusus*. Donne is transported 'in extasie' to Hell where Lucifer reserves an inner chamber for great and troublesome innovators. Since only one can be admitted, Ignatius Loyola, the founder of the Jesuits, defends his own right to entry against the claims of Copernicus, Paracelsus, Machiavelli, Columbus, and Philip Neri. At the end of the debate Ignatius is so clearly the victor that a worried Lucifer embarks him for the moon to found a 'Lunatique Church'; on the general principle that 'after the Jesuits have been there a little while, there will soon grow naturally a Hell in that world also'.

The general tone of the work is genial, although Donne allows himself some moments of standard controversial scurrility. He consistently makes fun of his own learning and of the dreariness of much contemporary controversy. He is, however, quite serious (and correct) in his feeling that Jesuit teachings were a threat to the absolute claims of Stuart monarchy.

## 1. [The Plea of Machiavelli]

. . . *Machiavel* succeeded, who having observed *Ignatius* his forward-nesse, and saucinesse, and how, uncal'd, he had thrust himselfe into the office of *Kings Atturney*, thought this stupid patience of *Copernicus* and *Paracelsus* (men which tasted too much of their Germany) unfit for a *Florentine*: and therefore had provided some venemous darts, out of his *Italian Arsenal*, to cast against this worne souldier of *Pampelune*, this *French-spanish* mungrell, *Ignatius*. But when he thought better upon it and observed that *Lucifer* ever approved whatsoever *Ignatius* sayd, he suddenly changed his purpose; and putting on another resolution, he determined to direct his speech to *Ignatius*, as to the principall person next to *Lucifer*, as well by this meanes to sweeten and mollifie him, as to make *Lucifer* suspect, that by these honors and specious titles offered to *Ignatius*, and entertained by him, his owne dignity might bee eclipsed or clouded; and that *Ignatius* by winning to his side politique men, exercised in civill businesses, might atempt some innovation in that kingdome. Thus therefore he began to speake. 'Dread *Emperour*, and you, his watchfull and diligent *Genius*, father *Ignatius*, *Arch-chancellor* of this *Court*, and highest *Priest* of this highest *Synagogue* (except the primacy of the *Romane Church* reach also unto this place) let me before I descend to my selfe, a little consider, speake, and admire your stupendious wisedome, and the government of this state. You may vouchsafe to remember (great *Emperour*) how long after the *Nazarens* death, you were forced to live a solitarie, a barren, and an Eremiticall life: till at last (as it was ever your fashion to imitate heaven) out of your aboundant love, you begot this deerely beloved sonne of yours, *Ignatius*, which stands at your right hand. And from both of you proceedes a spirit, whom you have sent into the world, who triumphing both with *Mitre* and *Crowne*, governes your Militant Church there. As for those sonnes of *Ignatius*, who either he left alive, or were borne after his death, and your spirit, the Bishop of *Rome*; how justly and properly may they be called *Equivocal* men . . . because they have brought into the world a new art of *Equivocation*. O wonderfull, and incredible *Hypercritiques*, who, not out of marble fragments, but out of the secretest Records of Hell itselfe: that is, out of the minds of *Lucifer*, the *Pope*, and *Ignatius*, (persons truly equivocall) have raised to life againe the language of the Tower of *Babel*, too long concealed, and brought us againe from understanding one an other. For my part (O noble paire of *Emperours*) that I may freely confesse the truth, all which I have done, wheresoever there shall be mention made of the Jesuites, can be reputed but childish; for this honor I hope will not be denied me, that I brought in an *Alphabet*, and provided certaine elements, & was some kind of schoolmaister in preparing them a way to higher undertakings; yet it grieves me, and makes me ashamed, that I should be ranked with this idle and Chymæricall *Copernicus*, or this cadaverous vulture, *Paracelsus*, I scorne that those gates, into which such men should conceive any hope of entrance, should not voluntarily flie open to mee: yet I can better endure the rashnesse and fellowship of *Paracelsus* than the other: because hee having beene conveniently practised in the butcheries, and mangling of men, hee had the reason to hope for favour of the Jesuites: For I my selfe went alwaies that way of bloud, and therefore I did ever preferre the sacrifices of the *Gentiles*, and of the *Jewes*, which were performed with effusion of bloud (whereby not only the people, but the Priests also were animated to bold enterprises) before the soft and wanton sacrifices of *Christians*. If I might have had my choyce, I should rather have wished, that the *Romane Church* had taken the *Bread*, than the *Wine*, from the people, since in the wine there is some colour, to imagine and represent blood. Neither did you, (most Reverend *Bishop* of this *Dioces*, *Ignatius*) abhorre from this way of blood. For having consecrated your first age to the wars, and growne somewhat unable to follow that course, by reason of a wound; you did presently begin to thinke seriously of a spirituall warre, against the *Church*, and found meanes to open waies, even into Kings chambers, for your executioners. Which dignitie, you did not reserve onely to your own *Order*, but (though I must confesse that the foundation, and the nourishment of this Doctrine remaines with you, and is peculiar to you,) out of your infinite liberalitie, you have vouchsafed sometime, to use the hands of other men in these imploiments. And therefore as well they, who have so often in vaine attempted it in *England*, as they which have brought their great purposes to effect in *Fraunce*, are indebted only to you for their courage and resolution. But yet although the entrance into this place may be decreed to none, but to Innovators, and to onely such of them as have dealt in *Christian* businesse; and of them also, to those only which have had the fortune to doe much harme, I cannot see but that next to the Jesuites, I must bee invited to enter, since I did not onely teach those wayes, by which, thorough *per-fidiousnesse* and *dissembling of Religion*, a man might possesse, and usurpe upon the liberty of free *Commonwealths*; but also did arme and furnish the people with my instructions, how when they were under this oppression, they might safeliest conspire, and remove a *tyrant*, or revenge themselves of their *Prince*, and redeeme their former losses; so that from both sides, both from *Prince* and *People*, I brought an aboundant harvest, and a noble encrease to this kingdome.'

## 2. [Ignatius *contra* Machiavelli]

'BUT to proceed now to the injuries, which this fellow [Machiavelli] hath done to the *Bishop* of *Rome*, although very much might be spoken, yet by this alone, his disposition may bee sufficiently discerned, that he imputes to the *Pope*, vulgar and popular sinnes, farre unworthy of his greatnesse. Weake praising, is a kind of Accusing, and wee detract from a mans honour, if when wee praise him for small things, and would seeme to have said all, we conceale greater. Perchance this man had seen some of the *Catalogues* of *Reserv'd Cases*, which every yeare the *Popes* encrease, and he might thinke, that the *Popes* did therefore reserve these sinnes to them-selves, that they only might commit them. But either hee is ignorant, or injurious to them. For, can they bee thought to have taken away the libertie of sinning from the people, who do not onely suffer men to keepe *Concubines*, but sometimes doe commaund them? who make *S. Peter* beholden to the *stewes*, for part of his revenue: and who excuse women from the infamous name of whore, till they have delivered themselves over to 23000 men? The Professors of which Religion teach, *that Universitie men, which keep whores in their chambers, may not be expeld for that, because it ought to be presumed before hand, that schollers will not live without them.* Shal he be thought to have a purpose of deterring others from sinne, which provides so well for their security, that he teaches, that he *may dispense in all the commaundements of the second Table, & in all moral law, and that those commandements of the second table can neither be called Principles, nor Conclusions necessarily deduced from Principles?* And therefore, (as they ever love that manner of teaching) hee did illustrate his *Rule* with an Example, & dispensed in a mariage between *Brother* and *Sister*, and hath hoorded up so many *Indulgencies* in one barne, the citie of *Rome*, that it is easie for any man in an houre, or two, to draw out Pardons inough for 100000 yeares. . . . And though it be true, that if in any of these Indulgences a certaine sum of money were limited to bee given (as for the most part it is;) a poore man, which could not give that money, though he were never so contrite for his sins, could have no benefit thereby: and though *Gerson* durst call those *Indulgences foolish*, and *superstitious*, which gave 20000 yeares pardon for rehearsing one praier, yet they do aboundantly testifie the *Popes* liberall disposition, and that he is not so covetous in reserving sinnes to himselfe; But if perchance once in an hundred yeares, some one of the scumme of the people be put to death for *Sodomy*; and that, not so much for the offence, as for usurping the right of the *Ecclesiastique* Princes, wee must not much lament nor grudge at that, since it is onely done to discontinue, and interrupt a præscription, to gaine which Title, the *Layety* hath ever beene very forward against the *Clergie*: for even in this kinde of his delicacies, the *Pope* is not so reserved and covetous, but that he allowes a taste thereof to his *Cardinals* . . . To these men certainly the Pope doth no more grudge the plurality of sins, than he doth of Benefices. And he hath beene content, that even Borgia should enjoy this dignity, so that hee hath heaped up, by his ingenious wickednesse, more sorts of sins in one Act, than (as far as I know) any the *Popes* themselves have attempted: For he did not only give the full reine to his licentiousnesse, but raging with a second ambition, hee would also change the Sex. Therein also his stomacke was not towardes young beardlesse boyes, nor such greene fruit: for hee did not thinke, that hee went farre inough from the right Sex, except hee had a manly, a reverend, and a bearded *Venus*. Neither staied he there; but his witty lust proceeded further: yet he sollicited not the *Minions* of the *Popes*; but striving to equall the licentiousnesse of *Sodomits*, which would have had the *Angels*; to come as neare them as hee could, hee tooke a *Cleargy-man*, one of the portion and lot of the *Lord*: and so made the maker of *God*, a *Priest*, subject to his lust; nor did hee seeke him out in a Cloyster, or Quire; but that his *Venus* might bee the more monstrous, hee would have her in a *Mitre*. And yet his prodigious lust was not at the height; as much as hee could he added: and having found a *Man*, a *Cleargy-man*, a *Bishop*, he did not sollicite him with entreaties, and rewards, but ravished him by force. Since then the *Popes* doe, out of the fulnesse of their power, come to those kindes of sinne, which have neither *Example* nor *Name*, insomuch that Pope *Paulus Venetus*, which used to paint himselfe, & desired to seeme a woman, was called the *Goddesse Cibele* (which was not without mysterie, since, prostitute boyes are sacred to that Goddesse,) and since they do not graunt ordinarily that liberty of practising sinnes, till they have used their owne right and priviledge of *Prevention* and *Anticipation*, This pratling fellow Machiavell doth but treacherously, and dishonestly prevaricate, and betraie the cause, if hee thinke hee hath done inough for the dignity of the *Popes*, when he hath affoorded to them sins common to all the world. The transferring of Empires, the ruine of Kingdomes, the Excommunications, and depositions of Kings, and devastations by fire and sword, should have bene produced as their marks and characters.'

## 3. An Apology for Jesuites

NOW is it time to come to the *Apology* for *Jesuites*: that is, it is time to leave speaking of them, for hee favours them most which saiest least of them; Nor can any man, though hee had declaimed against them till all the sand of the sea were run through his houre-glasse, lacke matter to adde of their practises. If any man have a mind to adde any thing to this *Apology*, hee hath my leave; and I have therefore left roome for three or foure lines: which is enough for such a paradox: and more than *Jungius*, *Scribanius*, *Gretzerus*, *Richeomus*, *Cydonius*, and all the rest which are used to *Apologies*, and almost tyred with defensive warre, are able to employ, if they will write onely *good* things, and *true*, of the *Jesuites*. Neither can they comfort themselves with this, That *Cato* was called to his answere foure and forty times: for hee was so many times acquitted, which both the *Parliaments* of *England* and *France* deny of the *Jesuites*. But if any man thinke this *Apology* too short, he may thinke the whole booke an *Apology*, by this *rule* of their owne. *That it is their greatest argument of innocency to be accused by us.* At this time, whilst they are yet somewhat able to do some harme, in some places, let them make much of this *Apology*. It will come to passe shortly, when as they have bene dispoyled and expelled at *Venice*, and shaked and fanned in *France*, so they will bee forsaken of other *Princes*, and then their owne weaknesse will bee their *Apology*, and they will grow harmelesse out of necessity, and that which Vegetius sayd of chariots armed with sithes and hookes, will be applied to the Jesuites, *at first they were a terror, and after a scorne.*

# ESSAYS IN DIVINITY

*Essays in Divinity* was first published, by John Donne the Younger, early in 1652, with a dedication to Sir Henry Vane the Younger. It was reissued later in the same year, with the dedication withdrawn, in company with the *Paradoxes and Problems*. It was not reprinted until 1855 when Dr. Augustus Jessopp produced an annotated edition. Many of Jessopp's notes were incorporated by Evelyn Simpson in her edition of 1952.

The date of composition is uncertain. The younger Donne asserted in his Address to the Reader that the *Essays* were 'the voluntary sacrifices of severall hours, when he had many debates betwixt God and himself, whether he were worthy, and competently learned to enter into Holy Orders'. From this Gosse deduced that Donne wrote them just before his ordination, and, absurdly, that they were designed to be laid before Archbishop Abbott as proof of orthodoxy. Evelyn Simpson pointed out that Donne had many such 'debates' long before he actually decided to take orders and was inclined to date the *Essays* around 1611, linking them with the two *Anniversaries*. As two of the works cited by Donne were not published until 1609, the *Essays* in their present form must have been composed after that date. A number of the authors Donne cites here are cited also in *Biathanatos*, *Pseudo-Martyr*, and *Ignatius His Conclave*, written between 1608 and 1611, and in the *Catalogus Librorum* which Evelyn Simpson thought was written in its first form in 1604–5 and revised 1610–11.[1]

The *Essays* are not meditations or prayers, though meditations and prayers are interspersed among them. They are dissertations of varying lengths on topics arising out of the first verse of each of the first two books of the Bible. Thus Book I discusses the Bible, Moses as author of the Pentateuch, Genesis, the notion of 'the beginning', God, the Name of God, Creation, Heaven and Earth, and concludes with a prayer. The second book is devoted to similar discussions arising out of the first verse of Exodus, and concludes with four prayers.

---

[1] It is possible that the *Essays* contain material of different dates. Biographical references in the prayers seem more appropriate to Donne's time at Pyrford or to the early years of his stay at Mitcham before he had rooms in the Strand. H. G.

# ESSAYS IN DIVINITY

## 1. Of God

MEN which seek God by reason, and naturall strength, (though we do not deny common notions and generall impressions of a soveraign power) are like Mariners which voyaged before the invention of the Compass, which were but Costers, and unwillingly left the sight of the land. Such are they which would arrive at God by this world, and contemplate him onely in his Creatures, and seeming Demonstration. Certainly, every Creature shewes God, as a glass, but glimeringly and transitiorily, by the frailty both of the receiver, and beholder: Our selves have his Image, as Medals, permanently, and preciously delivered. But by these meditations we get no further, than to know what he *doth*, not what he *is*. But as by the use of the Compass, men safely dispatch *Ulysses* dangerous ten years travell in so many dayes, and have found out a new world richer than the old; so doth Faith, as soon as our hearts are touched with it, direct and inform us in that great search of the discovery of Gods Essence, and the new *Hierusalem*, which Reason durst not attempt. And though the faithfullest heart is not ever directly, and constantly upon God, but that it sometimes descends also to Reason; yet it is [not] thereby so departed from him, but that it still looks towards him, though not fully to him: as the Compass is ever Northward, though it decline, and have often variations towards East, and West. By this faith, as by reason, I know, that God is all that which all men can say of all Good; I beleeve he is somewhat which no man can say nor know. For, *si scirem quid Deus esset, Deus essem.* For all acquired knowledg is by degrees, and successive; but God is impartible, and only faith which can receive it all at once, can comprehend him.

## 2. Prayer

*O Eternall and Almighty power, which being infinite, hast enabled a limited creature, Faith, to comprehend thee; And being, even to Angels but a passive Mirror and looking-glasse, art to us an Active guest and domestick,* (for thou hast said, I stand at the door and knock, if any man hear me, and open the doore, I will come in unto him, and sup with him, and he with me), *and so thou dwellst in our hearts; And not there only, but even in our mouths; for though thou beest greater, and more remov'd, yet humbler and more communicable than the Kings of* Egypt, *or* Roman *Emperours, which disdain'd their particular distinguishing Names, for* Pharaoh *and* Caesar, *names of confusion; hast contracted thine immensity, and shut thy selfe within Syllables, and accepted a Name from us; O keep and defend my tongue from misusing that Name in lightnesse, passion, or falshood; and my heart, from mistaking thy Nature, by an inordinate preferring thy Justice before thy Mercy, or advancing this before that. And as, though thy self hadst no beginning thou gavest a beginning to all things in which thou wouldst be served and glorified; so, though this soul of mine, by which I partake thee, begin not now, yet let this minute, O God, this happy minute of thy visitation, be the beginning of her conversion, and shaking away confusion, darknesse, and barrennesse; and let her now produce Creatures, thoughts, words, and deeds agreeable to thee. And let her not produce them, O God, out of any contemplation, or* (I cannot say Idæa, but) Chimera of *my worthinesse, either because I am a man and no worme, and within the pale of thy Church, and not in the wild forrest, and enlightned with some glimerings of Naturall knowledge; but meerely out of Nothing: Nothing* pre[e]*xistent in her selfe, but by power of thy Divine will and word. By which, as thou didst so make Heaven, as thou didst not neglect Earth, and madest them answerable and agreeable to one another, so let my Soul's Creatures have that temper and Harmony, that they be not by a misdevout consideration of the next life, stupidly and trecherously negligent of the offices and duties which thou enjoynest amongst us in this life; nor so anxious in these, that the other* (which is our better business, though this also must be attended) *be the less endeavoured. Thou hast, O God, denyed even to Angells, the ability of arriving from one Extreme to another, without passing the mean way between. Nor can we pass from the prison of our Mothers womb, to thy palace, but we must walk* (in that pace whereto thou *hast enabled us) through the street of this life, and not sleep at the first corner, nor in the midst. Yet since my soul is sent immediately from thee, let me (for her return) rely, not principally, but wholly upon thee and thy word: and for this body, made of preordained matter, and instruments, let me so use the materiall means of her sustaining, that I neither neglect the seeking, nor grudge the missing of the Conveniencies of this life: And that for fame, which is a mean Nature between them, I so esteem opinion, that I despise not others thoughts of me, since most men are such, as most men think they be: nor so reverence it, that I make it alwayes the rule of my Actions. And because in this world my Body was first made, and then my Soul, but in the next my soul shall be first, and then my body, In my Exterior and morall conversation let my first and presentest care be to give them satisfaction with whom I am mingled, because they may be scandaliz'd, but thou, which seest hearts, canst not: But for my faith, let my first relation be to thee, because of that thou art justly jealous, which they cannot be. Grant these requests, O God, if I have asked fit things fitly, and as many more, under the same limitations, as are within that prayer which (As thy Manna, which was meat for all tasts, and served to the appetite of him which took it, and was that which every man would) includes all which all can aske, Our* Father which art, *etc.*

# 3. [The true sense of Scripture]

I DO not (I hope) in undertaking the Meditation upon this verse,[1] incur the fault of them, who for ostentation and magnifying their wits, excerpt and tear shapeless and unsignificant rags of a word or two, from whole sentences, and make them obey their purpose in discoursing; The Souldiers would not divide our Saviours garment, though past his use and his propriety. No garment is so neer God as his word: which is so much his, as it is *he*. His flesh, though dignified with unexpressible priviledges, is not so near God, as his word: for that is *Spiritus Oris*. And in the Incarnation, the Act was onely of one Person, but the whole Trinity speaks in every word. They therefore which stub up these severall roots, and mangle them into chips,

---

1 The verse is 'Now these are the Names of the Children of Israel which came into Egypt, etc.' (Exod. i. 1).

in making the word of God not such, (for the word of God is not the word of God in any other sense than literall, and that also is not the literall, which the letter seems to present, for so to diverse understandings there might be diverse literall senses; but it is called literall, to distinguish it from the Morall, Allegoricall, and the other senses; and is that which the Holy Ghost doth in that place principally intend:) they, I say, do what they can this way, to make God, whose word it is pretended to be, no God. They which build, must take the solid stone, not the rubbish. Of which, though there be none in the word of God, yet often unsincere translations, to justifie our prejudices and foreconceived opinions, and the underminings and batteries of Hereticks, and the curious refinings of the Allegoricall Fathers, which have made the Scriptures, which are stronge toyles, to catch and destroy the bore and bear which devast our Lords vineyard, fine cobwebs to catch flies; And of strong [cables], by which we might anker in all storms of Disputation and Persecution, the threads of silkworms, curious vanities and excesses (for do not many among us study even the Scriptures only for ornament?) these, I say, may so bruse them, and raise so much dust, as may blinde our Eyes, and make us see nothing, by coveting too much. He which first invented the cutting of Marble, had (says *Pliny*) *importunum ingenium*; a wit that would take no answer nor denyal. So have they which break these Sentences, *importuna ingenia*, unseasonable and murmuring spirits. When God out of his abundance affords them whole Sentences, yea Chapters, rather than not have enough to break to their auditory, they will attempt to feed miraculously great Congregations with a loafe or two, and a few fishes; that is, with two or three incoherent words of a Sentence. I remember I have read of a General, who, having at last carryed a town, yet not meerly by force, but upon this article, That in sign of subjection they should admit him to take away one row of stones round about their wall, chose to take the undermost row, by which the whole wall ruined. So do they demolish Gods fairest Temple, his Word, which pick out such stones, and deface the integrity of it, so much, as neither that which they take, nor that which they leave, is the word of God. In the Temple was admitted no sound of hammer, nor in the building of this great patriarchal Catholick Church, of which every one of us is a little chappel, should the word be otherwise wrested or broken, but taken intirely as it is offered and presented.

## 4. [The Register of Scripture]

AMONGST men, all Depositaries of our Memories, all means which we have trusted with the preserving of our Names, putrifie and perish. Of the infinite numbers of the Medals of the Emperors, some one happy Antiquary, with much pain, travell, cost, and most faith, beleeves he hath recovered some one rusty piece, which deformity makes reverend to him, and yet is indeed the fresh work of an Impostor.

The very places of the *Obeliscs*, and *Pyramides* are forgotten, and the purpose why they were erected. Books themselves are subject to the mercy of the Magistrate: and as though the ignorant had not been enemie enough for them, the Learned unnaturally and treacherously contribute to their destruction, by rasure and mis-interpretation. *Caligula* would abolish *Homer*, *Virgil*, and all the Lawyers Works, and eternize himself and his time in Medals: The Senate, after his death, melted all them: Of their brasse [*Claudius*] his Wife *Messalina* made the Statue of her beloved Player; and where is that? But Names honour'd with a place in this book, cannot perish, because the Book cannot. Next to the glory of having his name entred into the *Book of Life*, this is the second, to have been matriculated in this Register, for an example or instrument of good. *Lazarus* his name is enrolled, but the wicked rich mans omitted.

## 5. [The Unity of the Church]

I ENCLINE to think, that another usefull document arises from this admitting of variety;[1] which seems to me to be this, that God in his eternall and ever-present omniscience, foreseeing that his universal, Christian, Catholick Church, imaged, and conceived, and

[1] Donne is discussing why the Children of Israel are given different names in Genesis and Exodus.

begotten by him in his eternall decree, born and brought to light when he travail'd and labored in those bitter agonies and throes of his passion, nourced ever more delicately and preciously than any natural children (for they are fed with their Mothers blood in her womb, but we with the blood of our most Blessed Saviour all our lives,) fore-seeing, I say, that this his dearly beloved Spouse, and Sister, and Daughter, the Church, should in her latter Age suffer many convulsions, distractions, rents, schisms, and wounds, by the severe and unrectified Zeal of many, who should impose necessity upon indifferent things, and oblige all the World to one precise forme of exterior worship, and Ecclesiastick policie; averring that every degree, and minute and scruple of all circumstances which may be admitted in either beleif or practice, is certainly, constantly, expressly, and obligatorily exhibited in the Scriptures; and that Grace, and Salvation is in this unity and no where else; his Wisdome was mercifully pleas'd, that those particular Churches, devout parts of the Universall, which, in our Age, keeping still the foundation and corner stone Christ Jesus, should piously abandon the spacious and specious super-edifications which the Church of *Rome* had built therupon, should from this variety of Names in the Bible it selfe, be provided of an argument, *That an unity and consonance in things not essentiall, is not so necessarily requisite as is imagined.* Certainly, when the Gentiles were assum'd into the Church, they entred into the same fundamentall faith and religion with the Jews, as *Musculus* truly notes; and this conjunction in the roote and foundation, fulfill'd that which was said, *Fiet unum Ovile, et unus Pastor*, One fold, and one shepherd. For, by that before, you may see that all Christs sheep are not alwayes in one fold, *Other sheep have I also, which are not of this fold.* So, all his sheep are of one fold, that is, *under one Shepherd, Christ*; yet not of one fold, that is, not *in one place*, nor form. For, that which was strayed and alone, was his sheep; much more any flock which hearken together to his voice, his Word, and feed together upon his Sacraments. Therefore that Church from which we are by Gods Mercy escaped, because upon the foundation, which we yet embrace together, Redemption in Christ, they had built so many stories high, as the foundation was, though not destroyed, yet hid and obscured; And their Additions

were of so dangerous a construction, and appearance, and misapply-
ableness, that to tender consciences they seem'd Idolatrous, and
are certainly scandalous and very slippery, and declinable into
Idolatry, though the Church be not in circumstantiall and deduced
points, at unity with us, nor it self; (for, with what tragick rage
do the Sectaries of *Thomas* and *Scotus* prosecute their differences?
and how impetuously doth *Molinas* and his Disciples at this day,
impugne the common doctrine of grace and freewill? And though
these points be not immediately fundamentall points of faith, yet
radically they are, and as neer the root as most of those things
wherein we and they differ;) yet though we branch out *East* and
*West,* that Church concurs with us in the root, and sucks her
vegetation from one and the same ground, *Christ Jesus;* who, as it is
in the *Canticle* lies between the brests of his Church, and gives suck
on both sides. And of that Church which is departed from us,
disunited by an opinion of a necessity that all should be united
in one form, and that theirs is it, since they keep their right foot
fast upon the Rock Christ, I dare not pronounce that she is not our
Sister; but rather as in the same *Song of Solomon's, We have a little
sister, and she hath no brests: if she be a wall, we will build upon her a silver
palace.* If therefore she be a wall, That is, *Because* she is a wall; for so
*Lyra* expounds those words, as on her part, she shall be safer from
ruine, if she apply her selfe to receive a *silver palace* of Order, and
that Hierarchy which is most convenient and proportionall to that
ground and state wherein God hath planted her; and she may not
transplant her self: So shall we best conserve the integrity of our
own body, of which she is a member, if we laboriously build upon
her, and not tempestuously and ruinously demolish and annull her;
but rather cherish and foment her vitall and wholsome parts, than
either cut, or suffer them to rot or moulder off. As naturall, so
politick bodies have *Cutem, et Cuticulam.* The little thin skin which
covers al our body, may be broken without pain or danger, and
may reunite it selfe, because it consists not of the chief and prin-
cipiant parts. But if in the skin it self, there be any solution or
division, which is seldome without drawing of blood, no art nor
good disposition of Nature, can ever bring the parts together again,
and restore the same substance, though it seem to the ey to have

sodder'd it self. It will ever seem so much as a deforming Scar, but is in truth a breach. Outward Worship is this *Cuticula*: and integrity of faith the skin it self. And if the first be touched with any thing too corrosive, it will quickly pierce the other; and so Schism, which is a departure from obedience, will quickly become Heresie, which is a wilfull deflexion from the way of faith. Which is not yet, so long as the main skin is inviolate: for so long that Church which despises another Church, is it self no other than that of which the *Psalm* speakes, *Ecclesia Malignantium*.

Thus much was to my understanding naturally occasioned and presented by this variety of Names in the Scriptures: For, if *Esau*, *Edom*, and *Seir* were but one man; *Jethro* and *Revel*, etc. but one man, which have no consonance with one another, and might thereby discredit and enervate any History but this, which is the fountain of truth; so Synagogue and Church is the same thing, and of the Church, *Roman* and *Reformed*, and all other distinctions of place, Discipline, or Person, but one Church, journying to one *Hierusalem*, and directed by one guide, Christ Jesus; In which, though this Unity of things not fundamentall, be not absolutely necessary, yet it were so comely and proportionall with the foundation it self, if it were at Unity in these things also, that though in my poor opinion, the form of Gods worship, established in the Church of *England* be more convenient, and advantageous than of any other Kingdome, both to provoke and kindle devotion, and also to fix it, that it stray not into infinite expansions and Subdivisions; (into the former of which, Churches utterly despoyl'd of Ceremonies, seem to me to have fallen; and the *Roman* Church, by presenting innumerable objects, into the later.) And though to all my thanksgivings to God, I ever humbly acknowledg, as one of his greatest Mercies to me, that he gave me my Pasture in this Park, and my milk from the brests of this Church, yet out of a fervent, and (I hope) not inordinate affection, even to such an Unity, I do zealously wish, that the whole catholick Church, were reduced to such Unity and agreement, in the form and profession Established, in any one of these Churches (though ours were principally to be wished) which have not by any additions destroyed the foundation and possibility of salvation in Christ Jesus; That then the Church, discharged of disputations, and misapprehensions, and this defensive warr, might contemplate Christ clearly and uniformely. For now he appears to her, as in *Cant. 2. 9. He standeth behind a wall, looking forth of the window, shewing himself through the grate.* But then, when all had one appetite, and one food, one nostrill and one purfume, the Church had obtained that which she then asked, *Arise ô North, and come ô South, and blow on my garden, that the spices thereof may flow out.* For then, that *savour of life unto life* might allure and draw those to us, whom our dissentions, more than their own stubborness with-hold from us.

## 6. [The mercy of God]

HIS Mercy is infinite in Extent: for it is in all places; yea, where there is no place: And it is infinite in Duration; For as it never begun, (for the Ideating of this world, which was from everlasting, was a work of mercy) and as the interruptions which by acts of Justice it seemes to suffer here, discontinue it not, (for though God say, *For a moment in mine anger I hid my face from thee*; yet he adds there, *yet with everlasting Mercy have I had compassion on thee*;) so also is it reasonable to think, that it shall never have end.

## 7. ['Let no smalnesse retard thee']

ALAS, our greatness is Hydroptick, not solid: we are not firm, but puffed, and swoln; we are the lighter, and the lesser for such greatness. *Alcibiades* bragg'd how he could walk in his own ground; all this was his, and no man a foot within him; and *Socrates* gave him a little map of the world, and bid him show him his territory there; and there an Ant would have overstrid it. Let no smalnesse retard thee: if thou beest not a Cedar to help towards a palace, if thou beest not Amber, Bezoar, nor liquid gold, to restore Princes; yet thou art a shrub to shelter a lambe, or to feed a bird; or thou art a plantane, to ease a childs smart; or a grasse to cure a sick dog. Love an asker better than a giver: which was good *Agapetus* counsel to *Justinian*: Yea rather, prevent the asking; and do not so much joyn and concur with misery, as to suffer it to grow to that strength, that it shall make thy brother ask, and put him to the danger of a denyall.

## 8. [Deliverances from Egypts]

ONLY to paraphrase the History of this Delivery, without amplifying, were furniture and food enough for a meditation of the best perseverence, and appetite, and digestion; yea, the least word in the History would serve a long rumination. If this be in the bark, what is in the tree? If in the superficiall grass, the letter; what treasure is there in the hearty and inward Mine, the Mistick and retired sense? Dig a little deeper, O my poor lazy soul, and thou shalt see that thou, and all mankind are delivered from an Egypt; and more miraculously than these. . . . Go one step lower, that is higher, and nearer to God, O my soul, in this Meditation, and thou shalt see, that even in this moment, when he affords thee these thoughts, he delivers thee from an Egypt of dulness and stupiditie. As often as he moves thee to pray to be delivered from the Egypt of sin, he delivers thee. And as often as thou promisest him not to return thither, he delivers thee. Thou hast delivered me, O God, from the Egypt of confidence and presumption, by interrupting my fortunes, and intercepting my hopes; And from the Egypt of despair by contemplation of thine abundant treasures, and my portion therein; from the Egypt of lust, by confining my affections; and from the monstrous and unnaturall Egypt of painfull and wearisome idleness, by the necessities of domestick and familiar cares and duties. Yet as an Eagle, though she enjoy her wing and beak, is wholly prisoner, if she be held by but one talon; so are we, though we could be delivered of all habit of sin, in bondage still, if Vanity hold us but by a silken thred. But, O God, as mine inward corruptions have made me mine own *Pharaoh*, and mine own *Egypt*; so thou, by the inhabitation of thy Spirit, and application of thy merit, hast made me mine own Christ; and contenting thy self with being my Medicine, allowest me to be my Physician.

## 9. [The Power of God]

OF all the wayes in which God hath expressed himselfe towards us, we have made no word which doth lesse signifie what we mean, than *Power*: for *Power*, which is but an ability to do, ever relates to some future thing: and God is ever a present, simple, and pure Act. But we think we have done much, and gone far, when we have made up the word *Omnipotence*, which is both wayes improper; for it is much too short, because *Omnipotence* supposes and confesses a matter and subject to work upon, and yet God was the same, when there was nothing. And then it over-reaches, and goes down-wards beyond God: for God hath not, or is not such an Omnipotence, as can do all things; for though squeamish and tenderer men think it more mannerly to say, *This thing cannot be done*, than, *God cannot do this thing*; yet it is all one: And if that be an Omnipotence, which is limited with the nature of the worker, or with the congruity of the subject, other things may incroach upon the word *Omnipotent*; that is, they can do all things which are not against their nature, or the nature of the matter upon which they work. *Beza* therefore might well enough say, That God could not make a body without place; And *Prateolus* might truly enough infer upon that, that the *Bezanites* (as he calls them) deny omnipotence in God; for both are true. And therefore I doubt not, but it hath some mysterie, that the word *Omnipotence* is not found in all the Bible; nor *Omnipotent* in the New Testament. And where it is in the Old, it would rather be interpreted *All-sufficient*, than *Almighty*; between which there is much difference. God is so *Al-sufficient*, that he is sufficient for all. . . . So that, as yet our understanding hath found no word, which is well proportioned to that which we mean by *power of God*.

## 10. [Miracles]

*Nature* is the *Common law* by which God governs us, and *Miracle* is his *Prerogative*. For Miracles are but so many *Non-obstantes* upon Nature. And Miracle is not like prerogative in any thing more than in this, that no body can tell what it is. For first, Creation and such as that, are not Miracles, because they are not (to speak in that language) *Nata fieri per alium modum.* And so, only that is Miracle, which might be done naturally, and is not so done. And then, lest we allow the Divell a power to do Miracles, we must say, that Miracle is *contra totam Naturam,* against the whole order and disposition of Nature . . . I can change some naturall things (as I can make a stone fly upward) a Physician more, and the Divell more than he; but only God can change all. And after that is out of necessity established, that *Miracle* is against the whole *Order* of Nature, I see not how there is left in God a power of Miracles. For, the Miracles which are produced to day, were determined and inserted into the body of the whole History of Nature (though they seem to us to be but interlineary and Marginall) at the beginning, and are as infallible and certain, as the most Ordinary and customary things. Which is evicted and approved by that which *Lactantius* says, and particularly proves, that all Christs Miracles were long before prophecied. So that truly nothing can be done against the Order of Nature. For, Saint *Augustine* says truly, That is Naturall to each thing, which God doth, from whom proceeds all Fashion, Number and Order of Nature: for that God, whose Decree is the Nature of every thing, should do against his own Decree, if he should do against Nature. As therefore if we understood all created Nature, nothing would be *Mirum* to us; so if we knew Gods purpose, nothing would be *Miraculum.*

# 11. Prayer

*O Eternall God, as thou didst admit thy faithfull servant* Abraham, *to make the granting of one petition an incouragement and rise to another, and gavest him leave to gather upon thee from fifty to ten; so I beseech thee, that since by thy grace, I have thus long meditated upon thee, and spoken of thee, I may now speak to thee. As thou hast enlightned and enlarged me to contemplate thy greatness, so, O God, descend thou and stoop down to see my infirmities and the Egypt in which I live; and (If thy good pleasure be such) hasten mine Exodus and deliverance, for I desire to be dissolved, and be with thee. O Lord, I most humbly acknowledg and confess thine infinite Mercy, that when thou hadst almost broke the staff of bread, and called a famine of thy word almost upon all the world, then thou broughtest me into this Egypt, where thou hadst appointed thy stewards to husband thy blessings, and to feed thy flock. Here also, O God, thou hast multiplied thy children in me, by begetting and cherishing in me reverent devotions, and pious affections towards thee, but that mine own corruption, mine own* Pharaoh *hath ever smothered and strangled them. And thou hast put me in my way towards thy land of promise, thy Heavenly* Canaan, *by removing me from the Egypt of frequented and populous, glorious places, to a more solitary and desart retiredness, where I may more safely feed upon both thy Mannaes, thy self in thy Sacrament, and that other, which is true Angells food, contemplation of thee. O Lord, I most humbly acknowledg and confess, that I feel in me so many strong effects of thy Power, as only for the Ordinariness and frequency thereof, they are not Miracles. For hourly thou rectifiest my lameness, hourly thou restorest my sight, and hourly not only deliverest me from the Egypt, but raisest me from the death of sin. My sin, O God, hath not onely caused thy descent hither, and passion here; but by it I am become that hell into which thou descendedst after thy Passion; yea, after thy glorification: for hourly thou in thy Spirit descendest into my heart, to overthrow there Legions of spirits of Disobedience, and Incredulity, and Murmuring. O Lord, I most humbly acknowledg and confesse, that by thy Mercy I have a sense of thy Justice; for not onely those afflictions with which it pleaseth thee to exercise mee, awaken me to consider how terrible thy severe justice is; but even the rest and security which thou affordest mee, puts me often into fear, that thou reservest and sparest me for a greater measure of punishment. O Lord, I most humbly acknowledg and confesse, that I have understood sin, by understanding thy laws and judgments; but have done against thy known and revealed will. Thou hast set up many candlesticks, and kindled many lamps in mee; but I have either blown them out, or carried them to guide me in by and forbidden ways. Thou hast given mee a desire of knowledg, and some meanes to it, and some possession of it; and I have arm'd my self with thy weapons against thee: Yet, O God, have mercy upon me, for thine own sake have mercy upon me. Let not sin and me be able to exceed thee, nor to defraud thee, nor to frustrate thy purposes: But let me, in despite of Me, be of so much use to thy glory, that by thy mercy to my sin, other sinners may see how much sin thou canst pardon. Thus show mercy to many in one: And shew thy power and al-mightinesse upon thy self, by casting manacles upon thine own hands, and calling back those Thunder-bolts which thou hadst thrown against mee. Show thy Justice upon the common Seducer and De-vourer of us all: and show to us so much of thy Judgments, as may instruct, not condemn us. Hear us, O God, hear us, for this contrition, which thou hast put into us, who come to thee with that watchword, by which thy Son hath assured us of access.* Our Father which art in Heaven, *etc.*

## 12. Prayer

*O Eternal God, who art not only first and last, but in whom, first and last is all one, who art not only all Mercy, and all Justice, but in whom Mercy and Justice is all one; who in the height of thy Justice, wouldest not spare thine own, and only most innocent Son; and yet in the depth of thy mercy, would'st not have the wretched'st liver come to destruction; Behold us, O God, here gathered together in thy fear, according to thine ordinance, and in confidence of thy promise, that when two or three are gathered together in thy name, thou wilt be in the midst of them, and grant them their petitions. We confess, O God, that we are not worthy so much as to confess; less to be heard, least of all to be pardoned our manifold sins and transgressions against thee. We have betrayed thy Temples to prophaness, our bodies to sensuality, thy fortresses to thine enemy, our soules to Satan. We have armed him with thy munition to fight against thee, by surrendring our eyes, and eares, all our senses, all our faculties to be exercised and wrought upon, and tyran-nized by him. Vanities and disguises have covered us, and thereby we are naked; licenciousness hath inflam'd us, and thereby we are frozen; voluptu-ousness hath fed us, and thereby we are sterved, the fancies and traditions of men have taught and instructed us, and thereby we are ignorant. These distempers, thou only, O God, who art true, and perfect harmonie, canst tune, and rectify, and set in order again. Doe so then, O most Mercifull Father, for thy most innocent Sons sake: and since he hath spread his armes upon the cross, to receive the whole world, O Lord, shut out none of us (who are now fallen before the throne of thy Majesty and thy Mercy) from the benefit of his merits; but with as many of us, as begin their conversion and newness of life, this minute, this minute, O God, begin thou thy account with them, and put all that is past out of thy remembrance. Accept our humble thanks for all thy Mercies; and, continue and enlarge them upon the whole Church, etc.*

## 13. Prayer

*O Most glorious and most gracious God, into whose presence our own consciences make us afraid to come, and from whose presence we cannot hide our selves, hide us in the wounds of thy Son, our Saviour Christ Jesus; And though our sins be as red as scarlet, give them there another redness, which may be acceptable in thy sight. We renounce, O Lord, all our confidence in this world; for this world passeth away, and the lusts thereof: Wee renounce all our confidence in our own merits, for we have done nothing in respect of that which we might have done, neither could we ever have done any such thing, but that still we must have remained unprofitable servants to thee; we renounce all confidence, even in our own confessions, and accusations of our self; for our sins are above number, if we would reckon them; above weight and measure, if we would weigh and measure them; and past finding out, if we would seek them in those dark corners, in which we have multiplied them against thee: yea we renounce all confidence even in our repentances; for we have found by many lamentable experiences, that we never perform our promises to thee, never perfect our purposes in our selves, but relapse again and again into those sins which again and again we have repented. We have no confidence in this world, but in him who hath taken possession of the next world for us, by sitting down at thy right hand. We have no confidence in our merits, but in him, whose merits thou hast been pleased to accept for us, and to apply to us, we have: no confidence in our own confessions and repentances, but in that blessed Spirit, who is the Author of them, and loves to perfect his own works and build upon his own foundations, we have: Accept them therefore, O Lord, for their sakes whose they are; our poor endeavours, for thy glorious Sons sake, who gives them their root, and so they are his; our poor beginnings of sanctification, for thy blessed Spirits sake, who gives them their growth, and so they are his: and for thy Sons sake, in whom only our prayers are acceptable to thee: and for thy Spirits sake which is now in us, and must be so whensoever we do pray acceptably to thee; accept our humble prayers for, etc.*

## 14. Prayer

*O Eternall and most merciful God, against whom, as we know and acknowledg that we have multiplied contemptuous and rebellious sins, so we know and acknowledg too, that it were a more sinfull contempt and rebellion, than all those, to doubt of thy mercy for them; have mercy upon us: In the merits and mediation of thy Son, our Saviour Christ Jesus, be mercifull unto us. Suffer not, O Lord, so great a waste, as the effusion of his blood, without any return to thee; suffer not the expence of so rich a treasure, as the spending of his life, without any purchace to thee; but as thou didst empty and evacuate his glory here upon earth, glorify us with that glory which his humiliation purchased for us in the kingdom of Heaven. And as thou didst empty that Kingdome of thine, in a great part, by the banishment of those Angels, whose pride threw them into everlasting ruine, be pleased to repair that Kingdom, which their fall did so far depopulate, by assuming us into their places, and making us rich with their confiscations. And to that purpose, O Lord, make us capable of that succession to thine Angels there; begin in us here in this life an angelicall purity, an angelicall chastity, an angelicall integrity to thy service, an Angelical acknowledgment that we alwaies stand in thy presence, and should direct al our actions to thy glory. Rebuke us not, O Lord, in thine anger, that we have not done so till now; but enable us now to begin that great work; and imprint in us an assurance that thou receivest us now graciously, as reconciled, though enemies; and fatherly, as children, though prodigals; and powerfully, as the God of our salvation, though our own consciences testifie against us. Continue and enlarge thy blessings upon the whole Church, etc.*

# DEVOTIONS UPON
# EMERGENT OCCASIONS

IN the winter of 1623 Donne fell dangerously ill and during this illness he composed the *Devotions* which was published in 1624. The *Devotions* is the most popular of Donne's works. There were two more editions in his lifetime and further editions appeared in 1634 and 1638. It was included in Alford's edition of Donne's works in 1839 and there were also editions in 1840 and 1841. The standard modern edition is by John Sparrow in 1923.

The form of the *Devotions* is rigid. It consists of twenty-three sections, each containing a meditation, an expostulation, and a prayer. The meditations describe with considerable realism the progress of Donne's illness which is summarized in a Latin poem prefixed to the whole work. We give this poem, and the first section *Insultus Morbi Primus* complete, to show the form of the whole. It is followed by passages selected by Evelyn Simpson.

# DEVOTIONS UPON EMERGENT OCCASIONS

## Stationes, *sive* Periodi *in* Morbo, *ad quas referuntur* Meditationes sequentes

1 Insultus *Morbi primus*; 2 Post, Actio laesa;
3 Decubitus *sequitur tandem*; 4 Medicusque *vocatur*;
5 Solus *adest*; 6 Metuit; 7 Socios *sibi jungier instat;*
8 *Et* Rex *ipse suum mittit;* 9 Medicamina scribunt;
10 Lente *et Serpenti satagunt occurrere Morbo.*
11 *Nobilibusque trahunt, a cincto corde, venenum,*
 Succis *et* Gemmis; *et quae generosa ministrant*
 Ars, *et* Natura, *instillant;* 12 *Spirante* Columba,
 *Supposita pedibus, revocantur ad ima* vapores;
13 *Atque* Malum Genium, *numeroso* stigmate, *fassus,*
 *Pellitur ad pectus, Morbique Suburbia,* Morbus:
14 *Idque notant* Criticis, Medici *evenisse* diebus.
15 *Interea* insomnes *Noctes ego duco Diesque:*
16 *Et properare meum, clamant, e turre propinqua*
 *Obstreperae* Campanae, aliorum *in funere, funus.*
17 *Nunc* lento sonitu *dicunt,* Morieris; 18 *At inde*
 Mortuus *es, sonitu* celeri, pulsuque agitato.
19 Oceano *tandem emenso,* aspicienda resurgit
 Terra; *vident, justis,* Medici, *jam* cocta *mederi*
 Se posse, *indiciis;* 20 Id agunt; 21 *Atque annuit* Ille
 *Qui per* eos *clamat, linquas jam* Lazare *lectum;*
22 *Sit* Morbi Fomes *tibi* Cura; 23 Metusque Relabi.

## 1. *Insultus Morbi Primus*

1. Insultus Morbi        *The first alteration, The first grudging of the*
   Primus;              *sicknesse.*

## I. Meditation.

VARIABLE, and therefore miserable condition of Man; this minute
I was well, and am ill, this minute. I am surpriz'd with a sodaine
change, and alteration to worse, and can impute it to no cause, nor
call it by any name. We study *Health*, and we deliberate upon our
*meats*, and *drink*, and *ayre*, and *exercises*, and we hew, and wee polish
every stone, that goes to that building; and so our *Health* is a long
and a regular work; But in a minute a Canon batters all, over-
throwes all, demolishes all; a *Sicknes* unprevented for all our diligence, unsuspected for all our curiositie; nay, undeserved, if we
consider only *disorder*, summons us, seizes us, possesses us, de-
stroyes us in an instant. O miserable condition of Man, which was
not imprinted by *God*, who as hee is *immortall* himselfe, had put a
*coale*, a *beame* of *Immortalitie* into us, which we might have blowen
into a *flame*, but blew it out, by our first sinne; wee beggard our
selves by hearkning after false riches, and infatuated our selves by
hearkning after false knowledge. So that now, we doe not onely die,
but die upon the Rack, die by the torment of sicknesse; nor that
onely, but are preafflicted, super-afflicted with these jelousies and
suspitions, and apprehensions of *Sicknes*, before we can cal it a
sicknes; we are not sure we are ill; one hand askes the other by the
pulse, and our eye asks our urine, how we do. O multiplied misery!
we die, and cannot enjoy death, because wee die in this torment of
sicknes; we are tormented with sicknes, and cannot stay till the
torment come, but preapprehensions and presages, prophecy those
torments, which induce that *death* before either come; and our
dissolution is conceived in these *first changes*, *quickned* in the *sicknes*
it selfe, and *borne* in *death*, which beares date from these first changes.
Is this the honour which Man hath by being a *litle world*, That he
hath these *earthquakes* in him selfe, sodaine shakings; these *lightnings*,
sodaine flashes; these *thunders*, sodaine noises; these *Eclypses*, sodain

offuscations, and darknings of his senses; these *Blazing stars*, sodaine fiery exhalations; these *Rivers of blood*, sodaine red waters? Is he a *world* to himselfe onely therefore, that he hath inough in himself, not only to destroy, and execute himselfe, but to presage that execution upon himselfe; to assist the sicknes, to antidate the sicknes, to make the sicknes the more irremediable, by sad apprehensions, and as if he would make a fire the more vehement, by sprinkling water upon the coales, so to wrap a hote fever in cold Melancholy, least the fever alone should not destroy fast enough, without this contribution, nor perfit the work (which is *destruction*) except we joynd an artificiall sicknes, of our owne *melancholy*, to our natural, our unnaturall fever. O perplex'd discomposition, O ridling distemper, O miserable condition of Man.

## I. Expostulation.

IF I were but meere *dust* and *ashes*, I might speak unto the *Lord*, for the *Lordes* hand made me of this *dust*, and the *Lords* hand shall recollect these *ashes*; the *Lords* hand was the wheele, upon which this vessell of clay was framed, and the *Lordes hand* is the *Urne*, in which these ashes shall be preserv'd. I am the *dust*, and the *ashes* of the *Temple* of the *H. Ghost*; and what Marble is so precious? But I am more than *dust* and *ashes*; I am my best part, I am my *soule*. And being so, the *breath* of God, I may breath back these pious *expostulations* to my God. *My God, my God,* why is not my *soule*, as sensible as my *body*? Why hath not my *soule* these apprehensions, these presages, these changes, these antidates, these jealousies, these suspitions of a *sinne*, as well as my body of a *sicknes*? why is there not alwayes a *pulse* in my *soule*, to beat at the approch of a tentation to sinne? why are there not always *waters* in mine eyes, to testifie to my spiritual sicknes? I stand in the way of tentations, (naturally, necessarily, all men doe so: for there is a *Snake in every path*, tentations in every vocation) but I go, I run, I flie into the wayes of tentation, which I might shun; nay, I breake into houses, wher the plague is; I presse into places of tentation, and tempt the *devill* himselfe, and solicite and importune them, who had rather be left unsolicited by me. I fall sick of *Sin*, and am bedded and bedrid,

buried and putrified in the practise of *Sin*, and all this while have
no presage, no pulse, no sense of my *sicknesse*; O heighth, O depth
of misery, where the first *Symptome* of the sicknes is *Hell*, and where
I never see the fever of lust, of envy, of ambition, by any other
light, than the darknesse and horror of *Hell* it selfe; and where the
first Messenger that speaks to me doth not say, *Thou mayst die*,
no nor *Thou must die*, but *Thou art dead*: and where the first notice,
that my *Soule* hath of her sicknes, is *irrecoverablenes, irremediablenes*:
but, O my God, *Job did not charge thee foolishly*, in his temporall
afflictions, nor may I in my spirituall. Thou has imprinted a *pulse* in
our *Soule*, but we do not examine it; a voice in our conscience, but
we do not hearken unto it. We talk it out, we drinke it out, we
sleepe it out; and when we wake, we doe not say with *Jacob, Surely
the Lord is in this place, and I knew it not*: but though we might know it,
we do not, we wil not. But will *God* pretend to make a *Watch*, and
leave out the *springe*? to make so many various wheels in the faculties
of the soule, and in the organs of the body, and leave out *Grace*, that
should move them? or wil *God* make a *springe*, and not *wind* it up? Infuse
his first *grace*, and not second it with more, without which we can no
more use his first *grace*, when we have it, than wee could dispose
our selves by *Nature*, to have it? But alas, that is not our case; we
are all *prodigall sonnes*, and not *disinherited*; wee have recieved our
portion, and mis-spent it, not bin denied it. We are *Gods tenants* heere,
and yet here, he, our *Land-lord* payes us *Rents*; not yearely, nor
quarterly: but hourely, and quarterly; *Every minute he renewes his
mercy*, but wee *will not understand, least that we should bee converted,
and he should heale us.*

### I. Prayer.

O ETERNALL, and most gracious *God*, who, considered in thy
selfe, art a *Circle*, first and last, and altogether; but considered in
thy working upon us, art a *direct line*, and leadest us from our
*beginning*, through all our wayes, to our end, enable me by thy
grace, to looke forward to mine end, and to looke backward to, to
the considerations of thy mercies afforded mee from my beginning;
that so by that practise of considering thy mercy, in my beginning

in this world, when thou plantedst me in the *Christian Church*, and thy mercy in the beginning in the other world, when thou writest me in the *Booke of life* in my *Election*, I may come to a holy consideration of thy *mercy*, in the beginning of all my actions here: that in all the beginnings, in all the accesses, and approches of spirituall sicknesses of *Sinn*, I may heare and hearken to that voice, *O thou Man of God, there is death in the pot*, and so refraine from that, which I was so hungerly, so greedily flying to. *A faithfull Ambassador is health*, says thy wise servant *Solomon*. Thy voice received, in the beginning of a sicknesse, of a sinne, is true health. If I can see that light betimes, and heare that voyce early, *Then shall my light breake forth as the morning, and my health shall spring forth speedily*.

Deliver mee therefore, O my God, from these vaine imaginations; that it is an overcurious thing, a dangerous thing, to come to that tendernesse, that rawnesse, that scrupulousnesse, to feare every *concupiscence*, every offer of *Sin*, that this suspicious, and jealous diligence will turne to an inordinate dejection of spirit, and a diffidence in thy care and providence; but keep me still establish'd, both in a constant assurance, that thou wilt speake to me at the beginning of every such sicknes, at the approach of every such *sinne*; and that, if I take knowledg of that voice then, and flye to thee, thou wilt preserve mee from falling, or raise me againe, when by naturall infirmitie I am fallen: doe this, *O Lord*, for his sake, who knowes our naturall infirmities, for he had them; and knowes the weight of our sinns, for he paid a deare price for them, thy *Sonne*, our *Saviour*, *Chr: Jesus*, *Amen*.

## 2. [The sickness grows worse]

NO man is so little, in respect of the greatest man, as the greatest in respect of *God*; for here, in that, wee have not so much as a *measure* to try it by; *proportion* is no measure for *infinitie*. He that hath no more of this world but a *grave*, hee that hath his grave but lent him, til a better man, or another man, must bee buried in the same grave, he that hath no *grave*, but a *dung-hill*, hee that hath no more *earth*, but that which he carries, but that which hee is, hee that hath not that *earth*, which hee is, but even in that, is anothers slave, hath as much proportion to *God*, as if all *Davids Worthies*, and all the *worlds Monarchs*, and all *imaginations Gyants* were kneaded and incorporated into one, and as though that one were the survivor of all the sonnes of men, to whom *God* had given the world. And therefore how little soever I bee, as *God calls things that are not, as though they were*, I, who am as though I were not, may call upon *God*, and say, *My God, my God*, why comes thine anger so fast upon me? Why dost thou melt me, scatter me, poure me like water upon the ground so instantly? Thou staidst for the first world, in *Noahs* time, 120 yeres; thou staidst for a rebellious generation in the wildernes, 40 yeres, wilt thou stay no minute for me? Wilt thou make thy *Processe*, and thy *Decree*, thy *Citation*, and thy *Judgement* but one act? Thy *Summons*, thy *Battell*, thy *Victorie*, thy *Triumph*, all but one act; and lead me captive, nay, deliver me captive to death, as soon as thou declarest me to be *enemy*, and so cut me off even with the drawing of thy sword out of the scabberd, and for that question, *How long was he sicke*? leave no other answere, but that the hand of death pressed upon him from the first minute? *My God, my God*, thou wast not wont to come in *whirlwinds*, but in soft and gentle ayre. Thy first breath breathed a *Soule* into mee, and shall thy breath blow it out? Thy breath in the *Congregation*, thy *Word* in the *Church*, breathes *communion*, and *consolation* here, and *consummation* hereafter; shall thy breath in this Chamber breathe *dissolution*, and *destruction*, *divorce*, and *separation*? Surely it is not thou; it is not thy hand. The devouring sword, the consuming fire, the winds from the wildernes, the diseases of the body, all that afflicted *Job*, were from the hand of *Satan*; it is not thou. It is thou, thou *my God*, who hast led mee so continually with thy hand, from the hand of my Nurce, as that I know, thou wilt not correct me, but with thine own hand. My parents would not give mee over to a *Servants* correction, nor my *God*, to *Satans*. I am *fallen into the hand of God*, with *David*, and with *David* I see that his *Mercies are great*. For by that mercy, I consider in my present state, not the haste, and the dispatch of the disease, in dissolving this body, so much, as the much more hast, and dispatch, which my *God* shal use, in recollecting, and reuniting this *dust* againe at the *Resurrection*. Then I shall heare his *Angels* proclaime the *Surgite Mortui, Rise yee dead.* Though I be dead, I shall heare the voice; the sounding of the voice, and the working of the voice shall be all one; and all shall rise there in a lesse *minute,* than any one dies here.

## 3. [The physician is sent for]

I HAVE not the *righteousnesse* of *Job,* but I have the desire of *Job, I would speake to the Almightie* and *I would reason with God. My God, my God,* how soone wouldest thou have me goe to the *Phisician,* and how farre wouldest thou have me go with the *Phisician?* I know thou hast made the *Matter,* and the *Man,* and the *Art,* and I goe not from *thee* when I go to the Phisician. Thou didst not make *clothes* before there was a shame of the nakednes of the body; but thou didst make *Phisick* before there was any grudging of any *sicknes;* for thou didst imprint a *medicinall* vertue in many *Simples,* even from the beginning; didst thou meane that wee should be *sicke,* when thou didst so? when thou madest them? No more than thou didst meane, that we should *sinne,* when thou madest us: thou foresawest both, but *causedst* neither. Thou, *Lord,* promisest heere trees, *whose fruit shall bee for meat, and their leaves for Medicine.* It is the voyce of thy Sonn, *Wilt thou bee made whole?* That drawes from the patient the confession that hee was ill, and could not make him selfe wel. And it is thine owne voyce, *Is there no Phisician?* That inclines us, disposes us to accept thine *Ordinance.* And it is the voyce of the Wise man, both for the *matter, Phisick* it selfe, *The Lord hath created Medicines out of the Earth, and hee that is wise, shall not abhorre them,* And for the *Arte,* and the *Person, The Phisician cutteth off a long disease.* In all these voyces, thou sendest us to those helpes, which thou hast afforded us in that. But wilt not thou avowe that voyce too, *Hee that hath sinned against his Maker, let him fall into the hands of the Phisician;* and wilt not thou affoord me an understanding of those wordes? Thou who sendest us for a blessing to the *Phisician,* doest not make it a curse to us, to go, when thou sendest. Is not the curse rather in this, that onely hee falls into the hands of the *Phisician,* that casts himself wholly, intirely upon the *Phisician,* confides in

him, relies upon him, attends all from him, and neglects that
*spirituall phisicke*, which thou also hast instituted in thy *Church*: so *to
fall into the hands of the Phisician*, is a *sinne*, and a *punishment* of former
sinnes; so, as *Asa* fell, who in his disease, *sought not to the Lord, but to
the Phisician*. Reveale therefore to me thy *Method*, O *Lord*, and see,
whether I have followed it; that thou mayest have glory, if I have,
and I pardon, if I have not, and helpe that I may. Thy *Method* is,
*In time of thy sicknesse, be not negligent*: Wherein wilt thou have my
diligence expressed? *Pray unto the Lord, and hee will make thee whole.*
O *Lord*, I doe; I pray, and pray thy servant *Davids* prayer, *Have
mercy upon mee, O Lord, for I am weake; Heale mee, O Lord, for my bones
are vexed*: I knowe, that even my weakenesse is a reason, a motive,
to induce thy mercie, and my sicknes an occasion of thy sending
health. When art thou so readie, when is it so seasonable to thee,
to commiserate, as in miserie? But is Prayer for health in season,
as soone as I am sicke? Thy *Method* goes further; *Leave off from sinne,
and order thy handes aright, and cleanse thy heart from all wickednesse*;
Have I, O *Lord*, done so? O *Lord*, I have; by thy Grace, I am come to
a holy detestation of my former sin; Is there any more? In thy
*Methode* there is more; *Give a sweet savor, and a memoriall of fine flower,
and make a fat offering, as not being*. And, *Lord*, by thy grace, I have
done that, sacrificed a little, of that litle which thou lentst me, to
them, for whom thou lentst it: and now in thy *Method*, and by thy
steps, I am come to that, *Then give place to the Phisician, for the Lord
hath created him, let him not goe from thee, for thou hast need of him*. I send
for the *Phisician*, but I will heare him enter with these wordes of
*Peter, Jesus Christ maketh thee whole*; I long for his presence, but I look
that the power of the Lord, should bee present to heale mee.

## 4. [The physician comes]

A s *Sicknes* is the greatest misery, so the greatest misery of sicknes, is
*solitude*; when the infectiousnes of the disease deterrs them who
should assist, from comming; even the *Phisician* dares scarse come.
*Solitude* is a torment which is not threatned in *hell* it selfe. Meere

*vacuitie*, the first *Agent*, *God*, the first *instrument* of *God*, *Nature*, will not admit; Nothing can be utterly *emptie*, but so neere a degree towards *Vacuitie*, as *Solitude*, to bee but one, they love not. When I am dead, and my body might infect, they have a remedy, they may bury me; but when I am but sick, and might infect, they have no remedy, but their absence, and my solitude. It is an *excuse* to them that are *great*, and pretend, and yet are loth to come; it is an *inhibition* to those who would truly come, because they may be made instruments, and pestiducts, to the infection of others, by their comming. And it is an *Outlawry*, an *Excommunication* upon the *Patient*, and seperats him from all offices not onely of *Civilitie*, but of *working Charitie*. A long sicknesse will weary friends at last, but a pestilentiall sicknes averts them from the beginning. *God* himself wold admit a *figure* of *Society*, as there is a plurality of persons in *God*, though there bee but one *God*; and all his externall actions testifie a love of *Societie*, and *communion*. In *Heaven* there are *Orders* of *Angels*, and *Armies* of *Martyrs*, and *in that house, many mansions;* in *Earth*, *Families*, *Cities*, *Churches*, *Colleges*, all *plurall things*; and lest either of these should not be company enough alone, there is an association of both, a *Communion of Saints*, which makes the *Militant*, and *Triumphant Church*, one Parish; So that *Christ*, was not out of his *Dioces*, when hee was upon the *Earth*, nor out of his *Temple*, when he was in our flesh. *God*, who sawe that all that hee made, was good, came not so neer seeing a *defect* in any of his works, as when he saw that it was not good, for man to bee *alone*, therefore *hee made him a helper*; and one that should helpe him so, as to increase the *number*, and give him *her owne*, and *more societie*. *Angels*, who do not propagate, nor multiply, were made at the first in an abundant number; and so were starres: But for the things of this world, their blessing was, *Encrease*; for I think, I need not aske leave to think, that there is no *Phenix*; nothing singular, nothing alone: Men that inhere upon *Nature* only, are so far from thinking, that there is anything *singular* in this world, as that they will scarce thinke, that this world it selfe is *singular*, but that every *Planet*, and every *Starre*, is another *world* like this; They finde reason to conceive, not onely a *pluralitie* in every *Species* in the world, but a *pluralitie of worlds*; so that the abhorrers of *Solitude*, are not solitary; for *God*, and *Nature*, and

*Reason* concurre against it. Now a man may counterfeyt the *Plague* in a *vowe*, and mistake a *Disease* for *Religion*; by such a retiring, and recluding of himselfe from all men, as to doe good to no man, to converse with no man. *God* hath two *Testaments*, two *Wils*; but this is a *Scedule*, and not of his, a *Codicill*, and not of his, not in the *body* of his *Testaments*, but *interlin'd*, and *postscrib'd* by others, that the way to the *Communion of Saints*, should be by such a *solitude*, as excludes all doing of good here. That is a *disease* of the *mind*; as the height of an infectious disease of the body, is *solitude*, to be left alone: for this makes an infectious bed, equall, nay worse than a *grave*, that thogh in both I be equally alone, in my bed I *know* it, and *feele* it, and shall not in my *grave*: and this too, that in my bedd, my soule is still in an infectious body, and shall not in my grave bee so.

## 5. ['Natures nest of boxes']

THIS is *Natures nest of Boxes*; The Heavens containe the *Earth*, the *Earth*, *Cities*, *Cities*, *Men*. And all these are *Concentrique*; the common *center* to them all, is *decay*, *ruine*; only that is *Eccentrique*, which was never made; only that place, or garment rather, which we can *imagine*, but not *demonstrate*, That light, which is the very emanation of the light of *God*, in which the *Saints* shall dwell, with which the *Saints* shall be appareld, only that bends not to this *Center*, to *Ruine*; that which was not made of *Nothing*, is not threatned with this annihilation. All other things are; even *Angels*, even our *soules*; they move upon the same *poles*, they bend to the same *Center*; and if they were not made immortall by *preservation*, their *Nature* could not keep them from sinking to this *center*, *Annihilation*. . . .

## 6. [Pestilent Vapours]

. . . BUT extend this *vapour*, rarifie it; from so narow a roome, as our *Naturall bodies*, to any *Politike body*, to a *State*. That which is *fume* in us, is in a State, *Rumor*, and these *vapours* in us, which wee consider here pestilent and infectious fumes, are in a State *infectious rumors*, detracting and dishonourable *Calumnies*, *Libels*. The *Heart* in that *body* is the *King*; and the *Braine*, his *Councell*; and the whole *Magistracie*, that ties all together, is the *Sinewes*, which proceed from thence; and the *life* of all is *Honour*, and just *respect*, and due *reverence*; and therfore, when these *vapors*, these venimous *rumors*, are directed against these *Noble parts*, the whole body suffers. But yet for all their priviledges, they are not priviledged from our *misery*; that as the *vapours* most pernitious to us, arise in our owne bodies, so do the most dishonorable *rumours*, and those that wound a *State* most, arise at home. What ill *ayre*, that I could have met in the street, what *Channell*, what *Shambles*, what *Dunghill*, what *vault*, could have hurt mee so much, as these home-bredd *vapours*? What *Fugitive*, what *Almes-man of any forraine State*, can doe so much harme as a *Detracter*, a *Libeller*, a scornefull *Jester* at home? For, as they that write of *poysons*, and of creatures naturally disposed to the ruine of Man, do as well mention the *Flea*, as the *Viper*, because the *Flea*, though hee kill none, hee does all the harme hee can; so even these libellous and licentious *Jesters* utter the venim they have, though sometimes *vertue*, and alwaies *power*, be a good *Pigeon*[1] to draw this *vapor* from the *Head*, and from doing any deadly harme there.

## 7. ['For whom the bell tolls']

Nunc lento sonitu dicunt,          *Now, this Bell tolling softly for another,*
Morieris.                          *saies to me, Thou must die.*

PERCHANCE hee for whom this *Bell* tolls, may be so ill, as that he knowes not it tolls for him; And perchance I may thinke my selfe so much better than I am, as that they who are about mee, and see my state, may have caused it to toll for mee, and I know not that. The *Church* is *Catholike*, *universall*, so are all her *Actions*; *All* that she does, belongs to *all*. When she *baptizes a child*, that action concernes mee; for that child is thereby connected to that

---

[1] His physicians had applied pigeons to the feet to draw vapours from the head.

*Head* which is my *Head* too, and engraffed into that *body*, whereof I am a *member*. And when she *buries a Man*, that action concernes me: All *mankinde* is of one *Author*, and is one *volume*; when one Man dies, one *Chapter* is not *torne* out of the *booke*, but *translated* into a better *language*; and every *Chapter* must be so *translated*; God employes several *translators*; some peeces are translated by *age*, some by *sicknesse*, some by *warre*, some by *justice*; but *Gods* hand is in every *translation*; and his hand shall binde up all our scattered leaves againe, for that *Librarie* where every *booke* shall lie open to one another: As therefore the *Bell* that rings to a *Sermon*, calls not upon the *Preacher* onely, but upon the *Congregation* to come; so this *Bell* calls us all: but how much more mee, who am brought so neere the *doore* by this *sicknesse*. There was a *contention* as farre as a *suite*, (in which both *pietie* and *dignitie*, *religion*, and *estimation*, were mingled) which of the religious *Orders* should ring to *praiers* first in the *Morning*; and it was *determined*, that *they should ring first that rose earliest*. If we understand aright the *dignitie* of this *Bell* that tolls for our *evening prayer*, wee would bee glad to make it ours, by rising early, in that *application*, that it might bee ours, as wel as his, whose indeed it is. The *Bell* doth toll for him that *thinkes* it doth; and though it *intermit* againe, yet from that *minute*, that that occasion wrought upon him, hee is united to *God*. Who casts not up his *Eie* to the *Sunne* when it rises? but who takes off his *Eie* from a *Comet* when that breakes out? Who bends not his *eare* to any *bell*, which upon any occasion rings? but who can remove it from that *bell*, which is passing a *peece of himselfe* out of this *world*? No man is an *Iland*, intire of it selfe; every man is a peece of the *Continent*, a part of the *maine*; if a *Clod* bee washed away by the *Sea*, *Europe* is the lesse, as well as if a *Promontorie* were, as well as if a *Mannor* of thy *friends* or of *thine owne* were; any mans *death* diminishes *me*, because I am involved in *Mankinde*; And therefore never send to know for whom the *bell* tolls; It tolls for *thee*. . . .

## 8. [The physicians, after a long and stormy voyage, see land]

MY *God*, my *God*, Thou art a *direct God*, may I not say a *literall God*, a *God* that wouldest bee understood *literally*, and according to the *plaine sense* of all that thou saiest? But thou art also (*Lord* I intend it to thy *glory*, and let no *prophane misinterpreter* abuse it to thy *diminution*) thou are a *figurative*, a *metaphoricall God too*: A *God* in whose words there is such a height of *figures*, such *voyages*, such *peregrinations* to fetch remote and precious *metaphors*, such *extentions*, such *spreadings*, such *Curtaines* of *Allegories*, such *third Heavens* of *Hyperboles*, so *harmonious eloquutions*, so *retired* and so *reserved expressions*, so *commanding perswasions*, so *perswading commandements*, such *sinewes* even in thy *milke*, and such *things* in thy *words*, as all *prophane Authors*, seeme of the seed of the *Serpent*, that *creepes*, thou art the *Dove*, that flies. O, what words but thine, can expresse the inexpressible *texture*, and *composition* of thy *word*; in which, to one man, that *argument* that binds his faith to beleeve that to bee the Word of *God*, is *the reverent simplicity* of the Word, and to another, the *majesty* of the Word; and in which two men, equally pious, may meet, and one wonder, that all should not understand it, and the other, as much, that any man should. So, *Lord*, thou givest us the same *earth*, to labour on and to lie in; a *house*, and a *grave*, of the same *earth*; so *Lord*, thou givest us the same *Word* for our *satisfaction*, and for our *Inquisition*, for our *instruction*, and for our *Admiration* too; for there are places, that thy servants *Hierom* and *Augustine* would scarce beleeve (when they grew warm by mutual letters) of one another, that they understood them, and yet both *Hierome* and *Augustine* call upon persons, whom they knew to bee farre weaker, than they thought one another (*old women and young maids*) to read thy *Scriptures*, without confining them, to these or those places. Neither art thou thus a *figurative*, a *metaphoricall God* in thy *word* only, but in thy *workes* too. The *stile* of thy *works*, the *phrase* of thine *actions*, is *metaphoricall*. The *institution* of thy whole *worship* in the *old Law*, was a continuall *Allegory*; *types* and *figures* overspread all; and *figures* flowed into *figures*, and powred themselves out into *farther figures; Circumcision* carried a *figure* of *Baptisme*, and *Baptisme* carries a *figure* of that *purity*, which we shall have in *perfection* in the *new Jerusalem*. Neither didst thou *speake* and *worke* in this *language*, onely in the time of thy *Prophets*; but since thou spokest in thy *Son*, it is so too. How often, how much more often doth thy *Sonne* call himself a *way*, and a *light*, and a *gate*, and a *Vine*, and *bread*, than the *Sonne of God*, or of *Man*? How much oftner doth he exhibit a *Metaphoricall Christ*, than a *reall*, a *literall*? This hath occasioned thine ancient *servants*, whose delight it was to write after thy *Copie*, to proceede the same way in their *expositions* of the *Scriptures*, and in their composing both of *publike liturgies*, and of *private prayers* to thee, to make their accesses to thee in such a kind of *language*, as thou wast pleased to speake to them, in a *figurative*, in a *Metaphoricall language*; in which manner I am bold to call the comfort which I receive now in this *sicknesse*, in the *indication* of the *concoction* and *maturity* thereof, in certaine *clouds*, and *recidences*, which the *Physitians* observe, a discovering of *land* from *Sea*, after a long, and tempestuous *voyage*.

# LETTERS

FAR more of Donne's letters have been preserved than of any other English writer of his own or earlier ages. In the absence of a modern edition, they have to be assembled from a wide variety of sources. The most important is the collection, published by his son, John Donne the Younger, *Letters to Several Persons of Honour* (1651). A further large number appeared in *A Collection of Letters made by Sir Tobie Mathews* (1660). Letters concerned with Donne's marriage survive in the Loseley Papers, now in the Folger Library at Washington. Transcripts of these were made by A. Kempe in *The Loseley Manuscripts* (1835), and Evelyn Simpson published the text of the letters in the Burley manuscript, unfortunately destroyed by fire after transcripts had been made, in the first edition of her *A Study of the Prose Works of John Donne* (1924). Other letters are extant in private hands and in record offices; some were printed for the first time by Mr. John Hayward in his edition of Donne's poetry and selected prose in 1929.

Evelyn Simpson left only rudimentary notes for this section of Donne's prose, and we have had to make our own selection. We are greatly indebted to Mr. I. H. Shapiro for reading our selection in proof and allowing us to quote him on dating and other problems. Donne's letters are in the old formal style of letter-writing, modelled on the classical epistle, and having some of the quality of an essay. Even so, they tell us much of Donne's mind and are an invaluable commentary on his life and poetry.

In printing letters from manuscript we have silently expanded manuscript contractions and supplemented punctuation. When a letter is dated we have included the date as it appears at the foot of the letter, and have given it in shortened form, in round brackets, at the head. In adding such dates to the heading, we have followed modern usage by which the year begins on 1 January, whereas, as will be seen, Donne followed the older usage by which the year began on 25 March. If a date has been supplied to an undated letter, we give it in square brackets in the heading, with a preceding mark of interrogation if the date is doubtful. We have given the name of the person addressed, in modern spelling, at the head of the letter, and expanded when the original has only initials. If the heading of the letter contains further information beyond the name of the addressee, we have given this in a footnote.

# LETTERS

## 1. [To . . .?]¹

Written from Plymouth          [August 1597]

Sir,

The first act of that play which I sayd I would go over the water to see is done and yet the people hisse. How it will end I know not *ast ego vicissim [risero].* It is true that Jonas was in a whales belly three dayes but hee came not voluntary as I did nor was troubled with the stinke of 150 land soldiers as wee; and I was there 20 dayes of so very very bad wether that even some of the marriners have beene drawen to thinke it were not altogether amisse to pray, and my self heard one of them say god help us. For all our paynes wee have seene the land of promise Spaine; whether wee shall enter or no I guess not; I think there is a blott in their tables but perchaunce tis not on our dice to hitt it. Wee are now againe at Plymouth quasi ply-mouth; for wee do nothing but eate and scarce that: I think when wee came in the burghers tooke us for the Spanish fleet for they have either hid or convayd all their mony. Never was extreame beggery so extreamely brave except when a company of mummers had lost theire box. I do not think that 77 Kelleys² could distill 10 l. out of all the towne. He that hath supt and hath 2 or 3s. is a king, for none hath a crowne; fayth, lands,

¹ 'This letter, which must have been written in August 1597, is the earliest-known prose letter of Donne's. It belongs to the same occasion which gave rise to his verse-letters, "The Storm" and "The Calm", written to his friend Christopher Brooke. The islands voyage of 1597 was less successful than the Cadiz expedition of the previous year, owing chiefly to the unfortunate weather which it experienced. A considerable fleet had been fitted out under the command of Essex, assisted by Howard and Raleigh, to destroy the new Spanish armada which was believed to be in preparation. Part of this fleet set out in June, but immediately encountered such tempests that it was forced to return to Plymouth, where the remainder of the expedition assembled. About the 9th of July the whole fleet put out to sea, and after a few days of fair weather it met so fierce a storm that all the vessels were driven back to the English coast. It reassembled at Plymouth and was there refitted for sea, but owing to the unfavourable weather it could not put forth again till 17 August.' (E.M.S., *Prose Works of John Donne*, 1948, pp. 304–5.) Mr. Shapiro informs us that he considers this letter to be very doubtfully Donne's.

² 'Edward Kelley (1555–95) was a well-known alchemist and charlatan, who was associated with John Dee in an attempt to produce the Philosophers' Stone.' (E.M.S., *Prose Works*, 1948, p. 304.)

jerkins, knighthoods, are reprobate pawnes and but for the much gay cloathes (which yet are much melted) I should thinke wee were in Utopia: all are so utterly coyneles. In one bad bare word the want is so generall that the lord generall wants, and till this day wee wanted the lord generall: you will pardone me if I write nothing ernest. Salute all whome thou lovest in my name and love me as I would deserve.

## 2. [To Sir Henry Wotton?]

[? 1600]¹

Sir,

I am no great voyager in other mens works: no swallower nor devowrer of volumes nor pursuant of authors. Perchaunce it is because I find borne in my self knowledg or apprehension enough, (for without forfeiture or impeachment of modesty I think I am bond to God thankfully to acknowledg it) to consyder him and my self: as when I have at home a convenient garden I covet not to walk in others broad medows or woods, especially because it falls not within that short reach which my foresight embraceth, to see how I should employ that which I already know; to travayle for inquiry of more were to labor to gett a stomach and then find no meat at home. To know how to live by the booke is a pedantery, and to do it is a bondage. For both hearers and players are more delighted with voluntary than with sett musike. And he that will live by precept shalbe long without the habite of honesty: as he that would every day gather one or two feathers might become brawne with hard lying before he make a feather bed of his gettings. That Erle of Arundell² that last dyed (that tennis ball whome fortune after tossing and banding brikwald into the hazard) in his

---

¹ 'This long and interesting letter with its references to Italian literature was probably written by Donne to Wotton, who took a great interest in the subject. In 1598 Lombardelli, a learned Sienese, published a small book in the form of a letter to Wotton, *I Fonti Toscani*, in which he spoke of Dante as one of the masters of Italian literature.... Dante was little read in England during the sixteenth and seventeenth centuries, but Donne evidently studied him early in life, for we find an allusion in the fourth Satire: "and in a trance Like his, who dreamt he saw hell, did advance It selfe on mee" (Grierson, i. 164).' (E.M.S., *Prose Works*, 1948, p. 315.) Mr. Shapiro very much doubts the assumption that this letter was written to Wotton.

² Philip Howard, Earl of Arundel, died in 1595 after ten years' imprisonment in the Tower for his adherence to the Roman faith, and for supposed complicity in plots against Elizabeth.

imprisonment used more than much reading, and to him that asked
him why he did so he answerd he read so much lest he should
remember something. I am as far from following his counsell as hee
was from Petruccios: but I find it true that after long reading
I can only tell you how many leaves I have read. I do therfore more
willingly blow and keep awake that smale coale which God hath
pleased to kindle in mee than farr off to gather a faggott of greene
sticks which consume without flame or heat in a black smoother:
yet I read something. But indeed not so much to avoyd as to enjoy
idlenes. Even when I begun to write these I flung away Dant the
Italian, a man pert enough to bee beloved and too much to bee
beeleeved: it angred me that Celestine a pope [so] far from the
manners of other popes, that he left even their seat, should by the
court of Dants witt bee attached and by him throwne into his
purgatory. And it angred me as much, that in the life of a pope he
should spy no greater fault, than that in the affectation of a cowardly
securyty he slipt from the great burthen layd upon him. Alas! what
would Dant have him do? Thus wee find the story related: he that
thought himself next in succession, by a trunke thorough a wall
whispered in Celestines eare counsell to remove the papacy: why
should not Dant be content to thinke that Celestine tooke this
for as imediate a salutacion and discourse of the holy ghost as
Abrahim did the commandment of killing his sonn? If he will needs
punish retyrednes thus, what hell can his witt devise for ambition?
And if white integryty merit this, what shall *Male* or *Malum* which
Seneca condems most, deserve? But as the chancellor Hatton being
told after a decree made, that his predecessor was of another opinion,
he answered hee had his genius and I had myne: So say I of authors
that they thinke and I thinke both reasonably yet posibly both
erroniously; that is manly: for I am so far from perswading yea
conselling you to beleeve others that I care not that you beleeve
not mee when I say that others are not to bee beleeved: only
beleeve that I love you and I have enough.

    I have studied philosophy, therefore marvayle not if I make such
accompt of arguments *que trahuntur ab effectibus.*

### 3. [To Sir Henry Wotton?]

[? 1600]¹

Sir,

Only in obedience I send you some of my paradoxes: I love you
and myself and them too well to send them willingly for they carry
with them a confession of their lightnes, and your trouble and my
shame. But indeed they were made rather to deceave tyme than her
daughter truth: although they have beene written in an age when
any thing is strong enough to overthrow her. If they make you to
find better reasons against them they do their office: for they are
but swaggerers: quiet enough if you resist them. If perchaunce
they be pretyly guilt, that is their best for they are not hatcht: they
are rather alarums to truth to arme her than enemies: and they
have only this advantadg to scape from being caled ill things
that they are nothings. Therefore take heed of allowing any of them
least you make another. Yet Sir though I know their low price,
except I receive by your next letter an assurance upon the religion
of your friendship that no coppy shalbee taken for any respect
of these or any other my compositions sent to you, I shall sinn
against my conscience if I send you any more. I speake that in
playnes which becomes (methinks) our honestyes; and therfore
call not this a distrustfull but a free spirit: I meane to acquaint you
with all myne: and to my satyrs there belongs some feare and to
some elegies, and these perhaps, shame. Against both which
affections although I be tough enough, yet I have a ridling disposition to bee ashamed of feare and afrayd of shame. Therefore
I am desirous to hyde them with out any over reconing of them or
their maker. But they are not worth thus much words in theyre
disprayse. I will step to a better subject, your last letter, to which I
need not tell I made no answere but I had need excuse it. All your
letter I embrace and beleeve it when it speakes of your self and

---

¹ 'This letter, which is undoubtedly Donne's, was probably written by him to Wotton
about 1600. Although we cannot date the *Paradoxes* exactly, they seem to be earlier than the
*Problems* and belong to the period when Donne was a young man at court in the service of
Egerton. . . . The reference to the *Satires* and *Elegies* would agree with this date. . . . In the
present letter Donne shows that he already felt a certain shame about them, caused, perhaps,
by the responsible post he now held as secretary to the grave Lord Keeper, and also by his
growing love for Ann More, whom he married in December 1601.' (E.M.S., *Prose Works*,
1948, p. 317.) Mr. Shapiro agrees that this letter 'is undoubtedly Donne's', but states that
it 'cannot have been written to Wotton'.

when of me too, if the good words which you speake of me bee ment of my intentions to goodnes: for else alas! no man is more beggerly in actuall vertue than I. I am sory you should (with any great ernestnes) desyre any thing of P. Aretinus, not that he could infect; but that it seemes you are alredy infected with the common opinion of him: beleeve me he is much lesse than his fame and was too well payd by the Roman church in that coyne which he coveted most where his bookes were by the counsell of Trent forbidden which if they had beene permitted to have beene worne by all long ere this had beene worne out: his divinyty was but a sirrope to enwrapp his prophane bookes to get them passage, yet in these bookes which have devine titles there is least harme as in his letters most good: his others have no other singularyty in them but that they are forbidden. The psalmes (which you aske) if I cannot shortly procure you one to poses I can and will at any tyme borrow for you: In the meane tyme Sir have the honor of forgiving two faults togeather: my not writing last tyme and my abrupt ending now.

## 4. To Sir George More

(2 February 1602)[1]

Sir,

If a very respective feare of your displeasure, and a doubt that my Lord whom I know owt of your worthiness to love yow much, would be so compassionate with yow as to add his anger to yours, did not so much increase my sicknes as that I cannot stir, I had taken the boldnes to have donne the office of this letter by wayting upon yow myself to have given yow truthe and clearnes of this matter be-tween your daughter and me, and to show to yow plainly the limits of our fault, by which I know your wisdome wyll proportion the

---

[1] Ann More, younger daughter of Sir George More of Loseley House, near Guildford, was born 27 May 1584. She became acquainted with Donne while living with her aunt, Sir George More's sister, who was married to Donne's employer, Sir Thomas Egerton. They were secretly married in December 1601. The news was broken to Sir George by the Earl of Northumberland. Sir George reacted violently, caused Egerton to dismiss Donne from his service, and had Donne, Samuel Brooke (who had officiated), and Christopher Brooke, who had given away the bride, committed to prison. It was an offence to marry a minor without her guardian's consent or to assist at such a marriage.

punishment. So long since as her being at York House this had foundacion, and so much then of promise and contract built upon yt, as withowt violence to conscience might not be shaken. At her lyeng in town this last Parliament, I found meanes to see her twice or thrice. We both knew the obligacions that lay upon us, and we adventurd equally, and about three weeks before Christmas we married. And as at the doinge, there were not usd above fyve persons, of which I protest to yow by my salvation, there was not one that had any dependence or relation to yow, so in all the passage of it did I forbear to use any suche person, who by furtheringe of yt might violate any trust or duty towards yow. The reasons why I did not foreacquaint yow with it (to deale with the same plainnes that I have usd) were these. I knew my present estate lesse than fitt for her, I knew (yet I knew not why) that I stood not right in your opinion. I knew that to have given any intimacion of yt had been to impossibilitate the whole matter. And then having these honest purposes in our harts, and those fetters in our consciences, me thinks we should be pardoned, if our fault be but this, that wee did not, by fore-revealinge of yt, consent to our hindrance and torment. Sir, I acknowledge my fault to be so great, as I dare scarse offer any other prayer to yow in mine own behalf than this, to beleeve this truthe, that I neyther had dishonest end nor meanes. But for her whom I tender much more than my fortunes or lyfe (els I would I might neyther joy in this lyfe, nor enjoy the next), I humbly beg of you that she may not to her danger feele the terror of your sodaine anger. I know this letter shall find yow full of passion; but I know no passion can alter your reason and wisdome, to which I adventure to commend these particulers; that yt is irremediably donne; that if yow incense my Lord yow destroy her and me; that yt is easye to give us happines, and that my endevors and industrie, if it please yow to prosper them, may soone make me somewhat worthyer of her. If any take the advantage of your displeasure against me, and fill yow with ill thoughts of me, my comfort is, that yow know that fayth and thanks are due to them onely, that speak when theyr informacions might do good; which now yt cannot work towards any party. For my excuse I can say nothing, except I knew what were sayd to yow. Sir, I have

truly told yow this matter, and I humbly beseeche yow so to deale
in yt as the persuasions of Nature, Reason, Wisdome, and Christianity shall inform yow; and to accept the vowes of one whom
yow may now rayse or scatter, which are that as my love ys directed
unchangeably upon her, so all my labors shall concur to her contentment, and to show my humble obedience to your self.

Yours in all duty and humblenes,<br>
J. DONNE

From my lodginge by the Savoy,
    2⁰ Februa: 1601.

To the right wor. Sir George
    More, kt.

## 5. To Sir George More

(11 February 1602)

Sir,

The inward accusacions in my conscience, that I have offended
yow beyond any ability of redeeming yt by me, and the feeling of
my Lord's heavy displeasure following yt, forceth me to wright,
though I know my fault make my letters very ungracious to yow.
Allmighty God, whom I call to witnesse that all my griefe ys that
I have in this manner offended yow and him, direct yow to beleeve
that which owt of an humble and afflicted hart I now wright to
yow. And since we have no meanes to move God, when he wyll
not hear our prayers, to hear them, but by prayeng, I humbly
beseech yow to allow by his gracious example, my penitence so
good entertainment, as yt may have a beeliefe and a pittie. Of
nothinge in this one fault that I hear sayd to me, can I disculpe
myselfe, but of the contemptuous and despightfull purpose towards
yow, which I hear ys surmised against me. But for my dutifull
regard to my late lady, for my religion, and for my lyfe, I refer my
selfe to them that may have observed them. I humbly beseech yow
to take off these waytes, and to put my fault into the balance alone,
as yt was donne without the addicon of these yll reports, and
though then yt wyll be too heavy for me, yett then yt will less
grieve yow to pardon yt. How litle and how short the comfort and

pleasure of destroyeng ys, I know your wisdome and religion informs yow. And though perchance yow intend not utter destruction, yett the way through which I fall towards yt is so headlong, that beeing thus push'd, I shall soone be at bottome, for yt pleaseth God, from whom I acknowledge the punishment to be just, to accompany my other ylls with so much sicknes as I have no refuge but that of mercy, which I beg of him, my Lord, and yow, which I hope yow wyll not repent to have afforded me, since all my endevors, and the whole course of my lyfe shal be bent, to make my selfe worthy of your favor and her love, whose peace of conscience and quiett I know must be much wounded and violenced if your displeasure sever us. I can present nothing to your thoughts which yow knew not before, but my submission, my repentance, and my harty desire to do any thing satisfactory to your just displeasure. Of which I beseech yow to make a charitable use and construction. From the Fleete, 11° Febr. 1601.

Yours in all faythfull duty and obedience,<br>
J. DONNE

To the right wor. Sir Geo.
More, kt.

## 6. To Sir Thomas Egerton

(12 February 1602)

To excuse my offence, or so much to resist the just punishment for ytt, as to move your Lordship to withdraw ytt, I thoughte till now were to aggravate my fault. But since yt hath pleasd God to joyne with yow in punishing thereof with increasing my sicknes, and that he gives me now audience by prayer, yt emboldneth me also to address my humble request to your Lordship, that yow would admit into your favorable consideracion how farr my intentions were from doing dishonor to your Lordships house; and how unable I am to escape utter and present destruction, if your Lordship judge onely the effect and deede. My services never had so muche worthe in them, as to deserve the favors, wherwith they were payd. But they had alwayes so much honesty, as that onely this hath staynd them. Your justice hath been mercifull in making me know my offence, and yt hath much profited me that I am dejected. Since then I ame so intirely yours that even your disfavors have wrought good upon me; I humbly beseeche yow that all my good may proceed from your Lordship. And that since Sir George More, whom I leave no humble way unsought to regaine, referrs all to your Lordship, yow would be pleased to lessen that correction which your just wisdome hath destind for me, and so to pitty my sicknes and other misery, as shall best agree with your honorable disposition. Allmighty God accompany all your Lordships purposes, and bless yow and yours with many good dayes. Fleet, 12° Febr. 1601.

Your Lordships most dejected and<br>poore servant,<br>J. DONNE

To the right honorable my very
   good Lord and Master Sir Thomas
   Egerton, knight, Lord keeper of
   the great Seale of England.


## 7. To Sir George More

(13 February 1602)

Sir,

From yow, to whom next to God I shall owe my health, by enjoyeng by your mediacion this mild change of imprisonment, I desire to derive all my good fortune and content in this world; and therefore with my most unfeyned thanks, present to yow my humble peticion, that yow would be pleasd to hope, that as that fault which was layd to me of having deceivd some gentlewomen before, and that of loving a corrupt religion, are vanishd and smoakd away (as I assure myself owt of theyr weaknes they are), and that as the devyll in the article of our death takes the advantage of our weaknes and fear, to aggravate our sinns to our conscience, so some uncharitable malice hath presented my debts doble at least. How many of the imputacions layd upon me would fall off, if I might shake and purge myself in your presence. But if that were donne, of this offence committed to yow I cannot acquit myself, of which yet I hope that God (to whom for that I hartily direct many prayers) wyll informe yow to make that use, that as of evyll manners good lawes growe, so owt of disobedience and boldnes yow wyll take occasion to show mercy and tendernes. And when yt shall please God to soften your hart so much towards us, as to pardon us, I beseech yow allso to undertake that charitable office of being my mediator to my Lord, whom as upon your just complaint yow found full of justice, I doubt not but yow shall also find full of mercy, for so ys the Almighty pattern of Justice and Mercy equally full of bothe. My conscience and such affection as in my conscience becomes an honest man, emboldneth me to make one request more, which ys, that by some kind and comfortable message yow would be pleas'd to give some ease of the afflictions which I know your daughter in her mind suffers, and that (if yt be not against your other purposes) I may with your leave wright to her, for without your leave I wyll never attempt anything concerning her. God so have mercy upon me, as I am unchangeably resolved to bend all my courses to make me fitt for her, which if God and my Lord and yow be pleased to strengthen, I hope neyther my debts which I can easily order nor any thing els shall interrupt. Allmighty God keepe yow in his favor, and restore me to his and yours. From my chamber, whither by your favor I ame come, 13° Feb. 1601. J. DONNE

To the right worshipfull
    Sir George More, knight.

## 8. To Sir George More

(March 1602)

Sir,

If I could fear that in so much worthynes as ys in yow there were no mercy, or yf these waights opprest onely my shoulders and my fortunes, and not my conscience and hers whose good is dearer to me by much than my lyfe, I should not thus troble yow with my letters; but when I see that this storme hath shakd me at roote in my Lord's favor, wher I was well planted, and have just reason to fear that those yll reports which malice hath raysd of me may have trobled hers, I can leave no honest way untryed to remedye these miseryes, nor find any way more honest than this, out of an humble and repentant hart, for the fault donne to yow, to beg both your pardon and assistance in my suite to my Lord. I should wrong you as much againe as I did, if I should think yow sought to destroy me, but though I be not hedlongly destroyd, I languish and rust dangerously. From seeking preferments abrode, my love and conscience restrains me; from hoping for them here my Lord's disgracings cut me off My emprisonments, and theyrs whose love to me brought them to yt, hath already cost me 40*l.* And the love of my frinds, though yt be not utterly grounded upon my fortunes, yet I know suffers somewhat in these long and uncertain disgraces of myne. I therfore humbly beseech yow to have so charitable a pitty, of what I have, and do, and must suffer, as to take to your selfe the comfort of having saved from such destruction as your just anger might have layd upon him, a sorowfull and honest man. I was bold in my last letter to beg leave of yow that I might wright to your daughter. Though I understand therupon, that after the Thursday yow were not displeased that I should, yet I have not, nor wyll not withowt your knowledge do yt. But now I beseech yow that I may, since I protest before God, yt is the greatest of my afflictions not to do yt. In all the world ys not more true sorrow than in my hart, nor more understanding of true repentance than in yours. And therfore God, whose pardon in such cases is never denyed, gives me leave to hope, that yow wyll favorably consider my necessityes. To his mercifull guiding and protection I commend yow, and cease to troble yow. Mar. 1601.

Yours in all humbleness,
and dutifull obedience,
J. DONNE

To the right worshipfull
Sir George More, knight.

# 9. To Sir Thomas Egerton

(1 March 1602)

That offence which was to God in this matter, his mercy hath assurd my conscience is pardoned. The commissioners who minister his anger and mercy, incline also to remitt yt. Sir George More, of whose learninge and wisdome I have good knowledge, and therfore good hope of his moderacion, hath sayd before his last goinge, that he was so far from being any cawse or mover of my punishment or disgrace, that if yt fitted his reputacion he would be a suter to your Lordship for my restorynge. All these irons are knock'd off, yett I perish in as heavy fetters as ever, whilst I languish under your Lordships anger. How soone my history is dispatched! I was carefully and honestly bred; enjoyd an indifferent fortune; I had (and I had understandinge enough to valew yt) the sweetnes and security of a freedome and independency; without markinge owt to my hopes any place of profitt. I had a desire to be your Lordships servant, by the favor which your good sonn's love to me obtein'd. I was 4 years your Lordships secretary, not dishonest nor gredy. The sicknes of which I dyed ys, that I begonne in your Lordships house this love. Wher I shal be buried I know not. It ys late now for me (but that necessity, as yt hath continually an autumne and a wytheringe, so yt hath ever a springe, and must put forthe,) to beginne that course, which some yeares past I purposd to travaile, though I could now do yt, not much disadvantageously. But I have some bridle upon me now, more than then, by my marriadge of this gentlewoman; in providing for whom I can and wyll show myself very honest, though not so fortunate. To seek preferment here with any but your Lordship were a madnes. Every great man to whom I shall address any such suite, wyll silently dispute the case, and say, would my Lord Keeper so disgraciously have imprisond him, and flung him away, if he had not donne some other great fault, of which we hear not. So that to the burden of my true weaknesses, I shall have this addicion of a very prejudiciall suspicion, that I ame worse than I hope your Lordship dothe think me, or would that the world should thinke. I have therfore no way before me; but must turn back to your Lordship, who knowes that redemtion was no less worke than creation. I know my fault so well, and so well acknowledge yt, that I protest I have not so much as inwardly grudged or startled at the punishment. I know your Lordships disposicion so well, as though in course of justice yt be of proofe against clamors of offenders, yet yt ys not strong inough to resist yt selfe, and I know yt selfe naturally enclines yt to pitty. I know myne own necessity, owt of which I humbly beg that your Lordship wyll so much entender your hart towards me, as to give me leave to come into your presence. Affliction, misery, and destruction are not there; and every wher els wher I ame, they are. 1° Martii, 1601.

> Your Lordships most poore and most
> penitent servant,
>
> J. DONNE

To the right honorable my very
   good Lord and master Sir Thomas
   Egerton, knight, Lord Keeper of
   the Great Seal of England.


## 10. To Sir Thomas Egerton

[? February or March 1602][1]

The honorable favor that your Lordship hath afforded me, in allowinge me the liberty of myne own chamber, hath given me leave so much to respect and love myself, that now I can desire to be well. And therfore for health, not pleasure (of which your Lordships displeasure hath dulld in me all tast and apprehension), I humbly beseeche your Lordship so much more to slacken my fetters, that as I ame by your Lordships favor myne own keeper, and surety, so I may be myne owne phisician and apothecary, which your Lordship shall worke, if yow graunt me liberty to take the ayre about this towne. The whole world ys a streight imprisonment to me, whilst I ame barrd your Lordships sight; but this favour may lengthen and better my lyfe, which I desire to preserve, onely in hope to redeeme by my sorrowe and desire to

---

1 This letter would seem to have been written either shortly before or soon after the last.

do your Lordship service, my offence past. Allmighty God dwell
ever in your Lordships hart, and fill yt with good desires, and
graunt them.

Your Lordships poorest servant,<br>
J. DONNE

To the right honorable my very
good Lord and Master Sir Thomas
Egerton, knight, Lord Keeper of
the Great Seale of England.

## 11. [To Sir Henry Goodyer][1]

[? 1604]

If you were here, you would not think me importune, if I bid you
good morrow every day; and such a patience will excuse my often
Letters. No other kinde of conveyance is better for knowledge, or
love: What treasures of Morall knowledge are in *Senecaes* Letters to
onely one *Lucilius*? and what of Naturall in *Plinies*? how much of the
storie of the time, is in *Ciceroes* Letters? And how all of these times,
in the Jesuites Eastern and Western Epistles? where can we finde so
perfect a Character of *Phalaris*, as in his own Letters, which are
almost so many writs of Execution? Or of *Brutus*, as in his privie
seals for monie? The Evangiles and Acts, teach us what to beleeve,
but the Epistles of the Apostles what to do. And those who have
endevoured to dignifie *Seneca* above his worth, have no way fitter,
than to imagine Letters between him and S. *Paul*. As they think also
that they have expressed an excellent person, in that Letter which
they obtrude, from our B. Saviour to King *Agabarus*. The Italians,
which are most discursive, and think the world owes them all
wisdome, abound so much in this kinde of expressing, that *Michel*

---

[1] This letter is headed 'To Sir G. M.', which Gosse expanded to 'Sir George More'.
It is written to a friend who has sent Donne a 'problem', and seems therefore to be addressed
to Goodyer and, from its tone, to have been written early in Donne's friendship with him;
see Letter 15, where Donne has sent Goodyer some problems. Mr. Shapiro says, 'the date
might be as early as 1604, or even 1603.' For an account of John Donne the Younger's
methods of editing, see R. E. Bennett, 'Donne's *Letters to Severall Persons of Honour*',
*P.M.L.A.*, March 1941. He claims that this and (among others) No. 34 were addressed
to Goodyer and summarizes earlier articles on Donne's Letters by himself, I. A. Shapiro, and
others.

*Montaigne* saies, he hath seen, (as I remember) 400 volumes of Italian Letters. But it is the other capacity which must make mine acceptable, that they are also the best conveyers of love. But, though all knowledge be in those Authors already, yet, as some poisons, and some medicines, hurt not, nor profit, except the creature in which they reside, contribute their lively activitie, and vigor; so, much of the knowledge buried in Books perisheth, and becomes ineffectuall, if it be not applied, and refreshed by a companion, or friend. Much of their goodnesse, hath the same period, which some Physicians of *Italy* have observed to be in the biting of their *Tarentola*, that it affects no longer, than the flie lives. For with how much desire we read the papers of any living now, (especially friends) which we would scarce allow a boxe in our cabinet, or shelf in our Library, if they were dead? And we do justly in it, for the writings and words of men present, we may examine, controll, and expostulate, and receive satisfaction from the authors; but the other we must beleeve, or discredit; they present no mean. Since then at this time, I am upon the stage, you may be content to hear me. And now that perchance I have brought you to it, (as *Thom. Badger* did the King) now I have nothing to say. And it is well, for the Letter is already long enough, else let this probleme supply, which was occasioned by you, of women wearing stones; which, it seems, you were afraid women should read, because you avert them at the beginning, with a protestation of cleanlinesse. *Martiall* found no way fitter to draw the Romane Matrons to read one of his Books, which he thinks most morall and cleanly, than to counsell them by the first Epigram to skip the Book, because it was obscene. But either you write not at all for women, or for those of sincerer palates. Though their unworthinesse, and your own ease be advocates for me with you, yet I must adde my entreaty, that you let goe no copy of my Problems, till I review them. If it be too late, at least be able to tell me who hath them.

*Yours,*

J. DONNE

## 12. To Sir Henry Goodyer

[1606][1]

Sir,

I live so farre removed, that even the ill news of your great losse (which is ever swiftest and loudest) found me not till now. Your letter speaks it not plain enough but I am so accustomed to the worst, that I am sure it is so in this. I am almost glad that I knew her so little: for I would have no more additions to sorrow. If I should comfort you, it were an almes acceptable in no other title, than when poor give to poor; for I am more needy of it than you. And I know you well provided of Christian, and learned, and brave defences against all humane accidents. I will make my best haste after your messenger: and if my self and the place had not been ill provided of horses, I had been the messenger, for you have taught me by granting more to deny no request.

*Your honest unprofitable friend*
J. DONNE

*Py[r]ford* 3 a clock
    just as yours came.

## 13. To Sir Henry Goodyer

[? January 1607][2]

Sir,

Though you escape my lifting up of your latch by removing, you cannot my Letters; yet of this Letter I do not much accuse my self, for I serve your Commandment in it, for it is only to convey to you this paper opposed to those, with which you trusted me. It is (I cannot say the waightyest, but truly) the saddest lucubration and nights passage that ever I had. For it exercised those hours, which, with extreme danger of her, whom I should hardly have

[1] Pyrford was the home of Sir Francis Wooley, cousin of Ann More, who gave Donne and his wife shelter after their marriage. This letter of condolence on the death of Goodyer's wife, who died in 1606, must have been written on a visit, since Donne moved to Mitcham in 1605. Sir Henry Goodyer, the younger, of Polesworth in Warwickshire was the recipient of a great many of Donne's extant letters and must have received far more than have survived. During the Mitcham period Donne appears to have written him a weekly letter every Tuesday.

[2] Gosse suggested that this letter refers to the birth of Donne's son, Francis, baptized at Mitcham 8 January 1607, who died in infancy.

abstained from recompensing for her company in this world, with accompanying her out of it, encreased my poor family with a son. Though her anguish, and my fears, and hopes, seem divers and wild distractions from this small businesse of your papers, yet because they all narrowed themselves, and met in *Via regia*, which is the consideration of our selves, and God, I thought it time not unfit for this dispatch. Thus much more than needed I have told you, whilest my fire was lighting at Tricombs 10 a clock.

*Yours ever intirely*
J. DONNE

## 14. To Mrs. Magdalen Herbert

(July 1607)[1]

Madam,

Your Favours to me are every where; I use them, and have them. I enjoy them at *London*, and leave them there; and yet, find them at *Micham*: Such Riddles as these become things unexpressible; and, such is your goodness. I was almost sorry to find your Servant here this day, because I was loth to have any witness of my not coming home last Night, and indeed of my coming this Morning: But, my not coming was excusable, because earnest business detain'd me; and my coming this day, is by the example of your St. *Mary Magdalen*, who rose early upon *Sunday*, to seek that which she lov'd most, and so did I. And, from her and my self, I return such thanks as are due to one to whom we owe all the good opinion, that they whom we need most, have of us—by this Messenger, and on this good day, I commit the inclosed *Holy Hymns* and *Sonnets* (which for the matter, not the workmanship, have yet escap'd the fire) to

---

[1] There is a slight error in the date: 11 July 1607 was a Saturday and the letter was plainly written on a Sunday (probably 12 July). Walton printed three further letters from Donne to Mrs. Herbert in an appendix to his *Life of Herbert*, dated 11 July (again probably a mistake for 12 July), 23 July, and 2 August 1607. They, like this, would seem to belong to the beginning of his close friendship with her, though it seems likely that they had met earlier at Oxford. See Sermon 54 for extracts from Donne's funeral sermon on Lady Danvers and biographical note. The sonnet enclosed with this letter was that beginning 'Her of your name, whose fair inheritance/*Bethina* was, and jointure *Magdalo*'; and Grierson suggested that the '*Holy Hymns* and *Sonnets*' it ushered to Mrs. Herbert's hands were the sonnets of '*La Corona*'.

your judgment, and to your protection too, if you think them worthy of it; and I have appointed this inclosed *Sonnet* to usher them to your happy hand.

> *Your unworthiest Servant,*
> *unless your accepting him*
> *have mended him.*
>                                    JO. DONNE

Micham,
   July 11,
   1607.

## 15. To Sir Henry Goodyer

[? 1607]¹

Sir,

   This *Tuesday* morning, which hath brought me to *London*, presents me with all your Letters. Me thought it was a rent day, I mean such as yours, and not as mine; and yet such too, when I considered how much I ought you for them, how good a mother, how fertill and abundant the understanding is, if she have a good father; and how well friendship performs that office. For that which is denied in other generations is done in this of yours: for here is superfetation, childe upon childe, and that which is more strange, twins at a latter conception. If in my second religion, friendship, I had a conscience, either *errantem* to mistake good and bad and indifferent, or *opinantem* to be ravished by others opinions or examples, or *dubiam* to adhere to neither part, or *scrupulosam* to encline to one, but upon reasons light in themselves, or indiscussed in me, (which are almost all the diseases of conscience) I might mistake your often, long, and busie Letters, and fear you did but intreat me to have mercy upon you and spare you; for you know our Court took the resolution, that it was the best way to dispatch the French Prince back again quickly, to receive him solemnly, ceremoniously, and expensively, when he hoped a domestique and durable entertainment. I never meant to excell you in weight nor price, but in number and bulk I thought I might, because he may cast up a greater summe who hath but forty small monies, than he with twenty Portuguesses. The memory

---

¹ Gosse suggested that the reference to the French Prince's visit is to the visit to England of the Prince de Joinville, brother of the Duke of Guise, in May and June 1607.

of friends, (I mean onely for Letters) neither enters ordinarily into busied men, because they are ever emploied within, nor into men of pleasure, because they are never at home. For these wishes therefore which you won out of your pleasure and recreation, you were as excusable to me if you writ seldome, as Sir *H. Wotton* is, under the oppression of businesse, or the necessity of seeming so; or more than he, because I hope you have both pleasure and businesse: onely to me, who have neither, this omission were sinne; for though writing be not of the precepts of friendship, but of the counsels, yet, as in some cases to some men counsels become precepts, and though not immediately from God, yet very roundly and quickly from his Church, (as selling and dividing goods in the first time, continence in the Romane Church, and order and decencie in ours) so to me who can do nothing else, it seems to binde my conscience to write; and it is sinne to doe against the conscience, though that erre. Yet no mans Letters might be better wanted than mine, since my whole Letter is nothing else but a confession that I should and would write. I owed you a Letter in verse before by mine owne promise, and now that you think that you have hedged in that debt by a greater by your Letter in verse, I think it now most seasonable and fashionable for me to break. At least, to write presently, were to accuse my self of not having read yours so often as such a Letter deserves from you to me. To make my debt greater (for such is the desire of all, who cannot or mean not to pay) I pray read these two problemes: for such light flashes as these have been my hawkings in my sorry journies. I accompany them with another ragge of verses, worthy of that name for the smalnesse, and age, for it hath long lien among my other papers, and laughs at them that have adventured to you: for I think till now you saw it not, and neither you, nor it should repent it. Sir, if I were any thing, my love to you might multiply it, and dignifie it: But infinite nothings are but one such; yet since even Chymera's have some name and titles, I am also

*Yours.*

# 16. To Sir Henry Goodyer

[1608][1]

ir,

I write not to you out of my poor Library, where to cast mine eye
ipon good Authors kindles or refreshes sometimes meditations not
infit to communicate to near friends; nor from the high way, where
am contracted, and inverted into my self; which are my two
rdinary forges of Letters to you. But I write from the fire side in
iy Parler, and in the noise of three gamesome children; and by
he side of her, whom because I have transplanted into a wretched
rtune, I must labour to disguise that from her by all such honest
devices, as giving her my company, and discourse, therefore I steal
from her, all the time which I give this Letter, and it is therefore
that I take so short a list, and gallop so fast over it; I have not been
out of my house since I received your pacquet. As I have much
quenched my senses, and disused my body from pleasure, and so
tried how I can indure to be mine own grave, so I try now how I
can suffer a prison. And since it is but to build one wall more about
our soul, she is still in her own Center, how many circumferences
soever fortune or our own perversnesse cast about her. I would I
could as well intreat her to go out, as she knows whither to go.
But if I melt into a melancholy whilest I write, I shall be taken in
the manner: and I sit by one too tender towards these impressions,
and it is so much our duty, to avoid all occasions of giving them sad
apprehensions, as S. *Hierome* accuses *Adam* of no other fault in
eating the Apple, but that he did it *Ne contristaretur delicias suas.*
I am not carefull what I write, because the inclosed Letters may
dignifie this ill-favoured bark, and they need not grudge so coarse
a countenance, because they are now to accompany themselves.
My man fetched them, and therefore I can say no more of them
than themselves say. Mistress *Meau[tys]* intreated me by her Letter
to hasten hers; as I think, for by my troth I cannot read it. My Lady
was dispatching in so much haste for *Twicknam*, as she gave no
word to a Letter which I sent with yours; of Sir *Tho. Bartlet*, I can

---

[1] The letter is headed 'A V. *Merced*', but it is certainly addressed to Goodyer and from
Mitcham. It must have been written in 1608 since it refers to the Countess of Bedford as at
Twickenham, and Jane Meautys, one of the young ladies who 'waited on her', married Donne's
old friend Sir William Cornwallis in 1609.

say nothing, nor of the plague, though your Letter bid me: but that he diminishes, the other increases, but in what proportion I am not clear. To them at *Hammersmith*, and Mistress *Herbert* I will do your command. If I have been good in hope, or can promise any little offices in the future probably, it is comfortable, for I am the worst present man in the world; yet the instant, though it be nothing, joynes times together, and therefore this unprofitableness, since I have been, and will still indevour to be so, shall not interrupt me now from being

*Your servant and lover*
J. DONNE

## 17. To Sir Henry Goodyer

[September 1608]¹

Sir,

    Every tuesday I make account that I turn a great hour-glass, and consider that a weeks life is run out since I writ. But if I aske my self what I have done in the last watch, or would do in the next, I can say nothing; if I say that I have passed it without hurting any, so may the Spider in my window. The primitive Monkes were excusable in their retirings and enclosures of themselves: for even of them every one cultivated his own garden and orchard, that is, his soul and body, by meditation, and manufactures; and they ought the world no more since they consumed none of her sweetnesse, nor begot others to burden her. But for me, if I were able to husband all my time so thriftily, as not onely not to wound my soul in any minute by actuall sinne, but not to rob and cousen her by giving any part to pleasure or businesse, but bestow it all upon her in meditation, yet even in that I should wound her more, and contract another guiltinesse: As the Eagle were very unnaturall if because she is able to do it, she should pearch a whole day upon a tree, staring in contemplation of the majestie and glory of the Sun, and let her young Eglets starve in the nest. Two of the most precious things which God hath afforded us here, for the agony and

---

¹ This letter is dated by a reference in a long postscript to the tragic death of a certain Captain Whitlock in September 1608.

exercise of our sense and spirit, which are a thirst and inhiation after the next life, and a frequency of prayer and meditation in this, are often envenomed, and putrefied, and stray into a corrupt disease: for as God doth thus occasion, and positively concurre to evill, that when a man is purposed to do a great sin, God infuses some good thoughts which make him choose a lesse sin, or leave out some circumstance which aggravated that; so the devill doth not only suffer but provoke us to some things naturally good, upon condition that we shall omit some other more necessary and more obligatory. And this is his greatest subtilty; because herein we have the deceitfull comfort of having done well, and can very hardly spie our errour because it is but an insensible omission, and no accusing act. With the first of these I have often suspected my self to be overtaken; which is, with a desire of the next life: which though I know it is not meerly out of a werinesse of this, because I had the same desires when I went with the tyde, and enjoyed fairer hopes than now: yet I doubt worldly encombrances have encreased it. I would not that death should take me asleep. I would not have him meerly seise me, and onely declare me to be dead, but win me, and overcome me. When I must shipwrack, I would do it in a Sea, where mine impotencie might have some excuse; not in a sullen weedy lake, where I could not have so much as exercise for my swimming. Therefore I would fain do something; but that I cannot tell what, is no wonder. For to chuse, is to do: but to be no part of any body, is to be nothing. At most, the greatest persons, are but great wens, and excrescences; men of wit and delightfull conversation, but as moales for ornament, except they be so incorporated into the body of the world, that they contribute something to the sustentation of the whole. This I made account that I begun early, when I understood the study of our laws: but was diverted by the worst voluptuousnes, which is an Hydroptique immoderate desire of humane learning and languages: beautifull ornaments to great fortunes; but mine needed an occupation, and a course which I thought I entred well into, when I submitted my self to such a service, as I thought might [have] imployed those poor advantages, which I had. And there I stumbled too, yet I would try again: for to this hour I am nothing, or so little, that I am scarce subject and argument good enough for one of mine own letters: yet I fear, that doth not ever proceed from a good root, that I am so well content to be lesse, that is dead. You, Sir, are farre enough from these descents, your vertue keeps you secure, and your naturall disposition to mirth will preserve you; but lose none of these holds, a slip is often as dangerous as a bruise, and though you cannot fall to my lownesse, yet in a much lesse distraction you may meet my sadnesse; for he is no safer which falls from an high tower into the leads, than he which falls from thence to the ground: make therefore to your self some mark, and go towards it *alegrement*. Though I be in such a planetary and erratique fortune, that I can do nothing constantly, yet you may finde some constancy in my constant advising you to it.

*Your hearty true friend*
J. DONNE

## 18. To Sir Henry Goodyer

[? 1608]¹

Sir,

This letter hath more merit, than one of more diligence, for I wrote it in my bed, and with much pain. I have occasion to sit late some nights in my study, (which your books make a pretty library) and now I finde that that room hath a wholesome emblematique use: for having under it a vault, I make that promise me, that I shall die reading, since my book and a grave are so near. But it hath another unwholesomenesse, that by raw vapors rising from thence, (for I can impute it to nothing else) I have contracted a sicknesse which I cannot name nor describe. For it hath so much of a continuall Cramp, that it wrests the sinews, so much of a Tetane, that it withdraws and puls the mouth, and so much of the Gout, (which they whose counsell I use, say it is) that it is not like to be cured, though I am too hasty in three days to pronounce it. If it be the Gout, I am miserable; for that affects dangerous parts, as my neck and brest, and (I think fearfully) my stomach, but it

---

¹ This letter seems close in date to the previous one, since this refers to the writing of 'A Litany', a poem which the other at times seems to echo. The 'Book' of which Donne is having copies made must be *Biathanatos*. There is an unfortunate *lacuna* in the text just as Donne turns to speak of a poem he has sent to Goodyer.

will not kill me yet; I shall be in this world, like a porter in a great house, ever nearest the door, but seldomest abroad: I shall have many things to make me weary, and yet not get leave to be gone. If I go, I will provide by my best means that you suffer not for me, in your bonds. The estate which I should leave behinde me of any estimation, is my poor fame, in the memory of my friends, and therefore I would be curious of it, and provide that they repent not to have loved me. Since my imprisonment in my bed, I have made a meditation in verse, which I call a Litany; the word you know imports no other than supplication, but all Churches have one forme of supplication, by that name. Amongst ancient annals I mean some 800 years, I have met two Letanies in Latin verse, which gave me not the reason of my meditations, for in good faith I thought not upon them then, but they give me a defence, if any man, to a Lay man, and a private, impute it as a fault, to take such divine and publique names, to his own little thoughts. The first of these was made by *Ratpertus* a Monk of *Suevia*; and the other by S. *Notker*, of whom I will give you this note by the way, that he is a private Saint, for a few Parishes; they were both but Monks, and the Letanies poor and barbarous enough; yet Pope *Nicolas* the 5, valued their devotion so much, that he canonized both their Poems, and commanded them for publike service in their Churches: mine is for lesser Chappels, which are my friends, and though a copy of it were due to you, now, yet I am so unable to serve my self with writing it for you at this time, (being some 30 staves of 9 lines) that I must intreat you to take a promise that you shall have the first, for a testimony of that duty which I owe to your love, and to my self, who am bound to cherish it by my best offices. That by which it will deserve best acceptation, is, That neither the Roman Church need call it defective, because it abhors not the particular mention of the blessed Triumphers in heaven; nor the Reformed can discreetly accuse it, of attributing more than a rectified devotion ought to doe. The day before I lay down, I was at *London*, where I delivered your Letter for Sr. *Ed. Conway*, and received another for you, with the copy of my Book, of which it is impossible for me to give you a copy so soon, for it is not of much lesse than 300 pages. If I die, it shall come to you in that fashion that your Letter desires it. If I warm

again, (as I have often seen such beggers as my indisposition is, end themselves soon, and the patient as soon) you and I shal speak together of that, before it be too late to serve you in that commandment. At this time I onely assure you, that I have not appointed it upon any person, nor ever purposed to print it: which later perchance you thought, and grounded your request thereupon. A Gent. that visited me yesterday told me that our Church hath lost Mr *Hugh Broughton*, who is gone to the Roman side. I have known before, that *Serarius* the Jesuit was an instrument from Cardinall *Baronius* to draw him to *Rome*, to accept a stipend, onely to serve the Christian Churches in controversies with the Jews, without indangering himself to change of his perswasion in particular deductions between these Christian Churches, or being enquired of, or tempted thereunto. And I hope he is no otherwise departed from us. If he be, we shall not escape scandall in it; because, though he be a man of many distempers, yet when he shall come to eat assured bread, and to be removed from partialities, to which want drove him, to make himself a reputation, and raise up favourers; you shall see in that course of opposing the Jews, he will produce worthy things: and our Church will perchance blush to have lost a Souldier fit for that great battell; and to cherish onely those single Duellisms, between *Rome* and *England*, or that more single, and almost self-homicide, between the unconformed Ministers, and Bishops. I writ to you last week that the plague increased; by which you may see that my Letters ................................
........................................ opinion of the song, not that I make such trifles for praise; but because as long as you speak comparatively of it with mine own, and not absolutely, so long I am of your opinion even at this time; when I humbly thank God, I ask & have, his comfort of sadder meditations; I doe not condemn in my self, that I have given my wit such evaporations, as those, if they be free from prophaneness, or obscene provocations. Sir you would pity me if you saw me write, and therefore will pardon me if I write no more: my pain hath drawn my head so much awry, and holds it so, that mine eie cannot follow mine hand: I receive you therefore into my prayers, with mine own weary soul, and commend my self to yours. I doubt not but next week I shall

be good news to you, for I have mending or dying on my side, which is two to one. If I continue thus, I shall have comfort in this, that my B. Saviour exercising his Justice upon my two worldly parts, my fortune, and body, reserves all his mercy for that which best tasts it, and most needs it, my soul. I professe to you truly, that my lothnesse to give over now, seems to my self an ill sign, that I shall write no more.

*Your poor friend, and Gods poor*
*patient,*

Jo. DONNE

## 19. To Sir Henry Goodyer

[? 1608–9][1]

Sir,

It should be no interruption to your pleasures, to hear me often say that I love you, and that you are as much my meditations as my self: I often compare not you and me, but the sphear in which your resolutions are, and my wheel; both I hope concentrique to God: for me thinks the new Astronomie is thus appliable well, that we which are a little earth, should rather move towards God, than that he which is fulfilling, and can come no whither, should move towards us. To your life full of variety, nothing is old, nor new to mine; and as to that life, all stickings and hesitations seem stupid and stony, so to this, all fluid slipperinesses, and transitory migrations seem giddie and featherie. In that life one is ever in the porch or postern, going in or out, never within his house himself: It is a garment made of remnants, a life raveld out into ends, a line discontinued, and a number of small wretched points, uselesse, because they concurre not: A life built of past and future, not proposing any constant present; they have more pleasures than we, but not more pleasure; they joy oftner, we longer; and no man but of so much understanding as may deliver him from being a fool, would change with a mad-man, which had a better proportion of wit in his often *Lucidis*. You know, they which dwell farthest from

---

[1] This and the following letter are connected by the reference to the Countess of Bedford's garden. She moved to Twickenham in 1608.

the Sun, if in any convenient distance, have longer daies, better appetites, better digestion, better growth, and longer life: And all these advantages have their mindes who are well removed from the scorchings, and dazlings, and exhalings of the worlds glory: but neither of our lives are in such extremes; for you living at Court without ambition, which would burn you, or envy, which would devest others, live in the Sun, not in the fire: And I which live in the Country without stupefying, am not in darknesse, but in shadow, which is not no light, but a pallid, waterish, and diluted one. As all shadows are of one colour, if you respect the body from which they are cast (for our shadows upon clay will be dirty, and in a garden green, and flowery) so all retirings into a shadowy life are alike from all causes, and alike subject to the barbarousnesse and insipid dulnesse of the Country: onely the emploiments, and that upon which you cast and bestow your pleasure, businesse, or books, gives it the tincture, and beauty. But truly wheresoever we are, if we can but tell our selves truly what and where we would be, we may make any state and place such; for we are so composed, that if abundance, or glory scorch and melt us, we have an earthly cave, our bodies, to go into by consideration, and cool our selves: and if we be frozen, and contracted with lower and dark fortunes, we have within us a torch, a soul, lighter and warmer than any without: we are therefore our own umbrella's, and our own suns. These, Sir, are the sallads and onions of *Micham*, sent to you with as wholesome affection as your other friends send Melons and *Quelque-choses* from Court and *London*. If I present you not as good diet as they, I would yet say grace to theirs, and bid much good do it you. I send you, with this, a Letter which I sent to the Countesse. It is not my use nor duty to doe so, but for your having of it, there were but two consents, and I am sure you have mine, and you are sure you have hers. I also writ to her Ladiship for the verses she shewed in the garden, which I did not onely to extort them, nor onely to keep my promise of writing, for that I had done in the other Letter, and perchance she hath forgotten the promise; nor onely because I think my Letters just good enough for a progresse, but because I would write apace to her, whilest it is possible to expresse that which I yet know of her, for by this growth I see how soon she will be ineffable.

## 20. To the Countess of Bedford

[? 1608–9][1]

*Happiest and worthiest Lady,*

I do not remember that ever I have seen a petition in verse, I would not therefore be singular, nor adde these to your other papers. I have yet adventured so near as to make a petition for verse, it is for those your Ladiship did me the honour to see in *Twicknam* garden, except you repent your making; and having mended your judgement by thinking worse, that is, better, because juster, of their subject. They must needs be an excellent exercise of your wit, which speake so well of so ill: I humbly beg them of your Ladiship, with two such promises, as to any other of your compositions were threatnings: that I will not shew them, and that I will not beleeve them; and nothing should be so used that comes from your brain or breast. If I should confesse a fault in the boldnesse of asking them, or make a fault by doing it in a longer Letter, your Ladiship might use your style and old fashion of the Court towards me, and pay me with a Pardon. Here therefore I humbly kisse your Ladiships fair learned hands, and wish you good wishes and speedy grants.

*Your Ladiships servant*
J. DONNE

## 21. To Sir Henry Goodyer

[1609][2]

Sir,

To you that are not easily scandalized, and in whom, I hope, neither my Religion nor Morality can suffer, I dare write my opinion of that Book in whose bowels you left me. It hath refreshed,

---

[1] Lucy, Countess of Bedford, daughter of John Harington, first Baron Harington of Exton, was a great patron of poets. Donne's friendship with her dates from around 1608 when she moved to Twickenham. Goodyer, through whom she acquired Twickenham, was no doubt responsible for bringing Donne to her notice, and Ben Jonson presented to her a copy of Donne's *Satires* with an introductory epigram. Donne wrote many letters to her in prose and verse and commemorated the death of her brother, the second Lord Harington, in 1614 in a long elegy. See Sermon 8 for an extract from a sermon preached before her.

[2] The book that Donne is commenting upon is Barlow's *An Answer to a Catholic Englishman* (1609), an answer to Parson's attack in 1608 on King James's *An Apology for the Oath of Allegiance* (1607). *Pseudo-Martyr*, Donne's contribution to the controversy over the Oath, was entered on the Stationers' Register 2 December 1609.

and given new justice to my ordinary complaint, That the Divines
of these times, are become meer Advocates, as though Religion
were a temporall inheritance; they plead for it with all sophistica-
tions, and illusions, and forgeries: And herein are they likest
Advocates, that though they be feed by the way, with Dignities,
and other recompenses, yet that for which they plead is none of
theirs. They write for Religion, without it. In the main point in
question, I think truly there is a perplexity (as farre as I see yet)
and both sides may be in justice, and innocence; and the wounds
which they inflict upon the adverse part, are all *se defendendo*: for,
clearly, our State cannot be safe without the Oath; since they
professe, that Clergie-men, though Traitors, are no Subjects, and
that all the rest may be none tomorrow. And, as clearly, the
Supremacy which the Roman Church pretend, were diminished,
if it were limited; and will as ill abide that, or disputation, as the
Prerogative of temporall Kings, who being the onely judges of their
prerogative, why may not Roman Bishops, (so enlightned as they
are presumed by them) be good witnesses of their own supremacie,
which is now so much impugned? But for this particular Author,
I looked for more prudence, and humane wisdome in him, in avoid-
ing all miscitings, or mis-interpretings, because at this time, the
watch is set, and every bodies hammer is upon that anvill; and to
dare offend in that kinde now, is, for a theef to leave the covert,
and meet a strong hue and cry in the teeth: and yet truly this man
is extremely obnoxious in that kinde; for, though he have answered
many things fully, (as no book ever gave more advantage than
that which he undertook) and abound in delicate applications, and
ornaments, from the divine and prophane authors, yet being
chiefly conversant about two points, he prevaricates in both. For,
for the matter, which is the first, he referres it intirely, and namely,
to that which Dr. *Morton* hath said therein before, and so leaves it
roundly: And for the person (which is the second) upon whom he
amasses as many opprobries, as any other could deserve, he pro-
nounceth, that he will account any answer from his adversary,
slander, except he do (as he hath done) draw whatsoever he saith
of him, from Authors of the same Religion, and in print: And so, he
having made use of all the Quodlibetaries, imputations against the

other, cannot be obnoxious himself in that kinde, and so hath provided safely. It were no service to you, to send you my notes upon the Book, because they are sandy, and incoherent ragges, for my memory, not for your judgement; and to extend them to an easinesse, and perspicuity, would make them a Pamphlet, not a Letter. I will therefore deferre them till I see you; and in the mean time, I will adventure to say to you, without inserting one unnecessary word, that the Book is full of falsifications in words, and in sense, and of falshoods in matter of fact, and of inconsequent and unscholarlike arguings, and of relinquishing the King, in many points of defence, and of contradiction of himself, and of dangerous and suspected Doctrine in Divinitie, and of silly ridiculous triflings, and of extreme flatteries, and of neglecting better and more obvious answers, and of letting slip some enormous advantages which the other gave, and he spies not. I know (as I begun) I speak to you who cannot be scandalized, and that neither measure Religion (as it is now called) by Unitie, nor suspect Unity, for these interruptions. Sir, not onely a Mathematique point, which is the most indivisible and unique thing which art can present, flowes into every line which is derived from the Center, but our soul which is but one, hath swallowed up a Negative, and feeling soul; which was in the body before it came, and exercises those faculties yet; and God himselfe, who only is one, seems to have been eternally delighted, with a disunion of persons. They whose active function it is, must endevour this unity in Religion: and we at our lay Altars (which are our tables, or bedside, or stools, wheresoever we dare prostrate our selves to God in prayer) must beg it of him: but we must take heed of making misconclusions upon the want of it: for, whether the Mayor and Aldermen fall out, (as with us and the Puritans; Bishops against Priests) or the Commoners voyces differ who is Mayor, and who Aldermen, or what their Jurisdiction, (as with the Bishop of *Rome*, or whosoever) yet it is still one Corporation.

Micham, Thursday *late*.

*Your very affectionate servant and lover*

J. DONNE

*Never leave the remembrance of my poor service unmentioned when you see the good Lady.*

## 22. To Sir Henry Goodyer

Sir,                                     [? 1609]¹

If a whole year be but *Annus ab Annulo*, because it returnes into
it self, what *Annulus* shall be diminutive enough, to express our
weekly revolutions? In chaines the least linkes have most curiosity,
but that can be no emblem of us: but they have also the most
strength, and that may. The first sphere onely which is resisted by
nothing, absolves his course every day; and so doth true friendship
well placed, often iterate in act or purpose, the same offices. But as
the lower spheres, subject to the violence of that, and yet naturally
encouraged to a reluctation against it, have therefore many distractions, and eccentricities, and some trepidations, and so return
but lamely, and lately to the same place, and office: so that friendship
which is not moved primarily by the proper intelligence, discretion,
and about the naturall center, vertue, doth perchance sometimes,
some things, somewhat like true friendship; but hath many
deviations, which are strayings into new loves, (not of other men;
for that is proper to true wise friendship, which is not a [marrying];
but of other things) and hath such trepidations as keep it from
shewing it self, where great persons do not love; and it returns to the
true first station and place of friendship planetarily, which is un-
certainly and seldome. I have ever seen in *London* and our Court,
as some colours, and habits, and continuances, and motions, and
phrases, and accents, and songs, so friends in fashion and in season:
and I have seen them as sodainly abandoned altogether, though I
see no change in them, nor know more why they were left, than
why they were chosen. To do things by example, and upon
confidence of anothers judgment may be some kinde of a second
wisdome; but it is but writing by a copy: or indeed it is the hardest
of all, and the issue of the first wisdome, for I cannot know that this
example should be followed, except I knew that it is good, and so
I judge my Judge. Our assent therefore, and arrest, must be upon
things, not persons. And when we are sure we are in the right way,
for great persons, we may be glad of their company, if they go our
way; we may for them change our place, but not our end, nor our

¹ This letter written from Mitcham would seem to be near in time to the last, since it
revolves the same ideas.

way, if there be but one, [as] in Religion. In persevering in it, it
concerns [us] much what our companions be, but very much what our
friends. In which I know I speak not dangerously nor mis-appliably
to you, as though I averted you from any of those friends, who are
of other impressions than you or I in some great circumstances of
Religion. You know I never fettered nor imprisoned the word
Religion; not straightning it Frierly, *ad Religiones factitias*, (as the
*Romans* call well their orders of Religion) nor immuring it in a
*Rome*, or a *Wittemberg*, or a *Geneva*; they are all virtuall beams of one
Sun, and wheresoever they finde clay hearts, they harden them,
and moulder them into dust; and they entender and mollifie waxen.
They are not so contrary as the North and South Poles; and that
they are connaturall pieces of one circle. Religion is Christianity,
which being too spirituall to be seen by us, doth therefore take an
apparent body of good life and works, so salvation requires an
honest Christian. These are the two Elements, and he which ele-
mented from these, hath the complexion of a good man, and a fit
friend. The diseases are, too much intention into indiscreet zeal,
and too much remisnesse and negligence by giving scandall:
for our condition and state in this, is as infirm as in our bodies;
where physitians consider only two degrees; sicknesse, and neutral-
ity; for there is no health in us. This, Sir, I use to say to you, rather
to have so good a witnesse and corrector of my meditations, than
to advise; and yet to do that too, since it is pardonable in a friend:
Not to slack you towards those friends which are religious in other
clothes than we; (for *Amici vitia si feras facis tua*, is true of such
faults) but to keep you awake against such as the place where you
must live will often obtrude, which are not onely naked, without
any fashion of such garments, but have neither the body of Religion,
which is morall honesty, and sociable faithfulness, nor the soul,
Christianity. I know not how this paper scaped last week which I send
now; I was so sure that I enwrapped it then, that I should be so still,
but that I had but one copy; forgive it as you use to do. From *Micham*
in as much haste, and with as ill Pen and Inke, as the letter can accuse
me of; but with the last and the next weeks heart and affection.

*Yours very truely and affectionately,*

J. DONNE

## 23. To Sir Edward Herbert

[? 1610]¹

Sir,

I make accompt that this book hath enough performed that which it undertook, both by argument and example. It shall therefore the lesse need to be it self another example of the Doctrine. It shall not therefore kill it self; that is, not bury it self; for if it should do so, those reasons, by which that act should be defended or excused, were also lost with it. Since it is content to live, it cannot chuse a wholsomer aire than your Library, where Authors of all complexions are [preserved]. If any of them grudge this book a room, and suspect it of new or dangerous doctrine, you who know us all, can best moderate. To those reasons which I know your love to me will make in my favour and discharge, you may adde this, that though this doctrine hath not been taught nor defended by writers, yet they, most of any sort of men in the world, have practised it.

*Your very true and earnest friend*
*and servant and lover*

J. DONNE

## 24. To a Friend²

[? 1611–12]

Sir,

There is a dangerous Rule in Law, *Socius socii mei, non est socius meus*. If it extend to Friendship, as well as to Familiaritie, I who can pretend no other title to your friendship, than that I am allowed some little interest in them, who have more in you, may well account my self to be within the danger of it. But, as in Divine, so in

---

¹ This letter is headed 'To the Noblest Knight, Sir Edward Herbert Lord of Cherbury; sent to him with his Book Biathanatos'. The autograph of the letter with a manuscript copy of *Biathanatos* was given by Lord Herbert to the Bodleian Library in 1642. Mrs. Simpson thought that this letter was written well before 1619, when Donne told Ker that *Biathanatos* had never been copied (see Letters 32), and that Donne had forgotten the existence of thi copy. Donne and Herbert were exchanging Verse-Letters in 1610.

² The friend appears to be abroad, where Donne hopes to see him 'this Summer', and is plainly a Catholic. It seems possible that this is a letter to Sir Toby Mathew, whom Donne met when abroad with Doncaster in 1619; see Letter 33. Mr. Shapiro agrees in thinking this letter is to Mathew and thinks it was written in the winter 1611–12 when Donne was abroad with Sir Robert Drury.

Morall things, where the beginning is from others, the assistance, and co-operation, is in our selves. I therefore, who could do nothing towards the begetting, would fain do somewhat towards the breeding and cherishing of such degrees of friendship, as formerly I had the honour to hold with you. If Letters be not able to do that office, they are yet able, at least to testifie, that he, who sends them, would be glad to do more, if he could. I have a great desire, not without some hope, to see you this Summer there; and I have more hope and more desire, to see you this next Winter here; and I have abundantly more of both, that, at least, we shall meet in Heaven. That we differ in our wayes, I hope we pardon one another. Men go to *China*, both by the Straights, and by the *Cape*. I never mis-interpreted your way; nor suffered it to be so, wheresoever I found it in discourse. For I was sure, you took not up your Religion upon trust, but payed ready money for it, and at a high Rate. And this taste of mine towards you, makes me hope for, and claime the same disposition in you towards me. I am sure, this messenger beares so many Letters to you, as if this of mine (which is written upon the first day of my comming to Town) should offer at any thing of the Times, it might perhaps shake your beliefe from somewhat, expressed in some of your other Letters, by my relating them diverselie. For it is but earlie daies with me here; and I see not things so distinctlie yet, as to lay them under such eyes as yours. This Letter doth therefore onely aske your safe conduct, for those others of mine, which are to follow, as the most constant testimonies of my love, etc.

## 25. To Mr. George Gerrard

(14 April 1612)[1]

Sir,

Neither your Letters, nor silence, needs excuse; your friendship is to me an abundant possession, though you remember me but twice in a year: He that could have two harvests in that time, might justly value his land at a high rate; but, Sir, as we doe not

---

[1] George Gerrard, after Goodyer Donne's closest friend, was second son of Sir William Gerrard of Dorney, Bucks. He became Master of the Charterhouse. In his will, Donne left 'to my kind friend Mr. George Garrard the picture of Mary Magdalene in my chamber'. Donne left England with Sir Robert and Lady Drury in November 1611 and was abroad until August 1612.

onely then thank our land, when we gather the fruit, but acknowledge that all the year she doth many motherly offices in preparing
it: so is not friendship then onely to be esteemed, when she is
delivered of a Letter, or any other reall office, but in her continuall
propensnesse and inclination to do it. This hath made me easie in
pardoning my long silences, and in promising my self your forgivenesse for not answering your Letter sooner. For my purpose
of proceeding in the profession of the law, so farre as to a title,
you may be pleased to correct that imagination, wheresoever you
finde it. I ever thought the study of it my best entertainment,
and pastime, but I have no ambition, nor designe upon the style. Of
my Anniversaries, the fault that I acknowledge in my self, is to have
descended to print any thing in verse, which though it have excuse
even in our times, by men who professe, and practise much gravitie;
yet I confesse I wonder how I declined to it, and do not pardon my
self: But for the other part of the imputation of having said too
much, my defence is, that my purpose was to say as well as I could:
for since I never saw the Gentlewoman, I cannot be understood to
have bound my self to have spoken just truths, but I would not be
thought to have gone about to praise her, or any other in rime;
except I took such a person, as might be capable of all that I could
say. If any of those Ladies think that Mistris *Drewry* was not so,
let that Lady make her self fit for all those praises in the book, and
they shall be hers. Sir, this messenger makes so much haste that
I cry you mercy for spending any time of this letter in other im-
ployment than thanking you for yours. I hope before *Christmas* to
see *England*, and kisse your hand, which shall ever, (if it disdain not
that office) hold all the keyes of the libertie and affection and all the
faculties of

*Your most affectionate servant,*

J. DONNE

*Paris* the 14 of
*Aprill*, here, 1612.

## 26. To Sir Robert More

Sir,                                             (10 August 1614)[1]

Since I had no other thinge in contemplacion when I purposed thys journey, than my health, me thinks yt ys a kinde of phisick to be so longe about that, and I grow weary of phisick quickly. I have therfore put off that purpose, at least tyll the King come into these parts. If your horse (which I returne by thys carryar of Gilford) have not found as good salads in our Covent Garden, as he should at Lothesley, yet I beleeve he hath had more ease than he should have had there. We are condemned to thys desart of London for all thys sommer, for yt ys company not houses which distinguishes between cityes and desarts. When I began to apprehend, that even to my-selfe, who can releive myself upon books, solitarines was a litle burdenous, I beleeved yt would be much more so to my wyfe, if she were left alone. So much company, therfore, as I ame, she shall not want; and we had not one another at so cheape a rate, as that we should ever be wearye of one another. Sir, when these places afford any thinge worthe your knowledge, I shall be your referendary. Now my errand ys onely to deliver my thanks and services, accompanyed with your poore sister's, to your selfe, and all your good company. 10 August. 1614.

Yours ever to be commanded
J. DONNE

I praie, Sir, give thys note enclosed to my lady your mother; it ys of some parcells which she commanded my wyfe to buy for her, which are sent down at thys tyme by the carryar.

*To the right wor. Sir Robert*
*More, knight, at Lothersley.*

## 27. To Sir Henry Goodyer

Sir,                                          (20 December 1614)

I writ to you yesterday taking the boldnesse to put a letter into the good Ladies pacquet for you. This morning I had this new

[1] Sir Robert More was Donne's brother-in-law.

occasion of writing, that Sir *Tho. Roe*, who brought this inclosed
Letter to me, and left it unsealed, intreated me to take the first
opportunity of sending it. Besides that which is in that letter (for
he read it to me) I came to the knowledg in *Yorkhouse* that my
L. Chancellor hath been moved, and incensed against you; and
asking Sir *Tho. Roe*, if he were directly or occasionally any cause
of that, he tells me thus much, that Sir *W. Lover*, and Sir *H. Carey*,
have obtained of my L. to have a Pursevant, and consequently a
Serjeant sent into the Countrey for you. My L. grounds this earnestnesse against you, upon some refusing to appear upon processe
which hath been taken out against you. And I perceive Sir *Ed. Eston*,
and both the other, admit consultations, of ways by petition to the
King, or Counsail, or L. Chamberlain, or any other. The great
danger, obliquely likely to fall, is that when it comes to light, how
you stand towards M. *Mathew*, you may lose the ease which you
have by colour of that extent, and he may lose the benefit, of having
had so much of his estate concealed. You will therefore at least
pardon my advising you, to place those sums, which by your
retiring I presume you do imploy upon payment of debts, in such
places as that these particular friends be not forced to leave being so.
I confesse, the going about to pay debts, hastens importunity. I
finde in my self, that where I was not asked money before, yet when
I offered to pay next Terme, they seem loth to afford me that time,
which might justly have been desperate before: but that which you
told me out of the Countrey, with the assistance which I hope to
finde here, (especially if your indevour may advance it at *Dorset*
house) I hope will inable me to escape clamor, and an ill conscience,
in that behalf. One thing more I must tell you; but so softly, that I
am loath to hear my self: and so softly, that if that good Lady were
in the room, with you and this Letter, she might not hear. It is, that
I am brought to a necessity of printing my Poems, and addressing
them to my L. Chamberlain. This I mean to do forthwith; not for
much publique view, but at mine own cost, a few Copies. I apprehend some incongruities in the resolution; and I know what I shall
suffer from many interpretations: but I am at an end, of much
considering that; and, if I were as startling in that kinde, as ever
I was, yet in this particular, I am under an unescapable necessity,

as I shall let you perceive, when I see you. By this occasion I am made a Rhapsoder of mine own rags, and that cost me more diligence, to seek them, than it did to make them. This made me aske to borrow that old book of you, which it will be too late to see, for that use, when I see you: for I must do this, as a valediction to the world, before I take Orders. But this is it, I am to aske you; whether you ever made any such use of the letter in verse, *A nostre Countesse chez vous*, as that I may not put it in, amongst the rest to persons of that rank; for I desire very very much, that something should bear her name in the book, and I would be just to my written words to my L. *Harrington*, to write nothing after that. I pray tell me as soon as you can, if I be at liberty to insert that: for if you have by any occasion applied any pieces of it, I see not, that it will be discerned, when it appears in the whole piece. Though this be a little matter, I would be sorry not to have an account of it, within as little after New years tide, as you could. I have something else to say, of M. *Villars*, but because I hope to see you here shortly, and because new additions, to the truths or rumours, which concern him, are likely to be made by occasion of this Masque, I forbear to send you the edition of this Mart, since I know it will be augmented by the next: of which, if you prevent it not by comming, you shall have, by letter an account from

*Your very affectionate*
*friend and servant*
J. DONNE

*Vigilia St. Tho.*
1614.

## 28. To Sir Edward Herbert

(23 January 1615)

Sir,

Because since I had the honor to see you, or hear from you, I have receyved such a change, as, if my unworthynes did not avile it, were an addition, I ame bold to present to you the knowledge thereof: because therby your power, and jurisdiction, which is entirely over mee, is somewhat enlardged. For, as if I should put any other stampe upon a peece of your gold, the gold were not the lesse yours, so (if there be not too much taken by mee, in that comparison) by havinge, by the orders of our churche, receyved a new character, I ame not departed from your title, and possession of mee. But, as I was ever, by my devotion, and your acceptance, your humble servant, so I ame become, by this addition, capable of the dignity, of beeinge

Your very humble<br>chapleyn<br>J. DONNE

23 Jan. 1614 which was
the very day wherein I
took orders.

## 29. To Sir Henry Goodyer

[? April 1615][1]

Sir,

At some later reading, I was more affected with that part of your Letter, which is of the book, and the namelesse Letters, than at first. I am not sorry, for that affection were for a jealousie or suspicion of a flexibilty in you. But I am angry, that any should think, you had in your Religion peccant humours, defective, or abundant, or that such a booke, (if I mistake it not) should be able to work upon you; my comfort is, that their judgment is too weak to endanger you, since by this it confesses, that it mistakes you, in thinking you irresolved or various: yet let me be bold to fear, that that sound true opinion, that in all Christian professions there is way to salvation (which I think you think) may have been so incommodiously or intempestively sometimes uttered by you; or else your having friends equally near you of all the impressions of Religion, may have testified such an indifferency, as hath occasioned some to further such inclinations, as they have mistaken to be in you. This I have feared, because hertofore the inobedient Puritans, and now the over-obedient Papists attempt you. It hath hurt very many, not in their conscience, nor ends, but in their reputation,

[1] Gosse suggested that the Countess referred to is the Countess of Huntingdon whom Donne approached at his ordination to pay his debts when disappointed by the smallness of the Countess of Bedford's gift. Goodyer had suggested that he should write a poem to the Countess. Mr. Shapiro disagrees with Gosse's date and suggests 1613-14.

and ways, that others have thought them fit to be wrought upon.
As some bodies are as wholesomly nourished as ours, with Akornes,
and endure nakednesse, both which would be dangerous to us, if
we for them should leave our former habits, though theirs were the
Primitive diet and custome: so are many souls well fed with such
formes, and dressings of Religion, as would distemper and mis-
become us, and make us corrupt towards God, if any humane
circumstance moved it, and in the opinion of men, though none.
You shall seldome see a Coyne, upon which the stamp were removed, though to imprint it better, but it looks awry and squint.
And so, for the most part, do mindes which have received divers
impressions. I will not, nor need to you, compare the Religions.
The channels of Gods mercies run through both fields; and they
are sister teats of his graces, yet both diseased and infected, but
not both alike. And I think, that as *Copernicisme* in the Mathe-
matiques hath carried earth farther up, from the stupid Center;
and yet not honoured it, nor advantaged it, because for the necessity of appearances, it hath carried heaven so much higher from it:
so the *Roman* profession seems to exhale, and refine our wills from
earthly [Dregs], and Lees, more than the Reformed, and so seems to
bring us nearer heaven; but then that carries heaven farther from
us, by making us pass so many Courts, and Offices of Saints in this
life, in all our petitions, and lying in a painfull prison in the next,
during the pleasure, not of him to whom we go, and who must be our
Judge, but of them from whom we come, who know not our case.
Sir, as I said last time, labour to keep your alacrity and dignity, in
an even temper: for in a dark sadnesse, indifferent things seem
abominable, or necessary, being neither; as trees, and sheep to
melancholique night-walkers have unproper shapes. And when you
descend to satisfie all men in your own religion, or to excuse others
to al; you prostitute your self and your understanding, though not
a prey, yet a mark, and a hope, and a subject, for every sophister in
Religion to work on. For the other part of your Letter, spent in the
praise of the Countesse, I am always very apt to beleeve it of her,
and can never beleeve it so well, and so reasonably, as now, when
it is averred by you; but for the expressing it to her, in that sort as
you seem to counsaile, I have these two reasons to decline it. That

that knowledge which she hath of me, was in the beginning of a graver course, than of a Poet, into which (that I may also keep my dignity) I would not seem to relapse. The Spanish proverb informes me, that he is a fool which cannot make one Sonnet, and he is mad which makes two. The other stronger reason, is my integrity to the other Countesse, of whose worthinesse though I swallowed your opinion at first upon your words, yet I have had since an explicit faith, and now a knowledge: and for her delight (since she descends to them) I had reserved not only all the verses, which I should make, but all the thoughts of womens worthinesse. But because I hope she will not disdain, that I should write well of her Picture, I have obeyed you thus far, as to write: but intreat you by your friendship, that by this occasion of versifying, I be not traduced, nor esteemed light in that Tribe, and that house where I have lived. If those reasons which moved you to bid me write be not constant in you still, or if you meant not that I should write verses; or if these verses be too bad, or too good, over or under her understanding, and not fit; I pray receive them, as a companion and supplement of this Letter to you; and as such a token as I use to send, which use, because I wish rather they should serve (except you wish otherwise) I send no other; but after I have told you, that here at a Christning at *Peckam*, you are remembred by divers of ours, and I commanded to tell you so, I kisse your hands, and so seal to you my pure love, which I would not refuse to do by any labour or danger.

*Your very true friend and servant*
J. DONNE

## 30. To his Mother (Mrs. Elizabeth Rainsford)

[? 1616][1]

*My most dear Mother,*

When I consider so much of your life, as can fall within my memorie and observation, I find it to have been a Sea, under a continuall

---

[1] The letter is headed 'To his Mother: comforting her after the death of her Daughter'. Elizabeth Heywood, daughter of John Heywood the playwright and epigrammatist, remained a staunch Catholic all her life. She died in 1632, having survived three husbands and six children. After the death of her third husband, Richard Rainsforth, she lived with Donne at the Deanery. Of the six children she had by her first marriage, three died in infancy and a

Tempest, where one wave hath ever overtaken another. Our most wise and blessed Saviour chuseth what way it pleaseth him, to conduct those which he loves, to his Haven, and eternall Rest. The way which he hath chosen for you, is strait, stormie, obscure, and full of sad apparitions of death, and wants, and sundry discomforts; and it hath pleased him, that one discomfort should still succeed, and touch another, that he might leave you no leasure, by anie pleasure or abundance, to [stray] or step out of that way, or almost to take breath in that way, by which he hath determined to bring you home, which is his glorious Kingdom. One of the most certain marks and assurances, that all these are his works, and to that good end, is your inward feeling and apprehension of them, and patience in them. As long as the Spirit of God distills and dews his cheerfulnesse upon your heart; as long as he instructs your understanding, to interpret his mercies and his judgments aright; so long your comfort must needs be as much greater than others, as your afflictions are greater than theirs. The happinesse which God afforded to your first young time, which was the love and care of my most dear and provident Father, whose soul, I hope, hath long since enjoyed the sight of our blessed Saviour, and had compassion of all our miseries in this world, God removed from you quickly. And hath since taken from you all the comfort, that that Marriage produced. All those children (for whose maintenance his industrie provided, and for whose education, you were so carefullie and so chargeablie diligent) he hath now taken from you. All that worth which he left, God hath suffered to be gone from us all. So that God hath seemed to repent, that he allowed any part of your life any earthly happinesse, that he might keep your Soul in continuall exercise, and longing, and assurance, of comming immediately to him. I hope therefore, my most dear Mother, that your experience of the calamities of this life, your continuall acquaintance with the visitations of the holy Ghost, which gives better inward comforts, than the world can outward discomforts,

fourth, her second son Henry, died in prison, where he had been committed for sheltering a priest, in 1593. Her daughter Anne married a Yorkshire Catholic, Avery Copley, who died in 1591, and married a second husband, William Lyly, some time before 1594; see R. C. Bald, *Donne and the Drurys*, 1959, for an account of Lyly. It is not known when Anne Lyly died; but this letter was written before the death of Donne's wife in 1617 and seems likely to be after he took orders.

your wisdom, to distinguish the value of this world from the next, and your religious fear of offending our mercifull God, by repining at any thing which he doth, will preserve you from any inordinate and dangerous sorrow, for this losse of my most beloved Sister. For my part, which am onely left now, to do the office of a child; though the poornesse of my fortune, and the greatnesse of my charge, hath not suffered me to expresse my duty towards you, as became me; yet, I protest to you before Almighty God, and his Angells and Saints in Heaven, that I do, and ever shall, esteem my self, to be as stronglie bound to look to you, and provide for your relief, as for my own poor wife and children. For, whatsoever I shall be able to do, I acknowledge to be a debt to you, from whom I had that education, which must make my fortune. This I speak not, as though I feared my father *Rainsford's* care of you, or his means to provide for you; for he hath been with me, and, as I perceive in him, a loving and industrious care to give you contentment; so, I see in his businesse, a happie and considerable forwardnesse. In the mean time, good Mother, take heed, that no sorrow nor dejection in your heart, interrupt or disappoint God's purpose in you; his purpose is, to remove out of your heart all such love of this world's happinesse, as might put Him out of possession of it. He will have you entirelie. And, as God is comfort enough, so Hee is inheritance enough. Joyne with God, and make his visitations and afflictions, as he intended them, mercies and comforts. And, for God's sake, pardon those negligences, which I have heretofore used towards you; and assist me, with your blessing to me, and all mine; and with your prayers to our blessed Saviour, that thereby both my mind and fortune, may be apt to do all my duties, especially those that belong to you.

God, whose omnipotent strength can change the nature of any thing, by his raising-Spirit of comfort, make your Povertie Riches, your Afflictions Pleasure, and all the Gall and Wormwood of your life, Hony and Manna to your taste, which he hath wrought, whensoever you are willing to have it so. Which, because I cannot doubt in you, I will forbear more lines at this time, and most humblie deliver my self over to your devotions, and good opinion of me, which I desire no longer to live, than I may have.

## 31. To the Countess of Montgomery

[March/April 1619][1]

Madam,

Of my ability to doe your Ladiship service, any thing may be an embleme good enough; for as a word vanisheth, so doth any power in me to serve you; things that are written are fitter testimonies, because they remain and are permanent: in writing this Sermon which your Ladiship was pleased to hear before, I confesse I satisfie an ambition of mine own, but it is the ambition of obeying your commandment, not onely an ambition of leaving my name in the memory, or in the Cabinet: and yet, since I am going out of the Kingdom, and perchance out of the world, (when God shall have given my soul a place in heaven) it shall the lesse diminish your Ladiship, if my poor name be found about you. I know what dead carkasses things written are, in respect of things spoken. But in things of this kinde, that soul that inanimates them, receives debts from them: The Spirit of God that dictates them in the speaker or writer, and is present in his tongue or hand, meets himself again (as we meet our selves in a glass) in the eies and hearts of the hearers and readers: and that Spirit, which is ever the same to an equall devotion, makes a writing and a speaking equall means to edification. In one circumstance, my preaching and my writing this Sermon is too equall: that that your Ladiship heard in a hoarse voyce then, you read in a coarse hand now: but in thankfulnesse I shall lift up my hands as clean as my infirmities can keep them, and a voyce as clear as his spirit shall be pleased to tune in my prayers in all places of the world, which shall either sustain or bury

> *Your Ladiships humble Servant*
> *in Christ Jesus*
>
> J. DONNE

[1] Susan Vere, daughter of the Earl of Oxford, married Sir Philip Herbert in 1605. He was shortly afterwards created Earl of Montgomery. The sermon this letter encloses was preached before her on 21 February 1619; see Potter and Simpson, *Sermons*, ii. 179. Donne went 'out of the Kingdom' in May 1619.

## 32. To Sir Robert Ker[1]

[April/May 1619]

Sir,

I had need do somewhat towards you above my promises; How weak are my performances, when even my promises are defective? I cannot promise, no not in mine own hopes, equally to your merit towards me. But besides the Poems, of which you took a promise, I send you another Book to which there belongs this History. It was written by me many years since; and because it is upon a misinterpretable subject, I have always gone so near suppressing it, as that it is onely not burnt: no hand hath passed upon it to copy it, nor many eyes to read it: onely to some particular friends in both Universities, then when I writ it, I did communicate it: And I remember, I had this answer, That certainly, there was a false thread in it, but not easily found: Keep it, I pray, with the same jealousie; let any that your discretion admits to the sight of it, know the date of it; and that it is a Book written by *Jack Donne*, and not by Dr. *Donne*: Reserve it for me, if I live, and if I die, I only forbid it the Presse, and the Fire: publish it not, but yet burn it not; and between those, do what you will with it. Love me still, thus farre, for your own sake, that when you withdraw your love from me, you will finde so many unworthinesses in me, as you grow ashamed of having had so long, and so much, such a thing as

*Your poor servant in Chr. Jes.*

J. DONNE

## 33. To Sir Toby Mathew

[September 1619][2]

Sir,

At *Ratisbone* I had your Letter from *Brussel's*; and, in it, you. For, my former knowledge of your ingenuitie, and mine own conscience

---

1 Headed in *Letters* 'To Sir Robert Carre *now Earle of* Ankerum, *with my Book* Biathanatos *at my going into* Germany'. See Letter 23 in which Donne sends a copy of *Biathanatos* to Edward Herbert. Donne left England with Doncaster on 12 May 1619 and was abroad until early in 1620.

2 The Letter is headed '*A Letter of much kindnesse from Doctor* Donne, *to* Sir Toby Mathew, *from* Colleyn'. The Doncaster embassy was at Cologne in mid-September 1619. Toby Mathew, the recusant son of Tobias Matthew, Archbishop of York, was abroad from 1608 and was the subject of many rumours. He was forgiven by King James and knighted in 1623 on his return to England.

of having demerited in nothing toward you, are assurances to me, that your professions are in earnest. I dare put my selfe upon the testimony of very many very good Companies in *England*, where your Person, and your Historie, have been the discourse, that I have never forsaken your honour and reputation. And you may be pleased to make this some argument of my disposition toward you, that when I have been told, that you have not been so carefull of me abroad, I have not been easie in beleeving it; and when at sometimes, the authoritie of the reporter, hath brought me to a half-belief of it, I have found other excuses in your behalfe, than a meer dis-affection to me: and now I am safelie returned to my first station again, not to beleeve it. If it could be possible that any occasion of doing you a reall service, might be presented me, you should see, that that Tree which was rooted in love, and alwaies bore leaves, readie to shadow and defend from others malice, would bear fruit also. You know, we say in the Schools, that Grace destroys not Nature: we may say too, that forms of Religion destroy not moralitie, nor civill offices. That which I add, I am farre from applying to you, but it is true, That we are fallen into so slack and negligent times, that I have been sometimes glad to hear, that some of my friends have differed from me in Religion. It is some degree of an union to be united in a serious meditation of God, and to make any Religion the rule of our actions. Our sweet and blessed Saviour bring us by his way, to his end! And be you pleased to be assured, that no man desires to renew, or continue, or encrease a friendship with you more than

## 34. [To Sir Henry Goodyer][1]

(4 October 1622)

Octob. *the* 4th 1622, *almost at midnight.*

Sir,

All our moralities are but our outworks, our Christianity is our Citadel; a man who considers duty but the dignity of his being a man, is not easily beat from his outworks, but from his Christianity

---

[1] This letter is headed 'To Sir Henry Wotton'. It is plainly to Goodyer, to whom Donne wrote three other letters on their common difficulties in providing dowries for their daughters. Wotton was unmarried. Walton cancelled Wotton's name in favour of Goodyer's in his copy of the *Letters*. See note to Letters, No. 11.

never; and therefore I dare trust you, who contemplates them both. Every distemper of the body now, is complicated with the spleen, and when we were young men we scarce ever heard of the spleen. In our declinations now, every accident is accompanied with heavy clouds of melancholy; and in our youth we never admitted any. It is the spleen of the minde, and we are affected with vapors from thence; yet truly, even this sadnesse that overtakes us, and this yeelding to the sadnesse, is not so vehement a poison (though it be no Physick neither) as those false waies, in which we sought our comforts in our looser daies. You are able to make rules to your self, and our B. Saviour continue to you an ability to keep within those rules. And this particular occasion of your present sadnesse must be helped by the rule, for, for examples you will scarce finde any, scarce any that is not encombred and distressed in his fortunes. I had locked my self, sealed and secured my self against all possibilities of falling into new debts, and in good faith, this year hath thrown me 400 l. lower than when I entred this house. I am a Father as well as you, and of children (I humbly thank God) of as good dispositions; and in saying so, I make account that I have taken my comparison as high as I could goe; for in good faith, I beleeve yours to be so: but as those my daughters (who are capable of such considerations) cannot but see my desire to accommodate them in this world, so I think they will not murmure if heaven must be their Nunnery, and they associated to the B. virgins there: I know they would be content to passe their lives in a Prison, rather than I should macerate my self for them, much more to suffer the mediocrity of my house, and my means, though that cannot preferre them: yours are such too, and it need not that patience, for your fortune doth not so farre exercise their patience. But to leave all in Gods hands, from whose hands nothing can be wrung by whining but by praying, nor by praying without the *Fiat voluntas tua*. Sir, you are used to my hand, and, I think have leisure to spend some time in picking out sense, in ragges; else I had written lesse, and in longer time. Here is room for an *Amen*; the prayer—so I am going to my bedside to make for all you and all yours, with

*Your true friend and servant in Chr. Jesus*

J. DONNE

## 35. To Sir Robert Ker

[April, May, or June 1623][1]

Sir,

Your way into *Spain* was Eastward, and that is the way to the land of Perfumes and Spices; their way hither is Westward, and that is the way to the land of Gold, and of Mynes. The Wise men, who sought Christ, laid down both their Perfumes, and their Gold, at the feet of Christ, the Prince of Peace. If All confer all to his glory, and to the peace of his Church, *Amen*. But now I consider in Cosmography better; they and we differ not in East and West: we are much alike Easterlie. But yet, *Oriens nomen ejus*, the East is one of Christ's names, in one Prophet; And, *Filius Orientis est Lucifer*, the East is one of the Devill's names, in another: and these two differ diametrically. And so in things belonging to the worship of God, I think we shall, *Amen*. But the difference of our scituation is in North and South; and you know, that though the labour of any ordinary Artificer in that Trade, will bring East and West together, (for if a flat Map be but pasted upon a round Globe, the farthest East, and the farthest West meet, and are all one) yet all this brings not North and South a scruple of a degree the nearer. There are things in which we may [meet]; and in that wherein we should not, my hope is in God, and in Him, in whom God doth so evidently work, we shall not meet, *Amen*. They have hotter daies in *Spain* than we have here, but our daies are longer; and yet we are hotter in our businesse here, and they longer about it there. God is sometimes called a Gyant, running a race; and sometimes is so slow-paced, as that a thousand years make but a day with God; and yet still the same God. He hath his purposes upon our noble and vehement affections, and upon their warie and sober discretions; and will use both to his glory. *Amen*.

Sir, I took up this Paper to write a Letter; but my imaginations were full of a Sermon before, for I write but a few hours before I am

---

[1] Sir Robert Ker, later first Earl of Ancrum and ancestor of the present Marquis of Lothian, to whom Donne left in his will the Lothian portrait, accompanied Prince Charles and Buckingham on their misguided and romantic visit to Spain to woo the Infanta from March to September 1623. A sermon which echoes this letter closely is dated by Mrs. Simpson April, May, or June 1623. Excerpts from it are given in Sermon 24.

to Preach, and so instead of a Letter I send you a Homily. Let it have thus much of a Letter, That I am confident in your love, and deliver my self over to your service. And thus much of a Homily, That you and I shall accompanie one another to the possession of Heaven, in the same way wherein God put us at first. *Amen.*

*Your very humble and very thank-*
*full servant in Christ, &c.*

## 36. To Sir Robert Ker

[January 1624][1]

Sir,

Though I have left my bed, I have not left my bed-side; I sit there still, and as a Prisoner discharged, sits at the Prison doore, to beg Fees, so sit I here, to gather crummes. I have used this leisure, to put the meditations had in my sicknesse, into some such order, as may minister some holy delight. They arise to so many sheetes (perchance 20.) as that without staying for that furniture of an Epistle, That my Friends importun'd me to Print them, I importune my Friends to receive them Printed. That, being in hand, through this long Trunke, that reaches from Saint *Pauls*, to Saint *James*, I whisper into your eare this question, whether there be any uncomlinesse, or unseasonablenesse, in presenting matter of Devotion, or Mortification, to that Prince, whom I pray God nothing may ever Mortifie, but Holinesse. If you allow my purposes in generall, I pray cast your eye upon the Title and the Epistle, and rectifie me in them: I submit substance, and circumstance to you, and the poore Author of both,

*Your very humble and very thankfull Servant*
*in Christ Jesus*

J. DONNE

---

1 The *Devotions* was entered in the Stationers' Register 9 January 1624 and appeared early in that year with the dedicatory epistle to the Prince of Wales which Donne here asks Ker to approve.

## 37. To the Queen of Bohemia

[1624][1]

Your Majesty hath had the patience heretofore to hear me deliver the messages of God to your self. In the hearing of me deliver my messages to God, I can hope for the continuance of your Majestie's patience. He is a very diffident man, that can doubt of that vertue in your Majestie; for of your great measure of that vertue, the World hath had more proofe than it needed. But I consider alwayes, that it had been in me a disloyall thing (I afford no milder a word to that fault) to have any way conjured to the exercising of your Majestie's patience; Therefore I have forborn, to thrust into your Majestie's presence my name, or any thing which hath proceeded from me, though alwayes the dignity of the subject, and sometimes the expresse commandment, sometimes the gracious alarum of your most royall Father, might have gon far in my excuse, in such a boldnesse to your Majestie. Now (for since I am doing a bold action, I may speak words that sound of boldnesse too) I surprise your Majestie, I take you at an advantage, I lay an obligation upon you, because that which your Brother's Highnesse hath received, your Majestie cannot refuse. By your own example you can suffer, by his example you may be pleased to accept this testimony of the zeal of your, &c.

[1] Princess Elizabeth, daughter of James I, married Frederick, Count Palatine, on 14 February 1613, and Donne celebrated their marriage by an Epithalamium. The Prince Palatine's acceptance of the Crown of Bohemia in 1619 was the spark that touched off the Thirty Years War. He was driven from his kingdom in 1620 and dubbed 'The Winter King', as his wife was called 'The Queen of Hearts'. Donne had preached before the Prince and Princess Palatine at Heidelberg on 16 June 1619, while on the Doncaster mission. Her reply to this letter sending her a copy of the *Devotions* (whose dedication her brother, the Prince of Wales, had accepted) is given below. In the following year Donne sent her a copy of the first sermon he preached before her brother, the new king, Charles I.

*A Letter from the Queen of* Bohemia, *in answer to the former.*
*Good Doctor.*

None should have cause to pitty me, nor my selfe to complain, had I met with no other exercise of my patience, than the hearing of you deliver (as you call them) the messages of God, unto me: which truly I never did, but with delight, and I hope some measure of edification. No doubt then but I shall read yours to him with pleasure, and I trust by his assistance, to whom they are directed, not without profit. For what I have already read, I give you hearty thanks; and if my better fortunes make progression with my reading (whereof I now begin to have good hope) I will not faile upon any good occasion to acknowledge this courtesie at your hands; and in the mean time I remaine yours, &c.

## 38. To Lady Kingsmill

(26 October 1624)[1]

Madam,

Those things which God dissolves at once, as he shall do the Sun, and Moon, and those bodies at the last conflagration, he never intends to reunite again; but in those things, which he takes in pieces, as he doth man, and wife, in these divorces, by death, and in single persons, by the divorce of body and soul, God hath another purpose, to make them up again. That piece which he takes to himself, is presently cast in a mould, and in an instant made fit for his use; for heaven is not a place of proficiency, but of present perfection. That piece which he leaves behinde in this world, by the death of a part thereof, growes fitter and fitter for him, by the good use of his corrections, and the intire conformity to his will. Nothing disproportions us, nor makes us so uncapable of being reunited to those whom we loved here, as murmuring, or not advancing the goodness of him, who hath removed them from hence. We would wonder, to see a man, who in a wood were left to his liberty, to fell what trees he would, take onely the crooked, and leave the streightest trees; but that man hath perchance a ship to build, and not a house, and so hath use of that kinde of timber: let not us, who know that in Gods house there are many Mansions, but yet have no modell, no designe of the forme of that building, wonder at his taking in of his materialls, why he takes the young, and leaves the old, or why the sickly overlive those, that had better health. We are not bound to think that souls departed have devested all affections towards them whom they left here; but we are bound to think, that for all their loves they would not be here again: Then is the will of God done in Earth, as it is in Heaven, when we neither pretermit his actions, nor resist them; neither pass them over in an inconsideration, as though God had no hand in them, nor go about to take them out of his hands, as though we could direct him to do them better. As Gods Scriptures are his will, so his actions are his will; both are

1 Lady Kingsmill, wife of Sir Henry Kingsmill of Sydmonton, Hampshire, was before her marriage Bridget White and one of Donne's correspondents. Mr. Shapiro informs us that Sir Henry died on 20 Oct. 1624, although the monument his wife erected to his memory gives the date of his death as 1625.

Testaments, because they testifie his minde to us. It is not lawfull
to adde a scedule to either of his wills: as they do ill, who adde
to his written will, the Scriptures, a scedule of Apocryphall books:
so do they also, who to his other will, his manifested actions, adde
Apochryphall conditions, and a scedule of such limitations as these,
If God would have stayed thus long, or, If God would have proceeded in this or this manner, I could have born it. To say that our
afflictions are greater than we can bear, is so near to despairing,
as that the same words express both; for when we consider *Caines*
words in that originall tongue in which God spake, we cannot tell
whether the words be, My punishment is greater than can be born;
or, My sin is greater than can be forgiven. But, Madame, you who
willingly sacrificed your self to God, in your obedience to him, in
your own sickness, cannot be doubted to dispute with him, about
any part of you, which he shall be pleased to require at your hands.
The difference is great in the loss, of an arme, or a head; of a child,
or a husband: but to them, who are incorporated into Christ, their
head, there can be no beheading; upon you, who are a member of
the spouse of Christ the Church, there can fall no widowhead, nor
orphanage upon those children, to whom God is father. I have not
another office by your husbands death; for I was your Chaplaine
before, in my daily prayers; but I shall inlarge that office with other
Collects, than before, that God will continue to you, that peace
which you have ever had in him, and send you quiet, and peaceable
dispositions in all them with whom you shall have anything to do,
in your temporall estate and matters of this world. *Amen.*

> *Your Ladiships very humble and*
> *thankfull servant in Christ*
> *Jesus* J. DONNE

*At my poor house at S.*
  *Pauls.* 26 *Octob.*
  1624.

## 39. To Sir Robert Ker

[April 1627][1]

Sir,

A few hours after I had the honour of your Letter, I had another from my Lord of *Bath* and *Wells*, commanding from the King a Copy of my Sermon. I am in preparations of that, with diligence, yet this morning I waited upon his Lordship, and laid up in him this truth, that of the B. of *Canterburies* Sermon, to this hour, I never heard syllable, nor what way, nor upon what points he went: And for mine, it was put into that very order, in which I delivered it, more than two moneths since. Freely to you I say, I would I were a little more guilty: Onely mine innocency makes me afraid. I hoped for the Kings approbation heretofore in many of my Sermons; and I have had it. But yesterday I came very near looking for thanks; for, in my life, I was never in any one peece, so studious of his service. Therefore, exceptions being taken, and displeasure kindled at this, I am afraid, it was rather brought thither, than met there. If you know any more, fit for me, (because I hold that unfit for me, to appear in my Masters sight, as long as this cloud hangs, and therefore, this day forbear my ordinary waitings) I beseech you to intimate it to

*Your very humble and very thankfull Servant*

J. DONNE

## 40. To Sir Robert Ker

[April 1627]

Sir,

I humbly thanke you, for this continuing me in your memory, and enlarging me so far, as to the memory of my Soveraign, and (I hope) my Master. My Tenets are always, for the preservation of the Religion I was born in, and the peace of the State, and the rectifying of the Conscience; in these I shall walke, and as I have from

---

[1] This and the following two letters refer to a sermon that Donne preached at Court on 1 April 1627. Laud, at this time Bishop of Bath and Wells, had quarrelled with Abbott, the Archbishop of Canterbury, who, early in 1627, preached a sermon advancing Puritanical views. In the state of tension and ill will existing Donne's sermon was regarded as supporting Abbott. To his dismay he received a letter from Laud demanding a copy.

you a new seal thereof, in this Letter, so I had ever evidence in mine own observation, that these ways were truly, as they are justly, acceptable in his Majesties eare. Our blessed Saviour multiply unto him all blessings; *Amen*.

*Your very true and intire servant in Christ Jesus*,
J. Donne

## 41. To Sir Robert Ker

[April 1627]

Sir,

I was this morning at your door, somewhat early; and I am put into such a distaste of my last Sermon, as that I dare not practise any part of it, and therefore though I said then, that we are bound to speake aloud, though we awaken men, and make them froward, yet after two or three modest knocks at the door, I went away. Yet I understood after, the King was gone abroad, and thought you might be gone with him. I came to give you an account of that, which this does as well. I have now put into my Lord of *Bath* and *Wells* hands the Sermon faithfully exscribed. I beseech you be pleased to hearken farther after it; I am still upon my jealousie, that the King brought thither some disaffection towards me, grounded upon some other demerit of mine, and tooke it not from the Sermon. For, as Cardinal *Cusanus* writ a Book *Cribratio Alchorani*, I have cribrated, and re-cribrated, and post-cribrated the Sermon, and must necessarily say, the King who hath let fall his eye upon some of my Poems, never saw, of mine, a hand, or an eye, or an affection, set down with so much study, and diligence, and labour of syllables, as in this Sermon I expressed those two points, which I take so much to conduce to his service, the imprinting of persuasibility and obedience in the subject, and the breaking of the bed of whisperers, by casting in a bone, of making them suspect and distrust one another. I remember I heard the old King say of a good Sermon, that he thought the Preacher never had thought of his Sermon, till he spoke it; it seemed to him negligently and extemporally spoken. And I knew that he had weighed every syllable, for halfe a year before, which made me conclude, that the King had before, some prejudice upon him. So, the best of my hope is, that some over bold allusions, or expressions in the way, might divert his Majesty, from vouchsafing to observe the frame, and purpose of the Sermon. When he sees the generall scope, I hope his goodnesse will pardon collaterall escapes. I intreated the B. to aske his Majesty, whether his displeasure extended so farre, as that I should forbear waiting, and appearing in his presence; and I had a return, that I might come. Till I had that, I would not offer to put my self under your roof. To day I come, for that purpose, to say prayers. And if, in any degree, my health suffer it, I shall do so, to morrow. If any thing fall into your observation before that, (because the B. is likely to speake to the King of it, perchance, this night) if it amount to such an increase of displeasure, as that it might be unfit for me to appear, I beseech you afford me the knowledge. Otherwise, I am likely to inquire of you personally, to morrow before nine in the morning, and to put into your presence then

*Your very humble and very true, and very*
*honest servant to God and the King and you*
J. DONNE

*I writ yesterday to my Lord Duke, by my Lord Carlile, who assured me*
*of a gracious acceptation of my putting my self in his protection.*

## 42. To Mrs. Cokayne

[? 1625–1628[1]]

*My noble dear Sister,*

I am come now, not onely to pay a Feavour every half year, as a Rent for my life; but I am called upon before the day, and they come sooner in the year than heretofore. This Feavour that I had

1 Ann Cokayne, mother of Sir Aston Cokayne, poet and dramatist, was the daughter of Sir John Stanhope of Elvaston. She married Thomas Cokayne of Ashbourne, Derbyshire, who deserted her, went crazy, and devoted himself to the composition of an English–Greek lexicon. Donne probably met Mrs. Cokayne through Goodyer. Gosse dated this letter in January 1631, in Donne's last illness. Mr. Shapiro says that it cannot be later than early in 1628 and may be as early as 1625–6.

now, I hoped, for divers daies, to have been but an exaltation of my damps and flashings, such as exercise me sometimes four or five daies, and passe away, without whining or complaint. But, I neglected this somewhat too long, which makes me (though, after I took it into consideration, the Feavour it self declined quickly) much weaker, than, perchance, otherwise I should have been. I had Doctor *Fox* and Doctor *Clement* with me, but, I thank God, was not much trouble to them. Ordinary means set me soon upon my leggs. And I have broke my close prison, and walk'd into the Garden; and (but that the weather hath continued so spitefully foul) make no doubt, but I might safely have done more. I eat, and digest well enough. And it is no strange thing, that I do not sleep well; for, in my best health, I am not much used to do so. At the same time, little *Betty* had a Feavour too; and, for her, we used Doctor *Wright*, who, by occasion, lies within two miles of us; and he was able to ease my sicknesse, with his report of your good health, which, he told us, he had received from you. But I found it not seconded in your own Letters, which I had the honour to receive by Mr. *Hazard*. My noble sister, I am afraid that Death will play with me so long, as he will forget to kill me; and suffer me to live in a languishing and uselesse age, a life, that is rather a forgetting that I am dead, than of living. We dispute whether the dead shall pray for the living: and because my life may be short, I pray with the most earnestnesse for you now. By the advantage of sicknesse, I return the oftner to that holy exercise, and in it joyn yours with mine own Soul. I would not have dignified my self, or my sicknesse with saying so much of either, but that it is in obedience to your Command, that I should do so. And though there lye upon me no Command, yet there lies a necessitie growing out of my respect, and a nobler root, than that my love to you, to enlarge myself, as farre as I have gone alreadie, in Mr. *Hazards* businesse. My noble Sister, when you carrie me up to the beginning, which it pleases you to call a promise to your self, and your noble Sister; I never slackned my purpose of performing that promise. But if my promise, which was, that I should be readie to assist him in any thing I could, were translated by you, or your noble Sister, or him, that I would give him the next Living in my gift, certainlie we speak not one language, or understand not one another, and I had thought we had; This which he imagined to be vacant, (for it is not yet, nor any way likely) is the first that fell to me, since I made that promise. And, my noble Sister, if a person of my place, from whom, one Scholler in each Universitie sucks something, and must be weaned by me, and who hath otherwise a latitude of importunate friends and verie many obligations, have a Living once in five or six yeares fall in his gift, (for it is so long since I gave any) and may not make a good choice with freedome then, it is hard; yet it is not my fortune to doe so now: for, now there is a living fallen (though not that); I am not left to my choice. For my Lord[s] *Carlile*, and *Percy* have chosen for me: but trulie such a man as I would have chosen; and for him, they laid an obligation upon me three yeares since, for the next that should fall: yet Mr. *Hazard* presses you to write for that, because he to whom my promise belongs, hath another before, but doth he or his Lord owe me any thing for that? yet Mr. *Hazard* importunes me, to presse that Chaplain of my Lord, that when he takes mine, he shall resign the other to him, which, as it is an ignorant request, (for if it be resign'd, it is not in his power to place it upon Mr. *Hazard*) so it is an unjust request, that I that give him fiftie pounds a year, should take from him fortie. But amongst Mr. *Hazards* manifold importunities, that that I took worst, was, that he should write of domestique things, and what I said of my Son, to you; and arme you with that plea, that my Son was not in Orders. But, my noble Sister, though I am far from drawing my Son immaturelie into Orders, or putting into his hands any Church with cure; yet there are many Prebends and other helps in the Church, which a man without taking Orders, may be capable of, and for some such I might change a Living with cure, and so begin to accommodate a Son in some preparation. But Mr. *Hazard* is too piercing. It is good counsell, (and as I remember I gave it him) that if a man deny him any thing, and accompany his deniall with a reason, he be not too searching, whether that be the true reason or no, but rest in the deniall: for many times it may be out of my power to doe a man a courtesie which he desires, and yet I not tied to tell him the true reason; Therefore out of his Letter to you, I continue my opinion, that he medled too far herein. I cannot shut my Letter, till (whilst we are upon this consideration of reasons of denialls) I tell you one Answer of his, which perchance may weaken your so great assurance of his modestie. I told him that my often sicknesses, had brought me to an inability of Preaching, and that I was under a necessitie of Preaching twelve or fourteen solemn Sermons every year, to great Auditories, at *Paules*, and to the Judges, and at Court; and that therefore I must think of conferring something upon such a man as may supplie my place in these Solemnities: And surely, said I, I will offer them no man in those cases which shall not be at least equall to my self; and, Mr. *Hazard*, I do not know your faculties. He gave me this answer, I will not make comparisons, but I do not doubt but I should give them satisfaction in that kind. Now, my noble Sister, whereas you repeat often, that you and your sister rested upon my word, and my worth; and, but for my word and my worth, you would not have proceeded so far: I must necessarily make my protestation, that my word and my worth is, herein, as chast, and untouch'd as the best Maidenhead in the world. For, my noble sister, Goes there no more to the giving of a Scholler a Church in *London*: but that he was a young Gentleman's School-master? You know the ticklishnesse of *London*-Pulpits, and how ill it would become me, to place a man in a *London*-Church that were not both a strong and a sound man. And, therefore, those things must come into consideration before he can have a Living from me; though there was no need of reflecting upon those things, when I made that generall promise, that I would assist his fortune in any thing. You end in a phrase of indignation and displeasure, rare in you towards me, therefore it affects me; which is, that he may part from me, as I received him at first, as though I were likely to hinder him. The heat that produced that word I know is past, and therefore, my most beloved Sister, give me leave to say to you, that he shall not part from me, but I shall keep him still in my care, and make you alwaies my judge of all omissions

*Your faithfull Friend, and*
*Servant.*

### 43. To Mrs. Cokayne

[August 1628]

*My noblest and lovingest Sister,*

Nothing returns oftner with more comfort to my memorie, than that you nor I ever asked any thing of one another, which we might not safelie grant; and we can ask nothing safelie, that implies an offence to God, or injury to any other person. I fall upon this consideration now, upon this occasion: Your Letter, upon the two and twentieth of *August*, which I received this day, laies a commandmant upon me, to give you an account of my state in health; you do but ask me how I do, and if your Letter had come yesterday, I could not have told you that. At my return from *Kent* to my gate, I found *Pegge* had the Pox; so I withdrew to [*Peckham*], and spent a fortnight there. And without comming home, when I could with some justice hope, that it would spread no farther amongst them, (as, I humbly thank God, it hath not, nor much disfigured her that had it) I went into *Bedfordshire*. There, upon my third *Sunday*, I was seized with a Feavour, which grew so upon me, as forced me to a resolution, of seeking my Physitian at *London*. Thither I came in a day, and a little piece; and within four miles of home, I was surprised with an accident in the Coach, which never befell me before, nor had been much in my contemplation, and therefore affected me much. It was a violent falling of the *Uvula*. Which when Doctor *Fox* (whom I found at *London*, and who had not been there in ten daies before) considered well, and perceived the feavour complicated with a Squinancie;[1] by way of prevention of both, he presentlie took blood; and so with ten-daies-starving in a close prison, that is, my bed, I am (blessed be God) returned to a convenient temper, and pulse, and appetite, and learn to eat, and this day met the acceptablest guest in the acceptablest manner, your Letter, walking in my chamber. All which I tell you with these particularities, lest my sicknesse might be presented by rumour worse, than God hath been pleased to make it: For, I humbly thank him, now I feel no present ill, nor have reason to fear worse. If I understand your Letter aright, much of your familie

[1] Quinzy.

is together; if it be so, entreat them, for your sake, to receive my service, which, by your hand, I present to them all. If they be otherwise severed, yet, in the ears of Almighty God, to whom, I know, they all daily pray, my daily Praiers for them all shall also meet them all. And that's the onely service which I can promise my self an ability to do to God's Church now, since this infirmity in my mouth and voice, is likelie to take me from any frequent exercise of my other duty of Preaching. But, God will either enable me, or pardon me. His will be done upon us all, as his goodnesse hath been overflowingly poured out upon

*Your poor Friend, and lovingest*
*Brother and Servant.*

## 44. To Mrs. Cokayne

[1629]¹

*My noble and vertuous Sister,*

If I had had such an occasion as this to have written to you, in the first year of our acquaintance, I had been likelie to have presented you with an Essay of Morall Comfort. Now my Letter may well be excused, if it amount to an Homilie. My profession and my willingnesse, to stay long upon so good an office, as to assist you, will bear it. Our souls are trulie said to be in everie part of our bodies; but yet, if any part of the bodie be cut off, no part of the soul perishes, but is suckt in to that soul that remains, in that that remains of the body. When any limb or branch of a family is taken away, the vertue, the love, and (for the most part) the patrimonie and fortune of him that is gone remaines with the Family. The family would not think it self the lesse, if any little quillet of ground had been evicted from it; nor must it, because a clod of earth, one person of the family, is removed. In these cases, there is nothing lost; one part, the soul, enjoyes a present gain; and the other, the body, expects a future. We think it good husbandry to place our childrens portions so, as that in so many years it may multiply to so much: Shall we not be as glad to lay their bodies there, where onely

---

¹ Mrs. Cokayne's son Thomas, who was born in January 1612, died at Bath in his eighteenth year.

they can be mellowed and ripened for glorification. The perversenesse of the father put you to such a necessity of hiding your sons,
as that this son is scarce more out of your sight, by being laid
under ground, than he was before. And perchance you have been
longer time, at some times, from meeting and seeing one another
in this world, than you shall be now from meeting in the glory of
the Resurrection. That may come sooner, than you looked he
should come from the *Bath*. A man truly liberall, or truly charitable,
will borrow monie to lend: For, if I be bound to assist another with
my meat, or with my mony, I may be as much bound to assist him
with my credit, and borrow to lend. We do but borrow Children
of God, to lend them to the world. And when I lend the world a
daughter in marriage, or lend the world a son in a profession, the
world does not alwaies pay me well again; my hopes are not alwaies
answered in that daughter or that son. But, of all that I lend to, the
Grave is my best pay-Master. The Grave shall restore me my
child, where he and I shall have but one Father; and pay me my
Earth, when that Earth shall be Amber, a sweet Perfume, in the
nostrills of his and my Saviour. Since I am well content to send one
sonne to the Church, the other to the Warrs; Why should I be loth
to send one part of either sonne to Heaven, and the other to the
Earth. Comfort your self in this, my noble Sister, that for those
years he lived, you were answerable to God for him; for yet, he was
so young, as a Mother's power might govern him; and so long he
was under your charge, and you accountable for him. Now, when
he was growing into those years, as needed a stronger hand, a
Father's care, and had not that; God hath cancelled your Bonds,
discharged you, and undertakes the office of a Father himself.
But, above all, comfort your self in this, That it is the declared
will of God. In sicknesses, and other worldlie crosses, there are
anxieties, and perplexities; we wish one thing to day, in the behalf
of a distressed child or friend, and another to morrow; because
God hath not yet declared his will. But when he hath done that,
in death, there is no room for anie anxietie, for anie perplexitie, no,
not for a wish; for we may not so much as pray for the dead. You
know, *David* made his child's Sicknesse his *Lent*, but his Death his
*Easter*: he fasted till the Child's death, but then he returned to his

repast, because then he had a declaration of God's will. I am farre from quenching in you, or discharging naturall affections; but, I know your easie apprehensions, and over-tendernesse in this kind. And, I know some persons in the world, that I wish may live, especially for this respect, because I know their death would over-affect you. In so noble and numerous a family as yours is, every year must necessarily present you some such occasion of sorrow, in the losse of some near friend. And therefore I, in the office of a Friend, and a Brother, and Priest of God, do not onelie look that you should take this patientlie, as a declaration of God's present will; but that you take it catechistically, as an instruction for the future; and that God, in this, tells you, That he will do so again, in some other your friends. For, to take any one crosse patiently, is but to forgive God for once; but, to surrender one's self entirely to God, is to be ready for all that he shall be pleased to do. And, that his pleasure may be either to lessen your crosses, or multiply your strength, shall be the prayer of

*Your Brother, and Friend, and*
*Servant, and Chaplain,*

JOHN DONNE

## 45. To Mr. George Gerrard

[? December 1630][1]

Sir,

This advantage you, and my other friends have, by my frequent Fevers, that I am so much the oftener at the gates of heaven, and this advantage by the solitude and close imprisonment that they reduce me to after, that I am thereby the oftener at my prayers; in which, I shall never leave out your happinesse; and, I doubt not, but amongst his many other blessings, God will adde to you some one for my prayers. A man would almost be content to dye, (if there were no other benefit in death) to hear of so much sorrow, and so much good testimony from good men, as I, (God be blessed

---

[1] This letter, which was printed in the second edition of Donne's *Poems* in 1635, as well as in the *Letters*, 1651, is in the *Poems* dated 7 January 1630 (i.e. 1631). But since it speaks of the arrangements that Donne has made for the sermon at Christmas at St. Paul's, it must have been written before Christmas.

for it) did upon the report of my death. Yet, I perceive it went not through all; for, one writ unto me, that some (and he said of my friends) conceived, that I was not so ill, as I pretended, but withdrew my self, to save charges, and to live at ease, discharged of preaching. It is an unfriendly, and God knows, an ill grounded interpretation: for in these times of necessity, and multitudes of poor there is no possibility of saving to him that hath any tendernesse in him; and for affecting my ease, I have been always more sorry, when I could not preach, than any could be, that they could not hear me. It hath been my desire, (and God may be pleased to grant it me) that I might die in the Pulpit; if not that, yet that I might take my death in the Pulpit, that is, die the sooner by occasion of my former labours. I thanke you, for keeping our *George* in your memory, I hope God reserves it for so good a friend as you are, to send me the first good newes of him. For the Diamond Lady, you may safely deliver *Roper*, whatsoever belongs to me, and he will give you a discharge for the money. For my L. *Percy*, we shall speake of it, when we meet at *London*; which, as I do not much hope before Christmas, so I do not much fear at beginning of Tearm; for I have intreated one of my fellowes to preach to my Lord Mayor, at *Pauls* upon Christmas day, and reserved Candlemas day to my self for that service, about which time also, will fall my Lent Sermon, except my Lord Chamberlaine beleeve me to be dead, and leave me out; for as long as I live, and am not speechlesse, I would not decline that service. I have better leasure to write, than you to read, yet I will not oppresse you with too much letter, God blesse you, and your sonne, as

*Your poor friend and humble servant in*
*Christ Jesus*

J. DONNE

## 46. To Mrs. Cokayne

(15 January 1631)

*My noblest sister,*

But that it is sweetned by your command, nothing could trouble me more, than to write of my self. Yet, if I would have it known, I must write it my self; for, I neither tell children, nor servants, my state. I have never good temper, nor good pulse, nor good appetite, nor good sleep. Yet, I have so much leasure to recollect my self, as that I can thinke I have been long thus, or often thus. I am not alive, because I have not had enough upon me to kill me, but because it pleases God to passe me through many infirmities before he take me either by those particular remembrances, to bring me to particular repentances, or by them to give me hope of his particular mercies in heaven. Therefore have I been more affected with Coughs in vehemence, more with deafenesse, more with toothach, more with the [uvula],[1] than heretofore. All this mellows me for heaven, and so ferments me in this world, as I shall need no long concoction in the grave, but hasten to the resurrection. Not onely to be nearer that grave, but to be nearer to the service of the Church, as long as I shall be able to do any, I purpose, God willing, to be at *London*, within a fortnight after your receit of this, as well because I am under the obligation of preaching at *Pauls* upon Candlemas day, as because I know nothing to the contrary, but that I may be called to Court, for Lent service; and my witnesse is in heaven, that I never left out S. *Dunstans*, when I was able to do them that service; nor will now; though they that know the state of that Church well, know that I am not so bound, as the world thinks, to preach there; for, I make not a shilling profit of S. *Dunstans* as a Church man, but as my L. of *Dorset* gave me the lease of the Impropriation, for a certain rent, and a higher rent, than my predecessor had it at. This I am fain to say often, because they that know it not, have defamed me, of a defectiveness towards that Church; and even that mistaking of theirs I ever have, and ever shall endevour to rectifie, by as often preaching there, as my condition of body will admit. All our company here is well, but not at home now, when I write; for, lest I should not have another return to *London*, before day of your Carrier, I write this, and rest

> *Your very affectionate servant,*
> *and friend, and brother,*
> J. DONNE

15 Jan. 1630.
  Abrey-hatch.

---

[1] Emended to 'uvula' from the meaningless 'vurbah' by Mr. Hayward. See Letter 43, where Donne complains of 'a violent falling of the *Uvula*'.

# SERMONS

ONE HUNDRED AND SIXTY of Donne's sermons are extant. A certain number were printed in his lifetime, either by royal command, or as sermons preached upon notable occasions; and, after separate publication, were in many cases bound together and republished as *Three*, *Foure*, or *Five Sermons*. A few are also extant in manuscript. But the great mass of the sermons, one hundred and forty-five, first appeared in print in three folio volumes: *LXXX Sermons* (1640), to which the first version of Walton's *Life of Donne* was prefixed, *Fifty Sermons* (1649), and *XXVI Sermons* (1661). All three volumes appeared under the auspices of Donne's eldest son, John Donne the Younger. Although many selections have been made from Donne's sermons, the only attempt, before the second half of this century, to reprint all the extant sermons was made by Henry Alford, afterwards Dean of Canterbury, in his six-volume edition of Donne's works in 1839. He modernized the text and followed the folio order.

The complete edition of *The Sermons of John Donne*, published by the University of California Press in ten volumes (1953–62), was planned in collaboration by George R. Potter of Berkeley and Evelyn Simpson. The collaboration was thoroughgoing; but in the main Professor Potter was to take responsibility for the text and notes of the first five volumes and Evelyn Simpson for the second five. In accordance with this arrangement, the first and the sixth volumes appeared together in 1953. In the following year Professor Potter died, leaving the second volume ready for the press and material for the third, fourth, and fifth. Evelyn Simpson declared her intention of completing the edition, on the lines George Potter and she had planned, and brought it to its conclusion in 1962. Since Evelyn Simpson was thus responsible for eight out of the ten volumes, and took responsibility for seeing a ninth through the press, we have quoted matter from the introductions as hers. But we know that she would have wished us to make clear that, although she was responsible for the final form of the edition, the fundamental work was done in collaboration, and the volumes published after Professor Potter's death owed much to his scholarship and industry.

The sermons in *LXXX Sermons* were arranged theologically, sermons on the feasts of the Church being followed by two series of sermons on the Psalms. Similarly, in *Fifty Sermons* sermons preached at occasions such as marriages, or at Lincoln's Inn, are brought together. By the time that he came to publish *XXVI Sermons* John Donne the Younger was scraping the bottom of the barrel and printing anything he could find in any order. One great merit of the California edition is that, owing to the editors' researches, all but a handful of the sermons are dated, and they are printed in chronological order. This allows a reader to study the development of Donne's mind and art as a preacher, as well as to have a keener sense of how he varied his matter and manner according to the audience he was addressing.

The headings of the sermons are taken from the Folios, as in the California edition, except that when the date given falls between 1 January and 24 March we have silently corrected it to conform with modern usage by which the year begins on 1 January. We follow the California edition in giving dates supplied by the editors in square brackets, and when the date is conjectural we prefix an interrogation mark. Unless square brackets are used, information in the notes is taken from Evelyn Simpson's introductory essays; when her actual words are used they are given in quotation marks.

# SERMONS

## 1. From a Sermon Preached to Queen Anne, at Denmarke-house, December 14. 1617[1]

### (i)

As the Prophets, and the other Secretaries of the holy Ghost in penning the books of Scriptures, do for the most part retain, and express in their writings some impressions, and some air of their former professions; those that had been bred in Courts and Cities, those that had been Shepheards and Heardsmen, those that had been Fishers, and so of the rest; ever inserting into their writings some phrases, some metaphors, some allusions, taken from that profession which they had exercised before; so that soul, that hath been transported upon any particular worldly pleasure, when it is intirely turn'd upon God, and the contemplation of his all-sufficiency and abundance, doth find in God fit subject, and just occasion to exercise the same affection piously, and religiously, which had before so sinfully transported, and possest it.

A covetous person, who is now truly converted to God, he will exercise a spiritual covetousness still, he will desire to have him all, he will have good security, the seal and assurance of the holy Ghost; and he will have his security often renewed by new testimonies, and increases of those graces in him; he will have witnesses enough; he will have the testimonie of all the world, by his good life and conversation; he will gain every way at Gods hand, he will have wages of God, for he will be his servant; he will have a portion from God, for he will be his Son; he will have a reversion, he will be sure that his name is in the book of life; he will have pawns, the

---

[1] On the text: 'I love them that love me, and they that seek me early shall find me' (Proverbs viii. 17).

'It is a sermon on human and divine love, and hence by age-old convention was particularly well adapted to a congregation that included a queen and many of her feminine attendants. . . . Also there unquestionably hovers over it the shadow of that other Anne, Donne's wife, whom he had lost four months earlier.'

seals of the Sacraments, nay, he will have a present possession; all that God hath promised, all that Christ hath purchased, all that the holy Ghost hath the stewardship and dispensation of, he will have all in present, by the appropriation and investiture of an actual and applying faith; a covetous person converted will be spiritually covetous still.

So will a voluptuous man, who is turned to God, find plenty and deliciousness enough in him, to feed his soul, as with marrow, and with fatness, as *David* expresses it; and so an angry and passionate man, will find zeal enough in the house of God to eat him up.

All affections which are common to all men, and those too, which in particular, particular men have been addicted unto, shall not only be justly employed upon God, but also securely employed, because we cannot exceed, nor go too far in imploying them upon him. According to this Rule, St. *Paul*, who had been so vehement a persecutor, had ever his thoughts exercised upon that; and thereupon after his conversion, he fulfils the rest of the sufferings of Christ in his flesh, he suffers most, he makes most mention of his suffering of any of the Apostles.

And according to this Rule too, *Salomon*, whose disposition was amorous, and excessive in the love of women, when he turn'd to God, he departed not utterly from his old phrase and language, but having put a new, and a spiritual tincture, and form and habit into all his thoughts, and words, he conveyes all his loving approaches and applications to God, and all Gods gracious answers to his amorous soul, into songs, and Epithalamions, and meditations upon contracts, and marriages between God and his Church, and between God and his soul; as we see so evidently in all his other writings, and particularly in this text, *I love them, &c.*

In which words is expressed all that belongs to love, all which, is to desire, and to enjoy; for to desire without fruition, is a rage, and to enjoy without desire is a stupidity: In the first alone we think of nothing, but that which we then would have; and in the second alone, we are not for that, when we have it; in the first, we are without it; in the second, we are as good as if we were without it, for we have no pleasure in it; nothing then can give us satisfaction, but where those two concurr, *amare* and *frui*, to love and to enjoy.

## (ii)

But can we love God when we will? do we not find, that in the love of some other things, or some courses of life, of some waies in our actions, and of some particular persons, that we would fain love them, and cannot? when we can object nothing against it, when we can multiply arguments, why we should love them, yet we cannot: but it is not so towards God; every man may love him, that will; but can every man have this will, this desire? certainly we cannot begin this love; except God love us first, we cannot love him; but God doth love us all so well, from the beginning, as that every man may see the fault was in the perversness of his own will, that he did not love God better. If we look for the root of this love, it is in the Father; for, though the death of Christ be towards us, as a root, as a cause of our love, and of the acceptableness of it, yet, *Meritum Christi est affectum amoris Dei erga nos*, the death of Christ was but an effect of the love of God towards us, *So God loved the world that he gave his Son*: if he had not lov'd us first, we had never had his Son; here is the root then, the love of the Father, and the tree, the merit of the Son; except there be fruit too, love in us, to them again, both root and tree will wither in us, howsoever they grew in God. *I have loved thee with an everlasting love*, (saies God) *therfore with mercy I have drawn thee*, if therefore we do not perceive, that we are drawn to love again by this love, 'tis not an everlasting love, that shines upon us.

All the sunshine, all the glory of this life, though all these be testimonies of Gods love to us, yet all these bring but a winters day, a short day, and a cold day, and a dark day, for except we love too, God doth not love with an everlasting love: God will not suffer his love to be idle, and since it profits him nothing, if it profits us nothing neither, he will withdraw it; *Amor Dei ut lumen ignis, ut splendor solis, ut odor lucis, non præbenti proficit, sed utenti*, The sun hath no benefit by his own light, nor the fire by his own heat, nor a perfume by the sweetness thereof, but only they who make their use, and enjoy this heat and fragrancy; And this brings us to our other part, to pass from loving to enjoying.

*Tulerunt Dominum meum*, They have taken away my Lord, and I know not where they have laid him; this was one strain of *Mary*

*Magdalens* lamentation, when she found not her Saviour in the monument: It is a lamentable case to be fain to cry so, *Tulerunt*, They have taken, other men have taken away Christ, by a dark and corrupt education, which was the state of our Fathers to the Roman captivity. But when the *abjecerunt Dominum*, which is so often complained of by God in the Prophets, is pronounced against thee, when thou hast had Christ offered to thee, by the motions of his grace, and seal'd to thee by his Sacraments, and yet wilt cast him so far from thee, that thou knowest not where to find him, when thou hast poured him out at thine eyes in prophane and counterfeit tears, which should be thy souls rebaptization for thy sins, when thou hast blown him away in corrupt and ill intended sighs, which should be *gemitus columbæ*, the voice of the Turtle, to sound thy peace and reconciliation with thy God; yea when thou hast spit him out of thy mouth in execrable and blasphemous oathes; when thou hast not only cast him so far, as that thou knowest not where to find him, but hast made so ordinary and so indifferent a thing of sin, as thou knowest not when thou didst lose him, no nor dost not remember that ever thou hadst him; no, nor dost not know that there is any such man, as *Dominus tuus*, a Jesus, that is, *thy Lord*; The *Tulerunt* is dangerous, when others hide Christ from thee; but the *Abjecerunt* is desperate, when thou thy self doest cast him away.

(iii)

To make haste, the circumstance only requir'd here, is that he be sought early; and to invite thee to it, consider how early he sought thee; It is a great mercy that he staies so long for thee; It was more to seek thee so early: Dost thou not feele that he seeks thee now, in offering his love and desiring thine? Canst not thou remember that he sought thee yesterday, that is, that some tentations besieged thee then, and he sought thee out by his Grace, and preserved thee? and hath he not sought thee so, so early, as from the beginning of thy life? nay, dost thou not remember that after thou hadst committed that sin, he sought thee by imprinting some remorse, some apprehension of his judgments, and so *miro & divino modo*, &

*quando te oderat diligebat*, by a miraculous and powerful working
of his Spirit, he threatned thee, when he comforted thee, he lov'd
thee when he chid thee, he sought thee when he drove thee from
him? He hath sought thee amongst the infinite numbers of false
and fashionall Christians, that he might bring thee out from the
hypocrite, to serve him in earnest, and in holyness, and in righteousness; he sought thee before that amongst the Herd of the nations
and Gentiles, who had no Church, to bring thee into his inclosures
and pastures, his visible Church, and to feed thee with his word and
sacraments; he sought thee before that, in the catalogue of all his
Creatures, where he might have left thee a stone, or a plant, or a
beast; and then he gave thee an immortal Soul, capable of all his
future blessings; yea, before this he sought thee, when thou wast
no where, nothing, he brought thee then, the greatest step of all,
from being nothing, to be a Creature; how early did he seek thee,
when he sought thee in *Adam's* confused loynes, and out of that
leavened and sowre loaf in which we were all kneaded up, out of
that *massa damnata*, that refuse and condemned lump of dough, he
sought and sever'd out that grain which thou shouldst be; yea
millions of millions of generations before all this he sought thee in
his own eternal Decree; And in that first Scripture of his, which is as
old as himself, in the book of life he wrote thy name in the blood of
that Lamb which was slain for thee, not only from the beginning
of this world, but from the writing of that eternal Decree of thy
Salvation. Thus early had he sought thee in the Church amongst
hypocrites; out of the Church amongst the Heathen; In his
Creatures amongst creatures of an ignoble nature, and in the first
vacuity, when thou wast nothing he sought thee so early as in
*Adam*, so early as in the book of life, and when wilt thou think it
a fit time to seek him?

## 2.  From a Sermon Preached at Lincolns Inne

[? Spring or Summer 1618][1]

FOR, this plurality, this multiplicity of sin, hath found first a spunginesse in the soul, an aptnesse to receive any liquor, to embrace any sin, that is offered to it; and after a while, a hunger and thirst in the soul, to hunt, and pant and draw after a tentation, and not to be able to endure any *vacuum*, any discontinuance, or intermission of sinne: and hee will come to think it a melancholique thing, still to stand in fear of Hell; a sordid, a *yeomanly* thing, still to be plowing, and weeding, and worming a conscience; a mechanicall thing, still to be removing logs, or filing iron, still to be busied in removing occasions of tentation, or filing and clearing particular actions: and, at last he will come to that case, which S. *Augustine* out of an abundant ingenuity, and tendernesse, and compunction, confesses of himself, *Ne vituperarer, vitiosior fiebam*, I was fain to sin, lest I should lose my credit, and be under-valued; *Et ubi non suberat, quo admisso, æquarer perditis*, when I had no means to doe some sins, whereby I might be equall to my fellow, *Fingebam me fecisse quod non feceram, ne viderer abjectior, quo innocentior*, I would bely my self, and say I had done that, which I never did, lest I should be under-valued for not having done it. *Audiebam eos exaltantes flagitia*, sayes that tender blessed Father, I saw it was thought wit, to make Sonnets of their own sinnes, *Et libebat facere, non libidine facti, sed libidine laudis*, I sinn'd, not for the pleasure I had in the sin, but for the pride that I had to write feelingly of it. O what a *Leviathan* is sin, how vast, how immense a body! And then, what a spawner, how numerous! Between these two, the *denying* of sins, which we have done, and the *bragging* of sins, which we have not done, what a space, what a compasse is there, for millions of millions of sins!

---

1 On the text: 'For mine iniquities are gone over my head, as a heavy burden, they are too heavy for me' (Ps. xxxviii. 4).

Donne was appointed Divinity Reader for Lincoln's Inn, where he had been a student, on 24 October 1616. He held office until 11 February 1622, when he resigned after accepting the Deanery of St. Paul's.

# 3. From a Lent-Sermon Preached at White-hall, February 12. 1619[1]

RELIGION is a serious thing, but not a sullen; Religious preaching is a grave exercise, but not a sordid, not a barbarous, not a negligent. There are not so eloquent books in the world, as the Scriptures: Accept those names of Tropes and Figures, which the Grammarians and Rhetoricians put upon us, and we may be bold to say, that in all their Authors, Greek and Latin, we cannot finde so high, and so lively examples, of those Tropes, and those Figures, as we may in the Scriptures: whatsoever hath justly delighted any man in any mans writings, is exceeded in the Scriptures. The style of the Scriptures is a diligent, and an artificial style; and a great part thereof in a musical, in a metrical, in a measured composition, in verse. The greatest mystery of our Religion, indeed the whole body of our Religion, the coming, and the Kingdome of a *Messias*, of a Saviour, of Christ, is conveyed in a Song, in the third chapter of *Habakkuk*: and therefore the Jews say, that that Song cannot yet be understood, because they say the *Messiah* is not yet come. His greatest work, when he was come, which was his union and marriage with the Church, and with our souls, he hath also delivered in a piece of a curious frame, *Solomons* Song of Songs. And so likewise, long before, when God had given all the Law, he provided, as himself sayes, a safer way, which was to give them a heavenly Song of his owne making: for that Song, he sayes there, he was sure they would remember. So the Holy Ghost hath spoken in those Instruments, whom he chose for the penning of the Scriptures, and so he would in those whom he sends for the preaching thereof: he would put in them a care of delivering God's messages, with consideration, with meditation, with preparation; and not barbarously, not suddenly, not occasionally, not extemporarily, which might derogate from the dignity of so great a service. That Ambassadour should open himself to a shrewd danger and surprisall, that should defer the thinking upon his Oration, till the Prince, to

---

[1] On the text : 'And lo, thou art unto them as a very lovely song, of one that hath a pleasant voice, and can play well on an instrument; for they hear thy words, but they do them not' (Ezek. xxxiii. 32).

whom he was sent, were reading his letters of Credit: And it is a late time of meditation for a Sermon, when the Psalm is singing. *Loquere Domine*, sayes the Prophet; speak, O Lord: But it was when he was able to say, *Ecce paratus*, Behold I am prepared for thee to speak in me: If God shall be believed, to speak in us, in our ordinary Ministry, it must be, when we have, so as we can, fitted our selves, for his presence.

## 4. From a Sermon Preached to the Lords upon Easter-day, at the Communion, The King being then dangerously sick at New-Market. [1619][1]

### (i)

WEE are all conceived in close Prison; in our Mothers wombes, we are close Prisoners all; when we are borne, we are borne but to the liberty of the house; Prisoners still, though within larger walls; and then all our life is but a going out to the place of Execution, to death. Now was there ever any man seen to sleep in the Cart, between New-gate, and Tyborne? between the Prison, and the place of Execution, does any man sleep? And we sleep all the way; from the womb to the grave we are never throughly awake; but passe on with such dreames, and imaginations as these, I may live as well, as another, and why should I dye, rather than another? but awake, and tell me, sayes this Text, *Quis homo?* who is that other that thou talkest of? *What man is he that liveth, and shall not see death?*

### (ii)

*Death and life are in the power of the tongue*, sayes *Solomon*, in another sense; and in this sense too, If my tongue, suggested by my heart, and by my heart rooted in faith, can say, *Non moriar, non moriar*; If I can say, (and my conscience doe not tell me, that I belye mine owne state) if I can say, That the blood of my Saviour runs in my veines, That the breath of his Spirit quickens all my purposes, that

---

1 On the text: 'What man is he that liveth, and shall not see death' (Ps. lxxxix. 48).

Queen Anne died early in March 1619, and later in the same month King James was seized with an attack of the stone and for a short time was thought to be in danger of death.

all my deaths have their Resurrection, all my sins their remorses, all my rebellions their reconciliations, I will harken no more after this question, as it is intended *de morte naturali*, of a naturall death, I know I must die that death, what care I? nor *de morte spirituali*, the death of sin, I know I doe, and shall die so; why despaire I? but I will finde out another death, *mortem raptus*, a death of rapture, and of extasie, that death which S. *Paul* died more than once, The death which S. *Gregory* speaks of, *Divina contemplatio quoddam sepulchrum animæ*, The contemplation of God, and heaven, is a kinde of buriall, and Sepulchre, and rest of the soule; and in this death of rapture, and extasie, in this death of the Contemplation of my interest in my Saviour, I shall finde my self, and all my sins enterred, and entombed in his wounds, and like a Lily in Paradise, out of red earth, I shall see my soule rise out of his blade, in a candor, and in an innocence, contracted there, acceptable in the sight of his Father.

## 5. A Sermon of Valediction at my going into Germany, at Lincolns-Inne, April 18. 1619[1]

WEE may consider two great virtues, one for the society of this life, Thankfulness, and the other for attaining the next life, Repentance; as the two pretious Mettles, Silver and Gold: Of Silver (of the virtue of thankfulness) there are whole Mines, books written by Philosophers, and a man may grow rich in that mettle, in that virtue, by digging in that Mine, in the Precepts of moral men; of this Gold (this virtue of Repentance) there is no Mine in the Earth; in the books of Philosophers, no doctrine of Repentance; this Gold is for the most part in the washes; this Repentance in matters of tribulation; but God directs thee to it in this Text, before thou come to those waters of Tribulation, remember now thy Creator before those evill dayes come, and then thou wilt

---

[1] On the text: 'Remember now thy Creator in the days of thy youth' (Eccles. xii. 1).

Donne left England, as chaplain to Lord Doncaster on his mission of mediation to the German Princes, on 12 May 1619, and was abroad until January 1620. An earlier version of this sermon is extant in several manuscript copies. It was printed by Evelyn Simpson (Nonesuch Press, 1932) and can also be found in an appendix to vol. ii of the *Sermons*.

repent the not remembring him till now. Here then the holy-Ghost takes the neerest way to bring a man to God, by awaking his memory; for, for the understanding, that requires long and cleer instruction; and the will requires an instructed understanding before, and is in it self the blindest and boldest faculty; but if the memory doe but fasten upon any of those things which God hath done for us, it is the neerest way to him. Remember therefore, and remember now, though the Memory be placed in the hindermost part of the brain, defer not thou thy remembring to the hindermost part of thy life, but doe that now *in die*, in the day, whil'st thou hast light, now *in diebus*, in the days, whilst God presents thee many lights, many means; and *in diebus juventutis*, in the days of thy youth, of strength, whilst thou art able to doe that which thou purposest to thy self; And as the word imports, *Bechurotheica*, *in diebus Electionum tuarum*, in the dayes of thy choice, whilst thou art able to make thy choyce, whilst the Grace of God shines so brightly upon thee, as that thou maist choose the way, and so powerfully upon thee, as that thou maist walke in that way. Now, *in this day*, and *in these dayes* Remember first the Creator, That all these things which thou laborest for, and delightest in, were created, made of nothing; and therfore thy memory looks not far enough back, if it stick only upon the Creature, and reach not to the Creator, Remember the Creator, and remember thy Creator; and in that, first that he made thee, and then what he made thee; He made thee of nothing, but of that nothing he hath made thee such a thing as cannot return to nothing, but must remain for ever; whether happy or miserable, that depends upon thy *Remembring thy Creator now in the dayes of thy youth*.

First *remember*; which word is often used in the Scripture for considering and taking care: for, God remembred *Noah* and every beast with him in the Ark; as the word which is contrary to that, forgetting, is also for the affection contrary to it, it is neglecting, *Can a woman forget her child, and not have compassion on the son of her womb?* But here we take not remembring so largly, but restrain it to the exercise of that one faculty, the memory; for it is *Stomachus animæ*. The memory, sayes St. *Bernard*, is the stomach of the soul, it receives and digests, and turns into good blood, all the benefits

formerly exhibited to us in particular, and exhibited to the whole
Church of God: present that which belongs to the understanding,
to that faculty, and the understanding is not presently setled in it;
present any of the prophecies made in the captivity, and a Jews
understanding takes them for deliverances from *Babylon*, and a
Christians understanding takes them for deliverances from sin and
death, by the Messias Christ Jesus; present any of the prophecies of
the Revelation concerning Antichrist, and a Papist will understand
it of a single, and momentane, and transitory man, that must last
but three yeer and a half; and a Protestant may understand it of a
succession of men, that have lasted so 1000. yeers already: present
but the name of Bishop or of elder, out of the Acts of the Apostle[s],
or their Epistles, and other men will take it for a name of equality,
and parity, and we for a name and office of distinction in the
Hierarchy of Gods Church. Thus it is in the understanding that's
often perplexed; consider the other faculty, the will of man, by
those bitternesses which have passed between the Jesuits and the
Dominicans, (amongst other things belonging to the will) whether
the same proportion of grace, offered to men alike disposed, must
necessarily work alike upon both their wills? And amongst persons
neerer to us, whether that proportion of grace, which doth convert
a man, might not have been resisted by perversness of his will?
By all these difficulties we may see, how untractable, and untame-
able a faculty the wil of man is. But come not with matter of law,
but matter of fact, *Let God make his wonderful works to be had in
remembrance*: present the history of Gods protection of his children,
from the beginning, in the ark, in both captivities, in infinite
dangers; present this to the memory, and howsoever the understanding be beclouded, or the will perverted, yet both Jew and
Christian, Papist and Protestant, Puritan and Protestant, are
affected with a thankfull acknowledgment of his former mercies and
benefits, this issue of that faculty of their memory is alike in them
all: And therefore God in giving the law, works upon no other
faculty but this, *I am the Lord thy God which brought thee out of the land
of Egypt*; He only presents to their memory what he had done for
them. And so in delivering the Gospel in one principal seal thereof,
the sacrament of his body, he recommended it only to their memory,

*Do this in remembrance of me.* This is the faculty that God desires to
work upon; And therefore if thine understanding cannot reconcile
differences in all Churches, if thy will cannot submit it self to
the ordinances of thine own Church, go to thine own memory;
for as St. *Bernard* calls that the stomach of the soul, we may be
bold to call it the Gallery of the soul, hang'd with so many, and
so lively pictures of the goodness and mercies of thy God to thee,
as that every one of them shall be a catachism to thee, to instruct
thee in all thy duties to him for those mercies: And as a well made,
and well plac'd picture, looks alwayes upon him that looks upon
it; so shall thy God look upon thee, whose memory is thus
contemplating him, and shine upon thine understanding, and
rectifie thy will too. If thy memory cannot comprehend his
mercy at large shewed to his whole Church, (as it is almost an
incomprehensible thing, that in so few yeers he made us of the
Reformation, equall even in number to our adversaries of the
Roman Church,) If thy memory have not held that picture of
our general deliverance from the Navy; (if that mercy be written
in the water and in the sands, where it was perform'd, and not in
thy heart) if thou remember not our deliverance from that artificiall
Hell, the Vault, (in which, though his instruments failed of their
plot, they did not blow us up; yet the Devil goes forward with his
plot, if ever he can blow out; if he can get that deliverance to be
forgotten.) If these be too large pictures for thy gallery, for thy
memory, yet every man hath a pocket picture about him, a manuall,
a bosome book, and if he will turn over but one leaf, and remember
what God hath done for him even since yesterday, he shall find
even by that little branch a navigable river, to sail into that great
and endless Sea of Gods mercies towards him, from the beginning
of his being.

Do but remember, but remember now: Of his own wil begat he
us with the word of truth, that we should be as the first fruits of
his creatures: That as we consecrate all his creatures to him, in
a sober, and religious use of them, so as the first fruits of all, we
should principally consecrate our selves to his service betimes. Now
there were three payments of first fruits appointed by God to
the Jews: The first was, *Primitiæ Spicarum*, of their Ears of Corn,

and this was early about *Easter*; The second was *Primitiæ panum*, of Loaves of Bread, after their corn was converted to that use; and this, though it were not so soon, yet it was early too, about *Whitsontide*; The third was *Primitiæ frugum*, of all their Fruits and Revenues; but this was very late in *Autumn*, at the fall of the leaf, in the end of the yeer. The two first of these, which were offered early, were offered partly to God, and partly to Man, to the Priest; but in the last, which came late, God had no part: He had his part in the corn, and in the loaves, but none in the latter fruits. Offer thy self to God; first, as *Primitias spicarum*, (whether thou glean in the world, or bind up whole sheaves, whether thy increase be by little and little, or apace;) And offer thy self, as *primitias panum*, (when thou hast kneaded up riches, and honor, and favour in a setled and established fortune) offer at thy *Easter*, whensoever thou hast any resurrection, any sense of raising thy soul from the shadow of death; offer at thy Pentecost, when the holy Ghost visits thee, and descends upon thee in a fiery tongue, and melts thy bowels by the power of his word; for if thou defer thy offering til thy fal, til thy winter, til thy death, howsoever they may be thy first fruits, because they be the first that ever thou gavest, yet they are such, as are not acceptable to God; God hath no portion in them, if they be not offered til then; offer thy self now; for that's an easie request; yea offer to thy self now, that's more easie; *Viximus mundo; vivamus reliquum nobis ipsis*; Thus long we have served the world; let us serve our selves the rest of our time, that is, the best part of our selves, our souls. *Expectas ut febris te vocet ad pœnitentiam?* Hadst thou rather a sickness should bring thee to God, than a sermon? hadst thou rather be beholden to a Physitian for thy salvation, than to a Preacher? thy business is to remember; stay not for thy last sickness, which may be a Lethargy in which thou mayest forget thine own name, and his that gave thee the name of a Christian, Christ Jesus himself: thy business is to remember, and thy time is now; stay not till that Angel come which shall say and swear, that time shall be no more.

Remember then, and remember now; *In Die*, in the day; The Lord will hear us *In die qua invocaverimus*, in the day that we shall call upon him; and *in quacunque die*, in what day soever we call, and *in quacunque die velociter exaudiet*, as soon as we call in any day. But all this is *Opus diei*, a work for the day; for in the night, in our last night, those thoughts that fall upon us, they are rather dreams, than true remembrings; we do rather dream that we repent, than repent indeed, upon our death-bed. To him that travails by night a bush seems a tree, and a tree seems a man, and a man a spirit; nothing hath the true shape to him; to him that repents by night, on his death-bed, neither his own sins, nor the mercies of God have their true proportion. Fool, saies Christ, this night they will fetch away thy soul; but he neither tels him, who they be that shall fetch it, nor whither they shall carry it; he hath no light but lightnings; a sodain flash of horror first, and then he goes into fire without light. *Numquid Deus nobis ignem paravit? non, sed Diabolo, et Angelis*: did God ordain hell fire for us? no, but for the Devil, and his Angels. And yet we that are vessels so broken, as that there is not a sheard left, to fetch water at the pit, that is, no means in our selves, to derive one drop of Christs blood upon us, nor to wring out one tear of true repentance from us, have plung'd our selves into this everlasting, and this dark fire, which was not prepared for us: A wretched covetousness, to be intruders upon the Devil; a wretched ambition, to be usurpers upon damnation. God did not make the fire for us; but much less did he make us for that fire; that is, make us to damn us. But now the Judgment is given, *Ite maledicti*, go ye accursed; but yet this is the way of Gods justice, and his proceeding, that his Judgments are not alwaies executed, though they be given. The Judgments and Sentences of Medes and Persians are irrevocable, but the Judgments and Sentences of God, if they be given, if they be published, they are not executed. The Ninevites had perished, if the sentence of their destruction had not been given; and the sentence preserv'd them; so even in this cloud of *Ite maledicti*, go ye accursed, we may see the day break, and discern beams of saving light, even in this Judgment of eternal darkness; if the contemplation of his Judgment brings us to remember him in that day, in the light and apprehension of his anger and correction.

For this circumstance is enlarged; it is not *in die*, but *in diebus*, not in one, but in many dayes; for God affords us many dayes, many lights to see and remember him by. This remembrance of God is our regeneration, by which we are new creatures; and therefore we may consider as many dayes in it, as in the first creation. The first day was the making of light; and our first day is the knowledg of him, who saies of himself, *ego sum lux mundi*, I am the light of the world, and of whom St. *John* testifies, *Erat lux vera*, he was the true light, that lighteth every man into the world. This is then our first day the true profession of Christ Jesus. God made light first, that the other creatures might be seen; *Frustra essent si non viderentur*, It had been to no purpose to have made creatures, if there had been no light to manifest them. Our first day is the light and love of the Gospel; for the noblest creatures of Princes, (that is, the noblest actions of Princes, war, and peace, and treaties) *frustra sunt*, they are good for nothing, they are nothing, if they be not shew'd and tried by this light, by the love and preservation of the Gospel of Christ Jesus: God made light first, that his other works might appear, and he made light first, that himself (for our example) might do all his other works in the light: that we also, as we had that light shed upon us in our baptism, so we might make all our future actions justifiable by that light, and not *Erubescere Evangelium*, not be ashamed of being too jealous in this profession of his truth. Then God saw that the light was good: the seeing implies a consideration; that so a religion be not accepted blindly, nor implicitly; and the seeing it to be good implies an election of that religion, which is simply good in it self, and not good by reason of advantage, or conveniency, or other collateral and by-respects. And when God had seen the light, and seen that it was good, then he severed light from darkness; and he severed them, *non tanquam duo positiva*, not as two essential, and positive, and equal things; not so, as that a brighter and a darker religion, (a good and a bad) should both have a beeing together, but *tanquam positivum et primitivum*, light and darkness are primitive, and positive, and figure this rather, that a true religion should be established, and continue, and darkness utterly removed; and then, and not till then, (till this was done, light severed from darkness) there was a day; And since God hath given us this day, the brightness of his Gospel, that this light is first presented, that is, all great actions begun with this consideration of the Gospel; since all other things are made by this light, that is, all have relation to the continuance of the Gospel, since God hath given us such a head, as is sharp-sighted in seeing the several lights, wise in discerning the true light, powerful in resisting forraign darkness; since God hath given us this day, *qui non humili-abit animam suam in die hac*, as *Moses* speaks of the dayes of Gods institution, he that will not remember God now in this day, is impious to him, and unthankful to that great instrument of his, by whom this day spring from on high hath visited us.

To make shorter dayes of the rest, (for we must pass through all the six dayes in a few minuts) God in the second day made the firmament to divide between the waters above, and the waters below; and this firmament in us, is *terminus cognoscibilium*, the limits of those things which God hath given man means and faculties to conceive, and understand: he hath limited our eyes with a firmament beset with stars, our eyes can see no farther: he hath limited our understanding in matters of religion with a starry firmament too; that is, with the knowledg of those things, *quæ ubique, quæ semper*, which those stars which he hath kindled in his Church, the Fathers and Doctors, have ever from the beginning proposed as things necessary to be explicitely believ'd, for the salvation of our souls; for the eternal decrees of God, and his unreveal'd mysteries, and the inextricable perplexities of the School, they are waters above the firmament: here *Paul* plants, and here *Apollo* waters; here God raises up men to convey to us the dew of his grace, by waters under the firmament; by visible sacraments, and by the word so preach'd, and so interpreted, as it hath been constantly, and unanimously from the beginning of the Church. And therefore this second day is perfited in the third, in the *congregentur aquæ*, let the waters be gathered together; God hath gathered all the waters, all the waters of life in one place; that is, all the doctrine necessary for the life to come, into his Church: And then *producet terra*, here in this world are produced to us all herbs and fruits, all that is necessary for the soul to feed upon. And in this third daies work God repeats here that testimony, *vidit quod bonum*, he saw that it was good; good, that here should be a gathering of waters in one place, that is, no doctrine receiv'd that had not been taught in the Church; and *vidit quod bonum*, he saw it was good, that all herbs

and trees should be produced that bore seed; all doctrines that were
to be proseminated and propagated, and to be continued to the
end, should be taught in the Church: but for doctrines which were
but to vent the passion of vehement men, or to serve the turns of
great men for a time, which were not seminal doctrines, doctrines
that bore seed, and were to last from the beginning to the end; for
these interlineary doctrines, and marginal, which were no part of
the first text, here's no testimony that God sees that they are good.
And, *In diebus istis*, if in these two daies, the day when God makes
thee a firmament, shewes thee what thou art, to limit thine understanding and thy faith upon, and the day where God makes thee a
sea, a collection of the waters, (showes thee where these necessary
things must be taught in the Church) if in those daies thou wilt
not remember thy Creator, it is an irrecoverable Lethargy.

In the fourth daies work, let the making of the Sun to rule the
day be the testimony of Gods love to thee, in the sunshine of
temporal prosperity, and the making of the Moon to shine by
night, be the refreshing of his comfortable promises in the darkness
of adversity; and then remember that he can make thy sun to set
at noon, he can blow out thy taper of prosperity when it burns
brightest, and he can turn the Moon into blood, he can make all the
promises of the Gospel, which should comfort thee in adversity,
turn into despair and obduration. Let the fift daies work, which was
the creation *Omnium reptibilium*, and *omnium volatilium*, of all creeping
things, and of all flying things, produc'd out of water, signifie and
denote to thee, either thy humble devotion, in which thou saist of
thy self to God, *vermis ego et non homo*, I am a worm and no man; or
let it be the raising of thy soul in that, *pennas columbæ dedisti*, that
God hath given thee the wings of a dove to fly to the wilderness, in a
retiring from, or a resisting of tentations of this world; remember
still that God can suffer even thy humility to stray, and degenerate
into an uncomly dejection and stupidity, and senselesness of the
true dignity and true liberty of a Christian: and he can suffer this
retiring thy self from the world, to degenerate into a contempt and
despising of others, and an overvaluing of thine own perfections.
Let the last day in which both man and beasts were made out of the
earth, but yet a living soul breath'd into man, remember thee that

this earth which treads upon thee, must return to that earth which
thou treadst upon; thy body, that loads thee, and oppresses thee to
the grave, and thy spirit to him that gave it. And when the Sabbath
day hath also remembered thee, that God hath given thee a temporal Sabbath, plac'd thee in a land of peace, and an ecclesiastical
Sabbath, plac'd in a Church of peace, perfect all in a spirituall
Sabbath, a conscience of peace, by remembring now thy Creator,
at least in one of these daies of the week of thy regeneration, either
as thou hast light created in thee, in the first day, that is, thy knowledg of Christ; or as thou hast a firmament created in thee the second
day, that is, thy knowledg what to seek concerning Christ, things
appertaining to faith and salvation; or as thou hast a sea created in
thee the third day, that is, a Church where all the knowledg is
reserv'd and presented to thee; or as thou hast a sun and moon in
the fourth day, thankfulness in prosperity, comfort in adversity, or
as thou hast *reptilem humilitatem*, or *volatilem fiduciam*, a humiliation
in thy self, or an exaltation in Christ in thy fift day, or as thou hast
a contemplation of thy mortality and immortality in the sixth day,
or a desire of a spiritual Sabbath in the seaventh, In those daies
remember thou thy Creator.

Now all these daies are contracted into less room in this text, *In
diebus Bechurotheica*, is either, *in the daies of thy youth*, or *electionum
tuarum*, in the daies of thy hearts desire, when thou enjoyest all that
thou couldest wish. First, therefore if thou wouldest be heard in
*Davids* prayer; *Delicta juventutis*; O Lord remember not the sins of
my youth; remember to come to this prayer, *In diebus juventutis*, in
the dayes of thy youth. *Job* remembers with much sorrow, how he
was in the dayes of his youth, when Gods providence was upon his
Tabernacle: and it is a late, but a sad consideration, to remember
with what tenderness of conscience, what scruples, what remorces
we entred into sins in our youth, how much we were afraid of all
degrees and circumstances of sin for a little while, and how indifferent things they are grown to us, and how obdurate we are
grown in them now. This was *Jobs* sorrow, and this was *Tobias*
comfort, when I was but young, all my Tribes fell away; but I alone
went after to *Jerusalem*. Though he lacked the counsail, and the
example of his Elders, yet he served God; for it is good for a man,

that he bear his yoke in his youth: For even when God had delivered
over his people purposely to be afflicted, yet himself complains in
their behalf, *That the persecutor laid the very heaviest yoke upon the
ancient*: It is a lamentable thing to fall under a necessity of suffering
in our age. *Labore fracta instrumenta, ad Deum ducis, quorum nullus
usus?* wouldest thou consecrate a Chalice to God that is broken?
no man would present a lame horse, a disordered clock, a torn
book to the King. *Caro jumentum*, thy body is thy beast; and wilt
thou present that to God, when it is lam'd and tir'd with excesse
of wantonness? when thy clock, (the whole course of thy time)
is disordered with passions, and perturbations; when thy book
(the history of thy life,) is torn, 1000. sins of thine own torn out
of thy memory, wilt thou then present thy self thus defac'd and
mangled to almighty God? *Temperantia non est temperantia in senectute, sed impotentia incontinentiæ*, chastity is not chastity in an old
man, but a disability to be unchast; and therefore thou dost not
give God that which thou pretendest to give, for thou hast no
chastity to give him. *Senex bis puer*, but it is not *bis juvenis*; an old
man comes to the infirmities of childhood again; but he comes not
to the strength of youth again.

Do this then *In diebus juventutis*, in thy best strength, and when
thy natural faculties are best able to concur with grace; but do it
*In diebus electionum*, in the dayes when thou hast thy hearts desire;
for if thou have worn out this word, in one sense, that it be too late
now, *to remember him in the dayes of youth*, (that's spent forgetfully)
yet as long as thou art able to make a new choise, to chuse a new
sin, that when thy heats of youth are not overcome, but burnt
out, then thy middle age chooses ambition, and thy old age chooses
covetousness; as long as thou art able to make thy choice thou art
able to make a better than this; God testifies that power, that he
hath given thee; *I call heaven and earth to record this day, that I have
set before you life and death; choose life*: If this choice like you not, *If it
seem evil unto you to serve the Lord*, saith *Josuah* then, *choose ye this day
whom ye will serve*. Here's the election day; bring that which ye
would have, into comparison with that which ye should have; that
is, all that this world keeps from you, with that which God offers
to you; and what will ye choose to prefer before him? for honor,

and favor, and health, and riches, perchance you cannot have them though you choose them; but can you have more of them than they have had, to whom those very things have been occasions of ruin? The Market is open till the bell ring; till thy last bell ring the Church is open, grace is to be had there: but trust not upon that rule, that men buy cheapest at the end of the market, that heaven may be had for a breath at last, when they that hear it cannot tel whether it be a sigh or a gasp, a religious breathing and anhelation after the next life, or natural breathing out, and exhalation of this; but find a spiritual good husbandry in that other rule, that the prime of the market is to be had at first: for howsoever, in thine age, there may be by Gods strong working, *Dies juventutis*, A day of youth, in making thee then a new creature; (for as God is *antiquissimus dierum*, so in his school no man is super-annated,) yet when age hath made a man impotent to sin, this is not *Dies electionum*, it is not a day of choice; but remember God now, when thou hast a choice, that is, a power to advance thy self, or to oppress others by evil means; now *in die electionum*, in those thy happy and sun-shine dayes, *remember him*.

This is then the faculty that is excited, the memory; and this is the time, now, now whilest ye have power of election: The object is, the Creator, *Remember the Creator*: First, because the memory can go no farther than the creation; and therefore we have no means to conceive, or apprehend any thing of God before that. When men therefore speak of decrees of reprobation, decrees of condemnation, before decrees of creation; this is beyond the counsail of the holy Ghost here, *Memento creatoris*, Remember the Creator, for this is to remember God a condemner before he was a creator: This is to put a preface to *Moses* his *Genesis*, not to be content with his *in principio*, to know that *in the beginning God created heaven and earth*, but we must remember what he did *ante principium*, before any such beginning was. *Moses* his *in principio*, that beginning, the creation we can remember; but St. *Johns in principio*, that beginning, eternity, we cannot; we can remember Gods *fiat* in *Moses*, but not Gods *erat* in St. *John*: what God hath done for us, is the object of our memory, not what he did before we were: and thou hast a good and perfect memory, if it remember all that the holy Ghost proposes in the

Bible; and it determines in the *memento Creatoris*: There begins the
Bible, and there begins the Creed, *I believe in God the Father*, *maker
of Heaven and Earth*; for when it is said, *The holy Ghost was not given,
because Jesus was not glorified*, it is not truly *Non erat datus*, but *non
erat*; for, *non erat nobis antequam operaretur*; It is not said there, the
holy Ghost was not given, but it is the holy Ghost was not: for
he is not, that is, he hath no being to us ward, till he works in us,
which was first in the creation: *Remember the Creator then*, because
thou canst remember nothing backward beyond him, and remember him so too, that thou maist stick upon nothing on this side of
him, That so neither *height*, *nor depth*, *nor any other creature may
separate thee from God*; not only not separate thee finally, but not
separate so, as to stop upon the creature, but to make the best of
them, thy way to the Creator; We see ships in the river; but all
their use is gone, if they go not to sea; we see men fraighted with
honor, and riches, but all their use is gone, if their respect be not
upon the honor and glory of the Creator; and therefore sayes the
Apostle, *Let them that suffer*, *commit their souls to God*, *as to a faithful
Creator*; that is, He made them, and therefore will have care of them.
This is the true contracting, and the true extending of the memory,
to *Remember the Creator*, and stay there, because there is no pros-
pect farther, and to *Remember the Creator*, and get thither, because
there is no safe footing upon the creature, til we come so far.

Remember then the Creator, and *remember thy Creator*, for, *Quis
magis fidelis Deo?* who is so faithful a Counsailor as God? *Quis
prudentior Sapiente?* who can be wiser than wisdome? *Quis utilior bono?*
or better than goodness? *Quis conjunctior Creatore?* or neerer than our
Maker? and therefore remember him. What purposes soever thy
parents or thy Prince have to make thee great, how had all those
purposes been frustrated, and evacuated if God had not made thee
before? this very being is thy greatest degree; as in Arithmatick
how great a number soever a man expresse in many figures, yet
when we come to number all, the very first figure is the greatest
and most of all; so what degrees or titles soever a man have in this
world, the greatest and the foundation of all, is, that he had a being
by creation: For the distance from nothing to a little, is ten thousand times more, than from it to the highest degree in this life: and

therefore *remember thy Creator*, as by being so, he hath done more for thee than all the world besides; and remember him also, with this consideration, that whatsoever thou art now, yet once thou wast nothing.

He created thee, *ex nihilo*, he gave thee a being, there's matter of exaltation, and yet all this from nothing; thou wast worse than a worm, there's matter of humiliation; but he did not create thee *ad nihilum*, to return to nothing again, and there's matter for thy consideration, and study, how to make thine immortality profitable unto thee; for it is a deadly immortality, if thy immortality must serve thee for nothing but to hold thee in immortal torment. To end all, that being which we have from God shall not return to nothing, nor the being which we have from men neither. As St. *Bernard* sayes of the Image of God in mans soul, *uri potest in gehenna, non exuri*, That soul that descends to hell, carries the Image [of] God in the faculties of that soul thither, but there that Image can never be burnt out, so those Images and those impressions, which we have received from men, from nature, from the world, the image of a Lord, the image of a Counsailor, the image of a Bishop, shall all burn in Hell, and never burn out; not only these men, but these offices are not to return to nothing; but as their being from God, so their being from man, shal have an everlasting being, to the aggravating of their condemnation. And therefore *remember thy Creator*, who, as he is so, by making thee of nothing, so he will ever be so, by holding thee to his glory, though to thy confusion, from returning to nothing; for the Court of Heaven is not like other Courts, that after a surfet of pleasure or greatness, a man may retire; after a surfet of sin there's no such retiring, as a dissolving of the soul into nothing; but God is from the beginning the Creator, he gave all things their being, and he is still thy Creator, thou shalt evermore have that being, to be capable of his Judgments.

Now to make up a circle, by returning to our first word, remember: As we remember God, so for his sake, let us remember one another. In my long absence, and far distance from hence, remember me, as I shall do you in the ears of that God, to whom the farthest East, and the farthest West are but as the right and left ear in one of us; we hear with both at once, and he hears in both at once; remember me, not my abilities; for when I consider my Apostleship that I was sent to you, I am in St. *Pauls quorum, quorum ego sum minimus*, the least of them that have been sent; and when I consider my infirmities, I am in his *quorum*, in another commission, another way, *Quorum ego maximus*; the greatest of them; but remember my labors, and endeavors, at least my desire, to make sure your salvation. And I shall remember your religious cheerfulness in hearing the word, and your christianly respect towards all them that bring that word unto you, and towards myself in particular far [a]bove my merit. And so as your eyes that stay here, and mine that must be far of, for all that distance shall meet every morning, in looking upon that same Sun, and meet every night, in looking upon that same Moon; so our hearts may meet morning and evening in that God, which sees and hears every where; that you may come thither to him with your prayers, that I, (if I may be of use for his glory, and your edification in this place) may be restored to you again; and may come to him with my prayer that what *Paul* soever plant amongst you, or what *Apollos* soever water, God himself will give the increase: That if I never meet you again till we have all passed the gate of death, yet in the gates of heaven, I may meet you all, and there say to my Saviour and your Saviour, that which he said to his Father and our Father, *Of those whom thou hast given me, have I not lost one.* Remember me thus, you that stay in this Kingdome of peace, where no sword is drawn, but the sword of Justice, as I shal remember you in those Kingdomes, where ambition on one side, and a necessary defence from unjust persecution on the other side hath drawn many swords; and Christ Jesus remember us all in his Kingdome, to which, though we must sail through a sea, it is the sea of his blood, where no soul suffers shipwrack; though we must be blown with strange winds, with sighs and groans for our sins, yet it is the Spirit of God that blows all this wind, and shall blow away all contrary winds of diffidence or distrust in Gods mercy; where we shall be all Souldiers of one Army, the Lord of Hostes, and Children of one Quire, the God of Harmony and consent: where all Clients shall retain but one Counsellor, our Advocate Christ Jesus, nor present him any other fee but his own blood, and yet every Client have a Judgment on his side, not only in a not guilty, in the remission of his sins, but in a *Venite benedicti*, in being

called to the participation of an immortal Crown of glory: where
there shall be no difference in affection, nor in mind, but we shall
agree as fully and perfectly in our *Allelujah*, and *gloria in excelsis*, as
God the Father, Son, and Holy Ghost agreed in the *faciamus
hominem* at first; where we shall end, and yet begin but then; where
we shall have continuall rest, and yet never grow lazie; where we
shall be stronger to resist, and yet have no enemy; where we shall
live and never die, where we shall meet and never part.

## 6.  From a Sermon Preached at White-Hall, April 2. 1620[1]

### (i)

THERE's no Simony in heaven, that a man can buy so much as a
door-keepers place in the Triumphant Church: There's no bribery
there, to fee Ushers for accesse; But God holds that ladder there,
whose foot stands upon the earth here, and all those good works,
which are put upon the lowest step of that Ladder here, that is,
that are done in contemplation of him, they ascend to him, and
descend again to us. Heaven and earth are as a musical Instrument;
if you touch a string below, the motion goes to the top: any good
done to Christs poor members upon earth, affects him in heaven.

### (ii)

It is not then with Riches in a family, as it is with a nail in a wall,
that the hard beating of it in, makes it the faster. It is not the hard
and laborious getting of money, the fixing of that in a strong wall,
the laying it upon lands, and such things as are vulgarly distinguished from moveables, (as though the world, and we were not
moveables) nor the beating that nail hard, the binding it with
Entailes, of Iron, and Adamant, and perpetuities of eternity, that
makes riches permanent, and sure; but it is the good purpose in

---

1 On the text: 'There is an evil sickness that I have seen under the sun: riches reserved
to the owners thereof, for their evil. And these riches perish by evil travail: and he begetteth
a son, and in his hand is nothing' (Eccles. v. [13 and 14]).

Two sermons on this text appear together in *XXVI Sermons*. They would seem to be
actually parts of a single sermon, divided by John Donne the Younger to make up the number
he had promised. The second extract here is from what is headed in the Folio 'The Second
Sermon Preached at White-hall upon Eccles. v. 12 and 13'.

the getting, and the good use in the having. And this good use is not, when thou makest good use of thy Money, but when the Common-wealth, where God hath given thee thy station, makes use of it: The Common-wealth must suck upon it by trade, not it upon the Common-wealth, by usury. Nurses that give suck to children, maintain themselves by it too; but both must be done; thou must be enriched so, by thy money, as that the state be not impoverished. This is the good use in having it; and the good purpose in getting it, is, that God may be glorified in it. Some errours in using of Riches, are not so dangerous; for some imploying of them in excesses, and superfluities, this is a rust without, it will be fil'd off with good counsel, or it will be worn off in time; in time we come to see the vanity of it: and when we leave looking at other mens cloaths, or thinking them the better men for their cloaths, why should we think, that others like us the better for our cloaths; those desires will decay in us. But an ill purpose in getting of them, that we might stand of our selves, and rely upon our Riches, this is a rust, a cancer at the heart, and is incurable. And therefore, if as the course, and progress of money hath been in the world from the beginning, (the observation is St. *Augustins*, but it is obvious to every man acquainted with history) That first the world used Iron money, and then Silver money, and last of all, Gold; If thy first purpose in getting, have been for Iron, (that thou have intended thy money to be thy strength, and defence in all calamities) And then for silver, (to provide thee abundance, and ornaments, and excesses) And then for gold, to hord, and treasure up in a little room; *Thesaurizasti iram*, thou hast treasured up the anger of God, against the day of anger.

# 7. From a Sermon Preached at Lincolns Inne. [?Easter Term 1620][1]

### (i)

AND yet as *Solomon* sends us to creatures, and to creatures of a low rank and station, to Ants and Spiders, for instruction, so Saint

---

[1] On the text: 'And though, after my skin, worms destroy this body, yet in my flesh shall I see God' (Job xix. 26).

*Gregory* sends us to creatures, to learne the Resurrection. *Lux quotidie moritur, & quotidie resurgit*; That glorious creature, that first creature, the light, dyes every day, and every day hath a resurrection. *In arbustis folia resurrectione erumpunt*; from the Cedar of *Libanus*, to the Hyssop upon the wall, every leafe dyes every yeare, and every yeare hath a Resurrection. *Ubi in brevitate seminis, tam immensa arbor latuit?* (as he pursues that meditation.) If thou hadst seen the bodies of men rise out of the grave, at Christs Resurrection, could that be a stranger thing to thee, than, (if thou hadst never seen, nor heard, nor imagined it before) to see an Oake that spreads so farre, rise out of an Akorne? Or if Churchyards did vent themselves every spring, and that there were such a Resurrection of bodies every yeare, when thou hadst seen as many Resurrections as years, the Resurrection would be no stranger to thee, than the spring is.

(ii)

As he that fears God, fears nothing else, so, he that sees God, sees every thing else: when we shall see God, *Sicuti est*, as he is, we shall see all things *Sicuti sunt*, as they are; for that's their Essence, as they conduce to his glory. We shall be no more deluded with outward appearances: for, when this sight, which we intend here comes, there will be no delusory thing to be seen. All that we have made as though we saw, in this world, will be vanished, and I shall see nothing but God, and what is in him; and him I shall see *In carne, in the flesh*, which is another degree of Exaltation in mine Exinanition.

I shall see him, *In carne sua, in his flesh*: And this was one branch in *Saint Augustines* great wish, That he might have seen Rome in her state, That he might have heard S. *Paul* preach, That he might have seen Christ in the flesh: *Saint Augustine* hath seen Christ in the flesh one thousand two hundred yeares; in Christs glorifyed flesh; but, it is with the eyes of his understanding, and in his soul. Our flesh, even in the Resurrection, cannot be a spectacle, a perspective glasse to our soul. We shall see the Humanity of Christ with our bodily eyes, then glorifyed; but, that flesh, though glorifyed, cannot make us see God better, nor clearer, than the soul alone hath done, all the time, from our death, to our resurrection.

But as an indulgent Father, or as a tender mother, when they go to see the King in any Solemnity, or any other thing of observation, and curiosity, delights to carry their child, which is flesh of their flesh, and bone of their bone, with them, and though the child cannot comprehend it as well as they, they are as glad that the child sees it, as that they see it themselves; such a gladnesse shall my soul have, that this flesh, (which she will no longer call her prison, nor her tempter, but her friend, her companion, her wife) that this flesh, that is, I, in the re-union, and redintegration of both parts, shall see God; for then, one principall clause in her rejoycing, and acclamation, shall be, that this flesh is her flesh; *In carne mea, in my flesh I shall see God.*

# 8. From a Sermon Preached to the Countesse of Bedford, then at Harrington house, January 7. 1621[1]

THE whole frame of the world is mortall, *Heaven and Earth passe away*: and upon us all, there is a irrecoverable Decree past, *statutum est, It is appointed to all men, that they shall once dye.* But when? quickly; If thou looke up into the aire, *remember that thy life is but a winde,* If thou see a cloud in the aire, aske St. *James* his question, *what is your life?* and give St. *James* his answer, *It is a vapour that appeareth and vanisheth away.* If thou behold a *Tree,* then *Job* gives thee a comparison of thy selfe; A *Tree* is an *embleme* of thy selfe; nay a Tree is the *originall,* thou art but the *copy,* thou are not so good as it: for, *There is hope of a tree* (as you reade there) *if the roote wax old, if the stock be dead, if it be cut down, yet by the scent of the waters, it will bud, but man is sick, and dyeth, and where is he?* he shall not wake againe, till heaven be no more. Looke upon the *water,* and we are as that, and as that spilt upon the ground: Looke to the *earth,* and we are not like that, but we are earth it self: At our Tables we feed upon the dead, and in the Temple we tread upon the dead: and when we meet in a Church, God hath made many *echoes,* many testimonies of our death, in the walls, and in the windowes, and he onely

---

[1] On the text: 'Lo, though he slay me, yet will I trust in him' (Job xiii. 15).
For a note on the Countess of Bedford, see Letter 20.

knowes, whether he will not make another testimony of our mortality, of the youngest amongst us, before we part, and make the very *place of our buriall*, our *deathbed*.

## 9. From a Sermon Preached [at Lincoln's Inn in Trinity Term 1621][1]

THE Lord then, the Son of God, had a *Sitio* in heaven, as well as upon the Crosse; He thirsted our salvation there; and in the midst of the fellowship of the Father from whom he came, and of the Holy Ghost, who came from him and the Father, and all the Angels, who came (by a lower way) from them all, he desired the conversation of Man, for Mans sake; He that was God *The Lord*, became *Christ*, a man, and he that was *Christ*, became *Jesus*, no man, a dead man, to save man: To save man, all wayes, in all his parts, And to save all men, in all parts of the world: To save his soule from hell, where we should have felt pains, and yet been dead, then when we felt them; and seen horrid spectacles, and yet been in darknes and blindnes, then when we saw them; And suffered unsufferable torments, and yet have told over innumerable ages in suffering them: To save this soule from that hell, and to fill that capacity which it hath, and give it a capacity which it hath not, to comprehend the joyes and glory of Heaven, this *Christ* became *Jesus*. To save this body from the condemnation of everlasting corruption, where the wormes that we breed are our betters, because they have a life, where the dust of dead Kings is blowne into the street, and the dust of the street blowne into the River, and the muddy River tumbled into the Sea, and the Sea remaunded into all the veynes and channels of the earth; to save this body from everlasting dissolution, dispersion, dissipation, and to make it in a glorious Resurrection, not onely a Temple of the holy Ghost, but a Companion of the holy Ghost in the kingdome of heaven, This *Christ* became this *Jesus*. To save this man, body and soule together, from the punishments

---

1 On the text: 'If any man love not the Lord Jesus Christ, let him be Anathema, Maranatha' (1 Cor. xvi. 22).

The editors of the *Sermons* conjecture that four undated sermons (nos. 38–41 in *LXXX Sermons*) headed 'Preached on Trinity Sunday' form a course of probably six sermons preached at Lincoln's Inn in Trinity Term 1621.

due to his former sinnes, and to save him from falling into future
sinnes by the assistance of his Word preached, and his Sacraments
administred in the Church, which he purchased by his bloud, is this
person, The *Lord*, the *Christ*, become this *Jesus*, this Saviour. To
save so, All wayes, In soule, in body, in both; And also to save all
men. For, to exclude others from that Kingdome, is a tyrannie, an
usurpation; and to exclude thy selfe, is a sinfull, and a rebellious
melancholy. But as melancholy in the body is the hardest humour
to be purged, so is the melancholy in the soule, the distrust of thy
salvation too. Flashes of presumption a calamity will quench, but
clouds of desperation calamities thicken upon us; But even in this
inordinate dejection thou exaltest thy self above God, and makest
thy worst better than his best, thy sins larger than his mercy.
Christ hath a Greek name, and an Hebrew name; *Christ* is Greeke,
*Jesus* is Hebrew; He had commission to save all nations, and he hath
saved all; Thou givest him another Hebrew name, and another
Greek, when thou makest his name *Abaddon*, and *Apollyon*, a
Destroyer; when thou wilt not apprehend him as a Saviour, and
love him so.

## 10.  From a Sermon Preached at Lincolns Inne[1]

THERE are many *tesseræ externæ*, outward badges and marks, by
which others may judge, and pronounce mee to bee a true Christian; But the *tessera interna*, the inward badge and marke, by which
I know this in my selfe, is joy; The blessednesse of heaven it selfe,
Salvation, and the fruits of Paradise, (that Paradise which cannot
be expressed, cannot be comprehended) have yet got no other name
in the subtilty of the Schools, nor in the fulnesse of the Scriptures,
but to be called the joys of heaven; Essentiall blessednesse is called
so, *Enter into thy Masters joy*, that is, into the Kingdome of heaven;
and accidentall happinesse added to that essentiall happinesse is
called so too: There is joy in heaven at the conversion of a sinner;

[1] On the text: 'Who now rejoice in my sufferings for you, and fill up that which is behind
of the afflictions of Christ in my flesh, for his body's sake which is the Church' (Col. i. 24).

The sermon gives no indication of its date. It must have been preached between October
1616 and February 1622, the period during which Donne held office as Reader, and from its
style seems unlikely to be early in that period.

and so in the *Revelation, Rejoyce ye heavens, and yee that dwell in them, for the accuser of our brethren is cast down;* There is now joy even in heaven, which was not there before; Certainly as that man shall never see the Father of Lights after this life, to whom the day never breaks in this life: As that man must never look to walk with the Lamb wheresover he goes in heaven, that ranne away from the Lamb whensoever he came towards him, in this life; so he shall never possesse the joyes of heaven hereafter, that feels no joy here; There must be joy here, which *Tanquam Cellulæ mellis* (as Saint *Bernard* says in his mellifluous language) as the honey-comb walles in, and prepares, and preserves the honey, and is as a shell to that kernell; so there must bee a joy here, which must prepare and preserve the joys of heaven itself, and be as a shell of those joys. For heaven and salvation is not a Creation, but a Multiplication; it begins not when wee dye, but it increases and dilates it self infinitely then; Christ himself, when he was pleased to feed all that people in the wildernesse, he asks first, *Quot panes habetis, how many loafes have you?* and then multiplyed them abundantly, as conduced most to his glory; but some there was before. *When thou goest to receive that bread, of which whosoever eats shall never dye,* the bread of life in the Land of life, Christ shall consider what joy thou broughtest with thee out of this world, and he shall extend and multiply that joy unexpressibly; but if thou carry none from hence, thou shalt find none there. Hee that were to travell into a far country, would study before, somewhat the map, and the manners, and the language of the Country; Hee that looks for the fulnesse of the joyes of heaven hereafter, will have a taste, an insight in them before he goe: And as it is not enough for him that would travail, to study any language indifferently (were it not an impertinent thing for him that went to lye in France, to study Dutch?); So if wee pretend to make the joys of heaven our residence, it is a madnesse to study the joys of the world; *The Kingdome of heaven is righteousnesse, and peace, and joy in the Holy Ghost,* says Saint *Paul*; And this Kingdome of heaven is *Intra nos,* says Christ, it is in us, and it is joy that is in us; but every joy is not this Kingdome, and therefore says the same Apostle, *Rejoyce in the Lord;* There is no other true joy, none but that; But yet says he there, *Rejoyce, and again, I*

*say rejoice*; that is, both again we say it, again, and again we call
upon you to have this spirituall joy, for without this joy ye have
not the earnest of the Spirit; And it is *again rejoyce*, bring all the
joys ye have, to a second examination, and see if you can rejoyce in
them again; Have you rejoyced all day in Feasts, in Musickes, in
Conversations? well, at night you must be alone, hand to hand with
God. *Again, I say rejoyce*, sleep not, till you have tryed whether your
joy will hold out there too. Have you rejoyced in the contemplation
of those temporall blessings which God hath given you? 'tis well,
for you may do so: But yet again I say *Rejoyce*; call that joy to an
accompt, and see whether you can rejoyce again, in such a use of
those blessings, as he that gave them to you, requires of you. Have
you rejoyced in your zeal of Gods service? that's a true rejoycing
in the Lord; But yet still rejoyce again, see that this joy be accompanyed with another joy; that you have zeal with knowledge:
*Rejoyce*, but rejoyce again, refine your joy, purge away all drosse,
and lees from your joy, there is no false joy enters into heaven,
but yet no sadnesse neither.


## 11. From a Sermon Preached at Saint Pauls upon Christmasse day. 1621[1]

F O R let no man thinke that *God* hath given him so much ease here,
as to save him by believing he knoweth not what, or why. *Knowledge* cannot save us, but we cannot be saved without Knowledge;
Faith is not on this side Knowledge, but beyond it; we must
necessarily come to *Knowledge* first, though we must not stay at it,
when we are come thither. For, a regenerate Christian, being now
a *new Creature*, hath also *a new facultie of Reason*: and so believeth the
Mysteries of Religion, out of another Reason, than as a meere
naturall Man, he believed naturall and morall things. He believeth

---

[1] On the text: 'He was not that light, but was sent to bear witness of that light' (John
i. 8).

King James sent his message to the Chapter of St. Paul's requiring them to elect Donne as
Dean on 19 November 1621. The Dean was required to preach on Christmas Day, Easter
Sunday, and Whitsunday, and could, as he chose, preach on other occasions. This is the first
of the splendid series of Christmas sermons that Donne preached in St. Paul's and his first
sermon as Dean.

them for their own sake, by *Faith*, though he take *Knowledge* of them before, by that common Reason, and by those humane Arguments, which worke upon other men, in naturall or morall things. Divers men may walke by the Sea side, and the same beames of the Sunne giving light to them all, one gathereth by the benefit of that light pebles, or speckled shells, for curious vanitie, and another gathers precious Pearle, or medicinall Ambar, by the same light. So the common light of reason illumins us all; but one imployes this light upon the searching of impertinent vanities, another by a better use of the same light, finds out the Mysteries of Religion; and when he hath found them, loves them, not for the lights sake, but for the naturall and true worth of the thing it self. Some men by the benefit of this light of Reason, have found out things profitable and usefull to the whole world; As in particular, *Printing*, by which the learning of the whole world is communicable to one another, and our minds and our inventions, our wits and compositions may trade and have commerce together, and we may participate of one anothers understandings, as well as of our Clothes, and Wines, and Oyles, and other Merchandize: So by the benefit of this light of reason, they have found out *Artillery*, by which warres come to quicker ends than heretofore, and the great expence of bloud is avoyded: for the numbers of men slain now, since the invention of Artillery, are much lesse than before, when the sword was the executioner. Others, by the benefit of this light have searched and found the secret corners of gaine, and profit, wheresoever they lie. They have found wherein the weakenesse of another man consisteth, and made their profit of that, by circumventing him in a bargain: They have found his riotous, and wastefull inclination, and they have fed and fomented that disorder, and kept open that leake, to their advantage, and the others ruine. They have found where was the easiest, and most accessible way, to sollicite the Chastitie of a woman, whether *Discourse*, *Musicke*, or *Presents*, and according to that discovery, they have pursued *hers*, and *their* own eternall destruction. By the benefit of this light, men see through the darkest, and most impervious places, that are, that is, *Courts of Princes*, and the greatest *Officers* in Courts; and can submit themselves to second, and to advance the humours of men in great place, and so make their profit of the weaknesses which they have discovered in these great men. All the wayes, both of *Wisdome*, and of *Craft* lie open to this light, this light of naturall reason: But when they have gone all these wayes by the benefit of this light, they have got no further, than to have walked by a tempestuous Sea, and to have gathered pebles, and speckled cockle shells. Their light seems to be great out of the same reason, that a Torch in a misty night, seemeth greater than in a clear, because it hath kindled and inflamed much thicke and grosse Ayre round about it. So the light and wisedome of worldly men, seemeth great, because he hath kindled an admiration, or an applause in Aiery flatterers, not because it is so in deed.

But, if thou canst take this light of reason that is in thee, this poore snuffe, that is almost out in thee, thy faint and dimme knowledge of God, that riseth out of this light of nature, if thou canst in those embers, those cold ashes, finde out one small coale, and wilt take the paines to kneell downe, and blow that coale with thy devout *Prayers*, and light thee a *little candle*, (a *desire* to reade that Booke, which they call the Scriptures, and the Gospell, and the Word of God;) If with that little candle thou canst creep humbly into low and poore places, if thou canst finde thy Saviour in a *Manger*, and in his *swathing clouts*, in his humiliation, and blesse God for that beginning, if thou canst finde him flying into Egypt, and finde in thy selfe a disposition to accompany him in a persecution, in a banishment, if not a bodily banishment, a locall banishment, yet a *reall, a spirituall banishment*, a banishment from those sinnes, and that sinnefull conversation, which thou hast loved more than thy *Parents*, or *Countrey*, or thine owne body, which perchance thou hast consumed, and destroyed with that sinne; if thou canst finde him contenting and containing himselfe at home in his fathers house, and not breaking out, no not about the worke of our salvation, till the due time was come, when it was to be done. And if according to that example, thou canst contain thy selfe in that station and vocation in which God hath planted thee, and not, through a hasty and precipitate *zeale*, breake out to an imaginary, and intempestive, and unseasonable *Reformation*, either in *Civill* or *Ecclesiasticall* businesse, which belong not to thee; if with this little poore light, these *first degrees* of *Knowledge* and *Faith*, thou canst follow him into the *Garden*, and gather up some of the droppes of his precious Bloud and sweat, which he shed for thy soule, if thou canst follow him to *Jerusalem*, and pick up some of those *teares*, which he shed upon that City, and upon thy soule; if thou canst follow him to the place of his scourging, and to his crucifying, and provide thee some of that balme, which must cure thy soule; if after all this, thou canst turne this little light inward, and canst thereby discerne where thy diseases, and thy wounds, and thy corruptions are, and canst apply those teares, and blood and balme to them, (all this is, That if thou attend the light of naturall reason, and cherish that, and exalt that, so that that bring thee to a *love of the Scriptures*, and that *love to a beleefe* of the truth thereof, and that *historicall faith* to a *faith of application, of appropriation*, that as all those things were certainly done, so they were certainly done *for thee*) thou shalt never envy the lustre and glory of the great lights of worldly men, which are great by the infirmity of others, or by their own opinion, great because others think them great, or because they think themselves so, but thou shalt finde, that howsoever they magnifie their lights, their wit, their learning, their industry, their fortune, their favour, and *sacrifice to their owne nets*, yet thou shalt see, that thou by thy small light hast gathered *Pearle* and *Amber*, and they by their great lights nothing but shels and pebles; they have determined the light of nature, upon the booke of nature, this world, and thou hast carried the light of nature higher, thy naturall reason, and even *humane arguments*, have brought thee to reade the Scriptures, and to that *love*, God hath set to the seale of *faith*. Their light shall set at noone; even in their heighth, some heavy crosse shall cast a damp upon their soule, and cut off all their succours, and devest them of all comforts, and thy light shall grow up, from a *faire hope*, to a modest assurance and *infallibility*, that that light shall never go out, nor the *works of darknesse*, nor the *Prince of darknesse* ever prevaile upon thee, but as thy light of *reason* is exalted by *faith* here, so thy light of *faith* shall be exalted into the light of *glory*, and fruition in the Kingdome of heaven.

## 12. From a Sermon Preached at White-hall, March 8. 1622[1]

### (i)

THIS is a Text of the Resurrection, and it is not Easter yet; but it is Easter Eve; All Lent, is but the Vigill, the Eve of Easter: to so long a Festivall as never shall end, the Resurrection, wee may well begin the Eve betimes. Forty yeares long was God grieved for that Generation which he loved; let us be content to humble our selves forty daies, to be fitter for that glory which we expect. In the Booke of God there are many *Songs*; there is but one *Lamentation*: And that one Song of *Solomon*, nay some one of *Davids* hundred and fiftie Psalmes, is longer than the whole booke of Lamentations. Make way to an everlasting Easter by a short Lent, to an undeterminable glory, by a temporary humiliation. You must weepe these teares, teares of contrition, teares of mortification, before God will wipe all teares from your eyes; You must dye this death, this death of the righteous, the death to sin, before this *last enemy*, *Death*, shalbe destroyed in you, and you made partakers of everlasting life in soule and body too.

### (ii)

As peace is of all goodnesse, so warre is an embleme, a Hieroglyphique, of all misery; And that is our second step in this paraphrase.

If the feete of them that preach peace, be beautifull, (And, *O how beautifull are the feete of them that preach peace?* The Prophet *Isaiah* askes the question, 52. 7. And the Prophet *Nahum* askes it, 1. 15. and the Apostle S. *Paul* askes it, *Rom.* 10. 15. They all aske it, but none answers it) who shall answer us, if we aske, How beautifull is his face, who is the Author of this peace, when we shall see that in the glory of Heaven, the Center of all true peace? It was the inheritance of Christ Jesus upon the earth, he had it at his birth, he brought it

---

[1] On the text: 'The last enemy that shall be destroyed, is death' (1 Cor. xv. 26).

This sermon was preached on the first Friday in Lent, the day on which Donne had been summoned for several years to preach before the King. James was not at Whitehall on this occasion, being ill at Theobalds.

with him, *Glory be to God on high, peace upon earth*. It was his purchase
upon earth, *He made peace* (indeed he bought peace) *through the blood
of his Crosse*. It was his Testament, when he went from earth; *Peace
I leave with you, my peace I give unto you*. Divide with him in that
blessed Inheritance, partake with him in that blessed Purchase,
enrich thy selfe with that blessed Legacy, his Peace.

Let the whole world be in thy consideration as one house; and
then consider in that, in the peacefull harmony of creatures, in the
peacefull succession, and connexion of causes, and effects, the peace
of Nature. Let this Kingdome, where God hath blessed thee with a
being, be the Gallery, the best roome of that house, and consider
in the two walls of that Gallery, the Church and the State, the peace
of a royall, and a religious Wisedome; Let thine owne family be a
Cabinet in this Gallery, and finde in all the boxes thereof, in the
severall duties of Wife, and Children, and servants, the peace of
vertue, and of the father and mother of all vertues, active discretion, passive obedience; and then lastly, let thine owne bosome
be the secret box, and reserve in this Cabinet, and find there the
peace of conscience, and truelie thou hast the best Jewell in the
best Cabinet, and that in the best Gallery of the best house that
can be had, peace with the Creature, peace in the Church, peace in
the State, peace in thy house, peace in thy heart, is a faire Modell,
and a lovely designe even of the heavenly Jerusalem which is *Visio
pacis*, where there is no object but peace.

## (iii)

[Death] comes equally to us all, and makes us all equall when it
comes. The ashes of an Oak in the Chimney, are no Epitaph of that
Oak, to tell me how high or how large that was; It tels me not what
flocks it sheltered while it stood, nor what men it hurt when it fell.
The dust of great persons graves is speechlesse too, it sayes nothing,
it distinguishes nothing: As soon the dust of a wretch whom thou
wouldest not, as of a Prince whom thou couldest not look upon, will
trouble thine eyes, if the winde blow it thither; and when a whirle-
winde hath blowne the dust of the Church-yard into the Church, and
the man sweeps out the dust of the Church into the Church-yard,

who will undertake to sift those dusts again, and to pronounce, This is the Patrician, this is the noble flowre, and this the yeomanly, this the Plebeian bran? So is the death of *Jesabel* (*Jesabel* was a Queen) expressed; *They shall not say, this is Jesabel*; not only not wonder that it is, nor pity that it should be, but they shall not say, they shall not know, This is *Jesabel*. It comes to all, to all alike; but not alike welcome to all. To die too willingly, out of impatience to wish, or out of violence to hasten death, or to die too unwillingly, to murmure at Gods purpose revealed by age, or by sicknesse, are equall distempers; and to harbour a disobedient loathnesse all the way, or to entertain it at last, argues but an irreligious ignorance; An ignorance, that death is in nature but *Expiratio*, a breathing out, and we do that every minute; An ignorance that God himself took a day to rest in, and a good mans grave is his Sabbath; An ignorance that *Abel* the best of those whom we can compare with him, was the first that dyed. Howsoever, whensoever, all times are Gods times: *Vocantur boni ne diutius vexentur a noxiis, mali ne diutius bonos persequantur*, God cals the good to take them from their dangers, and God takes the bad to take them from their triumph. And therefore neither grudge that thou goest, nor that worse stay, for God can make his profit of both; *Aut ideo vivit ut corrigatur, aut ideo ut per illum bonus exerceatur*; God reprieves him to mend him, or to make another better by his exercise; and not to exult in the misery of another, but to glorifie God in the ways of his justice, let him know, *Quantumcunque sero, subito ex hac vita tollitur, qui finem prævidere nescivit*: How long soever he live, how long soever he lie sick, that man dies a sudden death, who never thought of it. If we consider death in S. *Pauls Statutum est, It is decreed that all men must die*, there death is indifferent; If we consider it in his *Mori lucrum, that it is an advantage to die*, there death is good.

## (iv)

Death is the last, and in that respect the worst enemy. In an enemy, that appears at first, when we are or may be provided against him, there is some of that, which we call Honour: but in the enemie that reserves himselfe unto the last, and attends our weake estate, there is more danger. Keepe it, where I intend it, in that which is my spheare, the Conscience: If mine enemie meet me betimes in my youth, in an object of tentation, (so *Josephs* enemie met him in *Putifars* Wife) yet if I do not adhere to this enemy, dwell upon a delightfull meditation of that sin, if I doe not fuell, and foment that sin, assist and encourage that sin, by high diet, wanton discourse, other provocation, I shall have reason on my side, and I shall have grace on my side, and I shall have the History of a thousand that have perished by that sin, on my side; Even Spittles will give me souldiers to fight for me, by their miserable example against that sin; nay perchance sometimes the vertue of that woman, whom I sollicite, will assist me. But when I lye under the hands of that enemie, that hath reserved himselfe to the last, to my last bed, then when I shall be able to stir no limbe in any other measure than a Feaver or a Palsie shall shake them, when everlasting darknesse shall have an inchoation in the present dimnesse of mine eyes, and the everlasting gnashing in the present chattering of my teeth, and the everlasting worme in the present gnawing of the Agonies of my body, and anguishes of my minde, when the last enemie shall watch my remedilesse body, and my disconsolate soule there, there, where not the Physitian, in his way, perchance not the Priest in his, shall be able to give any assistance, And when he hath sported himselfe with my misery upon that stage, my death-bed, shall shift the Scene, and throw me from that bed, into the grave, and there triumph over me, God knowes, how many generations, till the Redeemer, my Redeemer, the Redeemer of all me, body as well as soule, come againe; As death is *Novissimus hostis*, the enemy which watches me, at my last weaknesse, and shall hold me, when I shall be no more, till that Angel come, *Who shall say, and sweare that time shall be no more*, in that consideration, in that apprehension, he is the powerfullest, the fearefulest enemy; and yet even there this enemy *Abolebitur*, he shall be destroyed.

# 13. From a Sermon Preached upon Easter-day. [1622]¹

## (i)

THE dead heare not Thunder, nor feele they an Earth-quake. If the Canon batter that Church walls, in which they lye buryed, it wakes not them, nor does it shake or affect them, if that dust, which they are, be thrown out, but yet there is a voyce, which the dead shall heare; *The dead shall heare the voyce of the Son of God,* (sayes the Son of God himself) *and they that heare shall live*; And that is the voyce of our Text. It is here called a clamour, a vociferation, a shout, and varied by our Translators, and Expositors, according to the origination of the word, to be *clamor hortatorius,* and *suasorius,* and *jussorius,* A voyce that carries with it a penetration, (all shall heare it) and a perswasion, (all shall beleeve it, and be glad of it) and a power, a command, (all shall obey it.) Since that voyce at the Creation, *Fiat,* Let there be a world, was never heard such a voyce as this, *Surgite mortui,* Arise ye dead. That was spoken to that that was meerely nothing, and this to them, who in themselves shall have no cooperation, no concurrence to the hearing or answering this voyce.

The power of this voyce is exalted in that it is said to be the *voyce of the Archangel.* Though legions of Angels, millions of Angels shall be employed about the Resurrection, to recollect their scattered dust, and recompact their ruined bodies, yet those bodies so recompact, shall not be able to heare a voyce. They shall be then but such bodies, as they were when they were laid downe in the grave, when, though they were intire bodies, they could not heare the voice of the mourner. But this voyce of the Archangel shall enable them to heare; The Archangel shall re-infuse the severall soules into their bodies, and so they shall heare that voyce, *Surgite mortui,* Arise ye that were dead, and they shall arise.

---

¹ On the text: 'Then we which are alive, and remain, shall be caught up together with them in the clouds, to meet the Lord in the air; and so shall we be ever with the Lord' (1 Thess. iv. 17).

This is the only undated Easter sermon in the Folio, and as Donne was required as Dean to preach every Easter Sunday and we have dated sermons for all the other Easters of his tenure of the Deanery, this must be placed in 1622 and be his first Easter sermon as Dean.

## (ii)

How barren a thing is Arithmetique? (and yet Arithmetique will tell you, how many single graines of sand, will fill this hollow Vault to the Firmament) How empty a thing is Rhetorique? (and yet Rhetorique will make absent and remote things present to your understanding) How weak a thing is Poetry? (and yet Poetry is a counterfait Creation, and makes things that are not, as though they were) How infirme, how impotent are all assistances, if they be put to expresse this Eternity?

## 14. From a Sermon Preached at the Spittle, Upon Easter-Munday. 1622[1]

### (i)

BUT he is *Idem Deus*; that God who hath begun, and proceeded, will persevere in mercy towards us. Our God is not out of breath, because he hath blown one tempest, and swallowed a Navy: Our God hath not burnt out his eyes, because he hath looked upon a Train of Powder: In the light of Heaven, and in the darkness of hell, he sees alike; he sees not onely all Machinations of hands, when things come to action; but all Imaginations of hearts, when they are in their first Consultations: past, and present, and future, distinguish not his *Quando*; all is one time to him: Mountains and Vallies, Sea and Land, distinguish not his *Ubi*; all is one place to him: *When I begin*, says God to *Eli*, *I will make an end*; not onely that all Gods purposes shall have their certain end, but that even then, when he begins, he makes an end: from the very beginning, imprints an infallible assurance, that whom he loves, he loves to the end: as a Circle is printed all at once, so his beginning and ending is all one.

1 On the text: 'For, God who commanded light to shine out of darkness, hath shined in our hearts, to give the light of the knowledge of the glory of God, in the face of Jesus Christ' (2 Cor. iv. 6).

The Lord Mayor and Aldermen attended sermons at Paul's Cross on Good Fridays and at the Spital Cross (that is the Cross by the Hospital of St. Mary, Bishopsgate) on the Mondays, Tuesdays, and Wednesdays after Easter. For the sermons at the Spital they were joined by the boys of Christ's Hospital. Donne's sermon at the Spital is the longest of his extant sermons and his editors reckon it would have taken close on two and a half hours to deliver.

## (ii)

Neither doe the Angels know *per species*, by those resultances and species, which rise from the Object, and pass through the Sense to the Understanding, for that's a deceiveable way, both by the indisposition of the Organ, sometimes, and sometimes by the depravation of the Judgment; and therefore, as the first is too high, this is too low a way for the Angels. Some things the Angels do know by the dignity of their Nature, by their Creation, which we know not; as we know many things which inferior Creatures do not; and such things all the Angels, good and bad know. Some things they know by the Grace of their confirmation, by which they have more given them, than they had by Nature in their Creation; and those things only the Angels that stood, but all they, do know. Some things they know by Revelation, when God is pleased to manifest them unto them; and so some of the Angels know that, which the rest, though confirm'd, doe not know. By Creation, they know as his Subjects; by Confirmation, they know as his servants; by Revelation, they know as his Councel. Now, *Erimus sicut Angeli*, says Christ, *There we shall be as the Angels*: The knowledge which I have by Nature, shall have no Clouds; here it hath: that which I have by Grace, shall have no reluctation, no resistance; here it hath: That which I have by Revelation, shall have no suspition, no jealousie; here it hath: sometimes it is hard to distinguish between a respiration from God, and a suggestion from the Devil. There our curiosity shall have this noble satisfaction, we shall know how the Angels know, by knowing as they know. We shall not pass from Author, to Author, as in a Grammar School, nor from Art to Art, as in an University; but, as that General which Knighted his whole Army, God shall Create us all Doctors in a minute. That great Library, those infinite Volumes of the Books of Creatures, shall be taken away, quite away, no more Nature; those reverend Manuscripts, written with Gods own hand, the Scriptures themselves, shall be taken away, quite away; no more preaching, no more reading of Scriptures, and that great School-Mistress, Experience, and Observation shall be remov'd, no new thing to be done, and in an instant, I shall know more, than they all could reveal unto me. I shall know, not only as I know already, that a Bee-hive, that an Ant-hill is the same Book in *Decimo sexto*, as a Kingdom is in *Folio*, That a Flower that lives but a day, is an abridgment of that King, that lives out his threescore and ten yeers; but I shall know too, that all these Ants, and Bees, and Flowers, and Kings, and Kingdoms, howsoever they may be Examples, and Comparisons to one another, yet they are all as nothing, altogether nothing, less than nothing, infinitely less than nothing, to that which shall then be the subject of my knowledge, for, *it is the knowledge of the glory of God.*

## 15. From a Sermon Preached at St. Pauls on Midsommer day. 1622[1]

THE grave it self shall be open againe; and *Aperti cœli*, The heavens shall be open, and I shall see the Sonne of man, the Sonne of God, and not see him at that distance, that *Stephen* saw him there, but see him, and sit down with him. I shall rise from the dead, from the darke station, from the prostration, from the prosternation of death, and never misse the sunne, which shall then be put out, for I shall see the Sonne of God, the Sunne of glory, and shine my self, as that sunne shines. I shall rise from the grave, and never misse this City, which shall be no where, for I shall see the City of God, the new *Jerusalem*. I shall looke up, and never wonder when it will be day, for, the Angell will tell me that *time shall be no more*, and I shall see, and see cheerefully that last day, the day of judgement, which shall have no *night*, never end, and be united to the *Antient of dayes*, to God himselfe, who had no *morning*, never began. There I shall beare witnesse for Christ, in ascribing the salvation of the whole world, *to him that sits upon the Throne, and to the Lamb*, and Christ shall bear witnesse for me, in ascribing his righteousnesse unto me, and in delivering me into his Fathers hands, with the same tendernesse, as he delivered up his owne soule, and in making me, who am a greater sinner, than they who crucified him on earth for me, as innocent, and as righteous as his glorious selfe, in the Kingdome of heaven.

[1] On the text: 'He was not that light, but was sent to bear witness of that light' (John i. 8).

Midsummer day (24 June) is the Feast of St. John the Baptist.

## 16. From a Sermon Preached at Hanworth, to my Lord of Carlile, and his company, being the Earles of Northumberland, and Buckingham, &c. Aug. 25. 1622[1]

HOW many times go we to Comedies, to Masques, to places of great and noble resort, nay even to Church onely to see the company? If I had no other errand to heaven, but the *communion of Saints*, the fellowship of the faithfull, to see that flock of *Lambs*, Innocent, unbaptized *children*, recompensed with the twice-baptized *Martyrs*, (baptized in *water*, and baptized in their owne *blood*) and that middle sort, the children baptized in blood, and not in the water, that rescued Christ Jesus, by their death, under *Herod*; to see the *Prophets* and the *Evangelists*, and not know one from the other, by their writings, for they all write the same things (for *prophecy* is but *antidated Gospell*, and *Gospell* but *postdated prophecy*;) to see holy *Matrons* saved by the bearing, and bringing up of children, and holy *Virgins*, saved by restoring their bodies in the integrity, that they received them, sit all upon one seate; to see *Princes*, and *Subjects* crowned all with one crowne, and *rich* and *poore* inherit one portion; to see this scene, this Court, this Church, this Catholique Church, not onely *Easterne* and *Westerne*, but *Militant* and *Triumphant* Church, all in one roome together, to see this *Communion of Saints*, this fellowship of the faithfull, is worth all the paynes, that that sight costs us in this world.

---

[1] On the Text: 'Every man may see it, man may behold it afar off' (Job xxxvi. 25).

[This sermon was preached before an aristocratic audience on an interesting occasion. James Hay, Viscount Doncaster, whom Donne had accompanied to Germany in 1619, was not created Earl of Carlisle until 13 September 1622. He married Lucy Percy, daughter of the Earl of Northumberland (the 'Wizard Earl') who had interceded with Donne's father-in-law, Sir George More, on the occasion of his clandestine marriage in 1601. Northumberland had just been released from the Tower, where he was imprisoned for sixteen years for complicity in the Gunpowder Plot, and Doncaster was anxious to reconcile him with the King's favourite, Buckingham, whom, like most of the old nobility, he detested. For this purpose he had invited his father-in-law and Buckingham with others of the nobility to his house at Hanworth and called on Donne to preach before them. See Jessopp, *John Donne* (1897), pp. 143–6.]

## 17. From a Sermon Preached to the Earle of Carlile, and his Company, at Sion. [? Autumn 1622]¹

WHEN all is done, the hell of hels, the torment of torments is the everlasting absence of God, and the everlasting impossibility of returning to his presence; *Horrendum est*, sayes the Apostle, *It is a fearefull thing to fall into the hands of the living God.* Yet there was a case, in which *David* found an ease, to fall into the hands of God, to scape the hands of men: *Horrendum est*, when Gods hand is bent to strike, *it is a fearefull thing, to fall into the hands of the living God*; but to fall out of the hands of the living God, is a horror beyond our expression, beyond our imagination.

That God should let my soule fall out of his hand, into a bottom-lesse pit, and roll an unremoveable stone upon it, and leave it to that which it finds there, (and it shall finde that there, which it never imagined, till it came thither) and never thinke more of that soule, never have more to doe with it. That of that providence of God, that studies the life and preservation of every weed, and worme, and ant, and spider, and toad, and viper, there should never, never any beame flow out upon me; that that God, who looked upon me, when I was nothing, and called me when I was not, as though I had been, out of the womb and depth of darknesse, will not looke upon me now, when, though a miserable, and a banished, and a damned creature, yet I am his creature still, and contribute some-thing to his glory, even in my damnation; that that God, who hath often looked upon me in my foulest uncleannesse, and when I had shut out the eye of the day, the Sunne, and the eye of the night, the Taper, and the eyes of all the world, with curtaines and windowes and doores, did yet see me, and see me in mercy, by making me see that he saw me, and sometimes brought me to a present remorse, and (for that time) to a forbearing of that sinne, should so turne himselfe from me, to his glorious Saints and Angels, as that no Saint nor Angel, nor Christ Jesus himselfe, should ever pray him to looke towards me, never remember him, that such a soule there is; that that God, who hath so often said to my soule,

---

¹ On the text: 'He that believeth not, shall be damned' (Mark xvi. 16).
Sion was the mansion of Carlisle's father-in-law, the Earl of Northumberland.

*Quare morieris?* Why wilt thou die? and so often sworne to my soule, *Vivit Dominus*, As the Lord liveth, I would not have thee dye, but live, will neither let me dye, nor let me live, but dye an everlasting life, and live an everlasting death; that that God, who, when he could not get into me, by standing, and knocking, by his ordinary meanes of entring, by his Word, his mercies, hath applied his judgements, and hath shaked the house, this body, with agues and palsies, and set this house on fire, with fevers and calentures, and frighted the Master of the house, my soule, with horrors, and heavy apprehensions, and so made an entrance into me; That that God should loose and frustrate all his owne purposes and practises upon me, and leave me, and cast me away, as though I had cost him nothing, that this God at last, should let this soule goe away, as a smoake, as a vapour, as a bubble, and that then this soule cannot be a smoake, nor a vapour, nor a bubble, but must lie in darknesse, as long as the Lord of light is light it selfe, and never a sparke of that light reach to my soule; What Tophet is not Paradise, what Brimstone is not Amber, what gnashing is not a comfort, what gnawing of the worme is not a tickling, what torment is not a marriage bed to this damnation, to be secluded eternally, eternally, eternally from the sight of God? Especially to us, for as the perpetuall losse of that is most heavy, with which we have been best acquainted, and to which wee have been most accustomed; so shall this damnation, which consists in the losse of the sight and presence of God, be heavier to us than others, because God hath so graciously, and so evidently, and so diversly appeared to us, in his pillar of fire, in the light of prosperity, and in the pillar of the Cloud, in hiding himselfe for a while from us; we that have seene him in the Execution of all the parts of this Commission, in his Word, in his Sacraments, and in good example, and not beleeved, shall be further removed from his sight, in the next world, than they to whom he never appeared in this. But *Vincenti & credenti*, to him that beleeves aright, and overcomes all tentations to a wrong beliefe, God shall give the accomplishment of fulnesse, and fulnesse of joy, and joy rooted in glory, and glory established in eternity, and this eternity is God; To him that beleeves and overcomes, God shall give himselfe in an everlasting presence and fruition, *Amen.*

## 18. From a Sermon Preached to the Honourable Company of the Virginian Plantation, 13° November. 1622[1]

THOSE of our profession that goe, you, that send them who goe, doe all an *Apostolicall* function. What action soever, hath in the first intention thereof, a purpose to propagate the Gospell of *Christ Jesus*, that is an *Apostolicall* action; Before the ende of the world come, before this mortality shall put on immortalitie, before the Creature shall be delivered of the bondage of corruption under which it groanes, before the Martyrs under the Altar shalbe silenc'd, before al things shal be subdued to *Christ*, his kingdome perfited, and the last Enemy Death destroied, the Gospell must be preached to those men to whom ye send; to all men. Further and hasten you this blessed, this joyfull, this glorious consummation of all, and happie reunion of all bodies to their Soules, by preaching the *Gospell* to those men. Preach to them Doctrinally, preach to them Practically; Enamore them with your *Justice*, and, (as farre as may consist with your security) your *Civilitie*; but inflame them with your *godlinesse*, and your *Religion*. Bring them to *love* and *Reverence* the name of that *King*, that sends men to teach them the wayes of *Civilitie* in this world, but to *feare* and *adore* the Name of that *King of Kings*, that sends men to teach them the waies of Religion, for the next world. Those amongst you, that are old now, shall passe out of this world with this great comfort, that you contributed to the beginning of that Common Wealth, and of that Church, though they live not to see the groath thereof to perfection: *Apollos* watred, but *Paul* planted; hee that begun the worke, was the greater man. And you that are young now, may live to see the Enemy as much empeach'd by that place, and your friends, yea Children, as well accommodated in that place, as any other. You shall have made this *Iland*, which is but as the *Suburbs* of the old world, a Bridge, a

---

[1] On the text: 'But ye shall receive power, after that the Holy Ghost is come upon you, and ye shall be witnesses unto me both in Jerusalem, and in all Judea, and in Samaria, and unto the uttermost part of the earth' (Acts i. 8).

Donne had attempted to secure the post of Secretary of Virginia in 1609, when his fortunes were at a very low ebb. This sermon to the Company has been called 'the first missionary sermon in English'. It was printed immediately after its delivery.

Gallery to the new; to joyne all to that world that shall never grow old, the Kingdome of heaven, You shall add persons to this Kingdome, and to the Kingdome of heaven, and adde names to the Bookes of our Chronicles, and to the Booke of Life.

## 19. From a Sermon Preached at St. Pauls, upon Christmas day. 1622[1]

IF you will reconcile things in heaven, and earth, with things in hell, that is a reconciling out of this Text. If you will mingle the service of God, and the service of this world, there is no reconciling of God and Mammon in this Text. If you will mingle a true religion, and a false religion, there is no reconciling of God and Belial in this Text. For the adhering of persons born within the Church of Rome, to the Church of Rome, our law sayes nothing to them if they come; But for reconciling to the Church of Rome, by persons born within the Allegeance of the King, or for perswading of men to be so reconciled, our law hath called by an infamous and Capitall name of Treason, and yet every Tavern, and Ordinary is full of such Traitors. Every place from jest to earnest is filled with them; from the very stage to the death-bed; At a Comedy they will perswade you, as you sit, as you laugh, And in your sicknesse they will perswade you, as you lye, as you dye. And not only in the bed of sicknesse, but in the bed of wantonnesse they perswade too; and there may be examples of women, that have thought it a fit way to gain a soul, by prostituting themselves, and by entertaining unlawfull love, with a purpose to convert a servant, which is somewhat a strange Topique, to draw arguments of religion from. Let me see a Dominican and a Jesuit reconciled, in doctrinall papistry, for freewill and predestination, Let me see a French papist and an Italian papist reconciled in State-papistry, for the Popes jurisdiction, Let me see the Jesuits, and the secular priests reconciled in England, and when they are reconciled to one another, let them presse reconciliation to their Church. To end all, Those men have their

---

[1] On the text: 'For, it pleased the Father, that in Him should all fulness dwell; and, having made peace through the blood of His cross, by Him, to reconcile all things to Himself, by Him, whether they be things in earth, or things in heaven' (Col. i. 19, 20).

bodies from the earth, and they have their soules from heaven; and
so all things in earth and heaven are reconciled: but they have their
Doctrine from the Devill; and for things in hell, there is no peace
made, and with things in hell, there is no reconciliation to be had
by the blood of his Crosse, except we will tread that blood under
our feet, and make a mock of Christ Jesus, and crucifie the Lord of
Life againe.

## 20. From a Sermon Preached upon Candlemas day. [?1623][1]

### (i)

THAT soule, that is accustomed to direct her selfe to God, upon
every occasion, that, as a flowre at Sun-rising, conceives a sense of
God, in every beame of his, and spreads and dilates it selfe towards
him, in a thankfulnesse, in every small blessing that he sheds
upon her; that soule, that as a flowre at the Suns declining,
contracts and gathers in, and shuts up her selfe, as though she
had received a blow, when soever she heares her Saviour wounded
by an oath, or blasphemy, or execration; that soule, who, whatsoever string be strucken in her, base or treble, her high or her
low estate, is ever tun'd toward God, that soule prayes sometimes
when it does not know that it prayes.

### (ii)

Pay this debt to thy selfe of looking into thy debts, of surveying,
of severing, of serving thy selfe with that which is truly thine, at
thy noone, in the best of thy fortune, and in the strength of thine
understanding; that when thou commest to pay thy other, thy
last debt to thy self, which is, to open a doore out of this world,
by the dissolution of body and soule, thou have not all thy money to
tell over when the Sun is ready to set, all the account to make of
every bag of money, and of every quillet of land, whose it is, and

---

[1] On the text: 'Render therefore to all men their dues' (Rom. xiii. 7).

The Folio adds 'The Text being part of the Epistle of that day, that yeare'. It occurs in
the Epistle for the fourth Sunday after Epiphany, which fell on Candlemas (2 February) only
in 1617 and 1623 during the years of Donne's ministry. The second date seems the likelier.

whether it be his that looks for it from thee, or his from whom it
was taken by thee; whether it belong to thine heire, that weepes
joyfull tears behinde the curtain, or belong to him that weeps
true, and bloody teares, in the hole in a prison. There will come a
time, when that land that thou leavest shall not be his land, when it
shall be no bodies land, when it shall be no land, for the earth must
perish; there will be a time when there shall be no Mannors, no
Acres in the world, and yet there shall lie Mannors and Acres upon
thy soul, when land shall be no more, when time shall be no more,
and thou passe away, not into the land of the living, but of eternall
death. Then the Accuser will be ready to interline the schedules of
thy debts, thy sins, and insert false debts, by abusing an over-
tendernesse, which may be in thy conscience then, in thy last
sicknesse, in thy death-bed: Then he will be ready to adde a cyphar
more to thy debts, and make hundreds thousands, and abuse the
faintnesse which may be in thy conscience then, in thy last sicknesse,
in thy death-bed. Then he will be ready to abuse even thy confidence in God, and bring thee to think, that as a Pirate ventures
boldly home, though all that he hath be stoln, if he be rich enough
to bribe for a pardon; so, howsoever those families perish whom
thou hast ruined, and those whole parishes whom thou hast de-
populated, thy soule may goe confidently home too, if thou bribe
God then, with an Hospitall or a Fellowship in a Colledge, or a
Legacy to any pious use in apparance, and in the eye of the world.

## 21. From a Sermon Preached at White-hall, the first Friday in Lent. 1623[1]

### (i)

HE wept as man doth weepe, and he wept as a man may weepe;
for these teares were *Testes naturæ, non Indices diffidentiæ*, They
declared him to be true man, but no distrustfull, no inordinate
man. In *Job* there is a question ask'd of God, *Hast thou eyes of
flesh, and doest thou see, as man sees?* Let this question be directed
to God manifested in Christ, and Christ will weepe out an

[1] On the text: 'Jesus wept' (John xi. 35).

answer to that question, I have eyes of flesh, and I do weep as man weepes. Not as sinfull man, not as a man, that had let fall his bridle, by which he should turne his horse: Not as a man that were cast from the rudder, by which he should steere his Ship: Not as a man that had lost his interest and power in his affections, and passions; Christ wept not so.

## (ii)

These men whom Jesus found weeping, and wept with them, were none of his kindred: They were Neighbours, and Christ had had a conversation, and contracted a friendship in that Family; *He loved Martha, and her sister, and Lazarus*, saies the Storie: and he would let the world see that he loved them: for so the Jewes argued that saw him weepe, *Behold how he loved them*; without outward declarations, who can conclude an inward love? to assure that, *Jesus wept*.

To an inordinatenesse of affections it never came; to a naturall tendernesse it did; and so far as to teares; and then who needs be ashamed of weeping? *Look away far from me, for I will weep bitterly*, sayes Hierusalem in *Esay*. But *look upon me*, sayes Christ in the Lamentations, *Behold and see if ever there were any sorrow, any teares like mine*: Not like his in value, but in the roote as they proceeded from naturall affection, they were teares of imitation, and we may, we must weepe teares like his teares. They scourged him, they crowned him, they nailed him, they pierced him, and then blood came; but he shed teares voluntarily, and without violence: The blood came from their ill, but the teares from his owne good nature: The blood was drawne, the teares were given. We call it a childish thing to weepe, and a womanish; and perchance we meane worse in that than in the childish; for therein we may meane falshood to be mingled with weaknesse. Christ made it an argument of his being man, to weepe, for though the lineaments of mans bodie, eyes and eares, hands and feet, be ascribed to God in the Scriptures, though the affections of mans mind be ascribed to him, (even sorrow, nay Repentance it selfe, is attributed to God) I doe not remember that ever God is said to have wept: It is for man. And when God shall come to that last Act in the glorifying of Man, when he promises, *to wipe all teares from his eyes*, what shall God have to doe with that eye that never wept?

## 22. From a Sermon Preached to the Nobility[1]

So therefore prayer is our first entry, for when it is said, *Ask and it shall be given*, it is also said, *Knock and it shall be opened*, showing that by prayer our entrance is. And not the entry onely, but the whole house: *My house is the house of prayer*. Of all the conduits and conveyances of Gods graces to us, none hath been so little subject to cavillations, as this of prayer. The Sacraments have fallen into the hands of flatterers and robbers. Some have attributed too much to them, some detracted. Some have painted them, some have withdrawn their naturall complexion. It hath been disputed, whether they be, how many they be, what they be, and what they do. The preaching of the word hath been made a servant of ambitions, and a shop of many mens new-fangled wares. Almost every meanes between God and man, suffers some adulteratings and disguises: But prayer least: And it hath most wayes and addresses. It may be mentall, for we may thinke prayers. It may be vocall, for we may speake prayers. It may be actuall, for we do prayers. For deeds have voyce; the vices of *Sodome* did cry, and the Almes of *Toby*. And if it were proper for St. *John*, in the first of the *Revelations* to turne back to see a voyce, it is more likely God will looke down, to heare a worke. So then to do the office of your vocation sincerely, is to pray. How much the favourites of Princes, and great personages labour, that they may be thought to have been in private conference with

1 On the text: 'Father forgive them, for they know not what they do' (Luke xxiii. 34).
This undated sermon is extant in two manuscripts as well as in *Fifty Sermons*. Its simple style, the facts that its marginal headings are in English, that Scripture references are in the body of the text, and that there are few patristic quotations suggest that Donne was preaching to a different type of audience from that which he addressed at Lincoln's Inn, St. Paul's, or Whitehall. 'Is it possible that we have here a solitary example of the sermons which Donne preached every summer during the vacation at his country livings of Sevenoaks or Blunham? When he visited there, we know that he generally stayed with the Earl of Dorset at Knole, or the Earl of Kent at the great house of Blunham. On these occasions the Earl with his wife, family, and part of the retinue of servants would be present at the Sunday morning service. A sermon preached on such an occasion could therefore be included by John Donne junior under the general heading "Preached to the Nobility".'

the Prince. And though they be forced to wait upon his purposes, and talk of what he will, how fain they would be thought to have solicited their own, or their Dependants businesse. With the Prince of Princes, this every man may doe truly; and the sooner, the more begger he is: for no man is heard here, but *in forma pauperis.*

Here we may talk long, welcomely, of our own affaires, and be sure to speed. You cannot whisper so low alone in your Chamber, but he heares you, nor sing so lowd in the Congregation, but he distinguishes you. He grudges not to be chidden and disputed with, by *Job. The Arrows of the Almighty are in me, and the venim thereof hath drunk up my spirit. Is my strength, the strength of stones, or is my flesh of brasse, &c.* Not to be directed and counselled by *Jonas*: who was angry and sayd; Did not I say, when I was in my Country, thou wouldest deale thus? And when the Lord sayd, *Doest thou well to be angry?* He replyed, *I doe well to be angry to the death.* Nor almost to be threatned and neglected by *Moses: Doe this, or blot my name out of thy book.* It is an Honour to be able to say to servants, Doe this: But to say to God, *Domine fac hoc,* and prevail, is more; And yet more easie. God is replenishingly every where; but most contractedly, and workingly in the Temple. Since then every rectified man, is the temple of the Holy Ghost, when he prays; it is the Holy Ghost it selfe that prays; and what can be denyed, where the Asker gives? He plays with us, as children, shewes us pleasing things, that we may cry for them, and have them. Before we call, he answers, and when we speak, he heares: so *Esay* 65. 24. Physicians observe some symptomes so violent, that they must neglect the disease for a time, and labour to cure the accident; as burning fevers, in Dysenteries. So in the sinfull consumption of the soule, a stupidity and indisposition to prayer, must first be cured. For, *Ye lust, and have not, because ye aske not,* Jam. 4. 2. The adulterous Mother of the three great brothers, *Gratian, Lombard,* and *Comestor,* being warned by her Confessour, to be sorry for her fact, sayd, she could not, because her fault had so much profited the Church. At least, sayd he, be sorry that thou canst not be sorry. So whosoever thou be, that canst not readily pray, at least pray, that thou mayst pray. For, as in bodily, so in spirituall diseases, it is a desperate state, to be speechlesse.

## 23. From a Sermon Preached upon All-Saints Day.
## [? 1623¹]

NONE of us hath got the victory over flesh and blood, and yet we
have greater enemies than flesh and blood are. Some disciplines,
some mortifications we have against flesh and blood; we have S.
*Pauls probatum est*, his medicine, (if we will use it) *Castigo corpus, I
keep under my body, and bring it into subjection;* for that we have
some assistance; Even our enemies become our friends; poverty
or sicknesse will fight for us against flesh and blood, against our
carnall lusts; but for these powers and principalities, I know not
where to watch them, how to encounter them. I passe my time
sociably and merrily in cheerful conversation, in musique, in feast-
ing, in Comedies, in wantonnesse; and I never heare all this while of
any power or principality, my Conscience spies no such enemy in
all this. And then alone, between God and me at midnight, some
beam of his grace shines out upon me, and by that light I see this
Prince of darknesse, and then I finde that I have been the subject,
the slave of these powers and principalities, when I thought not of
them. Well, I see them, and I try then to dispossesse my selfe of
them, and I make my recourse to the powerfullest exorcisme that is,
I turne to hearty and earnest prayer to God, and I fix my thoughts
strongly (as I thinke) upon him, and before I have perfected one
petition, one period of my prayer, a power and principality is got
into me againe. *Spiritus soporis*, The spirit of slumber closes mine eyes,
and I pray drousily; Or *spiritus vertiginis*, the spirit of deviation, and
vaine repetition, and I pray giddily, and circularly, and returne
againe and againe to that I have said before, and perceive not that
I do so; and *nescio cujus spiritus sim*, (as our Saviour said, rebuking his
Disciples, who were so vehement for the burning of the Samaritans,
*you know not of what spirit you are*) I pray, and know not of what spirit
I am, I consider not mine own purpose in prayer; And by this
advantage, this doore of inconsideration, enters *spiritus erroris*, The
seducing spirit, the spirit of error, and I pray not onely negligently,

¹ On the text: 'And I saw another angel ascending from the east, which had the seal of
the living God, and he cried with a loud voice to the four angels, to whom power was given
to hurt the earth, and the sea, saying, Hurt ye not the earth, neither the sea, neither the
trees, till we have sealed the servants of our God in their foreheads' (Rev. vii. 2, 3).

but erroniously, dangerously, for such things as disconduce to the glory of God, and my true happinesse, if they were granted. Nay, even the Prophet *Hosea's spiritus fornicationum*, enters into me, *The spirit of fornication*, that is, some remembrance of the wantonnesse of my youth, some mis-interpretation of a word in my prayer, that may beare an ill sense, some unclean spirit, some power or principality hath depraved my prayer, and slackned my zeale. And this is my greatest misery of all, that when that which fights for me, and fights against me too, sicknesse, hath laid me upon my last bed, then in my weakest estate, these powers and principalities shall be in their full practise against me. And therefore it is one great advancement of thy deliverance, to be brought by this Angel, that is, by the Ministery of the Gospel of Christ, to know that thou hast Angels to thine enemies; And then another is to know their number, and so the strength of their confederacy; for, in the verse before the Text, they are expressed to be foure, (*I saw foure Angels, &c.*)

Foure legions of Angels, foure millions, nay, foure Creations of Angels could do no more harme, than is intended in these foure; for, (as it is said in the former verse) *They stood upon the foure corners of the earth*, they bestrid, they cantoned the whole world. Thou hast opposite Angels enow to batter thee every where, and to cut off and defeat all succours, all supplies, that thou canst procure, or propose to thy selfe; absolute enemies to one another will meet and joyne to thy ruine, and even presumption will induce desperation. We need not be so literall in this, as S. *Hierome*, (who indeed in that followed *Origen*) to thinke that there is a particular evill Angel over every sin; That because we finde that mention of *the spirit of error*, and *the spirit of slumber*, and *the spirit of fornication*, we should therefore thinke that Christ meant by *Mammon*, a particular spirit of Covetousnesse, and that there be severall princes over severall sins. This needs not; when thou art tempted, never aske that Spirits name; his name is *legio*, for he is many. Take thy selfe at the largest, as thou art a world, there are foure Angels at thy foure corners; Let thy foure corners be thy worldly profession, thy calling, and another thy bodily refection, thy eating, and drinking, and sleeping, and a third thy honest and allowable recreations, and a fourth thy religious service of God in this place, (which two last, that is, recreation, and religion, God hath been pleased to joyn together in the Sabbath, in which he intended his own glory in our service of him, and then the rest of the Creature too) let these foure, thy calling, thy sleeping, thy recreation, thy religion be the foure corners of thy world, and thou shalt find an Angel of tentation at every corner; even in thy sleep, even in this house of God thou hast met them. The Devill is no Recusant; he will come to Church, and he will lay his snares there; *When that day comes, that the Sonnes of God present themselves before the Lord, Satan comes also among them.* Not onely so, as S. *Augustin* confesses he met him at Church, to carry wanton glances between men and women, but he is here, sometimes to work a mis-interpretation in the hearer, sometimes to work an affectation in the speaker, and many times doth more harme by a good Sermon than by a weake, by possessing the hearers with an admiration of the Preachers gifts, and neglecting Gods Ordinance. And then it is not onely their naturall power, as they are Angels, nor their united power, as they are many, nor their politique power, that in the midst of that confusion which is amongst them, yet they agree together to ruine us, but (as it follows in our text) it is *potestas data,* a particular power, which, besides their naturall power, God, at this time, put into their hands; (*He cryed to the foure Angels, to whom power was given to hurt*).

## 24. From a Sermon Preached at S. Pauls, upon Easter-day in the Evening. 1624[1]

### (i)

IN the first book of the Scriptures, that of Genesis, there is danger in departing from the letter; In this last book, this of the Revelation, there is as much danger in adhering too close to the letter. The literall sense is always to be preserved; but the literall sense is not always to be discerned: for the literall sense is not always

[1] On the text: 'Blessed and holy is he that hath part in the first resurrection' (Rev. xx. 6). Donne was gravely ill in the late autumn of 1623. During his illness he composed the *Devotions,* the 'Hymn to God the Father', and probably also the 'Hymn to God, my God, in my sickness'. This Easter sermon is the first he preached after his recovery.

that, which the very Letter and Grammer of the place presents, as where it is literally said, *That Christ is a Vine*, and literally, *That his flesh is bread*, and literally, *That the new Jerusalem is thus situated, thus built, thus furnished*: But the literall sense of every place, is the principall intention of the Holy Ghost, in that place: And his principall intention in many places, is to expresse things by allegories, by figures; so that in many places of Scripture, a figurative sense is the literall sense, and more in this book than in any other. As then to depart from the literall sense, that sense which the very letter presents, in the book of Genesis, is dangerous, because if we do so there, we have no history of the Creation of the world in any other place to stick to; so to binde our selves to such a literall sense in this book, will take from us the consolation of many spirituall happinesses, and bury us in the carnall things of this world. . . . Thus far then the text is literall, That this Resurrection in the text, is different from the generall Resurrection. The first differs from the last: And thus far it is figurative, allegoricall, mysticall, that it is a spirituall Resurrection, that is intended. But wherein spirituall? or of what spirituall Resurrection? In the figurative exposition of those places of Scripture, which require that way oft to be figuratively expounded, that Expositor is not to be blamed, who not destroying the literall sense, proposes such a figurative sense, as may exalt our devotion, and advance our edification; And as no one of those Expositors did ill, in proposing one such sense, so neither do those Expositors ill, who with those limitations, that it destroy not the literall sense, that it violate not the analogy of faith, that it advance devotion, do propose another and another such sense. So doth that preacher well also, who to the same end, and within the same limit, makes his use of both, of all those expositions; because all may stand, and it is not evident in such figurative speeches, which is the literall, that is, the principall intention of the Holy Ghost.

## (ii)

Here saies S. *Augustine*, when the soule considers the things of this world, *Non veritate certior, sed consuetudine securior*; She rests upon such things as she is not sure are true, but such as she sees, are ordinarily received and accepted for truths: so that the end of her knowledge is not Truth, but opinion, and the way, not Inquisition, but ease: But saies he, when she proceeds in this life, to search into heavenly things, *Verberatur luce veritatis*, The beames of that light are too strong for her, and they sink her, and cast her downe, *Et ad familiaritatem tenebrarum suarum, non electione sed fatigatione convertitur*; and so she returnes to her owne darknesse, because she is most familiar, and best acquainted with it; *Non electione*, not because she loves ignorance, but because she is weary of the trouble of seeking out the truth, and so swallowes even any Religion to escape the paine of debating, and disputing; and in this lazinesse she sleeps out her lease, her terme of life, in this death, in this grave, in this body.

But then in her Resurrection, her measure is enlarged, and filled at once; There she reads without spelling, and knowes without thinking, and concludes without arguing; she is at the end of her race, without running; In her triumph, without fighting; In her Haven, without sayling: A free-man, without any prentiship; at full yeares, without any wardship; and a Doctor, without any proceeding: She knowes truly, and easily, and immediately, and entirely, and everlastingly; Nothing left out at first, nothing worne out at last, that conduces to her happinesse. What a death is this life? what a resurrection is this death? For though this world be a sea, yet (which is most strange) our Harbour is larger than the sea; Heaven infinitely larger than this world. For, though that be not true, which *Origen* is said to say, That at last all shall be saved, nor that evident, which *Cyril* of Alexandria saies, That without doubt the number of them that are saved, is far greater than of them that perish, yet surely the number of them, with whom we shall have communion in Heaven, is greater than ever lived at once upon the face of the earth: And of those who lived in our time, how few did we know? and of those whom we did know, how few did we care much for? In Heaven we shall have Communion of Joy and Glory with all, alwaies; *Ubi non intrat inimicus, nec amicus exit*, Where never any man shall come in that loves us not, nor go from us that does.

## (iii)

God, who hath spoken to us by his *Son*, works upon us by his *Son* too; He was our Creation, he was our Redemption, he is our Resurrection. And that man trades in the world without money, and goes out of the world without recommendation, that leaves out Christ Jesus. To be a good Morall man, and refer all to the law of Nature in our hearts, is but *Diluculum*, The dawning of the day; To be a godly man, and refer all to God, is but *Crepusculum*, A twylight; But the Meridionall brightnesse, the glorious noon, and heighth, is to be a Christian, to pretend to no spirituall, no temporall blessing, but for, and by, and through, and in our only Lord and Saviour Christ Jesus; for he is this first Resurrection, and *Blessed and holy is he, that hath part in this first Resurrection.*

## 25. From a Sermon Preached to the Earl of Exeter, and his company, in his Chappell at Saint Johns, 13. June. 1624[1]

THERE are an infinite number of *Stars* more than we can distinguish, and so, by Gods grace, there may be an infinite number of soules saved, more than those, of whose salvation, we discerne the *ways*, and the *meanes*. Let us embrace the way which God hath given us, which is, the knowledge of his Sonne, *Christ Jesus*: what other way God may take with others, how he wrought upon *Job*, and *Naaman*, and such others as were not in the *Covenant*, let us not inquire too curiously, determine too peremptorily, pronounce too uncharitably: God be blessed, for his declaring his good-wil towards *us*, and *his will be done* his way upon others.

[1] On the text: 'After this, I beheld, and lo, a great multitude, which no man could number, of all nations, and kindreds, and people, and tongues, stood before the throne, and before the Lamb, clothed with white robes, and palms in their hands' (Rev. vii. 9).

## 26. From an Anniversary Sermon Preached at St. Dunstans, upon the commemoration of a Parishioner, a Benefactor to that Parish. [? 29 June 1624][1]

So, if he who is *Serpens serpens humi*, the Serpent condemned to creep upon the ground, doe transforme himselfe into a flying Serpent, and attempt our nobler faculties, there is *Serpens exaltatus*, a Serpent lifted up in the wildernesse to recover all them that are stung, and feel that they are stung with this Serpent, this flying Serpent, that is, these high and continued sinnes. The creeping Serpent, the groveling Serpent, is Craft; the exalted Serpent, the crucified Serpent, is Wisdome. All your worldly cares, all your crafty bargaines, all your subtill matches, all your diggings into other mens estates, all your hedgings in of debts, all your planting of children in great allyances; all these diggings, and hedgings and plantings savour of the earth, and of the craft of that Serpent, that creeps upon the earth: But crucifie this craft of yours, bring all your worldly subtilty under the Crosse of Christ Jesus, husband your farmes so, as you may give a good account to him, presse your debts so, as you would be pressed by him, market and bargaine so, as that you would give all, to buy that field, in which his treasure, and his pearle is hid, and then you have changed the Serpent, from the Serpent of perdition creeping upon the earth, to the Serpent of salvation exalted in the wildernesse. Creeping wisedome, that still looks downward, is but craft; Crucified wisedome, that looks upward, is truly wisedome. Between you and that ground Serpent God hath kindled a war; and the nearer you come to a peace with him, the farther ye go from God, and the more ye exasperate the

---

[1] On the text: 'And dust shalt thou eat all the days of thy life' (Gen. iii. 14).

The reversion of the living of St. Dunstan's-in-the-West was given to Donne soon after he took orders by Richard, third Earl of Dorset. He succeeded on the death of the incumbent on 1 March 1624. He appointed a curate, Matthew Griffiths, to do the ordinary clerical duties, and installed him in the vicarage; but he took pains to preach fairly regularly himself. Among his parishioners was Izaak Walton, who had a linen-draper's shop in Fleet Street, west of Chancery Lane.

Professor Baird Whitlock found an entry in the St. Dunstan's records for 29 June 1624: 'paid to Mr. Deane for a sermon for Mr. Adams xs'. The 29th of June was the day (year unknown) of the funeral of the Mr. Adams who had left money for these commemorative sermons. Donne preached the Adams sermon again in 1626, 1627, and 1628. Evelyn Simpson accepted Professor Whitlock's suggestion that this was the first of these sermons.

Lord of Hosts, and you whet his sword against your own souls. A truce with that Serpent, is too near a peace; to condition with your conscience for a time, that you may continue in such a sin, till you have paid for such a purchase, married such a daughter, bought such an annuity, undermined and eaten out such an unthrift, this truce, (though you mean to end it before you die) is too near a peace with that Serpent, between whom and you, God hath kindled an everlasting war. A cessation of Arms, that is, not to watch all his attempts and tentations, not to examine all your particular actions, A Treaty of Peace, that is, to dispute and debate in the behalf and favour of a sin, to palliate, to disguise, to extenuate that sin, this is too near a peace with this Serpent, this creeping Serpent. But in the other Serpent, the crucified Serpent, God hath reconciled to himself, all things in heaven, and earth, and hell. You have peace in the assistance of the Angels of heaven, Peace in the contribution of the powerfull prayers, and of the holy examples of the Saints upon earth, peace in the victory and triumph over the power of hell, peace from sins towards men, peace of affections in your selves, peace of conscience towards God. From your childhood you have been called upon to hold your peace; To be content is to hold your peace; murmure not at God, in any corrections of his, and you doe hold this peace. That creeping Serpent, Satan, is war, and should be so; The crucified Serpent Christ Jesus is peace, and shall be so for ever. The creeping Serpent eats our dust, the strength of our bodies in sicknesses, and our glory in the dust of the grave: The crucified Serpent hath taken our flesh, and our blood, and given us his flesh, and his blood for it; And therefore, as *David*, when he was thought base, for his holy freedome in dancing before the Ark, said he would be more base; so, since we are all made of *red earth*, let him that is red, be more red; Let him that is red with the blood of his own soul, be red again in blushing for that rednesse, and more red in the Communion of the blood of Christ Jesus; whom we shall eat all the days of our life, and be mystically, and mysteriously, and spiritually, and Sacramentally united to him in this life, and gloriously in the next.

## 27. From a Sermon Preached upon the Penitentiall Psalmes.[1] [?1624-5]

### (i)

EASINES of conversation in a woman, seemes no great harme; Adorning themselves to please those with whom they converse, is not much more; To heare them, whom they are thus willing to please, praise them, and magnifie their perfections, is little more than that; To allow them to sue, and solicit for the possession of that which they have so much praised, is not much more neither; Nor will it seeme much at last, to give them possession of that they sue for; nay it will seeme a kinde of injustice to deny it them. We hide lesser sinnes with greater, greater with lesser; Nay we hide the devill with God, wee hide all the weeks sins with a Sabbaths solemnity: And as in the Romane Church, they poysoned God, (when they had made their Bread-god, they poysoned the Emperour with that bread) so this is a Possessing of God, a making the devill to enter into God, when we hide our sins with an outward sanctity, and call God to witnesse and testifie to the Congregation, that we are saints, when we are devils; for this is a suborning of God, and a drawing of God himselfe into a perjury. We hide our sinnes in his house, by hypocrisie, all our lives, and we hide them at our deaths, perchance with an Hospitall. And truely wee had need doe so, when we have impoverished God, in his children, by our extorsions, and wounded him, and lam'd him, in them, by our oppressions, wee had need provide God an Hospitall. As men that rob houses thrust in a child at the window, and he opens greater doores for them, so lesser sins make way for greater. *De minimis non curat Lex*, The law is faine to passe over small faults; but *De minimis curat lux*, That light of grace, by which a sinner disposes himselfe to confession, must discover every sinne, and hide none, suffer none to hide it selfe, nor lie hidden under others. When God

---

[1] On the text: 'I acknowledged my sin unto thee, and mine iniquity have I not hid. I said, I will confess my transgressions unto the Lord, and thou forgavest the iniquity of my sin' (Ps. xxxii. 5).

*LXXX Sermons* includes (Nos. 56–63) an undated series of eight sermons on the penitential psalms which seems likely to have been a course of sermons. Evelyn Simpson suggests that the most likely time for such a course would be Advent and Lent 1624 and 1625.

speaks so much of *Behemoth*, and *Leviathan*, the great land and sea-oppressors, he calls us to the consideration of the insupportable-nesse of great sinnes; but in the plaines of Egypt by *haile*, and *locusts*, and *lice*, little and contemptible things, hee calls us to the consideration of these vermine of the soule, lesser and unconsidered sins.

(ii)

I consider often that passionate humiliation of S. *Peter*, *Exi a me Domine*, *He fell at Jesus knees, saying, Depart from me, for I am a sinfull man, O Lord*; And I am often ready to say so, and more; Depart from me, O Lord, for I am sinfull inough to infect thee; As I may perse-cute thee in thy Children, so I may infect thee in thine Ordinances; Depart, in withdrawing thy word from me, for I am corrupt inough to make even thy saving Gospel, the savor of death unto death; Depart, in withholding thy Sacrament, for I am leprous inough to taint thy flesh, and to make the balme of thy blood, poyson to my soule; Depart, in withdrawing the protection of thine Angels from me, for I am vicious inough to imprint corruption and rebellion into their nature. And if I be too foule for God himselfe to come neare me, for his Ordinances to worke upon me, I am no companion for my selfe, I must not be alone with my selfe; for I am as apt to take, as to give infection; I am a reciprocall plague; passively and actively contagious; I breath corruption, and breath it upon my selfe; and I am the Babylon that I must goe out of, or I perish.

(iii)

Here enters the fulnesse of his mercy, at one leafe of this doore; well expressed at our doore, in that *Ecce sto, & pulso*, Behold, I stand at the doore and knock; for, first he comes; here is no mention of our calling of him before; He comes of himselfe; And then he suffers not us to be ignorant of his comming, he comes so, as that he mani-fests himself, *Ecce*, Behold; And then he expects not that we should wake with that light, and look out of our selves, but he knocks, solicits us, at least, with some noyse at our doores, some calamities upon our neighbours; And againe he appeares not, like a lightning that passes away as soon as it is seene, that no man can reade by it,

nor work by it, nor light a candle, nor kindle a coale by it, but he
stands at the doore, and expects us, all day; not only with a patience,
but with a hunger to effect his purpose upon us; he would come in,
and sup with us, accept our diet, our poore endeavours; And then,
would have us sup with him, (as it is there added) would feast us
with his abundant Graces, which he brings even home to our
doores; But those he does not give us at the doore; not till we have
let him in, by the good use of his former grace; And as he offers
this fulnesse of his mercy, by these meanes before, so by way of Pardon, and Remission, if we have been defective in opening the doore
upon his standing and knocking, this fulnesse is fully expressed
in this word of this Text, as our two Translations, (neither departing from the naturall signification of the word) have rendred it.


## 28. From a Sermon Preached upon the Penitentiall Psalmes. [? 1624-5[1]]

### (i)

As in the former Circumstance, we noted that it was the *They*, that
aggravated it, it was not an *An, an Adulterer, an Ambitious man*, but
a *The, The wicked*, whom God enwrapped in this irrecoverable, this
undeterminable sorrow: so here, it is not a *This*, or *That*, This
wicked, or that wicked man, but *The wicked*, every wicked man is
surrounded with this sorrow. He can propose no comfort in a
decimation, as in popular Rebellions, where nine may be spared,
and the tenth man hanged; No, nor so much hope as to have nine
hanged, and the tenth spared; He is not in Sodoms case, That a few
righteous might have saved the wicked; But he feeles a necessity
of applying to himselfe, that, *If Noah, Daniel, and Job were in the
midst of them, as I live, saith the Lord God, they should deliver neither Son,
nor Daughter. Jussisti Domine, & sic est, ut pæna sit sibi omnis inordinatus
animus*; It is thy pleasure O God, and thy pleasure shall be infallibly

[1] On the text: 'Many sorrows shall be to the wicked; but he that trusteth in the Lord,
Mercy shall compass him about.
'Be glad in the Lord, and rejoice ye righteous; and shout for joy all ye that are upright
in heart' (Ps. xxxii. 10, 11).

accomplished, that every wicked person should be his owne Executioner. He is *Spontaneus Dæmon*, as S. *Chrysostome* speaks, an In-mate,
an in-nate Devill; a bosome devill, a selfe-Devill; That as he could
be a tempter to himselfe, though there were no Devill, so he could
be an Executioner to himselfe, though there were no Satan, and a
Hell to himselfe, though there were no other Torment. Sometimes
he staies not the Assises, but prevents the hand of Justice; he
destroies himselfe before his time. But when he staies, he is evermore condemned at the Assises. Let him sleepe out as much of the
morning as securely as he can; embellish, and adorne himselfe as
gloriously as he can; dine as largely and as delicately as he can;
weare out as much of the afternoone, in conversation, in Comedies,
in pleasure, as hee can; sup with as much distension, and inducement
of drousinesse as he can, that he may scape all remorse, by falling
asleepe quickly, and fall asleepe with as much discourse, and
musicke, and advantage as he can, he hath a conscience that will
survive, and overwatch all the company; he hath a sorrow that
shall joyne issue with him when he is alone, and both God, and the
devill, who doe not meet willingly, shall meet in his case, and be
in league, and be on the sorrowes side, against him. The anger of
God, and the malice of the devill, shall concurre with his sorrow,
to his farther vexation. No one wicked person, by any diversion or
cunning, shall avoid this sorrow, for it is in the midst, and in the
end of all his forced contentments; *Even in laughing, the heart is
sorrowfull, and the end of that mirth is heavinesse.*

## (ii)

This is the roote of our three Branches, the foundation of our
three Stories; the bagge of our three summes, in this portion, *Mercy,
Compassing mercy*; and then the Branches themselves, the roomes,
the summes are but these three words, expressing and exalting one
affection, *Be glad, Rejoyce*, and *Shout for joy*; Which joy, is first an
inward love of the Law of God, *Thy testimonies have I taken as an
heritage for ever, for they are the joy of my heart*: It is not *Dant*, but
*Sunt*, not that they Bring joy, but that they Are joy; There is no
other joy but the delight in the Law of the Lord: For all other joy,
the Wise King said, *Of laughter, thou art mad, and of joy, what is this*

*that thou dost?* True joy is the earnest which we have of heaven, It is the treasure of the soule, and therefore should be laid in a safe place, and nothing in this world is safe to place it in: And therefore with the Spouse we say, *We will be glad in thee, we will remember thy love more than wine.* Let others seek their joy in wine, in society, in conversation, in musique; for mee, *Thou hast put gladnesse into my heart, more than in the time that their corne and their wine increased.*

*Rejoyce therefore in the Lord alwayes, and againe I say, rejoyce:* Againe, that is, Rejoyce in the second manner of expressing it, by externall declarations. Goe chearfully, and joyfully forward, in the works of your callings. Rejoyce in the blessings of God without murmuring, or comparing with others. And establish thy joy so, in an honest, and religious manner of getting, that thy joy may descend to thine heire, as well as thy land. No land is so well fenced, no house so well furnished, as that, which hath this joy, this testimony of being well gotten. For, *This thou knowest of old, since man was placed upon earth, that the Triumphing of the wicked is short, and the joy of the Hypocrite but for a moment.*

And then the last degree is louder than this, *Jubilate, Shout for joy;* Declare thy joy in the eares of other men. As the Angels said to the Shepheards, *I bring you tidings of great joy, which shall be unto all people,* So be thou a chearfull occasion of glorifying God by thy joy. *Declare his loving kindnesse unto the sons of men;* Tell them what he hath done for thy soule, thy body, thy state. Say, *With this staffe came I over Jordane:* Be content to tell whose Son thou wast, and how small thy beginning. Smother not Gods blessings, by making thy selfe poore, when he who is truly poore, begges of thee, for that Gods sake, who gave thee all that thou hast. Hold up a holy chearfulnesse in thy heart; Goe on in a chearfull conversation; and let the world see, that all this growes out of a peace, betwixt God and thee, testified in the blessings of this world; and then thou art that Person, and then thou hast that Portion, which growes out of this root, in this Text, *Mercy shall compasse him about that trusteth in the Lord.*

## 29. From a Sermon Preached at Pauls, upon Christmas Day, in the Evening. 1624[1]

### (i)

WE begin with that which is elder than our beginning, and shall over-live our end, The mercy of God. *I will sing of thy mercy and judgement*, sayes *David*; when we fixe our selves upon the meditation and modulation of the mercy of God, even his judgements cannot put us out of tune, but we shall sing, and be chearefull, even in them. As God made grasse for beasts, before he made beasts, and beasts for man, before he made man: As in that first generation, the Creation, so in the regeneration, our re-creating, he begins with that which was necessary for that which followes, Mercy before Judgement. Nay, to say that mercy was first, is but to post-date mercy; to preferre mercy but so, is to diminish mercy; The names of first or last derogate from it, for first and last are but ragges of time, and his mercy hath no relation to time, no limitation in time, it is not first, nor last, but eternall, everlasting; Let the Devill make me so far desperate as to conceive a time when there was no mercy, and he hath made me so far an Atheist, as to conceive a time when there was no God; if I despoile him of his mercy, any one minute, and say, now God hath no mercy, for that minute I discontinue his very Godhead, and his beeing. Later Grammarians have wrung the name of mercy out of misery; *Misericordia præsumit miseriam*, say these, there could be no subsequent mercy, if there were no precedent misery; But the true roote of the word mercy, through all the Prophets, is *Racham*, and *Racham* is *diligere*, to love; as long as there hath been love (and *God is love*) there hath been mercy: And mercy considered externally, and in the practise and in the effect, began not at the helping of man, when man was fallen and become miserable, but at the making of man, when man was nothing. So then, here we consider not mercy as it is radically in God, and an essentiall attribute of his, but productively in us, as it is an action, a working upon us, and that more especially, as God takes all

[1] On the text: 'Therefore the Lord shall give you a sign; Behold, a virgin shall conceive, and bear a son, and shall call his name Immanuel' (Isa. vii. 14): part of the first lesson, that evening.

occasions to exercise that action, and to shed that mercy upon us: for particular mercies are feathers of his wings, and that prayer, *Lord let thy mercy lighten upon us, as our trust is in thee,* is our birdlime; particular mercies are that cloud of Quailes which hovered over the host of Israel, and that prayer, *Lord let thy mercy lighten upon us,* is our net to catch, our Gomer to fill of those Quailes. The aire is not so full of Moats, of Atomes, as the Church is of Mercies; and as we can suck in no part of aire, but we take in those Moats, those Atomes; so here in the Congregation we cannot suck in a word from the preacher, we cannot speak, we cannot sigh a prayer to God, but that that whole breath and aire is made of mercy. But we call not upon you from this Text, to consider Gods ordinary mercy, that which he exhibites to all in the ministery of his Church; nor his miraculous mercy, his extraordinary deliverances of States and Churches; but we call upon particular Consciences, by occasion of this Text, to call to minde Gods occasionall mercies to them; such mercies as a regenerate man will call mercies, though a naturall man would call them accidents, or occurrences, or contingencies; A man wakes at midnight full of unclean thoughts, and he heares a passing Bell; this is an occasionall mercy, if he call that his own knell, and consider how unfit he was to be called out of the world then, how unready to receive that voice, *Foole, this night they shall fetch away thy soule.* The adulterer, whose eye waites for the twy-light, goes forth, and casts his eyes upon forbidden houses, and would enter, and sees a *Lord have mercy upon us* upon the doore; this is an occasionall mercy, if this bring him to know that they who lie sick of the plague within, passe through a furnace, but by Gods grace, to heaven; and hee without, carries his own furnace to hell, his lustfull loines to everlasting perdition. What an occasionall mercy had *Balaam,* when his Asse Catechized him? What an occasionall mercy had one Theefe, when the other catechized him so, *Art thou not afraid being under the same condemnation?* What an occasionall mercy had all they that saw that, when the Devil himself fought for the name of Jesus, and wounded the sons of *Sceva* for exorcising in the name of Jesus, with that indignation, with that increpation, *Jesus we know, and Paul we know, but who are ye?* If I should declare what God hath done (done occasionally) for my soule,

where he instructed me for feare of falling, where he raised me
when I was fallen, perchance you would rather fixe your thoughts
upon my illnesse, and wonder at that, than at Gods goodnesse,
and glorifie him in that; rather wonder at my sins, than at his
mercies, rather consider how ill a man I was, than how good a God
he is. If I should inquire upon what occasion God elected me, and
writ my name in the book of Life, I should sooner be afraid that it
were not so, than finde a reason why it should be so. God made
Sun and Moon to distinguish seasons, and day, and night, and we
cannot have the fruits of the earth but in their seasons: But God
hath made no decree to distinguish the seasons of his mercies; In
paradise, the fruits were ripe, the first minute, and in heaven it is
alwaies Autumne, his mercies are ever in their maturity. We ask
*panem quotidianum*, our daily bread, and God never sayes you should
have come yesterday, he never sayes you must againe to morrow,
but *to day if you will heare his voice*, to day he will heare you. If some
King of the earth have so large an extent of Dominion, in North,
and South, as that he hath Winter and Summer together in his
Dominions, so large an extent East and West, as that he hath day
and night together in his Dominions, much more hath God mercy
and judgement together: He brought light out of darknesse, not
out of a lesser light; he can bring thy Summer out of Winter, though
thou have no Spring; though in the wayes of fortune, or understanding, or conscience, thou have been benighted till now,
wintred and frozen, clouded and eclypsed, damped and benummed,
smothered and stupified till now, now God comes to thee, not as in
the dawning of the day, not as in the bud of the spring, but as the
Sun at noon to illustrate all shadowes, as the sheaves in harvest, to
fill all penuries, all occasions invite his mercies, and all times are his
seasons.

(ii)

One of the most convenient Hieroglyphicks of God, is a Circle;
and a Circle is endlesse; whom God loves, hee loves to the end: and
not onely to their own end, to their death, but to his end, and his end
is, that he might love them still. His hailestones, and his thunder-
bolts, and his showres of bloud (emblemes and instruments of

his Judgements) fall downe in a direct line, and affect and strike some one person, or place: His Sun, and Moone, and Starres, (Emblemes and Instruments of his Blessings) move circularly, and communicate themselves to all. His Church is his chariot; in that, he moves more gloriously, than in the Sun; as much more, as his begotten Son exceeds his created Sun, and his Son of glory, and of his right hand, the Sun of the firmament; and this Church, his chariot, moves in that communicable motion, circularly; It began in the East, it came to us, and is passing now, shining out now, in the farthest West. As the Sun does not set to any Nation, but withdraw it selfe, and returne againe; God, in the exercise of his mercy, does not set to thy soule, though he benight it with an affliction. Remember that our Saviour Christ himselfe, in many actions and passions of our humane nature, and infirmities, smother-ed that Divinity, and suffered it not to worke, but yet it was alwayes in him, and wrought most powerfully in the deepest danger; when he was absolutely dead, it raised him again: If Christ slumbred the God-head in himselfe, The mercy of God may be slumbred, it may be hidden from his servants, but it cannot be taken away, and in the greatest necessities, it shall break out. The Blessed Virgin was overshadowed, but it was with the Holy Ghost that overshadowed her: Thine understanding, thy conscience may be so too, and yet it may be the work of the Holy Ghost, who moves in thy darknesse, and will bring light even out of that, knowledge out of thine ignor-ance, clearnesse out of thy scruples, and consolation out of thy Dejection of Spirit. *God is thy portion*, sayes *David*; *David* does not speak so narrowly, so penuriously, as to say, God hath given thee thy portion, and thou must look for no more; but, *God is thy portion*, and as long as he is God, he hath more to give, and as long as thou art his, thou hast more to receive. Thou canst not have so good a Title, to a subsequent blessing, as a former blessing; where thou art an ancient tenant, thou wilt look to be preferred before a stranger; and that is thy title to Gods future mercies, if thou have been formerly accustomed to them. The Sun is not weary with sixe thousand yeares shining; God cannot be weary of doing good; And therefore never say, God hath given me these and these temporall things, and I have scattered them wastfully, surely he will give me no more; These and these spirituall graces, and I have neglected them, abused them, surely he will give me no more; For, for things created, we have instruments to measure them; we know the compasse of a Meridian, and the depth of a Diameter of the Earth, and we know this, even of the uppermost spheare in the heavens: But when we come to the Throne of God himselfe, the Orbe of the Saints, and Angels that see his face, and the vertues, and powers that flow from thence, we have no balance to weigh them, no instruments to measure them, no hearts to conceive them: So, for temporall things, we know the most that man can have; for we know all the world; but for Gods mercy, and his spirituall graces, as that language in which God spake, the Hebrew, hath no superlative, so, that which he promises, in all that he hath spoken, his mercy hath no superlative; he shewes no mercy, which you can call his Greatest Mercy, his Mercy is never at the highest; whatsoever he hath done for thy soule, or for any other, in applying himselfe to it, he can exceed that. Onely he can raise a Tower, whose top shall reach to heaven: The Basis of the highest building is but the Earth; But though thou be but a Tabernacle of Earth, God shall raise thee peece by peece, into a spirituall building; And after one Story of Creation, and another of Vocation, and another of Sanctification, he shall bring thee up, to meet thy selfe, in the bosome of thy God, where thou wast at first, in an eternall election: God is a circle himselfe, and he will make thee one; Goe not thou about to square eyther circle, to bring that which is equall in it selfe, to Angles, and Corners, into dark and sad suspicions of God, or of thy selfe, that God can give, or that thou canst receive no more Mercy, than thou hast had already.

### (iii)

God does not furnish a roome, and leave it darke; he sets up lights in it; his first care was, that his benefits should be seene; he made light first, and then creatures, to be seene by that light: He sheds himselfe from my mouth, upon the whole auditory here; he powres himselfe from my hand, to all the Communicants at the table; I can say to you all here, *The grace of our Lord Jesus Christ be with you, and remaine with you all*; I can say to them all there, *The Body of our Lord Jesus Christ which was given for you, preserve you to ever-lasting life*: I can bring it so neare; but onely the worthy hearer, and the worthy receiver, can call this Lord, this Jesus, this Christ, *Immanuel, God with us*; onely that Virgin soule, devirginated in the blood of *Adam*, but restored in the blood of the Lambe, hath this *Ecce*, this testimony, this assurance, that God is with him; they that have this *Ecce*, this testimony, in a rectified conscience, are Godfathers to this child Jesus, and may call him *Immanuel, God with us*; for, as no man can deceive God, so God can deceive no man; God cannot live in the darke himselfe, neither can he leave those, who are his, in the darke: If he be with thee, he will make thee see, that he is with thee; and never goe out of thy sight, till he have brought thee, where thou canst never goe out of his.

## 30. From a Sermon Preached at S. Pauls, The Sunday after the Conversion of S. Paul. 1625[1]

CHRIST, who in his humane nature hath received from the Father all Judgement, and power, and dominion over this world, hath received all this, upon that condition that he shall governe in this manner, *Aske of me, and I shall give thee the Heathen for thine inheritance*, sayes the Father; How is he to use them, when he hath them? Thus, *Thou shalt breake them with a rod of iron, and dash them in pieces like a potters vessell*. Now, God meant well to the Nations, in this bruising and breaking of them; God intended not an annihilation of the Nations, but a reformation; for Christ askes the Nations for an Inheritance, not for a triumph; therefore it is intended of his way of governing them; and his way is to bruise and beat them; that is, first to cast them downe, before he can raise them up, first to breake them before he can make them in his fashion. *Novit Dominus vul-nerare ad amorem*; The Lord, and onely the Lord knowes how to wound us, out of love; more than that, how to wound us into love; more than all that, to wound us into love, not onely with him that wounds us, but into love with the wound it selfe, with the very

---

[1] On the text: 'And he fell to the earth, and heard a voice, saying, Saul, Saul, why persecutest thou me?' (Acts ix. 4).

affliction that he inflicts upon us; The Lord knowes how to strike us so, as that we shall lay hold upon that hand that strikes us, and kisse that hand that wounds us. *Ad vitam interficit, ad exaltationem prosternit*, sayes the same Father; No man kills his enemy therefore, that his enemy might have a better life in heaven; that is not his end in killing him: It is Gods end; Therefore he brings us to death, that by that gate he might lead us into life everlasting; And he hath not discovered, but made that Northerne passage, to passe by the frozen Sea of calamity, and tribulation, to Paradise, to the heavenly Jerusalem. There are fruits that ripen not, but by frost; There are natures, (there are scarce any other) that dispose not themselves to God, but by affliction. And as Nature lookes for the season for ripening, and does not all before, so Grace lookes for the assent of the soule, and does not perfect the whole worke, till that come. It is Nature that brings the season, and it is Grace that brings the assent; but till the season for the fruit, till the assent of the soule come, all is not done.

Therefore God begun in this way with *Saul*, and in this way he led him all his life. *Tot pertulit mortes, quot vixit dies*, He dyed as many deaths, as he lived dayes; for so himselfe sayes, *Quotidie morior, I die daily*; God gave him sucke in blood, and his owne blood was his daily drink; He catechized him with calamities at first, and calamities were his daily Sermons, and meditations after; and to author-ize the hands of others upon him, and to accustome him to submit himself to the hands of others without murmuring, Christ himself strikes the first blow, and with that, *Cecidit, he fell*, (which was our first consideration, in his humiliation) and then, *Cecidit in terram, He fell to the ground*, which is our next.

I take no farther occasion from this Circumstance, but to arme you with consolation, how low soever God be pleased to cast you, Though it be to the earth, yet he does not so much cast you downe, in doing that, as bring you home. Death is not a banishing of you out of this world; but it is a visitation of your kindred that lie in the earth; neither are any nearer of kin to you, than the earth it selfe, and the wormes of the earth. You heap earth upon your soules, and encumber them with more and more flesh, by a super-fluous and luxuriant diet; You adde earth to earth in new purchases,

and measure not by Acres, but by Manors, nor by Manors, but by
Shires; And there is a little Quillet, a little Close, worth all these,
A quiet Grave. And therefore, when thou readest, That God makes
thy bed in thy sicknesse, rejoyce in this, not onely that he makes
that bed, where thou dost lie, but that bed where thou shalt lie;
That that God, that made the whole earth, is now making thy bed
in the earth, a quiet grave, where thou shalt sleep in peace, till the
Angels Trumpet wake thee at the Resurrection, to that Judgement
where thy peace shall be made before thou commest, and writ, and
sealed, in the blood of the Lamb.

## 31. From a Sermon Preached at White-hall, March 4. 1625[1]

THAT which God commanded by his Word, to be done at some
times (that we should humble our soules by fasting) the same God
commands by his Church, to be done now: In the Scriptures you
have *Præceptum*, The thing it self, What; In the Church, you have
the *Nunc*, The time, When. The Scriptures are Gods Voyce; The
Church is his Eccho; a redoubling, a repeating of some particular
syllables, and accents of the same voice. And as we harken with
some earnestnesse, and some admiration at an Eccho, when perchance we doe not understand the voice that occasioned that
Eccho; so doe the obedient children of God apply themselves to the
Eccho of his Church, when perchance otherwise, they would lesse
understand the voice of God, in his Scriptures, if that voice were
not so redoubled unto them. This fasting then, thus enjoyned by
God, for the generall, in his Word, and thus limited to this Time,
for the particular, in his Church, is indeed but a continuation of a
great Feast: Where, the first course (that which we begin to serve
in now) is Manna, food of Angels, plentifull, frequent preaching;
but the second course, is the very body and blood of Christ Jesus,
shed for us, and given to us, in that blessed Sacrament, of which

---

[1] On the text: 'And He said unto him, Why callest thou me good? There is none good but
one; that is, God' (Matt. xix. 17).

4 March 1625 was the first Friday in Lent, Donne's usual day for preaching at Whitehall.

himselfe makes us worthy receivers at that time. Now, as the end of all bodily eating, is Assimilation, that after all other concoctions, that meat may be made *Idem corpus*, the same body that I am; so the end of all spirituall eating, is Assimilation too, That after all Hearing, and all Receiving, I may be made *Idem spiritus cum Domino*, the same spirit, that my God is: for, though it be good to Heare, good to Receive, good to Meditate, yet, (if we speake effectually, and consummatively) why call we these good? there is nothing good but One, that is, Assimilation to God.

## 32. From the First Sermon Preached to King Charles, at Saint James, 3° April. 1625[1]

So then, in the *Text*, we have a *Rule* implyed, *Something is left to the righteous to doe, though some Foundations bee destroyed*; for the words are words of *Consultation*, and *consultation* with *God*; when Man can afford no Counsayle, *God* can, and will direct those that are his, the righteous, what to doe. The words give us the *Rule*, and *Christ* gives us the *Example* in himselfe. First, hee continues his *Innocencie*, and *avowes* that; the destroying of *Foundations*, does not destroy his *Foundation*, *Innocence*: still hee is able to confound his adversaries, with that, *Which of you can convince mee of sinne?* And then, hee *prayes* for the remooving of the persecution, *Transeat Calix*, let this Cup passe. When that might not bee, hee *prayes* even for them, who inflicted this persecution, *Pater ignosce*, Father forgive them; And when all is done, hee *suffers* all that can bee done unto him: And hee calls his whole Passion, *Horam suam*, it spent *nights* and *dayes*; his whole life was a continuall Passion; yet how long soever, he calls it but an *Houre*, and how much soever it were *their* act, the act of their malignitie that did it, yet hee calls it *his*, because it was the act of his owne *Predestination* as *God*, upon himselfe as *Man*; And hee calls it by a more acceptable Name than that, hee calles his Passion

---

1 On the text: 'If the foundations be destroyed, what can the righteous do?' (Ps. xi. 3.)

Donne was commanded to preach the first sermon at Court of the new reign at a day's notice. The King listened attentively and devoutly and ordered the sermon to be published. Donne began his sermon by reminding his congregation that this was a Psalm used in the office of Martyrs and with a long disquisition on martyrdom.

*Calicem suum*, his Cup, because hee brought not onely a patience to it, but a delight and a joy in it; for, *for the joy that was set before him, hee endured the Crosse*. All this then the righteous can doe, though *Foundations bee destroyed*; Hee can *withdrawe* himselfe, if the duties of his place make not his residence necessarie; If it doe, hee can *pray*; and then hee can *suffer*; and then hee can *rejoyce* in his sufferings; and hee can make that *protestation, Our God is able to deliver us, and hee will deliver us; but if not, wee will serve no other Gods*. For, the righteous hath evermore this refuge, this assurance, that though some *Foundations* bee destroyed, all cannot bee: for first, *The foundation of God stands sure, and hee knowes who are his*; Hee is safe in *God*; and then he is safe in his owne *Conscience*, for, *The Righteous is an everlasting foundation*; not onely that he *hath* one, but *is* one; and not a temporary, but an everlasting *Foundation*: So that *foundations* can never bee so destroyed, but that hee is safe in *God*, and safe in *himselfe*.

For such things then, as concerne the *foundation* of the first *House*, the *Church*, Bee not apt to call *Super-Edifications, Foundations*; Collaterall Divinitie, Fundamentall Divinitie; Problematicall, Disputable, Controvertible poynts, poynts Essentiall, and Articles of Faith. Call not *Super-Edifications, Foundations*, nor call not the *furniture* of the *House, Foundations*; Call not *Ceremoniall*, and *Rituall* things, *Essentiall* parts of Religion, and of the worship of *God*, otherwise than as they imply *Disobedience*; for *Obedience* to lawfull Authoritie, is alwayes an *Essentiall* part of Religion. Doe not *Anti-date* Miserie; doe not *Prophesie* Ruine; doe not *Concurre* with Mischiefe, nor *Contribute* to Mischiefe so farre, as to *over-feare* it before, nor to misinterprete their *wayes*, whose *Ends* you cannot knowe; And doe not call the cracking of a pane of glasse, a *Destroying of foundations*. But every man doing the particular duties of his distinct Calling, for the preservation of *Foundations, Praying*, and *Preaching*, and *Doing*, and *Counsailing*, and *Contributing* too, *Foundations* beeing never destroyed, the Righteous shall doe still, as they have done, enjoy *God* manifested in *Christ*, and *Christ* applyed in the *Scriptures*, which is the *foundation* of the first *House*, the *Church*.

For things concerning the *Foundation* of the second *House*, the *Commonwealth*, which is the *Lawe*, Dispute not *Lawes*, but obey them when they are made; In those *Councells*, where *Lawes* are made, or reformed, dispute; but there also, without particular interest, without private affection, without personall relations. Call not every entrance of such a *Judge*, as thou thinkest insufficient, a *corrupt* entrance; nor every *Judgement*, which hee enters, and thou understandest not, or likest not, a *corrupt* Judgement. As in *Naturall* things, it is a weakenesse to thinke, that every thing that I knowe not how it is done, is done by *Witch-craft*, So is it also in *Civill* things, if I know not why it is done, to thinke it is done for *Money*. Let the *Law* bee sacred to thee, and the Dispensers of the *Law*, reverend; Keepe the *Lawe*, and the *Lawe* shall keepe thee; And so *Foundations* being never destroyed, the Righteous shall doe still, as they have done, enjoy their Possessions, and Honours, and themselves, by the overshadowing of the *Lawe*, which is the *Foundation* of the second *House*, the *State*.

For those things which concerne the *Foundations* of the third *House*, the *Family*, Call not light faults by heavie Names; Call not all sociablenesse, and Conversation, Disloyaltie in thy Wife; Nor all levitie, or pleasurablenesse, Incorrigiblenesse in thy Sonne; nor all negligence, or forgetfulnesse, Perfidiousnesse in thy Servant; Nor let every light disorder within doores, shut thee out of doores, or make thee a stranger in thine owne House. In a smoakie roome, it may bee enough to open a Windowe, without leaving the place; In Domestique unkindnesses, and discontents, it may bee wholesomer to give them a Concoction at home in a discreete patience, or to give them a vent at home, in a moderate rebuke, than to thinke to ease them, or put them off, with false divertions abroad. As *States* subsist in part, by keeping their weakenesses from being knowen, so is it the quiet of *Families*, to have their *Chauncerie*, and their *Parliament* within doores, and to compose and determine all emergent differences there: for so also, *Foundations* beeing kept undestroyed, the righteous shall doe, as they should doe, enjoy a *Religious* Unitie, and a *Civill* Unitie, the same Soule towards *God*, the same heart towards one another, in a holy, and in a happy *Peace*, and *Peace* is the *foundation* of this third *House*, The *Family*.

Lastly, for those things which concerne the *Foundations* of the fourth *House*, *Our selves*, Mis-interprete not *Gods* former Corrections upon thee, how long, how sharpe soever: Call not his Phisicke, poyson, nor his Fish, Scorpions, nor his Bread, Stone: Accuse not *God*, for that hee hath done, nor suspect not *God*, for that hee may doe, as though *God* had made thee, onely because hee lacked a man, to damne. In all scruples of *Conscience*, say with Saint *Peter*, *Domine quo vadam*, Lord, *whither shall I goe*, *Thou hast the Word of eternall life*, And *God* will not leave thee in the darke: In all oppression from potent Adversaries, say with *David*, *Tibi soli peccavi: Against thee*, *O Lord, onely have I sinned*, And *God* will not make the malice of another man his Executioner upon thee. Crie to him; and if hee have not heard thee, crie lowder, and crie oftner; The first way that *God* admitted thee to him was by Water, the water of *Baptisme*; Goe still the same way to him, by Water, by repentant *Teares*: And remember still, that when *Ezechias* wept, *Vidit lachrymam*, God saw *his Teare*, His Teare in the *Singular: God* sawe his first teare, every severall teare: If thou thinke *God* have not done so by thee, Continue thy teares, till thou finde hee doe. The first way that *Christ* came to thee, was in *Blood*; when hee submitted himselfe to the *Lawe*, in *Circumcision*; And the last thing that hee bequeathed to thee, was his *Blood*, in the Institution of the Blessed *Sacrament*; Refuse not to goe to him, the same way too, if his glorie require that *Sacrifice*. If thou pray, and hast an apprehension that thou hearest *God* say, hee will not heare thy prayers, doe not beleeve that it is hee that speakes; If thou canst not chuse but beleeve that it is hee, let mee say, in a pious sense, doe not beleeve him: *God* would not bee beleeved, in denouncing of Judgements, so absolutely, so peremptorily, as to bee thought to speake unconditionally, illimitedly: *God* tooke it well at *Davids* hands, that when the *Prophet* had tolde him, *The childe shall surely die*, yet hee beleeved not the *Prophet* so peremptorily, but that hee proceeded in Prayer to *God*, for the life of the childe. Say with *David*, *Thou hast beene a strong Tower to mee; I will abide in thy Tabernacle*, *Et non Emigrabo*, I will never goe out, I know thou hast a *Church*, I know I am in it, and I will never depart from it; and so *Foundations* beeing never destroyed, the righteous shall doe, as the righteous have alwayes done, enjoy the *Evidence*, and the *Verdict*, and the *Judgement*, and the *Possession* of a good *Conscience*, which is the *Foundation* of this fourth *House*. First, governe this first *House*, *Thy selfe*, well; and as *Christ* sayde, hee shall say againe, *Thou hast*

*beene faithfull in a little, take more*; Hee shall enlarge thee in the next
House, Thy *Family*, and the next, The *State*, and the other, The
*Church*, till hee say to thee, as hee did to *Jerusalem*, after all his other
Blessings, *Et prosperata es in Regnum, Now I have brought thee up to a
Kingdome*, A Kingdome, where not onely no *Foundations* can bee
destroyed, but no stone shaked; and where the Righteous know
alwayes what to doe, to glorifie *God*, in that incessant Acclamation,
*Salvation to our God, who sits upon the Throne, and to the Lambe*; And to
this *Lambe of God*, who hath taken away the *sinnes* of the world, and
but changed the *Sunnes* of the world, who hath complicated two
wondrous workes in one, To make *our Sunne* to set at Noone, and to
make *our Sunne* to rise at Noone too, That hath given him *Glorie*,
and not taken away our *Peace*, That hath exalted him to Upper-
roomes, and not shaked any *Foundations* of ours, To this *Lambe of
God*, the glorious *Sonne of God*, and the most Almightie *Father*, and
the *Blessed Spirit* of Comfort, three Persons and one *God*, bee ascribed
by us, and the whole *Church*, the *Triumphant Church*, where the
*Father* of blessed *Memorie* raignes *with God*, and the *Militant Church*,
where the *Sonne* of blessed *Assurance* raignes *for God*, All Power,
Praise, Might, Majestie, Glory, and Dominion, now, and for ever.
*Amen.*

## 33. From a Sermon Preached at S. Pauls, in the Evening, upon Easter-day. 1625[1]

BUT it is, *Ne miremini hoc, Wonder not at this*; but yet, there are
things, which we may wonder at. *Nil admirari*, is but the Philosophers wisdome; He thinks it a weaknesse, to wonder at any thing,
That any thing should be strange to him: But Christian Philosophy
that is rooted in humility, tels us, in the mouth of *Clement* of
*Alexandria, Principium veritatis est res admirari*, The first step to faith,
is to wonder, to stand, and consider with a holy admiration, the

---

[1] On the text: 'Marvel not at this; for the houre is coming, in which, all that are in the
graves, shall hear his voice; and shall come forth, they that have done good, unto the resurrection of life; and they that have done evil, unto the resurrection of damnation' (John v.
28, 29).

waies and proceedings of God with man: for, Admiration, wonder, stands as in the midst, betweene knowledge and faith, and hath an eye towards both. If I know a thing, or beleeve a thing, I do no longer wonder: but when I finde that I have reason to stop upon the consideration of a thing, so, as that I see enough to induce admiration, to make me wonder, I come by that step, and God leads me by that hand, to a knowledge, if it be of a naturall or civill thing, or to a faith, if it be of a supernaturall, and spirituall thing.

And therefore be content to wonder at this, That God would have such a care to dignifie, and to crown, and to associate to his own everlasting presence, the body of man. God himself is a Spirit, and heaven is his place; my soul is a spirit, and so proportioned to that place; That God, or Angels, or our Soules, which are all Spirits, should be in heaven, *Ne miremini*, never wonder at that. But since we wonder, and justly, that some late Philosophers have removed the whole earth from the Center, and carried it up, and placed it in one of the Spheares of heaven, That this clod of earth, this body of ours should be carried up to the highest heaven, placed in the eye of God, set down at the right hand of God, *Miramini hoc*, wonder at this; That God, all Spirit, served with Spirits, associated to Spirits, should have such an affection, such a love to this body, this earthly body, this deserves this wonder. The Father was pleased to breathe into this body, at first, in the Creation; The Son was pleased to assume this body himself, after, in the Redemption; The Holy Ghost is pleased to consecrate this body, and make it his Temple, by his sanctification; In that *Faciamus hominem, Let us*, all us, *make man*, that consultation of the whole Trinity in making man, is exercised even upon this lower part of man, the dignifying of his body. So far, as that amongst the ancient Fathers, very many of them, are very various, and irresolved, which way to pronounce, and very many of them cleare in the negative, in that point, That the soule of man comes not to the presence of God, but remaines in some out-places till the Resurrection of the body: That observation, that consideration of the love of God, to the body of man, withdrew them into that error, That the soul it self should lack the glory of heaven, till the body were become capable of that glory too.

They therefore oppose God in his purpose of dignifying the body

of man, first, who violate, and mangle this body, which is the Organ
in which God breathes; And they also which pollute and defile this
body, in which Christ Jesus is apparelled; and they likewise who
prophane this body, which the Holy Ghost, as the high Priest,
inhabites, and consecrates.

Transgressors in the first kinde, that put Gods Organ out of
tune, that discompose, and teare the body of man with violence,
are those inhumane persecutors, who with racks, and tortures, and
prisons, and fires, and exquisite inquisitions, throw downe the
bodies of the true Gods true servants, to the Idolatrous worship of
their imaginary Gods; that torture men into hell, and carry them
through the inquisition into damnation. S. *Augustine* moves a
question, and institutes a disputation, and carries it somewhat
problematically, whether torture be to be admitted at all, or no.
That presents a faire probability, which he sayes against it: we
presume, sayes he, that an innocent man should be able to hold his
tongue in torture; That is no part of our purpose in torture, sayes
he, that hee that is innocent, should accuse himselfe, by confession,
in torture. And, if an innocent man be able to doe so, why should
we not thinke, that a guilty man, who shall save his life, by holding
his tongue in torture, should be able to doe so? And then, where is
the use of torture? *Res fragilis, & periculosa quæstio*, sayes that Lawyer,
who is esteemed the law, alone, *Ulpian*: It is a slippery triall, and
uncertaine, to convince by torture: For, many times, sayes S.
*Augustine* againe, *Innocens luit pro incerto scelere certissimas pœnas*; He
that is yet but questioned, whether he be guilty or no, before that
be knowne, is, without all question, miserably tortured. And
whereas, many times, the passion of the Judge, and the covetousnesse of the Judge, and the ambition of the Judge, are calamities
heavy enough, upon a man, that is accused, in this case of torture,
*Ignorantia Judicis est calamitas plerumque innocentis*, sayes that Father,
for the most part, even the ignorance of the Judge, is the greatest
calamity of him that is accused: If the Judge knew that he were
innocent, he should suffer nothing; If he knew he were guilty, he
should not suffer torture; but because the Judge is ignorant, and
knowes nothing, therefore the Prisoner must bee racked, and
tortured, and mangled, sayes that Father.

# 34. From a Sermon Preached at Denmark house, some few days before the body of King James, was removed from thence, to his buriall, Apr. 26. 1625[1]

HERE, at your coming hither now, you have *two glasses*, wherein you may see your selves from head to foot; One in the Text, your *Head, Christ Jesus*, represented unto you, in the name and person of *Solomon, Behold King Solomon crowned, &c.* And another, under your feet, in the dissolution of this great *Monarch*, our *Royall Master*, now layd lower by death than any of us, his Subjects and servants.

First then, behold your selves in that first glasse, *Behold King Solomon*; *Solomon* the sonne of *David*, but not the Son of *Bathsheba*, but of a better mother, the most blessed *Virgin Mary*. For, *Solomon*, in this text, is not a *proper* Name, but an *Appellative*; a significative word: *Solomon* is *pacificus*, the *Peacemaker*, and our peace is made in, and by Christ Jesus: and he is that *Solomon*, whom we are called upon to see here. Now, as Saint *Paul* says, that *he would know nothing but Christ*, (that's his first abridgement) and then he would know nothing of Christ, but *him crucifyed*, (and that's the re-abridgement) so we seek no other glasse, to see our selves in, but Christ, nor any other thing in this glasse, but his *Humiliation*. What need we? Even that, his lowest humiliation, his death, is expressed here, in three words of exaltation, It is a *Crown*, it is a *Mariage*, it is the *gladnesse of heart*: *Behold King Salomon crowned, &c.*

The Crown, which we are called to see him crowned with, *his mother* put upon him; The Crown which his *Father gave him*, was that glory, wherewith he was glorifyed, with the Father, *from all eternity*, in his *divine nature*: And the Crown wherewith his Father crowned his *Humane nature*, was the glory given to that, in his

[1] On the text: 'Go forth ye daughters of Sion, and behold King Solomon, with the crown, wherewith his mother crowned him, in the day of his espousals, and in the day of the gladness of his heart' (Song of Sol. iii. 11).

Evelyn Simpson quotes Jessopp: 'A greater contrast than this beautiful sermon offers to the fulsome and almost prophane oration which the Bishop of Lincoln (Williams) delivered at Westminster Abbey can hardly be imagined.' She adds: 'It is only by comparing Donne's sermons with those of his immediate contemporaries that we can realize how comparatively sober and restrained was the eulogy which Donne delivered on the dead king.' Donne's choice of text is 'a delicate allusion to the fact that James for his learning and his pacific policy had been called "the British Solomon"', but Donne devotes most of his sermon to Christ as prefigured by Solomon.

*Ascension. His Mother* could give him no such Crown: she her selfe had no Crown, but that, which *he* gave her. The Crown that *she* gave him, was that substance, that he received from her, *our flesh, our nature,* our *humanity*; and this, *Athanasius,* and this, Saint *Ambrose,* calls the *Crown,* wherewith *his Mother crowned him,* in this text, his infirm, his humane nature. Or, *the Crown wherewith his Mother crowned him,* was that Crown, to which, that infirme nature which he tooke from her, submitted him, which was his *passion,* his *Crown of thornes*; for so *Tertullian,* and divers others take this Crown of his, from her, to be his *Crown of thorns: Woe to the Crown of pride, whose beauty is a fading flower,* says the Prophet; But blessed be this Crown of Humiliation, whose flower cannot fade. Then was there truly a *Rose* amongst *Thorns,* when through his Crown of *Thorns,* you might see his title, *Jesus Nazarenus*: for, in that very name *Nazarenus,* is involved the signification of a *flower*; the very word signifies a *flower. Esay's* flower in the Crown of pride fades, and is removed; This flower in the Crown of Thornes fades not, nor could be removed; for, for all the importunity of the Jews, *Pilate* would not suffer *that title* to be removed, or to be changed; still *Nazarenus* remained, and still a rose amongst thorns. You know the curse of the earth, *Thorns and thistles shall it bring forth unto thee*; It did so to our *Solomon* here, it brought forth thornes to Christ, and he made a *Crown* of those thorns, not onely for *himself,* but for us too, *Omnes aculei mortis, in Dominici Corporis tolerantia, obtusi sunt,* All the thorns of life and death, are broken, or blunted upon the head of our *Solomon,* and now, even our *thorns,* make up *our Crown,* our tribulation in life, our dissolution in death, conduce to our glory: *Behold him crowned with his Mothers Crown,* for even that brought him to his *Fathers Crown,* his humiliation to exaltation, his passion to glory.

*Behold* your *Solomon, your Saviour* again, and you shall see another *beam* of Comfort, in your tribulations from his; for even this *Humiliation* of his, is called his *Espousals,* his *marriage, Behold him crowned in the day of his Espousals.* His Spouse is the *Church,* His marriage is the *uniting* of himselfe to this Spouse, in his becomming *Head of the Church.* The great City, the heavenly Jerusalem, is called *The Bride,* and *The Lambs wife,* in the *Revelation*: And he is the *Head* of this body, the *Bridegroom* of this Bride, the Head of this Church, as he is *The first-borne of the Dead*; Death, that dissolves all ours, made up this marriage. His Death is his Marriage, and upon his Death flowed out from his side, those two *Elements of the Church, water* and *bloud*; The Sacraments of *Baptisme*, and of the *Communion* of himself. Behold then this *Solomon crowned* and *married*; both words of *Exaltation*, and *Exultation*, and both by *Death*; and trust him for working the same effects upon thee; That thou (*though by Death*) shalt be *crowned* with a Crown of Glory, and *married* to him, in whose right and merit thou shalt have that Crown.

And *Behold* him once again, and you shall see not a *beam*, but a *stream* of comfort; for this day, which is the day of his death, he calls here *The day of the gladnesse of his heart*. Behold him crowned in the day of the gladnesse of his heart. The fulnesse, the compasse, the two *Hemispheres* of Heaven, are often designed to us, in these two names, *Joy* and *Glory*: If the *Crosse* of Christ, the *Death* of Christ, present us both these, how neare doth it bring, how fully doth it deliver Heaven it self to us in this life? And then we heare the Apostle say, *We see Jesus, for the suffering of Death, crowned with Honour and Glory*: There is *half* Heaven got by *Death*, *Glory*. And then, *for the joy that was set before him, he indured the Crosse*; There is the *other half*, *Joy*; All Heaven purchased by Death. And therefore, *if any man suffer as a Christian, let him not be ashamed*, saith the Apostle; but *let him glorifie God*, *In isto Nomine*, as the *vulgate* read it; *In that behalfe*, as we translate it. But, *In isto Nomine*, saith S. *Augustine*: Let us glorifie God, in that Name; *Non solum in nomine Christiani, sed Christiani patientis*, not onely because he is a *Christian* in his *Baptisme*, but a Christian in a *second Baptisme*, a *Baptisme of bloud*; not onely as he hath received Christ, in accepting his *Institution*, but because he hath conformed himself to Christ, in fulfilling his *sufferings*. And therefore, though we admit *naturall* and *humane sorrow*, in the calamities which overtake us, and surround us in this life: (for as *all glasses* will gather drops and tears from externall causes, so this very glasse which we looke upon now, our *Solomon* in the Text, our *Saviour*, had those *sadnesses of heart* toward his Passion, and *Agonies* in his passion) yet *count it all Joy when you fall into tentations*, saith the Apostle: *All Joy*, that is, both the *interest*, and the *principall*, hath the *earnest* and the *bargain*; for if you can conceive joy in your tribulations in this world, how shall that joy be multiplied unto you, when no tribulation shall be mingled with it? There is not a better evidence, nor a more binding earnest of everlasting Joy in the next world, than to find *Joy of heart* in the *tribulations* of this; fixe thy self therefore upon this first glasse, this *Solomon*, thy Saviour, *Behold King Solomon crownd, &c.* and by conforming thy self to his *holy sadnesse*, and *humiliation*, thou shalt also become like him, in his Joy, and Glory.

But then the hand of God, hath *not set up*, but *laid down another Glasse*, wherein thou maist see thy self; a glasse that reflects thy self, and nothing but thy selfe. Christ, who was the other glasse, *is like thee in every thing*, but not absolutely, for *sinne* is *excepted*; but in this glasse presented now (*The Body of our Royall*, but *dead Master and Soveraigne*) we cannot, we doe not except sinne. Not onely the greatest man is subject to *naturall infirmities*, (Christ himself was so) but the holiest man is subject to *Originall and Actuall sinne*, as thou art, and so a fit glasse for thee, to see thyself in. *Jeat* showes a man his face, as well as *Crystall*; nay, a Crystall glasse will not show a man his face, except it be steeled, except it be darkned on the backside: Christ as he was a pure *Crystall* glasse, as he was *God*, had not been a glasse for us, to have seen ourselves in, except he had been *steeled, darkened with our humane nature*; Neither was he ever so throughly darkened, as that he could present us wholly to our selves, because he had no *sinne*, without seeing of which we do not see our selves. Those therefore that are like thee in all things, subject to humane *infirmities*, subject to *sinnes*, and yet are translated, and *translated* by *Death*, to everlasting *Joy*, and *Glory*, are nearest and clearest glasses for thee, to see thy self in; and such is this glasse, which God hath proposed to thee, in this house. And therefore, change the word of the Text, in a letter or two, from *Egredimini*, to *Ingredimini*; never go forth to see, but *Go in and see a Solomon crowned with his mothers crown, &c.* And when you shall find that hand that had signed to one of you a *Patent* for *Title*, to another for *Pension*, to another for *Pardon*, to another for *Dispensation, Dead*: That hand that settled Possessions by his *Seale*, in the *Keeper*, and rectified *Honours* by the *sword*, in his *Marshall*, and distributed relief to the *Poore*, in his *Almoner*, and *Health* to the *Diseased*, by his *immediate*

*Touch*, Dead: That Hand that ballanced his *own three Kingdomes* so equally, as that none of them complained of one another, nor of him, and carried the *Keyes* of all the Christian world, and locked up, and let out *Armies* in their due season, Dead; how poore, how faint, how pale, how momentany, how transitory, how empty, how frivolous, how Dead things, must you necessarily thinke *Titles*, and *Possessions*, and *Favours*, and all, when you see that Hand, which was the *hand of Destinie*, of *Christian Destinie*, of the *Almighty God*, lie dead? It was not so *hard* a hand when we touched it last, nor so *cold* a hand when we kissed it last: That hand which was wont *to wipe all teares from all our eyes*, doth now but presse and squeaze us as so many spunges, filled one with one, another with another cause of teares. Teares that can have no other banke to bound them, but the declared and manifested *will of God*: For, till our teares flow to that heighth, that they might be called a *murmuring* against the declared will of God, it is against our Allegiance, it is *Disloyaltie*, to give our teares any stop, any termination, any measure. It was a great part of *Annaes prayse*, *That she departed not from the Temple*, *day nor night*; visit Gods Temple often in the day, meet him in his owne House, and depart not from his *Temples*, (The *dead bodies* of his Saints are his Temples still) even at *midnight*; at midnight remember them, who resolve into dust, and make them thy glasses to see thy self in. Looke now especially upon him whom God hath presented to thee now, and with as much cheerfulnesse as ever thou heardst him say, *Remember my Favours*, or *remember my Commandements*; heare him say now with the wise man, *Remember my Judgement*, *for thine also shall be so; yesterday for me, and to day for thee*; He doth not say *to morrow*, but *to Day*, *for thee*. Looke upon him as a beame of that Sunne, as an abridgement of that *Solomon* in the Text; for every Christian truely reconciled to God, and *signed* with his hand in the *Absolution*, and *sealed* with his bloud in the *Sacrament*, (and this was his case) is a beame, and an abridgement of *Christ* himselfe.

*Behold him* therefore *Crowned with the Crown that his Mother gives him: His Mother*, *The Earth*. In antient times, when they used to reward Souldiers with particular kinds of *Crowns*, there was a great dignity *in Corona graminea*, in a Crown of Grasse: That denoted a Conquest, or a Defence of that land. He that hath but *Coronam*

*Gramineam*, a turfe of grasse in *a Church yard*, hath a Crown from his *Mother*, and even in that buriall taketh *seisure* of the *Resurrection*, as by a turfe of grasse men give seisure of land. *He is crowned in the day of his Marriage*; for though it be a day of *Divorce* of us from him, and of *Divorce* of his body from his soul, yet neither of these Divorces breake the Marriage: His *soule* is married to him that made it, and his body and soul shall meet again, and all we, both then in that Glory where we shall acknowledge, that there is no way to this *Marriage*, but this *Divorce*, nor to *Life*, but by *Death*. And lastly, he is *Crowned in the day of the gladnesse of his heart*: He leaveth that heart, which was accustomed to the halfe joyes of the earth, in the earth; and he hath enlarged his heart to a greater capacity of Joy, and Glory, and God hath filled it according to that new capacity. And therefore, to end all with the Apostles words, *I would not have you to be ignorant, Brethren, concerning them, which are asleepe, that ye sorrow not, as others that have no hope; for if ye beleeve that Jesus died, and rose again, even so, them also, which sleepe in him, will God bring with him.* But when you have performed this *Ingredimini*, that you have gone in, and mourned upon him, and performed the *Egredimini*, you have gone forth, and laid his Sacred body, in Consecrated Dust, and come then to another *Egredimini*, to a going forth in many severall wayes: some to the service of their *new Master*, and some to the enjoying of their Fortunes conferred by their old; some to the raising of new *Hopes*, some to the burying of old, and all; some to new, and busie endeavours in Court, some to contented retirings in the Countrey; let none of us, goe so farre from him, or from one another, in any of our wayes, but that all we that have served him, may meet once a day, the first time we see the Sunne, in the eares of almighty God, with humble and hearty prayer, that he will be pleased to hasten that day, in which it shall be *an addition*, even to the joy of that place, as perfect as it is, and as infinite as it is, to see that face againe, and to see those eyes open there, which we have seen closed here. Amen.

# 35. From a Sermon Preached at S. Pauls, May 8. 1625[1]

NEITHER hath God onely reserved this treasure and dignity of man to the next world, but even here he hath made him *filium Dei*, The Sonne of God, and *Semen Dei*, The seed of God, and *Consortem divinæ naturæ*, Partaker of the divine Nature, and *Deos ipsos*, Gods themselves, for *Ille dixit Dii estis*, he hath said we are Gods. So that, as though the glory of heaven were too much for God alone, God hath called up man thither, in the ascension of his Sonne, to partake thereof; and as though one God were not enough for the administration of this world, God hath multiplied gods here upon Earth, and imparted, communicated, not onely his power to every Magistrate, but the Divine nature to every sanctified man. *David* asks that question with a holy wonder, *Quid est homo? What is man that God is so mindfull of him?* But I may have his leave, and the holy Ghosts, to say, since God is so mindfull of him, since God hath set his minde upon him, What is not man? Man is all.

Since we consider men in the place that they hold, and value them according to those places, and aske not how they got thither, when we see Man made The Love of the Father, The Price of the Sonne, The Temple of the Holy Ghost, The Signet upon Gods hand, The Apple of Gods eye, Absolutely, unconditionally we cannot annihilate man, not evacuate, not evaporate, not extenuate man to the levity, to the vanity, to the nullity of this Text (*Surely men altogether, high and low, are lighter than vanity.*) For, man is not onely a contributary Creature, but a totall Creature; He does not onely make one, but he is all; He is not a piece of the world, but the world it selfe; and next to the glory of God, the reason why there is a world.

[1] On the text: 'Surely men of low degree are vanity, and men of high degree are a lie; to be laid in the balance they are altogether lighter than vanity' (Ps. lxii. 9).

This sermon is subtitled in the Folio 'The first of the Prebend of *Cheswicks* five Psalmes; which five are appointed for that Prebend; as there are five other, for every other of our thirty Prebendaries'. The Psalter was divided among thirty Prebendaries, each of whom was supposed to recite his five Psalms daily and make them the subject of his meditation. Donne as Prebend of Chiswick was allotted Psalms lxii to lxvi.

## 36. From a Sermon Preached upon Whitsunday. [?1625][1]

### (i)

HEAVEN is Glory, and heaven is Joy; we cannot tell which most; we cannot separate them; and this comfort is joy in the Holy Ghost. This makes all *Jobs* states alike; as rich in the first Chapter of his Booke, where all is suddenly lost, as in the last, where all is abundantly restored. This Consolation from the Holy Ghost makes my mid-night noone, mine Executioner a Physitian, a stake and pile of Fagots, a Bone-fire of triumph; this consolation makes a Satyr, and Slander, and Libell against me, a Panegyrique, and an Elogy in my praise; It makes a *Tolle* an *Ave*, a *Væ* an *Euge*, a *Crucifige* an *Hosanna*; It makes my death-bed, a mariage-bed, And my Passing-Bell, an Epithalamion.

### (ii)

As the world is the whole frame of the world, God hath put into it a reproofe, a rebuke, lest it should seem eternall, which is, a sensible decay and age in the whole frame of the world, and every piece thereof. The seasons of the yeare irregular and distempered; the Sun fainter, and languishing; men lesse in stature, and shorter-lived. No addition, but only every yeare, new sorts, new species of wormes, and flies, and sicknesses, which argue more and more putrefaction of which they are engendred. And the Angels of heaven, which did so familiarly converse with men in the beginning of the world, though they may not be doubted to perform to us still their ministeriall assistances, yet they seem so far to have deserted this world, as that they do not appeare to us, as they did to those our Fathers. S. *Cyprian* observed this in his time, when writing to *Demetrianus*, who imputed all those calamities which afflicted the world then, to the impiety of the Christians who would not joyne with them in the worship of their gods, *Cyprian* went no farther for

---

1 On the text: 'And when he is come, he will reprove the world of sin, and of righteousness, and of judgement. Of sin, because ye believe not on me. Of righteousness, because I go to my Father, and ye see me no more. Of judgement, because the prince of this world is judged' (John xvi. 8, 9, 10, 11).

the cause of these calamities, but *Ad senescentem mundum,* To the age and impotency of the whole world; And therefore, sayes he, *Imputent senes Christianis, quod minus valeant in senectutum;* Old men were best accuse Christians, that they are more sickly in their age, than they were in their youth; Is the fault in our religion, or in their decay? *Canos in pueris videmus, nec ætas in senectute desinit, sed incipit a senectute;* We see gray haires in children, and we do not die old, and yet we are borne old. Lest the world (as the world signifies the whole frame of the world) should glorifie it selfe, or flatter, and abuse us with an opinion of eternity, we may admit usefully (though we do not conclude peremptorily) this observation to be true, that there is a reproofe, a rebuke born in it, a sensible decay and mortality of the whole world.

## 37. From the second of my Prebend Sermons upon my five Psalmes. Preached at S. Pauls, January 29. 1626[1]

### (i)

LET me wither and weare out mine age in a discomfortable, in an unwholesome, in a penurious prison, and so pay my debts with my bones, and recompence the wastfulnesse of my youth, with the beggery of mine age; Let me wither in a spittle under sharpe, and foule, and infamous diseases, and so recompence the wantonnesse of my youth, with that loathsomnesse in mine age; yet, if God with-draw not his spirituall blessings, his Grace, his Patience, If I can call my suffering his Doing, my passion his Action, All this that is temporall, is but a caterpiller got into one corner of my garden, but a mill-dew fallen upon one acre of my Corne; The body of all, the substance of all is safe, as long as the soule is safe. But when I shall trust to that, which wee call a good spirit, and God shall deject, and empoverish, and evacuate that spirit, when I shall rely upon a morall constancy, and God shall shake, and enfeeble, and enervate, destroy and demolish that constancy; when I shall

---

[1] On the text: 'Because thou hast been my help, therefore in the shadow of thy wings will I rejoice' (Ps. lxiii. 7).

think to refresh my selfe in the serenity and sweet ayre of a good
conscience, and God shall call up the damps and vapours of hell
it selfe, and spread a cloud of diffidence, and an impenetrable crust
of desperation upon my conscience; when health shall flie from me,
and I shall lay hold upon riches to succour me, and comfort me in
my sicknesse, and riches shall flie from me, and I shall snatch after
favour, and good opinion, to comfort me in my poverty; when even
this good opinion shall leave me, and calumnies and misinformations
shall prevaile against me; when I shall need peace, because there is
none but thou, O Lord, that should stand for me, and then shall
finde, that all the wounds that I have, come from thy hand, all the
arrowes that stick in me, from thy quiver; when I shall see, that
because I have given my selfe to my corrupt nature, thou hast
changed thine; and because I am all evill towards thee, therefore
thou hast given over being good towards me; When it comes to this
height, that the fever is not in the humors, but in the spirits, that
mine enemy is not an imaginary enemy, fortune, nor a transitory
enemy, malice in great persons, but a reall, and an irresistible, and
an inexorable, and an everlasting enemy, The Lord of Hosts himselfe, The Almighty God himselfe, the Almighty God himselfe
onely knowes the waight of this affliction, and except hee put in
that *pondus gloriæ*, that exceeding waight of an eternall glory, with
his owne hand, into the other scale, we are waighed downe, we are
swallowed up, irreparably, irrevocably, irrecoverably, irremediably.

(ii)

I would always raise your hearts, and dilate your hearts, to a
holy Joy, to a joy in the Holy Ghost. There may be a just feare, that
men doe not grieve enough for their sinnes; but there may bee a
just jealousie, and suspition too, that they may fall into inordinate
griefe, and diffidence of Gods mercy; And God hath reserved us to
such times, as being the later times, give us even the dregs and
lees of misery to drinke. For, God hath not onely let loose into the
world a new spirituall disease; which is, an equality, and an
indifferency, which religion our children, or our servants, or our
companions professe; (I would not keepe company with a man that
thought me a knave, or a traitor; with him that thought I loved not

my Prince, or were a faithlesse man, not to be beleeved, I would not associate my selfe; And yet I will make him my bosome companion, that thinks I doe not love God, that thinks I cannot be saved) but God hath accompanied, and complicated almost all our bodily diseases of these times, with an extraordinary sadnesse, a predominant melancholy, a faintnesse of heart, a chearlesnesse, a joylesnesse of spirit, and therefore I returne often to this endeavor of raising your hearts, dilating your hearts with a holy Joy, Joy in the holy Ghost, for *Under the shadow of his wings*, you may, you should, *rejoyce*.

If you looke upon this world in a Map, you find two Hemisphears, two half worlds. If you crush heaven into a Map, you may find two Hemisphears too, two half heavens; Halfe will be Joy, and halfe will be Glory; for in these two, the joy of heaven, and the glory of heaven, is all heaven often represented unto us. And as of those two Hemisphears of the world, the first hath been knowne long before, but the other, (that of America, which is the richer in treasure) God reserved for later Discoveries; So though he reserve that Hemisphear of heaven, which is the Glory thereof, to the Resurrection, yet the other Hemisphear, the Joy of heaven, God opens to our Discovery, and delivers for our habitation even whilst we dwell in this world. As God hath cast upon the unrepentant sinner two deaths, a temporall, and a spirituall death, so hath he breathed into us two lives; for so, as the word for death is doubled, *Morte morieris*, *Thou shalt die the death*, so is the word for life expressed in the plurall, *Chaiim*, *vitarum*, *God breathed into his nostrils the breath of lives*, of divers lives. Though our naturall life were no life, but rather a continuall dying, yet we have two lives besides that, an eternall life reserved for heaven, but yet a heavenly life too, a spirituall life, even in this world; And as God doth thus inflict two deaths, and infuse two lives, so doth he also passe two Judgements upon man, or rather repeats the same Judgement twice. For, that which Christ shall say to thy soule then at the last Judgement, *Enter into thy Masters joy*, Hee sayes to thy conscience now, *Enter into thy Masters joy*. The everlastingnesse of the joy is the blessednesse of the next life, but the entring, the inchoation is afforded here. For that which Christ shall say then to us, *Venite benedicti*, *Come ye blessed*, are words intended to persons that are comming, that are upon the way, though not at home; Here in this world he bids us *Come*, there in the next, he shall bid us *Welcome*.

## 38. From a Sermon Preached to the King in my Ordinary wayting at White-hall, 18. Aprill. 1626[1]

### (i)

WHO but my selfe can conceive the sweetnesse of that salutation, when the Spirit of God sayes to me in a morning, Go forth to day and preach, and preach consolation, preach peace, preach mercy, And spare my people, spare that people whom I have redeemed with my precious Blood, and be not angry with them for ever; Do not wound them, doe not grinde them, do not astonish them with the bitternesse, with the heavinesse, with the sharpnesse, with the consternation of my judgements. *David* proposes to himselfe, that he would *Sing of mercy, and of judgement*; but it is of mercy first; and not of judgement at all, otherwise than it will come into a song, as joy and consolation is compatible with it. It hath falne into disputation, and admitted argument, whether ever God inflicted punishments by his good Angels; But that the good Angels, the ministeriall Angels of the Church, are properly his instruments, for conveying mercy, peace, consolation, never fell into question, never admitted opposition.

How heartily God seemes to utter, and how delightfully to insist upon that, which he sayes in *Esay*, *Consolamini, consolamini populum meum*, *Comfort ye, comfort ye my people*, And *Loquimini ad cor*, *Speake to the heart of Jerusalem, and tell her, Thine iniquities are pardoned*? How glad Christ seemes that he had it for him, when he gives the sick man that comfort, *Fili confide, My son be of good comfort, thy sins are forgiven thee*? What a Coronation is our taking of Orders, by which God makes us a Royall Priesthood? And what an inthronization is the comming up into a Pulpit, where God invests his servants with

[1] On the text: 'In my Fathers house are many mansions; if it were not so, I would have told you' (John xiv. 2).

his Ordinance, as with a Cloud, and then presses that Cloud with a *Væ si non*, woe be unto thee, if thou doe not preach, and then enables him to preach peace, mercy, consolation, to the whole Congregation. That God should appeare in a Cloud, upon the Mercy Seat, as he promises *Moses* he will doe, That from so poore a man as stands here, wrapped up in clouds of infirmity, and in clouds of iniquity, God should drop raine, poure downe his dew, and sweeten that dew with his honey, and crust that honied dew into Manna, and multiply that Manna into Gomers, and fill those Gomers every day, and give every particular man his Gomer, give every soule in the Congregation, consolation by me; That when I call to God for grace here, God should give me grace for grace, Grace in a power to derive grace upon others, and that this Oyle, this Balsamum should flow to the hem of the garment, even upon them that stand under me; That when mine eyes looke up to Heaven, the eyes of all should looke up upon me, and God should open my mouth, to give them meat in due season; That I should not onely be able to say, as Christ said to that poore soule, *Confide fili*, My son be of good comfort, but *Fratres & Patres mei*, My Brethren, and my Fathers, nay *Domini mei*, and *Rex meus*, My Lords, and my King be of good comfort, your sins are forgiven you; That God should seale to me that Patent, *Ite prædicate omni Creaturæ*, *Goe and preach the Gospell to every Creature*, be that creature what he will, That if God lead me into a Congregation, as into his Arke, where there are but eight soules, but a few disposed to a sense of his mercies, and all the rest (as in the Arke) ignobler creatures, and of brutall natures and affections, That if I finde a licentious Goat, a supplanting Fox, an usurious Wolfe, an ambitious Lion, yet to that creature, to every creature I should preach the Gospel of peace and consolation, and offer these creatures a Metamorphosis, a transformation, a new Creation in Christ Jesus, and thereby make my Goat, and my Fox, and my Wolfe, and my Lion, to become *Semen Dei*, The seed of God, and *Filium Dei*, The child of God, and *Participem Divinæ Naturæ*, Partaker of the Divine Nature it selfe; This is that which Christ is essentially in himselfe, This is that which ministerially and instrumentally he hath committed to me, to shed his consolation upon you, upon you all; Not as his Almoner to drop his consolation upon one soule, nor as his Treasurer to issue his consolation to a whole Congregation, but as his Ophir, as his Indies, to derive his gold, his precious consolation upon the King himselfe.

(ii)

God hath a progresse house, a removing house here upon earth, His house of prayer; At this houre, God enters into as many of these houses, as are opened for his service at this houre: But his standing house, his house of glory, is that in Heaven, and that he promises them. God himselfe dwelt in Tents in this world, and he gives them a House in Heaven. A House, in the designe and survay whereof, the Holy Ghost himselfe is figurative, the Fathers wanton, and the School-men wilde. The Holy Ghost, in describing this House, fills our contemplation with foundations, and walls, and gates, of gold, of precious stones, and all materialls, that we can call precious. The Holy Ghost is figurative; And the Fathers are wanton in their spirituall elegancies, such as that of S. *Augustins*, (if that booke be his) *Hiems horrens*, *Æstas torrens*, And, *Virent prata*, *vernant sata*, and such other harmonious, and melodious, and mellifluous cadences of these waters of life. But the School-men are wild; for as one Author, who is afraid of admitting too great a hollownesse in the Earth, lest then the Earth might not be said to be solid, pronounces that Hell cannot possibly be above three thousand miles in compasse, (and then one of the torments of Hell will be the throng, for their bodies must be there, in their dimensions, as well as their soules) so when the School-men come to measure this house in heaven, (as they will measure it, and the Master, God, and all his Attributes, and tell us how Allmighty, and how Infinite he is) they pronounce, that every soule in that house shall have more roome to it selfe, than all this world is. We know not that; nor see we that the consolation lyes in that; we rest in this, that it is a House, It hath a foundation, no Earth-quake shall shake it, It hath walls, no Artillery shall batter it, It hath a roofe, no tempest shall pierce it. It is a house that affords security, and that is one beame; And it is *Domus patris*, His Fathers house, a house in which he hath interest, and that is another beame of his Consolation.

It was his Fathers, and so his; And his, and so ours; for we are not joynt purchasers of Heaven with the Saints, but we are co-heires with Christ Jesus. We have not a place there, because they have done more than enough for themselves, but because he hath done enough for them and us too. By death we are gathered to our Fathers in nature; and by death, through his mercy, gathered to his Father also. Where we shall have a full satisfaction, in that wherein S. *Philip* placed all satisfaction, *Ostende nobis patrem*, *Lord, shew us thy Father, and it is enough*. We shall see his Father, and see him made ours in him.

And then a third beame of this Consolation is, That in this house of his Fathers, thus by him made ours, there are *Mansions*; In which word, the Consolation is not placed, (I doe not say, that there is not truth in it) but the Consolation is not placed in this, That some of these Mansions are below, some above staires, some better seated, better lighted, better vaulted, better fretted, better furnished than others; but onely in this, That they are *Mansions*; which word, in the Originall, and Latin, and our Language, signifies a *Remaining*, and denotes the perpetuity, the everlastingnesse of that state. A state but of one Day, because no Night shall over-take, or determine it, but such a Day, as is not of a thousand yeares, which is the longest measure in the Scriptures, but of a thousand millions of millions of generations: *Qui nec præceditur hesterno, nec excluditur crastino*, A day that hath no *pridie*, nor *postridie*, yesterday doth not usher it in, nor to morrow shall not drive it out. *Methusalem*, with all his hundreds of yeares, was but a Mushrome of a nights growth, to this day, And all the foure Monarchies, with all their thousands of yeares, And all the powerfull Kings, and all the beautifull Queenes of this world, were but as a bed of flowers, some gathered at six, some at seaven, some at eight, All in one Morning, in respect of this Day. In all the two thousand yeares of Nature, before the Law given by *Moses*, And the two thousand yeares of Law, before the Gospel given by Christ, And the two thousand of Grace, which are running now, (of which last houre we have heard three quarters strike, more than fifteen hundred of this last two thousand spent) In all this six thousand, and in all those, which God may be pleased to adde, *In domo patris*, In this House of his Fathers, there was never heard quarter clock to strike, never seen minute glasse to turne. No time lesse than it selfe would serve to expresse this time, which is intended in this word *Mansions*; which is also exalted with another beame, that they are *Multa, In my Fathers House there are many Mansions*.

In this Circumstance, an Essentiall, a Substantiall Circumstance, we would consider the joy of our society, and conversation in heaven, since society and conversation is one great element and ingredient into the joy, which we have in this world. We shall have an association with Christ himselfe; for *where he is*, it is his promise, *that we also shall be*. We shall have an association with the Angels, and such a one, as we shall be such as they. We shall have an association with the Saints, and not onely so, to be such as they, but to be they: And with all *who come from the East, and from the West, and from the North, and from the South, and sit down with Abraham, and Isaac, and Jacob in the kingdome of heaven*. Where we shall be so far from being enemies to one another, as that we shall not be strangers to one another: And so far from envying one another, as that all that every one hath, shall be every others possession: where all soules shall be so intirely knit together, as if all were but one soule, and God so intirely knit to every soule, as if there were as many Gods as soules.

## 39. From a Sermon Preached to the Houshold at White-hall, April 30. 1626[1]

### (i)

THE Wise-man in *Ecclesiasticus* institutes his meditation thus: *There is one that hath great need of help, full of poverty, yet the eye of the Lord looked upon him for good, and set him up from his low estate, so that many that saw it, marvelled at it*. Many marvelled, but none reproached the Lord, chid the Lord, calumniated the Lord, for doing so. And if the Lord will look upon a sinner, and raise that bedrid man; if he will look with that eye, that pierces deeper than the eye of heaven, the Sun, (and yet with a look of that eye, the womb of the earth conceives) if he will look with that eye, that conveys more warmth

---

[1] On the text: 'I am not come to call the righteous, but sinners to repentance' (Matt. ix. 13).

The phrase 'to the houshold' implies that the King was not present.

than the eye of the Ostrich, (and yet with a look of that eye, that Bird is said to hatch her young ones, without sitting) that eye that melted *Peter* into water, and made him flow towards Christ; and rarified *Matthew* into air, and made him flee towards Christ; if that eye vouchsafe to look upon a Publican, and redeem a *Goshen* out of an *Egypt*, hatch a soul out of a carnal man, produce a saint out of a sinner, shall we marvel at the matter? marvel so, as to doubt Gods power? shall any thing be impossible to God? or shall we marvel at the manner, at any way by which Christ shall be pleased to convey his mercy? *Miraris eum peccatorum vinum bibere, qui pro peccatoribus sanguinem fudit?* shall we wonder that Christ would live with sinners, who was content to die for sinners? Wonder that he would eat the bread and Wine of sinners, that gave sinners his own flesh to eat, and his own blood to drink? Or if we do wonder at this, (as, indeed, nothing is more wonderful) yet let us not calumniate, let us not mis-interpret any way, that he shall be pleased to take, to derive his mercy to any man: but, (to use *Clement* of *Alexandria's* comparison) as we tread upon many herbs negligently in the field, but when we see them in an Apothecaries shop, we begin to think that there is some vertue in them; so howsoever we have a perfect hatred, and a religious despite against a sinner, as a sinner; yet if Christ Jesus shall have been pleased to have come to his door, and to have stood, and knock'd, and enter'd, and sup'd, and brought his dish, and made himself that dish, and seal'd a reconciliation to that sinner, in admitting him to that Table, to that Communion, let us forget the Name of Publican, the Vices of any particular profession; and forget the name of sinner, the history of any mans former life; and be glad to meet that man now in the arms, and to grow up with that man now in the bowels of Christ Jesus; since Christ doth not now begin to make that man his, but now declares to us, that he hath been his, from all eternity: For in the Book of Life, the name of *Mary Magdalen* was as soon recorded, for all her incontinency, as the name of the blessed Virgin, for all her integrity; and the name of St. *Paul* who drew his sword against Christ, as soon as St. *Peter*, who drew his in defence of him: for the Book of life was not written successively, word after word, line after line, but delivered as a Print, all together. There the greatest sinners were as soon recorded, as the most righteous; and here Christ comes *to call, not the righteous* at all, *but* onely *sinners to repentance.*

(ii)

Christ saves no man against his will. There is a word crept into the later School, that deludes many a man; they call it *Irresistibility*; and they would have it mean, that when God would have a man, he will lay hold upon him, by such a power of grace, as no perversness of that man, can possibly resist. There is some truth in the thing, soberly understood: for the grace of God is more powerful than any resistance of any man or devil. But leave the word, where it was hatcht, in the School, and bring it not home, not into practice: for he that stays his conversion upon that, God, at one time or other, will lay hold upon me by such a power of Grace, as I shall not be able to resist, may stay, till Christ come again, to *preach to the Spirits that are in prison.* Christ beats his Drum, but he does not Press men; Christ is serv'd with Voluntaries. There is a *Compelle intrare*, A forcing of men to come in, and fill the house, and furnish the supper: but that was an extraordinary commission, and in a case of Necessity: Our ordinary commission is, *Ite, prædicate*; *Go, and preach the Gospel*, and bring men in so: it is not, *Compelle intrare*, Force men to come in: it is not, Draw the Sword, kindle the Fire, winde up the Rack: for, when it was come to that, that men were forc'd to come in, (as that Parabolical story is reported in this Evangelist) *the house was fill'd*, and the supper was furnisht, (the Church was fill'd and the Communion-table frequented) but it was *with good and bad too*: for men that are forc'd to come hither, they are not much the better in themselves, nor we much the better assur'd of their Religion, for that: Force and violence, pecuniary and bloudy Laws, are not the right way to bring men to Religion, in cases where there is nothing in consideration, but Religion meerly. 'Tis true, there is a *Compellite Manere*, that hath all justice in it; when men have been baptiz'd, and bred in a Church, and embrac'd the profession of a Religion, so as that their allegiance is complicated with their Religion, then it is proper by such Laws to compel them to remain and continue in that Religion; for in the Apostacy, and Defection of such men, the State hath a detriment, as well as the Church; and therefore the temporal sword may be drawn as well as the spiritual; which is the case between those of the Romish perswasion, and us: their Laws work directly upon our Religion; they draw blood meerly for that, ours work directly upon their allegiance, and punish only where pretence of Religion colours a Defection in allegiance. But Christs end being meerly spiritual, to constitute a Church, *Non venit Occurrere*, as he came not to meet man, man was not so forward; so he came not to compel man, to deal upon any that was so backward; for, *Venit vocare, He came to call*.

## 40. From a Sermon Preached upon Whitsunday. [?1626]¹

THE holy Ghost *reproves thee*, convinces thee, *of judgement*, that is, offers thee the knowledge that such a Church there is; A Jordan to wash thine originall leprosie in Baptisme; A City upon a mountaine, to enlighten thee in the works of darknesse; a continuall application of all that Christ Jesus said, and did, and suffered, to thee. Let no soule say, she can have all this at Gods hands immediatly, and never trouble the Church; That she can passe her pardon between God and her, without all these formalities, by a secret repentance. It is true, beloved, a true repentance is never frustrate: But yet, if thou wilt think thy selfe a little Church, a Church to thy selfe, because thou hast heard it said, That thou art a little world, a world in thy selfe, that figurative, that metaphoricall representation shall not save thee. Though thou beest a world to thy self, yet if thou have no more corn, nor oyle, nor milk, than growes in thy self, or flowes from thy self, thou wilt starve; Though thou be a Church in thy fancy, if thou have no more seales of grace, no more absolution of sin, than thou canst give thy self, thou wilt perish. *Per solam Ecclesiam sacrificium libenter accipit Deus*: Thou maist be a Sacrifice in thy chamber, but God receives a Sacrifice more cheere-

---

¹ On the text: 'And when he is come, he will reprove the world of sin, and of righteousness, and of judgement.

'Of sin, because ye believe not on me.

'Of righteousness, because I go to my Father, and ye see me no more.

'Of judgement, because the prince of this world is judged' (John xvi. 8, 9, 10, 11).

fully at Church. *Sola, quæ pro errantibus fiducialiter intercedit*, Only the Church hath the nature of a surety; Howsoever God may take thine own word at home, yet he accepts the Church in thy behalfe, as better security. Joyne therefore ever with the Communion of Saints; *Et cum membrum sis ejus corporis, quod loquitur omnibus linguis, crede te omnibus linguis loqui*, Whilst thou art a member of that Congregation, that speaks to God with a thousand tongues, beleeve that thou speakest to God with all those tongues. And though thou know thine own prayers unworthy to come up to God, because thou liftest up to him an eye, which is but now withdrawne from a licentious glancing, and hands which are guilty yet of unrepented uncleannesses, a tongue that hath but lately blasphemed God, a heart which even now breaks the walls of this house of God, and steps home, or runs abroad upon the memory, or upon the new plotting of pleasurable or profitable purposes, though this make thee thinke thine own prayers uneffectuall, yet beleeve that some honester man than they selfe stands by thee, and that when he prayes with thee, he prayes for thee; and that, if there be one righteous man in the Congregation, thou art made the more acceptable to God by his prayers; and make that benefit of this reproofe, this conviction of the Holy Ghost, That he convinces thee *De judicio*, assures thee of an orderly Church established for thy reliefe, and that the application of thy self to this judgement, The Church, shall enable thee to stand upright in that other judgement, the last judgement, which is also enwrapped in the signification of this word of our Text, *Judgement*, and is the conclusion for this day.

## 41. From the third of my Prebend Sermons upon my five Psalmes: Preached at S. Pauls, November 5. 1626. In Vesperis[1]

UPON this earth, a man cannot possibly make one step in a straight, and a direct line. The earth it selfe being round, every step wee make upon it, must necessarily bee a segment, an arch of a circle. But yet though no piece of a circle be a straight line, yet if we take

---

1 On the text: 'And all the upright in heart shall glory' (Ps. lxiv. 10).

any piece, nay if wee take the whole circle, there is no corner, no angle in any piece, in any intire circle. A perfect rectitude we cannot have in any wayes in this world; In every Calling there are some inevitable tentations. But, though wee cannot make up our circle of a straight line, (that is impossible to humane frailty) yet wee may passe on, without angles, and corners, that is, without disguises in our Religion, and without the love of craft, and falsehood, and circumvention in our civill actions. A Compasse is a necessary thing in a Ship, and the helpe of that Compasse brings the Ship home safe, and yet that Compasse hath some variations, it doth not looke directly North; Neither is that starre which we call the North-pole, or by which we know the North-pole, the very Pole it selfe; but we call it so, and we make our uses of it, and our conclusions by it, as if it were so, because it is the neerest starre to that Pole. He that comes as neere uprightnesse, as infirmities admit, is an upright man, though he have some obliquities. To God himselfe we may alwayes go in a direct line, a straight, a perpendicular line; For God is verticall to me, over my head now, and verticall now to them, that are in the East, and West-Indies; To our Antipodes, to them that are under our feet, God is verticall, over their heads, then when he is over ours.

## 42. From a Sermon Preached at the funerals of Sir William Cokayne Knight, Alderman of London, December 12. 1626[1]

### (i)

GOD made the first Marriage, and man made the first Divorce; God married the Body and Soule in the Creation, and man divorced the Body and Soule by death through sinne, in his fall. God doth not admit, not justifie, not authorize such Super-inductions upon such Divorces, as some have imagined; That the soule departing from one body, should become the soule of another body, in a perpetuall revolution and transmigration of soules through bodies, which

---

[1] On the text: 'Lord if thou hadst been here, my brother had not died' (John xi. 21).

For a less favourable view of the career of Cokayne than that given by Donne in this sermon and by the notice of him in *D.N.B.*, see Astrid Friis, *Alderman Cockayne's Project and the Cloth Trade* (Copenhagen and London, 1927).

hath been the giddinesse of some Philosophers to think; Or that
the body of the dead should become the body of an evill spirit, that
that spirit might at his will, and to his purposes informe, and
inanimate that dead body; God allowes no such Super-inductions,
no such second Marriages upon such divorces by death, no such
disposition of soule or body, after their dissolution by death. But
because God hath made the band of Marriage indissoluble but by
death, farther than man can die, this divorce cannot fall upon man;
As farre as man is immortall, man is a married man still, still in
possession of a soule, and a body too; And man is for ever immortall
in both; Immortall in his soule by Preservation, and immortall in his
body by Reparation in the Resurrection. For, though they be
separated *a Thoro & Mensa*, from Bed and Board, they are not
divorced; Though the soule be at the *Table of the Lambe*, in Glory,
and the body but at the table of *the Serpent, in dust*; Though the
soule be *in lecto florido*, in that bed which is alwayes green, in an
everlasting spring, in *Abrahams bosome*; And the body but in that
green-bed, whose covering is but a yard and a halfe of Turfe, and a
Rugge of grasse, and the sheet but a winding sheet, yet they are
not divorced; they shall returne to one another againe, in an in-
separable re-union in the Resurrection.

### (ii)

And how imperfect is all our knowledge? What one thing doe
we know perfectly? Whether wee consider Arts, or Sciences, the
servant knows but according to the proportion of his Masters
knowledge in that Art, and the Scholar knows but according to the
proportion of his Masters knowledge in that Science; Young men
mend not their sight by using old mens Spectacles; and yet we
looke upon Nature, but with *Aristotles* Spectacles, and upon the
body of man, but with *Galens*, and upon the frame of the world, but
with *Ptolomies* Spectacles. Almost all knowledge is rather like a
child that is embalmed to make Mummy, than that is nursed to
make a Man; rather conserved in the stature of the first age, than
growne to be greater; And if there be any addition to knowledge,
it is rather a new knowledge, than a greater knowledge; rather
a singularity in a desire of proposing something that was not

knowne at all before, than an emproving, an advancing, a multiplying of former inceptions; and by that meanes, no knowledge comes
to be perfect. One Philosopher thinks he is dived to the bottome,
when he sayes, he knows nothing but this, That he knows nothing;
and yet another thinks, that he hath expressed more knowledge
than he, in saying, That he knows not so much as that, That he
knows nothing. S. *Paul* found that to be all knowledge, To know
Christ; And Mahomet thinks himselfe wise therefore, because he
knows not, acknowledges not Christ, as S. *Paul* does. Though a man
knew not, that every sin casts another shovell of Brimstone upon him
in Hell, yet if he knew that every riotous feast cuts off a year, and
every wanton night seaven years of his seventy in this world, it
were some degree towards perfection in knowledge. He that purchases a Mannor, will thinke to have an exact Survey of the Land:
But who thinks of taking so exact a survey of his Conscience, how
that money was got, that purchased that Mannor? We call that a
mans meanes, which he hath; But that is truly his meanes, what
way he came by it. And yet how few are there, (when a state comes
to any great proportion) that know that; that know what they have,
what they are worth? We have seen great Wills, dilated into glorious
uses, and into pious uses, and then too narrow an estate to reach
to it; And we have seen Wills, where the Testator thinks he hath
bequeathed all, and he hath not knowne halfe his own worth. When
thou knowest a wife, a sonne, a servant, a friend no better, but that
that wife betrayes thy bed, and that sonne thine estate, and that
servant thy credit, and that friend thy secret, what canst thou say
thou knowest? But we must not insist upon this Consideration of
knowledge; for, though knowledge be of a spirituall nature, yet
it is but as a terrestriall Spirit, conversant upon Earth; Spirituall
things, of a more rarified nature than knowledge, even faith it selfe,
and all that grows from that in us, falls within this Rule, which we
have in hand, That even in spirituall things, nothing is perfect.

(iii)

And to make a Prayer a right Prayer, there go so many essentiall
circumstances, as that the best man may justly suspect his best
Prayer: for, since Prayer must bee of faith, Prayer can be but so

perfect, as the faith is perfect; and the imperfections of the best
faith we have seene. Christ hath given us but a short Prayer; and
yet we are weary of that. Some of the old Heretiques of the Primitive
Church abridged that Prayer, and some of our later Schismatiques
have annihilated, evacuated that Prayer: The Cathari then, left
out that one Petition, *Dimitte nobis, Forgive us our trespasses*, for they
thought themselves so pure, as that they needed no forgivenesse,
and our new men leave out the whole Prayer, because the same
Spirit that spake in Christ, speakes in their extemporall prayers,
and they can pray, as well as Christ could teach them. And (to
leave those, whom we are bound to leave, those old Heretiques,
those new Schismatiques) which of us ever, ever sayes over that
short Prayer, with a deliberate understanding of every Petition as
we passe, or without deviations, and extravagancies of our thoughts,
in that halfe-minute of our Devotion? We have not leasure to speake
of the abuse of prayer in the Roman Church; where they wil antidate
and postdate their prayers; Say to morrows prayers to day, and to
dayes prayers to morrow, if they have other uses and employments
of the due time betweene; where they will trade, and make merchandise of prayers by way of exchange, My man shall fast for me,
and I will pray for my man; or my Atturney, and Proxy shall pray
for us both, at my charge; nay, where they will play for prayers,
and the loser must pray for both; To this there belongs but a holy
scorne, and I would faine passe it over quickly. But when we
consider with a religious seriousnesse the manifold weaknesses of
the strongest devotions in time of Prayer, it is a sad consideration.
I throw my selfe downe in my Chamber, and I call in, and invite
God, and his Angels thither, and when they are there, I neglect
God and his Angels, for the noise of a Flie, for the ratling of a Coach,
for the whining of a doore; I talke on, in the same posture of praying;
Eyes lifted up; knees bowed downe; as though I prayed to God; and,
if God, or his Angels should aske me, when I thought last of God
in that prayer, I cannot tell: Sometimes I finde that I had forgot
what I was about, but when I began to forget it, I cannot tell. A
memory of yesterdays pleasures, a feare of to morrows dangers, a
straw under my knee, a noise in mine eare, a light in mine eye, an
any thing, a nothing, a fancy, a Chimera in my braine, troubles me

in my prayer. So certainely is there nothing, nothing in spirituall
things, perfect in this world.

## (iv)

I need not call in new Philosophy, that denies a settlednesse, an
acquiescence in the very body of the Earth, but makes the Earth to
move in that place, where we thought the Sunne had moved; I
need not that helpe, that the Earth it selfe is in Motion, to prove
this, That nothing upon Earth is permanent; The Assertion will
stand of it selfe, till some man assigne me some instance, something
that a man may rely upon, and find permanent. Consider the greatest
Bodies upon Earth, The Monarchies; Objects, which one would
thinke, Destiny might stand and stare at, but not shake; Consider
the smallest bodies upon Earth, The haires of our head, Objects,
which one would thinke, Destiny would not observe, or could not
discerne; And yet Destiny, (to speak to a naturall man) And God,
(to speake to a Christian) is no more troubled to make a Monarchy
ruinous, than to make a haire gray. Nay, nothing needs be done to
either, by God, or Destiny; A Monarchy will ruine, as a haire will
grow gray, of it selfe. In the Elements themselves, of which all sub-
elementary things are composed, there is no acquiescence, but a
vicissitudinary transmutation into one another; Ayre condensed
becomes water, a more solid body, and Ayre rarified becomes fire,
a body more disputable, and in-apparant. It is so in the Conditions
of men too; A Merchant condensed, kneaded and packed up in a
great estate, becomes a Lord; And a Merchant rarified, blown up by
a perfidious Factor, or by a riotous Sonne, evaporates into ayre, into
nothing, and is not seen. And if there were any thing permanent and
durable in this world, yet we got nothing by it, because howsoever
that might last in it selfe, yet we could not last to enjoy it. . . .

The world is a great Volume, and man the Index of that Booke;
Even in the body of man, you may turne to the whole world; This
body is an Illustration of all Nature; Gods recapitulation of all that
he had said before, in his *Fiat lux*, and *Fiat firmamentum*, and in all
the rest, said or done, in all the six dayes. Propose this body to thy
consideration in the highest exaltation thereof; as it is the *Temple of
the Holy Ghost*: Nay, not in a Metaphor, or comparison of a Temple,

or any other similitudinary thing, but as it was really and truly the very body of God, in the person of Christ, and yet this body must wither, must decay, must languish, must perish. When *Goliah* had armed and fortified this body, And *Jezabel* had painted and perfumed this body, and *Dives* had pampered and larded this body, as God said to *Ezekiel*, when he brought him to the *dry bones*, *Fili hominis*, *Sonne of Man*, *doest thou thinke these bones can live*? They said in their hearts to all the world, Can these bodies die? And they are dead. *Jezabels* dust is not Ambar, nor *Goliahs* dust *Terra sigillata*, Medicinall; nor does the Serpent, whose meat they are both, finde any better relish in *Dives* dust, than in *Lazarus*. But as in our former part, where our foundation was, That in nothing, no spirituall thing, there was any perfectnesse, which we illustrated in the weaknesses of Knowledge, and Faith, and Hope, and Charity, yet we concluded, that for all those defects, God accepted those their religious services; So in this part, where our foundation is, That nothing in temporall things is permanent, as we have illustrated that, by the decay of that which is Gods noblest piece in Nature, The body of man; so we shall also conclude that, with this goodnesse of God, that for all this dissolution, and putrefaction, he affords this Body a Resurrection.

The Gentils, and their Poets, describe the sad state of Death so, *Nox una obeunda*, That it is one everlasting Night; To them, a Night; But to a Christian, it is *Dies Mortis*, and *Dies Resurrectionis*, The day of Death, and The day of Resurrection; We die in the light, in the sight of Gods presence, and we rise in the light, in the sight of his very Essence. Nay, Gods corrections, and judgements upon us in this life, are still expressed so, *Dies visitationis*, still it is a Day, though a *Day of visitation*; and still we may discerne God to be in the action. The *Lord of Life* was the first that named *Death*; *Morte morieris*, sayes God, Thou shalt die the Death. I doe the lesse feare, or abhorre Death, because I finde it in his mouth; Even a malediction hath a sweetnesse in his mouth; for there is a blessing wrapped up in it; a mercy in every correction, a Resurrection upon every Death. When *Jezabels* beauty, exalted to that height which it had by art, or higher than that, to that height which it had in her own opinion, shall be infinitely multiplied upon every Body; And as

God shall know no man from his own Sonne, so as not to see the very righteousnesse of his own Sonne upon that man; So the Angels shall know no man from Christ, so as not to desire to looke upon that mans face, because the most deformed wretch that is there, shall have the very beauty of Christ himselfe; So shall *Goliahs* armour, and *Dives* fulnesse, be doubled, and redoubled upon us. And every thing that we can call good, shall first be infinitely exalted in the goodnesse, and then infinitely multiplied in the proportion, and againe infinitely extended in the duration. And since we are in an action of preparing this dead Brother of ours to that state, (for the Funerall is the Easter-eve, The Buriall is the depositing of that man for the Resurrection) As we have held you, with Doctrine of Mortification, by extending the Text, from *Martha* to this occasion; so shall we dismisse you with Consolation, by a like occasionall inverting the Text, from passion in *Martha's* mouth, *Lord, if thou hadst been here, my Brother had not dyed*, to joy in ours, *Lord, because thou wast here, our Brother is not dead.*

The Lord was with him in all these steps; with him in his life; with him in his death; He is with him in his funerals, and he shall be with him in his Resurrection; and therefore, because the Lord was with him, our Brother is not dead. He was with him in the beginning of his life, in this manifestation, That though he were of Parents of a good, of a great Estate, yet his possibility and his expectation from them, did not slacken his own industry; which is a Canker that eats into, nay that hath eat up many a family in this City, that relying wholly upon what the Father hath done, the Sonne does nothing for himselfe. And truly, it falls out too often, that he that labours not for more, does not keepe his own. God imprinted in him an industrious disposition, though such hopes from such parents might have excused some slacknesse, and God prospered his industry so, as that when his Fathers estate came to a distribution by death, he needed it not. God was with him, as with *David* in a Dilatation, and then in a Repletion; God enlarged him, and then he filled him; He gave him a large and a comprehensive understanding, and with it, A publique heart; And such as perchance in his way of education, and in our narrow and contracted times, in which every man determines himselfe in himselfe, and scarce looks farther, it would be hard to finde many Examples of such largenesse. You have, I thinke, a phrase of Driving a Trade; And you have, I know, a practise of Driving away Trade, by other use of money; And you have lost a man, that drove a great Trade, the right way in making the best use of our home-commodity. To fetch in Wine, and Spice, and Silke, is but a drawing of Trade; The right driving of trade, is, to vent our owne outward; And yet, for the drawing in of that, which might justly seeme most behoofefull, that is, of Arts, and Manufactures, to be imployed upon our owne Commodity within the Kingdome, he did his part, diligently, at least, if not vehemently, if not passionately. This City is a great Theater, and he Acted great and various parts in it; And all well; And when he went higher, (as he was often heard in Parliaments, at Councell tables, and in more private accesses to the late King of ever blessed memory) as, for that comprehension of those businesses, which he pretended to understand, no man doubts, for no man lacks arguments and evidences of his ability therein, So for his manner of expressing his intentions, and digesting and uttering his purposes, I have sometimes heard the greatest Master of Language and Judgement, which these times, or any other did, or doe, or shall give, (that good and great King of ours) say of him, That he never heard any man of his breeding, handle businesses more rationally, more pertinently, more elegantly, more perswasively; And when his purpose was, to do a grace to a Preacher, of very good abilities, and good note in his owne Chappell, I have heard him say, that his language, and accent, and manner of delivering himselfe, was like this man. This man hath God accompanied all his life; and by performance thereof seemes to have made that Covenant with him, which he made to *Abraham, Multiplicabo te vehementer, I will multiply thee exceedingly.* He multiplied his estate so, as was fit to endow many and great Children; and he multiplied his Children so, both in their number, and in their quality, as they were fit to receive a great Estate. God was with him all the way, In *a Pillar of Fire,* in the brightnesse of prosperity, and in the *Pillar of Clouds* too, in many darke, and sad, and heavy crosses: So great a Ship, required a great Ballast, So many blessings, many crosses; And he had them, and sailed on his course the steadier for them; The *Cloud* as well as the

*Fire*, was a *Pillar* to him; His crosses, as well as his blessings established his assurance in God; And so, in all the course of his life, *The Lord was here*, and therefore *our Brother is not dead*; not dead in the evidences and testimonies of life; for he, whom the world hath just cause to celebrate, for things done, when he was alive, is alive still in their celebration.

The Lord was here, that is, with him at his death too. He was served with the Processe here in the City, but his cause was heard in the Country; Here he sickned, There he languished, and dyed there. In his sicknesse there, those that assisted him, are witnesses, of his many expressings, of a religious and a constant heart towards God, and of his pious joyning with them, even in the holy declaration of kneeling, then, when they, in favour of his weaknesse, would disswade him from kneeling. I must not defraud him of this testimony from my selfe, that into this place where we are now met, I have observed him to enter with much reverence, and compose himselfe in this place with much declaration of devotion. And truly it is that reverence, which those persons who are of the same ranke that he was in the City, that reverence that they use in this place, when they come hither, is that that makes us, who have now the administration of this Quire, glad, that our Predecessors, but a very few yeares before our time, (and not before all our times neither) admitted these Honourable and worshipfull Persons of this City, to sit in this Quire, so, as they do upon Sundayes: The Church receives an honour in it; But the honour is more in their reverence, than in their presence; though in that too: And they receive an honour, and an ease in it; and therefore they do piously towards God, and prudently for themselves, and gratefully towards us, in giving us, by their reverent comportment here, so just occasion of continuing that honour, and that ease to them here, which to lesse reverend, and unrespective persons, we should be lesse willing to doe. To returne to him in his sicknesse; He had but one dayes labour, and all the rest were Sabbaths, one day in his sicknesse he converted to businesse; Thus; He called his family, and friends together; Thankfully he acknowledged Gods manifold blessings, and his owne sins as penitently: And then, to those who were to have the disposing of his estate, joyntly with his Children, he recommended his servants, and the poore, and the Hospitals, and the Prisons, which, according to his purpose, have beene all taken into consideration; And after this (which was his Valediction to the world) he seemed alwaies loath to returne to any worldly businesse, His last Commandement to Wife and Children was Christs last commandement to his Spouse the Church, in the Apostles, *To love one another.* He blest them, and the Estate devolved upon them, unto them: And by Gods grace shall prove as true a Prophet to them in that blessing, as he was to himselfe, when in entring his last bed, two dayes before his Death, he said, *Help me off with my earthly habit, and let me go to my last bed.* Where, in the second night after, he said, *Little know ye what paine I feele this night, yet I know, I shall have joy in the morning;* And in that morning he dyed. The forme in which he implored his Saviour, was evermore, towards his end, this, *Christ Jesus, which dyed on the Crosse, forgive me my sins; He have mercy upon me:* And his last and dying words were the repetition of the name of Jesus; And when he had not strength to utter that name distinctly and perfectly, they might heare it from within him, as from a man a far off; even then, when his hollow and remote naming of Jesus, was rather a certifying of them, that he was with his Jesus, than a prayer that he might come to him. And so *The Lord was here,* here with him in his Death; and because *the Lord was here, our Brother is not dead;* not dead in the eyes and eares of God; for as the blood of *Abel* speaks yet, so doth the zeale of Gods Saints; and their last prayers (though we heare them not) God continues still; and they pray in Heaven, as the Martyrs under the Altar, even till the Resurrection.

He is with him now too; Here in his Funerals. Buriall, and Christian Buriall, and Solemne Buriall are all evidences, and testimonies of Gods presence. God forbid we should conclude, or argue an absence of God, from the want of Solemne Buriall, or Christian Buriall, or any Buriall; But neither must we deny it, to be an evidence of his favour and presence, where he is pleased to afford these. So God makes that the seale of all his blessings to *Abraham, That he should be buried in a good age;* God established *Jacob* with that promise, *That his Son Joseph should have care of his Funerals:* And *Joseph* does cause his servants, *The Physitians, to embalme him, when he was dead.* Of Christ it was Prophecied, *That he should have a glorious Buriall*; And therefore Christ interprets well that profuse, and prodigall piety of the Woman that poured out the Oyntment upon him, *That she did it to Bury him*; And so shall *Joseph* of Arimathea be ever celebrated, for his care in celebrating Christs Funerals. If we were to send a Son, or a friend, to take possession of any place in Court, or forraine parts, we would send him out in the best equipage: Let us not grudge to set downe our friends, in the Antichamber of Heaven, the Grave, in as good manner, as without vainegloriousnesse, and wastfulnesse we may; And, in inclining them, to whom that care belongs, to expresse that care as they doe this day, *The Lord is with him*, even in this Funerall; And because *The Lord is here, our brother is not dead*; Not dead in the memories and estimation of men.

And lastly, that we may have God present in all his Manifestations, *Hee that was, and is, and is to come*, was with him, in his life and death, and is with him in this holy Solemnity, and shall bee with him againe in the Resurrection. God sayes to *Jacob, I will goe downe with thee into Egypt, and I will also surely bring thee up againe.* God goes downe with a good man into the Grave, and will surely bring him up againe. When? The Angel promised to returne to *Abraham* and *Sarah*, for the assurance of the birth of *Isaac, according to the time of life*; that is, in such time, as by nature a woman may have a childe. God will returne to us in the Grave, *according to the time of life*; that is, in such time, as he, by his gracious Decree, hath fixed for the Resurrection. And in the meane time, no more than the God-head departed from the dead body of our Saviour, in the grave, doth his power, and his presence depart from our dead bodies in that darknesse; But that which *Moses* said to the whole Congregation, I say to you all, both to you that heare me, and to him that does not, *All ye that did cleave unto the Lord your God, are alive, every one of you, this day*; Even hee, whom we call dead, is alive this day. In the presence of God, we lay him downe; In the power of God, he shall rise; In the person of Christ, he is risen already. And so into the same hands that have received his soule, we commend his body; beseeching his blessed Spirit, that as our charity enclines us to hope confidently of his good estate, our faith may assure us of the same happinesse, in our owne behalfe; And that for all our sakes, but especially for his own glory, he will be pleased to hasten the consummation of all, in that kingdome which that Son of God hath purchased for us, with the inestimable price of his incorruptible blood. *Amen.*

## 43. From a Sermon Preached at S. Pauls upon Christmas day. 1626[1]

### (i)

THE whole life of Christ was a continuall Passion; others die Martyrs, but Christ was born a Martyr. He found a *Golgotha,* (where he was crucified) even in Bethlem, where he was born; For, to his tendernesse then, the strawes were almost as sharp as the thornes after; and the Manger as uneasie at first, as his Crosse at last. His birth and his death were but one continuall act, and his Christmas-day and his Good Friday, are but the evening and morning of one and the same day. And as even his birth, is his death, so every action and passage that manifests Christ to us, is his birth; for, *Epiphany* is *manifestation;* And therefore, though the Church doe now call Twelf-day Epiphany, because upon that day Christ was manifested to the Gentiles, in those Wise men who came then to worship him, yet the Ancient Church called this day, (the day of Christs birth) the Epiphany, because this day Christ was manifested to the world, by being born this day. Every manifestation of Christ to the world, to the Church, to a particular soule, is an Epiphany, a Christmas-day.

### (ii)

Thus was our Saviour presented to God; And in this especially was that fulfilled, *the glory of the later house shall be greater than the glory of the former;* The later Temple exceeded the former in this, that the Lord, the God of this house, was in the house bodily, as one of the congregation; And the little body of a sucking childe, was a Chappell in that Temple, infinitely more glorious than the

[1] On the text: 'Lord now lettest thou thy servant depart in peace, according to thy word: for mine eyes have seen thy salvation' (Luke ii. 29, 30).

Temple it selfe. How was the joy of *Noah* at the return of the Dove into the Ark, multiplied upon *Simeon* at the bringing of this Dove into the Temple? At how cheape a price was Christ tumbled up and down in this world? It does almost take off our pious scorn of the low price, at which *Judas* sold him, to consider that his Father sold him to the world for nothing; and then, when he had him again, by this new title of primogeniture and presentation, he sold him to the world again, if not for a Turtle, or for a Pigeon, yet at most for 5. shekels, which at most is but 10. shillings.

And yet you have had him cheaper than that, today in the Sacrament: whom hath Christ cost 5. shekels there? As Christ was presented to God in the Temple, so is hee presented to God in the Sacrament; not sucking, but bleeding. And God gives him back again to thee. And at what price? upon this exchange; Take his first born, Christ Jesus, and give him thine. Who is thine? *Cor primogenitum*, says S. *Augustine*: The heart is the first part of the body that lives; Give him that; And then, as it is in nature, it shall be in grace too, the last part that dyes; for it shall never dye; *If a man eat the bread that commeth down from heaven, he shall not die*, sayes Christ. If a man in exchange of his heart receive Christ Jesus himselfe, he can no more die than Christ Jesus himselfe can die. That which *Æschines* said to *Socrates*, admits a faire accomodation here; He saw every body give *Socrates* some present, and he said, Because I have nothing else to give, I will give thee my selfe. Do so, sayes Socrates, and I will give thee back again to thy self, better than when I received thee. If thou have truly given thy selfe to him in the Sacrament, God hath given thee thy selfe back, so much mended, as that thou hast received thy self and him too; Thy selfe, in a holy liberty, to walk in the world in a calling, and himself, in giving a blessing upon all the works of thy calling, and imprinting in thee a holy desire to do all those works to his glory.

### (iii)

My body is my prison; and I would be so obedient to the Law, as not to break prison; I would not hasten my death by starving, or macerating this body: But if this prison be burnt down by continuall feavers, or blowen down with continuall vapours, would any man be so in love with that ground upon which that prison stood, as to desire rather to stay there, than to go home? Our prisons are fallen, our bodies are dead to many former uses; Our palate dead in a tastlesnesse; Our stomach dead in an indigestiblenesse; our feete dead in a lamenesse, and our invention in a dulnesse, and our memory in a forgetfulnesse; and yet, as a man that should love the ground, where his prison stood, we love this clay, that was a body in the dayes of our youth, and but our prison then, when it was at best; wee abhorre the graves of our bodies; and the body, which, in the best vigour thereof, was but the grave of the soule, we over-love. *Pharaohs* Butler, and his Baker went both out of prison in a day; and in both cases, *Joseph*, in the interpretation of their dreames, calls that, (their very discharge out of prison) a lifting up of their heads, a kinde of preferment: Death raises every man alike, so far, as that it delivers every man from his prison, from the incumbrances of this body: both Baker and Butler were delivered of their prison; but they passed into divers states after, one to the restitution of his place, the other to an ignominious execution. Of thy prison thou shalt be delivered whether thou wilt or no; thou must die; Foole, this night thy soule may be taken from thee; and then, what thou shalt be to morrow, prophecy upon thy selfe, by that which thou hast done to day; If thou didst depart from that Table in peace, thou canst depart from this world in peace. And the peace of that Table is, to come to it *in pace desiderii*, with a contented minde, and with an enjoying of those temporall blessings which thou hast, without macerating thy self, without usurping upon others, without murmuring at God; And to be at that Table, *in pace cogitationum*, in the peace of the Church, without the spirit of contradiction, or inquisition, without uncharitablenesse towards others, without curiosity in thy selfe: And then to come from that Table *in pace domestica*, with a bosome peace, in thine own Conscience, in that seale of thy reconciliation, in that Sacrament; that so, riding at that Anchor, and in that calme, whether God enlarge thy voyage, by enlarging thy life, or put thee into the harbour, by the breath, by the breathlesnesse of Death, either way, East or West, thou maist depart in peace, according to his word, that is, as he shall be pleased to manifest his pleasure upon thee.

## 44. From the fourth of my Prebend Sermons upon my five Psalmes: Preached at S. Pauls, 28 January. 1627[1]

*G O D S House is the house of Prayer*; It is his Court of Requests; There he receives petitions, there he gives Order upon them. And you come to God in his House, as though you came to keepe him company, to sit downe, and talke with him halfe an houre; or you come as Ambassadors, covered in his presence, as though ye came from as great a Prince as he. You meet below, and there make your bargaines, for biting, for devouring Usury, and then you come up hither to prayers, and so make God your Broker. You rob, and spoile, and eat his people as bread, by Extortion, and bribery, and deceitfull waights and measures, and deluding oathes in buying and selling, and then come hither, and so make God your Receiver, and his house a den of Thieves. His house is *Sanctum Sanctorum*, The holiest of holies, and you make it onely *Sanctuarium*; It should be a place sanctified by your devotions, and you make it onely a Sanctuary to priviledge Malefactors, A place that may redeeme you from the ill opinion of men, who must in charity be bound to thinke well of you, because they see you here. *Offer this to one of your Princes*, (as God argues in the Prophet) and see, if he will suffer his house to be prophaned by such uncivill abuses; And, *Terribilis Rex*, *The Lord most high is terrible, and a great King over all the earth*; and, *Terribilis super omnes Deos, More terrible than all other Gods*. Let thy Master be thy god, or thy Mistresse thy god, thy Belly be thy god, or thy Back be thy god, thy fields be thy god, or thy chests be thy god, *Terribilis super omnes Deos*, The Lord is terrible above all gods, *A great God, and a great King above all gods*. You come, and call upon him by his name here, But *Magnum & terribile, Glorious and fearefull is the name of the Lord thy God*. And, as if the Son of God were but the Son of some Lord, that had beene your Schoole-fellow in your youth, and so you continued a boldnesse to him ever after, so, because you have beene brought up with Christ from your cradle,

[1] On the text: 'By terrible things in righteousness wilt thou answer us, O God of our salvation; who art the confidence of all the ends of the earth, and of them that are afar off, upon the sea' (Ps. lxv. 5).

and catechized in his name, his name becomes lesse reverend unto you, and *Sanctum & terribile*, Holy, and reverend, Holy and terrible should his name be.

## 45. From a Sermon Preached upon Candlemas day. [?1627][1]

### (i)

THE Church, which is the Daughter of God, and Spouse of Christ, celebrates this day, the Purification of the blessed Virgin, the Mother of God: And she celebrates this day by the name, vulgarly, of *Candlemas day*. It is *dies luminarium*, the day of lights; The Church took the occasion of doing so, from the Gentiles; At this time of the yeare, about the beginning of February, they celebrated the feast of *Februus*, which is their *Pluto*; And, because that was the God of darknesse, they solemnized it, with a multiplicity of Lights. The Church of God, in the outward and ceremoniall part of his worship, did not disdain the ceremonies of the Gentiles; Men who are so severe, as to condemne, and to remove from the Church, whatsoever was in use amongst the Gentiles before, may, before they are aware, become Surveyors, and Controllers upon Christ himself, in the institution of his greatest seales: for Baptisme, which is the Sacrament of purification by washing in water, and the very Sacrament of the Supper it self, religious eating, and drinking in the Temple, were in use amongst the Gentiles too. It is a perverse way, rather to abolish Things and Names, (for vehement zeale will work upon Names as well as Things) because they have been abused, than to reduce them to their right use. We dealt in the reformation of Religion, as Christ did in the institution thereof; He found ceremonies amongst the Gentiles, and he took them in, not because he found them there, but because the Gentiles had received them from the Jews, as they had their washings, and their religious meetings to eat and drink in the Temple, from the Jews

---

[1] On the text: 'Blessed are the pure in heart, for they shall see God' (Matt. v. 8).

Donne's daughter, Lucy, died early in January 1627. Evelyn Simpson suggests that the third passage excerpted from this sermon here bears an allusion to his loss, which is recalled again in the Easter sermon for 1627 (No. 47).

Passeover. Christ borrowed nothing of the Gentiles, but he took
his own where he found it: Those ceremonies, which himself had
instituted in the first Church of the Jews, and the Gentiles had
purloined, and prophaned, and corrupted after, he returned to a
good use againe. And so did we in the Reformation, in some ceremonies which had been of use in the Primitive Church, and
depraved and corrupted in the Romane. For the solemnizing of this
Day, Candlemas-day, when the Church did admit Candles into the
Church, as the Gentiles did, it was not upon the reason of the
Gentiles, who worshipped therein the God of darknesse, *Februus*,
*Pluto*; but because he who was the light of the world, was this day
presented and brought into the Temple, the Church admitted
lights. The Church would signifie, that as we are to walk in the
light, so we are to receive our light from the Church, and to
receive Christ, and our knowledge of him, so as Christ hath notified
himself to us. So it is a day of purification to us, and a day of lights,
and so our Text fits the Day, *Blessed are the pure in heart, for they shall
see God.*

(ii)

If we consider the Sermon in Saint *Matthew*, and the Sermon in
S. *Luke*, the purpose and the scope of both, the matter and the
forme of both, the body and the parts of both, the phrase and the
language of both, is for the most part the same, and yet Christ
forbore not to preach it twice.

This excuses no mans ignorance, that is not able to preach
seasonably, and to break, and distribute the bread of life according
to the emergent necessities of that Congregation, at that time;
Nor it excuses no mans lazinesse, that will not employ his whole
time upon his calling; Nor any mans vain-glory, and ostentation,
who having made a Pye of Plums, without meat, offers it to sale
in every Market, and having made an Oration of Flowres, and
Figures, and Phrases without strength, sings it over in every
Pulpit: It excuses no mans ignorance, nor lazinesse, nor vain-glory,
but yet it reproaches their itching and curious eares, to whom any
repetition of the same things is irksome and fastidious. You may
have heard an answer of an Epigrammatist applyable to this purpose;

When he read his Epigrams in an Auditory, one of the hearers
stopped him, and said, Did not I heare an Epigram to this purpose
from you, last yeare? Yes, sayes he, it is like you did; but is not
that vice still in you this yeare, which last yeares Epigram repre-
hended? If your curiosity bring you to say to any Preacher, Did not
I heare this Point thus handled in your Sermon, last yeare? Yes,
must he say, and so you must next yeare againe, till it appeare in
your amendment, that you did heare it. The Devill maintaines a
Warre good cheap, if he may fight with the same sword, and we
may not defend with the same buckler; If he can tempt a Son with
his Fathers covetousnesse, and a Daughter with her Mothers
wantonnesse, if he need not vary the sin, nor the tentation, must
wee vary our Doctrine? This is indeed to put new Wine into old
vessels, new Doctrine into eares, and hearts not disburdened of old
sins. We say, as the Spouse sayes, *Vetera & nova*, we prepare old and
new, all that may any way serve your holy taste, and conduce to
your spirituall nourishment; And he is not a Preacher sufficiently
learned, that must of necessity preach the same things againe, but
he is not a Preacher sufficiently discreet neither, that forbeares any
thing therefore, because himselfe, or another in that place, hath
handled that before. Christ himselfe varied his Sermon very little,
if this in S. *Matthew*, and that in S. *Luke*, were divers Sermons.

(iii)

The farthest that any of the Philosophers went in the discovery
of Blessednesse, was but to come to that, *Nemo ante obitum*, to
pronounce that no man could be called Blessed before his death;
not that they had found what kind of better Blessednesse they went
to after their death, but that still till death they were sure, every
man was subject to new miseries, and interruptions of any thing
which they could have called Blessednesse. The Christian Philosophy goes farther; It showes us a perfecter Blessednesse than they
conceived for the next life, and it imparts that Blessednesse to this
life also: The pure in heart are blessed already, not onely comparatively, that they are in a better way of Blessednesse, than
others are, but actually in a present possession of it: for this world

and the next world, are not, to the pure in heart, two houses, but two roomes, a Gallery to passe thorough, and a Lodging to rest in, in the same House, which are both under one roofe, Christ Jesus; The Militant and the Triumphant, are not two Churches, but this the Porch, and that the Chancell of the same Church, which are under one Head, Christ Jesus; so the Joy, and the sense of Salvation, which the pure in heart have here, is not a joy severed from the Joy of Heaven, but a Joy that begins in us here, and continues, and accompanies us thither, and there flowes on, and dilates it selfe to an infinite expansion, (so, as if you should touch one corne of powder in a traine, and that traine should carry fire into a whole City, from the beginning it was one and the same fire) though the fulness of the glory thereof be reserved to that which is expressed in the last branch, *Videbunt Deum, They shall see God.*

## 46. From a Sermon Preached to the King at White-hall, the first Sunday in Lent. [?11 February 1627][1]

### (i)

TRACE God *in thy self*, and thou shalt find it so. If thou beest drowzie now, and unattentive, curious or contentious, or quarrel-some now, now God leaves thee in that indisposition, and that is a judgement: But it was his Mercy that brought thee hither before. In every sinne thou hast some remorse, some *reluctation*, before thou do that sinne; and that *pre-reluctation*, and *pre-remorse* was Mercy. If thou hadst no such remorse in thy last sinne, before the sinne, and hast it now, this is the effect of Gods former mercy, and former good purpose upon thee, to let thee see that thou needest the assistance of his Minister, and of his Ordinance, to enable thee to lay hold on Mercy when it is offered thee. Can any calamity fall upon thee, in which thou shalt not be bound to say, I have had blessings in a greater measure than this? If thou have had losses, yet thou hast more, out of which God took that. If all be lost,

[1] On the text: 'For the child shall die a hundred years old; but the sinner, being a hundred years old, shall be accursed' (Isa. lxv. 20).

perchance thou art but where thou begunst at first, at nothing. If thou begunst upon a good heighth, and beest fallen from that, and fallen low, yet as God prepared a *Whale* to transport *Jonas*, before *Jonas* was cast into the *Sea*, God prepared thee a holy *Patience*, before he reduced thee to the exercise of that Patience. *If thou* couldest apprehend nothing done for thy self, yet all the mercies that God hath exhibited to *others*, are former mercies to thee, in the *Pattern*, and in the *Seal*, and in the *Argument* thereof: They have had them, therefore thou shalt. All Gods *Prophecies*, are thy *Histories*: whatsoever he hath promised others, he hath done in his purpose for thee: And all Gods *Histories* are thy *Prophesies*; all that he hath done for others, he owes thee. Hast thou *a hardnesse* of heart? knowest thou not that Christ hath wept before to entender that hardnesse? hast thou a *palenesse* of soul, in the apparition of God in fire, and in judgement? knowest thou not, that Christ hath *bled* before, to give a vigour, and a vegetation, and a verdure to that palenesse? is thy sinne *Actuall* sinne? knowest thou not, that there is a Lamb bleeding before upon the Altar, to expiate that? Is thy terrour from thy inherence, and encombrance of *Originall* sinne? knowest thou not, that the effect of *Baptism* hath blunted the sting of that sinne before? art thou full of sores, putrid and ulcerous sores? full of wounds, through and through piercing wounds? full of diseases, namelesse and complicate diseases? knowest thou not that there is a holy Charm, a blessed Incantation, by which thou art, though not invulnerable, yet invulnerable *unto death*, wrapt up in the eternall Decree of thine *Election*? that's thy pillar, the *assurance of thine Election*: If thou shake that, if thou cast down that Pillar, if thou distrust thine Election, with *Samson*, who pulled down pillars in his blindnesse, in thy blindnesse thou destroyest thy self. Begin where thou wilt at any Act in thy self, at any act in God, yet there was mercy before that, for his mercy is eternall, eternall even towards thee. *I could* easily think that that, that past between *God* and *Moses* in their long conversation; that that, that past between *Christ* and *Moses* in his transfiguration; that that, that past between Saint *Paul* and the *Court of Heaven* in his extasie was instruction and manifestation on one part, and admiration and application on the other part of the mercy of God. Earth cannot receive, Heaven cannot give such another universall soul to all: all persons, all actions, as Mercy. And were I *the childe of this Text*, that were to live *a hundred yeares*, I would ask no other marrow to my bones, no other wine to my heart, no other light to mine eyes, no other art to my understanding, no other eloquence to my tongue, than the power of apprehending for my self, and the power of deriving and conveying upon others by my Ministery, the Mercy, the early Mercy, the everlasting Mercy of yours, and my God.

## (ii)

How men do bear it, we know not; what passes between God and those men, upon whom the curse of God lieth, in their dark *horrours at midnight*, they would not have us know, because it is part of their curse, to envy God that glory. But we may consider in some part the insupportablenesse of that weight, if we proceed but so farre, as to accomodate to God, that which is ordinarily said of naturall things, *Corruptio optimi pessima*; when the best things change their nature, they become worst. When God, who is all sweetnesse, shall have learned frowardnesse from us, as *David* speaks; and being all rectitude, shall have learned perversenesse and crookednesse from us, as *Moses* speaks; and being all providence, shall have learned negligence from us: when God who is all Blessing, hath learned to curse of us, and being of himself spread as an universall Hony-combe over All, takes in an impression, a tincture, an infusion of gall from us, what extraction of Wormwood can be so bitter, what exaltation of fire can be so raging, what multiplying of talents can be so heavy, what stiffnesse of destiny can be so inevitable, what confection of gnawing worms, of gnashing teeth, of howling cries, of scalding brimstone, of palpable darknesse, can be so, so insupportable, so inexpressible, so in-imaginable, as the curse and malediction of God? *And therefore* let not us by our works provoke, nor by our words teach God to curse. Lest if *with the same tongue that we blesse God, we curse Men*; that is, seem to be in Charity in our Prayers here, and carry a ranckerous heart, and venemous tongue home with us God come to say (and Gods *saying* is *doing*) *As he loved cursing, so let it come unto him; as he clothed himself with cursing, as with a garment, so let it be as a girdle, wherewith he is girded continually*: When a man curses out of *Levity*, and makes a loose habit of that sinne, God shall so gird it to him, as he shall never devest it. The Devils grammar is *Applicare Activa Passivis*, to apply Actives to Passives; where he sees an inclination, to subminister a temptation; where he seeth a froward choler, to blow in a curse. And Gods grammar is to *change* Actives into Passives: where a man delights in cursing, to make that man accursed. And if God do this to them who do but curse men, will he do lesse to them, who blaspheme himself? where man wears out *Æternum suum*, (as Saint *Gregory* speaketh) his own eternity, his own hundred yeares; that is, his whole life, in cursing and blaspheming, God shall also extend his curse, *In æterno suo*, in his eternity, that is, for *ever*. Which is that, that falls to the bottome, as the heaviest of all, and is our last consideration; that all the rest, that there is a curse deposited in the Scriptures, denounced by the Church, avowed by God, reduced to execution, and that insupportable in this life, is infinitely aggravated by this, that he shall be *accursed for ever*.

This is the *Anathema Maran-atha*, accursed *till the Lord come*; and when the Lord cometh, he cometh not to reverse, nor to alleviate, but to ratifie and aggravate that curse. As soon as Christ curst the *fig-tree*, it withered, and it never recovered: for saith that Gospell, he curst it *In æternum*, for ever. In the course of our sinne, the *Holy Ghost* hath put here a number of yeares, a hundred yeares: We sinne long, as long as we can, but yet sinne hath an end. But in this curse of God in the Text, there is no number; it is an *indefinite* future; *He shall be accursed*: A mile of cyphers or figures, added to the former hundred, would not make up a minute of this eternity. Men have calculated how many particular graines of sand, would fill up all the vast space between the Earth and the Firmament: and we find, that a few lines of cyphers will designe and expresse that number. But if every grain of sand were that number, and multiplied again by that number, yet all that, all that inexpressible, inconsiderable number, made not up one minute of this eternity; neither would this curse, be a minute the shorter for having been indured so many Generations, as there were grains of sand in that number. Our *Esse*, our *Being*, is from Gods saying, *Dixit & facti*, God spoke, and we were made: our *Bene esse*, our *Well-being*, is from Gods saying too;

*Bene-dicit* God blesses us, in speaking gratiously to us. Even our *Ill-being*, our condemnation is from Gods saying also: for *Malediction* is *Damnation*. So far God hath gone with us that way, as that our Being, our well-being, our ill-being is from his saying: But God shall never come to a *Non esse*, God shall never say to us, *Be nothing*, God shall never succour us with an *annihilation*, nor give us the ease of resolving into nothing, for this curse flowes on into an *everlasting* future, *He shall be accurst*, he shall be so for *ever*. In a true sense we may say, that Gods *fore-knowledge* growes lesse and lesse every day; for his fore-knowledge is of *future* things, and many things which were future heretofore are past, or present now; and therefore cannot fall under his fore-knowledge: His fore-knowledge in that sense, growes lesse, and decaieth. But his eternity decayeth in no sense; and as long as his eternity lasts, as long as God is God, God shall never see that soul, whom he hath accurst, delivered from that curse, or eased in it.

But we are now in the work of an houre, and no more. If there be a minute of sand left, (There is not) If there be a minute of patience left, heare me say, This minute that is left, is that eternitie which we speake of; upon this minute dependeth that eternity: And this minute, God is in this Congregation, and puts his eare to every one of your hearts, and hearkens what you will bid him say to your selves: whether he shall blesse you for your acceptation, or curse you for your refusall of him this minute: for this minute makes up your *Century*, your hundred yeares, your eternity, because it may be your last minute. We need not call that a *Fable*, but a *Parable*, where we heare, That a Mother to still her froward childe told him, she would cast him to the Wolf, the Wolf should have him; and the Wolf which was at the doore, and within hearing, waited, and hoped he should have the childe indeed: but the childe being still'd, and the Mother pleased, then she saith, so shall we kill the Wolf, the Wolf shall have none of my childe, and then the Wolf stole away. No metaphor, no comparison is too high, none too low, too triviall, to imprint in you a sense of Gods everlasting goodnesse towards you. God bids your Mother the Church, and us her Servants for your Souls, to denounce his judgements upon your sinnes, and we do it; and the executioner *Satan*, beleeves us, before you beleeve us, and is ready on his part. Be you also ready on your part, to lay hold upon those conditions, which are annext to all Gods maledictions, Repentance of former, *preclusion* against *future sinnes*, and we shall be alwayes ready, on our part to assist you with the *Power* of our *Intercession*, to deliver you with the *Keies* of our *Absolution*, and to establish you with the *seales* of *Reconcilation*, and so disappoint that *Wolf*, that roaring *Lion*, that seeks whom he may devour: Go in Peace, and be this your Peace, to know this, *Maledictus qui pendet in Cruce*, God hath laid the whole curse belonging to us upon him, that hangs upon the Crosse; But *Benedictus qui pendet in pendentem*; To all them that hang upon him, that hangeth there, God offereth now, all those blessings, which he that hangeth there hath purchased with the inestimable price of his Incorruptible blood; And to this glorious *Sonne* of God, who hath suffered all this, and to the most Almighty *Father*, who hath *done* all this, and to the *blessed Spirit of God*, who offereth now to *apply* all this, be ascribed by us, and by the whole Church, All power, praise, might, majesty, glory, and dominion, now and for evermore *Amen*.

## 47. From a Sermon Preached at S. Pauls, upon Easter-day. 1627[1]

### (i)

THERE is nothing that God hath established in a constant course of nature, and which therefore is done every day, but would seeme a Miracle, and exercise our admiration, if it were done but once; Nay, the ordinary things in Nature, would be greater miracles, than the extraordinary, which we admire most, if they were done but once; The standing still of the Sun, for *Josuahs* use, was not, in it selfe, so wonderfull a thing, as that so vast and immense a body as the Sun, should run so many miles, in a minute; The motion of the Sun were a greater wonder than the standing still, if all were to begin againe; And onely the daily doing takes off the admiration.

---

[1] On the text: 'Women received their dead raised to life again: and others were tortured, not accepting a deliverance, that they might obtain a better resurrection' (Heb. xi. 35).

See note to No. 45.

But then God having, as it were, concluded himself in a course of nature, and written downe in the booke of Creatures, Thus and thus all things shall be carried, though he glorifie himselfe sometimes, in doing a miracle, yet there is in every miracle, a silent chiding of the world, and a tacite reprehension of them, who require, or who need miracles.

### (ii)

But yet, (which is a last consideration, and our conclusion of this part) this being thus put onely in women, in the weaker sexe, that they desired, that they rejoyced in this resuscitation of the dead, may well intimate thus much unto us, that our virility, our holy manhood, our true and religious strength, consists in the assurance, that though death have divided us, and though we never receive our dead raised to life again in this world, yet we do live together already, in a holy Communion of Saints, and shal live together for ever, hereafter, in a glorious Resurrection of bodies. Little know we, how little a way a soule hath to goe to heaven, when it departs from the body; Whether it must passe locally, through Moone, and Sun, and Firmament, (and if all that must be done, all that may be done, in lesse time than I have proposed the doubt in) or whether that soule finde new light in the same roome, and be not carried into any other, but that the glory of heaven be diffused over all, I know not, I dispute not, I inquire not. Without disputing, or inquiring, I know, that when Christ sayes, *That God is not the God of the dead*, he saies that to assure me, that those whom I call dead, are alive. And when the Apostle tels me, *That God is not ashamed to be called the God of the dead*, he tels me that to assure me, That Gods servants lose nothing by dying.

He was but a Heathen that said, If God love a man, *Juvenis tollitur*, He takes him young out of this world; And they were but Heathens, that observed that custome, To put on mourning when their sons were born, and to feast and triumph when they dyed. But thus much we may learne from these Heathens, That if the dead, and we, be not upon one floore, nor under one story, yet we are under one roofe. We think not a friend lost, because he is gone into another roome, nor because he is gone into another Land;

And into another world, no man is gone; for that Heaven, which God created, and this world, is all one world. If I had fixt a Son in Court, or married a daughter into a plentifull Fortune, I were satisfied for that son and that daughter. Shall I not be so, when the King of Heaven hath taken that son to himselfe, and maried himselfe to that daughter, for ever? I spend none of my Faith, I exercise none of my Hope, in this, that I shall have my dead raised to life againe.

This is the faith that sustaines me, when I lose by the death of others, or when I suffer by living in misery my selfe, That the dead, and we, are now all in one Church, and at the resurrection, shall be all in one Quire. But that is the resurrection which belongs to our other part; That resurrection which wee have handled, though it were a resurrection from death, yet it was to death too; for those that were raised again, died again. But the Resurrection which we are to speak of, is for ever; They that rise then, shall see death no more, for it is (sayes our Text) *A better Resurrection.*

### (iii)

Beloved, There is nothing so little in heaven, as that we can expresse it; But if wee could tell you the fulnesse of a soul there, what that fulnesse is; the infinitenesse of that glory there, how far that infinitenesse goes; the Eternity of that happinesse there, how long that happinesse lasts; if we could make you know all this, yet this *Better Resurrection* is a heaping, even of that Fulnesse, and an enlarging, even of that Infinitenesse, and an extention, even of that eternity of happinesse; For, all these, this Fulnesse, this Infinitenesse, this Eternity are in all the Resurrections of the Righteous, and this is a *better Resurrection*; We may almost say, it is something more than Heaven; for, all that have any Resurrection to life, have all heaven; And something more than God; for, all that have any Resurrection to life, have all God; and yet these shall have a better Resurrection. Amorous soule, ambitious soule, covetous soule, voluptuous soule, what wouldest thou have in heaven? What doth thy holy amorousnesse, thy holy covetousnesse, thy holy ambition, and voluptuousnesse most carry thy desire upon? Call it what thou wilt; think it what thou canst; think it something that thou canst not think; and all this thou shalt have, if thou have any Resurrection unto life; and yet there is a *Better Resurrection*. When I consider what I was in my parents loynes (a substance unworthy of a word, unworthy of a thought) when I consider what I am now, (a Volume of diseases bound up together, a dry cynder, if I look for naturall, for radicall moisture, and yet a Spunge, a bottle of overflowing Rheumes, if I consider accidentall; an aged childe, a gray-headed Infant, and but the ghost of mine own youth) When I consider what I shall be at last, by the hand of death, in my grave, (first, but Putrifaction, and then, not so much as putrifaction, I shall not be able to send forth so much as an ill ayre, not any ayre at all, but shall be all insipid, tastlesse, savourlesse dust; for a while, all wormes, and after a while, not so much as wormes, sordid, senslesse, namelesse dust) When I consider the past, and present, and future state of this body, in this world, I am able to conceive, able to expresse the worst that can befall it in nature, and the worst that can be inflicted upon it by man, or fortune; But the least degree of glory that God hath prepared for that body in heaven, I am not able to expresse, not able to conceive.

## 48. From a Sermon Preached at Saint Pauls Crosse, 6 May. 1627[1]

GOD is the Father of man, otherwise than he is of other creatures. He is the Father of all Creatures; so *Philo* cals all Creatures *sorores suas*, his sisters; but then, all those sisters of man, all those daughters of God are not alike maried. God hath placed his Creatures in divers rankes, and in divers conditions; neither must any man thinke, that he hath not done the duty of a Father, if he have not placed all his Sonnes, or not matched all his daughters, in a condition equall to himselfe, or not equall to one another. God hath placed

[1] On the text: 'For, the children of Israel shall abide many days, without a king, and without a Prince, and without a sacrifice, and without an image, and without an ephod, and without teraphim' (Hos. iii. 4).

creatures in the heavens, and creatures in the earth, and creatures in the sea, and yet, all these creatures are his children, and when he looked upon them all, in their divers stations, he saw, *omnia valde bona*, that all was very well; And that Father that imploies one Sonne in learning, another to husbandry, another to Merchandise, pursues Gods example, in disposing his children, (his creatures) diversly, and all well. Such creatures as the *Raine*, (though it may seem but an imperfect, and ignoble creature, fallen from the wombe of a cloud) have God for their Father; (*God is the Father of* the *Raine.*) And such creatures as *light*, have but God for their Father. God is *Pater luminum*, the Father of lights. Whether we take lights there to be the *Angels*, created with the light, (some take it so) or to be the severall lights set up in the heavens, Sun, and Moon and Stars, (some take it so) or to be the light of *Grace* in *infusion* by the Spirit, or the light of the *Church*, in manifestation, by *the word*, (for, all these acceptations have convenient Authors, and worthy to be followed) God is the Father of lights, of all lights; but so he is of raine, and clouds too. And God is the *Father of glory*; (as Saint *Paul* styles him) of all glory; whether of those beames of glory which he sheds upon us here, in the blessings, and preferments of this life, or that *waight of glory* which he reserves for us, in the life to come. From that inglorious drop of raine, that falls into the dust, and rises no more, to those glorious Saints who shall rise from the dust, and fall no more, but, as they arise at once to the fulnesse of *Essentiall* joy, so arise daily in *accidentiall* joyes, all are the children of God, and all alike of kin to us. And therefore let us not measure our avowing, or our countenancing of our kindred, by their measure of honour, or place, or riches in this world, but let us looke how fast they grow in the root, that is, in the same worship of the same God, who is ours, and their Father too.

## 49. From a Sermon Preached at Saint Pauls[1]

### (i)

FOR our first consideration, of Gods lothnesse to lose us, this is argument enough, That we are here now, *now* at the participation of that grace, which God alwayes offers to al such Congregations as these, gathered in his name. For, I pray God there stand any one amongst us here now, that hath not done something since *yesterday*, that made him unworthy of being here to day; and who, if he had been left under the damp, and mist of *yesterdayes sinne*, without the light of *new grace*, would never have found way hither of himself. If God be weary of me, and would faine be rid of me, he needs not repent that he wrapped me up in the *Covenant*, and derived me of *Christian parents*, (though he gave me a great help in *that*) nor repent that he bred me in a *true Church*, (though he afforded me a great assistance in *that*) nor repent that he hath brought me *hither* now, to the participation of his *Ordinances*, (though thereby also I have a great advantage) for, if God be weary of me, and would be rid of me, he may finde enough in me now, and here, to let me perish. A present *levity* in me that speake, a present *formality* in you that heare, a present *Hypocrisie* spread over us all, would justifie God, if now, and here, he should forsake us. When our blessed Saviour sayes, *When the Son of man comes, shall he finde faith upon earth?* we need not limit that question so, if he come to a *Westminster*, to an *Exchange*, to an *Army*, to a *Court*, shall he finde *faith* there? but if he come to a *Church*, if he come hither, shall he finde *faith* here? If (as Christ speaks in another sense, That *Judgement should begin at his owne house*,) the great and generall judgement should begin now at this *his house*, and that the first that should be taken up in the clouds, to meet the Lord Jesus, should be we, that are met now in this his house,

---

[1] On the text: 'Beware of the concision' (Phil. iii. 2).

Evelyn Simpson says of this and the following three sermons, all undated, which she placed together in volume x, that they can be 'considered together as in some way a defence of the Church of England against the attacks of Romanists and Separatists'. In the two Whitehall sermons (Nos. 51 and 52) the defence is mainly against Roman attacks. It was largely in Court circles that the Church of Rome made headway in the reign of Charles I. Donne's audience at St. Paul's was more likely to be influenced by Puritan attacks. We have excerpted passages from these four sermons as examples of Donne's controversial style and placed them together among the sermons of 1627, since Evelyn Simpson notes that in many of the sermons of 1626 to 1627 Donne strikes an unusually controversial note.

would we be glad of that acceleration, or would we thank him for that haste? Men *of little faith*, I feare we would not. *There was a day, when the Sonnes of God presented themselves before the Lord, and Satan came also amongst them*; one Satan amongst many Sonnes of God. Blessed Lord, is not our case far otherwise? do not we, (we, who, as we are but *we*, are all the Sonnes of Satan) present our selves before thee, and yet, thou Lord art amongst us? Is not the spirit of slumber and *wearinesse* upon one, and the spirit of *detraction*, and mis-interpretation upon another; upon one the spirit of *impenitence* for former sinnes, and the spirit of *recidivation* into old, or of *facility* and opennesse to admit tentations into new upon another? We, as we are but *we*, are all the Sonnes of Satan, and thou Lord, the onely Sonne of God, onely amongst us. If thou Lord wert weary of me, and wouldest be rid of me, (may many a soule here say) Lord thou knowest, and I know many a *midnight*, when thou mightest have been rid of me, if thou hadst left me to my selfe then. But *vigilavit Dominus*, the Lord vouchsafed to *watch* over me, and *deliciæ ejus*, the delight of the Lord was to be with me; And what is there in me, but his *mercy*? but then, what is there in his mercy, that that may not reach *to all*, as well as to *me*? The Lord is loth to lose any, the Lord would not the death of *any*; not of *any sinner*; much lesse if he do not see him, nor consider him so; the Lord would not lose him, *though a sinner*, much lesse *make* him a sinner, that he might be lost: *Vult omnes*, the Lord would have all men come unto him, and be saved.

## (ii)

Seeing is hearing, in Gods first language, the language of *works*. But then God translates himself, in particular *works*; *nationally*, he speaks in particular judgements, or deliverances to one *nation*; and, *domestically*, he speaks that language to a particular family; and so *personally* too, he speaks to every particular soul. God will speak unto me, in that voice, and in that way, which I am most delighted with, and hearken most to. If I be *covetous*, God wil tel me that heaven is a pearle, a treasure. If cheerfull and affected with mirth, that heaven is all *Joy*. If ambitious, and hungry of preferment, that it is all *Glory*. If sociable, and conversable, that it is a *communion of Saints*. God will make a *Fever* speake to me, and tell me his minde, that there is no health but in *him*; God will make the *disfavour*, and frowns of *him* I depend upon, speake to me, and tell me his minde, that there is no safe dependence, no assurance but in *him*; God will make a *storme* at Sea, or a *fire* by land, speake to me, and tell mee his minde, that there is no perpetuity, no possession but in *him*; nay, God will make my *sinne* speake to me, and tell me his minde; even my sinne shall bee a Sermon, and a Catechisme to me; God shall suffer mee to fall into some such sinne, as that by some circumstances in the sinne, or consequences from the sinne, I shall be drawn to hearken unto him; and whether I heare *Hosannaes*, acclamations, and commendations, or *Crucifiges*, exclamations and condemnations from the world, I shall stil finde the voice and tongue of God, though in the mouth of the Devill, and his instruments. God is a declaratory God. The whole yeare, is, to his Saints, a continuall *Epiphany*, one day of manifestation. In every minute that strikes upon the *Bell*, is a syllable, nay a syllogisme from God. And, and in my *last Bell*, God shall speake too; that Bell, when it tolls, shall tell me I am going, and when it rings out, shall tell you I am gone into the hands of that God, who is the God of the living and not of the dead, for, they dye not that depart in him.

## 50. From a Sermon Preached at Saint Pauls[1]

### (i)

WHEN our adversaries do so violently, so impetuously cry out, that we have no Church, no Sacrament, no Priesthood, because none are sent, that is, none have a right calling, for *Internall calling*, who are called by the Spirit of God, they can be no Judges, and for *Externall calling*, we admit them for Judges, and are content to be tried by their own *Canons*, and their own evidences, for our Mission and vocation, our sending and our calling to the Ministery. If they require a necessity of lawfull Ministers to the constitution of a Church, we require it with as much earnestnesse as they; *Ecclesia non est quæ non habet sacerdotem*, we professe with Saint *Hierome*, It is

[1] On the text: 'We pray ye in Christ's stead, be ye reconciled to God' (2 Cor. v. 20). See note to No. 49.

no Church that hath no Priest. If they require, that this spirituall power be received from them, who have the same power in themselves, we professe it too, *Nemo dat quod non habet*, no man can confer other power upon another, than he hath himself. If they require *Imposition of hands*, in conferring Orders, we joyn hands with them. If they will have it a Sacrament, men may be content to let us be as liberall of that name of Sacrament, as *Calvin* is; and he says of it, *Institut. l.* 4. c. 14. para. 20. *Non invitus patior vocari Sacramentum, ita inter ordinaria Sacramenta non numero*, I am not loth, it should be called a Sacrament, so it be not made an ordinary, that is, a generall Sacrament; and how ill hath this been taken at some of our mens hands, to speak of more such Sacraments, when indeed they have learnt this manner of speech, and difference of Sacraments, not onely from the ancient Fathers, but from *Calvin* himself, who always spoke with a holy warinesse, and discretion. Whatsoever their own authors, their own Schools, their own Canons doe require to be essentially and necessarily requisite in this Mission in this function, we, for our parts, and as much as concerns our Church of *England*, admit it too, and professe to have it. And whatsoever they can say for their Church, that from their first Conversion, they have had an orderly derivation of power from one to another, we can as justly and truly say of our Church, that ever since her first being of such a Church, to this day, she hath conserved the same order, and ever hath had, and hath now, those Ambassadours sent, with the same Commission, and by the same means, that they pretend to have in *their* Church. And being herein convinced, by the evidence of undeniable Record, which have been therefore shewed to some of their Priests, not being able to deny that such a Succession and Ordination, we have had, from the hands of such as were made Bishops according to their Canons, now they pursue their common beaten way, That as in our Doctrine, they confesse we affirm no Heresie, but that we deny some Truths, so in our Ordination, and sending, and Calling, when they cannot deny, but that from such a person, who is, by their own Canons, able to confer Orders, we, in taking our Orders, (after their own manner) receive the Holy Ghost, and the power of binding and loosing, yet, say they, we receive not the full power of Priests, for, we receive onely a power *in Corpus mysticum,* upon the mysticall body of Christ, that is, the persons that constitute the visible Church, but we should receive it *in Corpus verum,* a power upon the very naturall body, a power of Consecration, by way of *Transubstantiation.* They may be pleased to pardon, this, rather *Modesty,* than *Defect,* in us, who, so we may work fruitfully, and effectually upon the *mysticall* body of Christ, can be content that his reall, and true body work upon us. Not that we have no interest to work upon the reall body of Christ, since he hath made us Dispensers even of that, to the faithfull, in the Sacrament; but for such a power, as exceeds the *Holy Ghost,* who in the *incarnation* of Christ, when he overshadowed the blessed Virgin, did but make man of the woman, who was one part disposed by nature thereunto, whereas these men make man, and God too of bread, naturally wholly indisposed to any such change, for this power we confesse it is not in our Commission; and their Commission, and ours was all one; and the Commission is manifest in the Gospel; and, since they can charge us with no rasures, no expunctions, we must charge them with interlinings, and additions, to the first Commission. But for that power, which is to work upon you, to whom we are sent, we are defective in nothing, which they call necessary thereunto.

## (ii)

A man might get into that feast, without his wedding garment; so a man may get into the Church, to bee a visible part of a Christian Congregation, without this acceptation of reconciliation, that is the *particular apprehension,* and application of Christ; but hee is still subject to a remove, and to that question of confusion, *Quomodo intrasti,* How came you in? That man in the Gospell could have answered to that question, directly, I came in by the invitation, and conduct of thy servants, I was called in, I was led in; So they that come hither without this wedding garment, they may answer to Christs *Quomodo intrasti,* How camest thou in? I came in by faithfull *parents,* to whom, and their seed thou hast sealed a Covenant; I was admitted by thy *Servants* and Ministers in *Baptisme,* and have been led along by them, by comming to hear them preach thy word, and doing the other externall offices of a Christian. But there is more in this question; *Quomodo intrasti,* is not onely how *didst* thou come in, but how *durst* thou come in? If thou camest to my feast, without any purpose to eate, and so to discredit, to accuse either my meat, or the dressing of it, to quarrell at the *Doctrine,* or at the *Discipline* of my Church, *Quomodo intrasti,* How didst thou, How durst thou come in? If thou camest with a purpose to poison my meat, that it might infect others, with a determination to goe forward in thy sinne, whatsoever the Preacher say, and so encourage others by thy example, *Quomodo intrasti,* How durst thou come in? If thou camest in with thine own provision in thy pocket, and didst not relie upon mine, and think that thou canst be saved without *Sermons,* or *Sacraments, Quomodo intrasti,* How durst thou come in? Him that came in there, without this Wedding garment, the Master of the Feast cals *Friend;* but scornfully, *Friend how camest thou in?* But he cast him out. God may call us *Friends,* that is, admit, and allow us the estimation and credit of being of his *Church,* but at one time or other, hee shall minister that Interrogatory, *Friend, how came you in?* and for want of that Wedding garment, and for want of wearing it in the sight of men, (for it is not said that that man had no such Wedding garment at home, in his Wardrobe, but that hee had none *on*) for want of *Sanctification* in a holy life, God shall deliver us over to the execution of our own consciences, and eternall condemnation.

## 51. From a Sermon Preached at White-hall[1]

BUT in the other way of treading down grasse, (that is, the word of God) by the Additions and Traditions of men, the *Italian Babylon Rome* abounded, superabounded, overflowed, surrounded all. And this is much more dangerous than the other; for this mingling of humane additions, and traditions, upon equall necessity, and equall obligation as the word of God it selfe, is a kneading, an incorporating of *grasse and earth* together, so, as that it is impossible for the weake sheep, to avoid eating the meat of the *Serpent, Dust shalt thou*

---

[1] On the text: 'And as for my flock, they eat that, which ye have trodden with your feet, and they drink that which ye have fouled with your feet' (Ezek. xxxiv. 19).

See note to No. 49.

*eate all the days of thy life*. Now man upon his transgression, was not accursed, nor woman; The sheep were not accursed; But the earth was, and the Serpent was; and now this kneading, this incorporating of earth with grasse, traditions with the word, makes the sheep to eate the cursed meat of the cursed Serpent, *Dust shalt thou eat all the days of thy life*.

Now, in this treading down this grasse, this way, this suppressing it by traditions, be pleased to consider these *two applications*; some traditions doe destroy the word of God, extirpate it, annihilate it, as when a *Hog* doth root up the grass; In which case, not onely that turfe withers, and is presently useless, and unprofitable to the sheep, but if you dig never so low after, down to the Center of the earth, it is impossible ever to finde any more grass under it: so some traditions doe utterly oppose the word of God, without having under them, any mysterious signification, or any occasion or provocation of our devotion, which is the ordinary pretext of traditions, and *Ceremoniall additions* in their Church. And of this sort was that amongst the *Jews*, of which our *blessed Saviour* reproches them, that whereas by the law, children were to relieve decayed parents, they had brought in a tradition, of *Commutation*, of *Compensation*, that if those children gave a *gift* to the *Priest*, or compounded with the Priest, they were discharged of the former obligation. And of this sort are many traditions in the *Roman Church*; where, not onely the doctrines of *men* but the doctrine of *Devills*, (as the Apostle calls the forbidding of *Mariage*, and of *meats*) did not onely tread down, but root up the true grass.

The other sort of Traditions, and Ceremonies, doe not as the Hog, root up the grass, but as a *Mole*, cast a slack, and thin earth upon the face of the grass. Now, if the shepheard, or husbandman be present to scatter this earth againe, the sheep receive no great harme, but may safely feed upon the wholesome grass, that is under; but if the sheep, who are not able to scatter this earth, nor to finde the grass that lies under, be left to their own weakness, they may as easily starve in this case, as in the other; The *Mole* may damnifie them as much as the *Hog*. And of this sort, are those traditions, which induce *Ceremonies* into the Church, in *vestures*, in *postures* of the body, in *particular* things, and words, and actions, in

Baptisme or Mariage, or any other thing to be transacted in the Church. These ceremonies are not the institutions of *God* immediately, but they are a kind of light earth, that hath *under it* good and usefull significations, which when they be understood conduce much to the encrease and advancement of our devotion, and of the glory of God. And this is the iniquity that we complaine of in the *Roman Church*, that when we accuse them of multiplying impertinent, and insupportable ceremonies, they tell us, of some mysterious and pious signification, in the institution thereof at first; They tell us this, and it is sometimes true; But neither in Preaching nor practise, doe they scatter this earth to their own sheep, or shew them the grass that lies under, but suffer the people, to inhere, and arrest their thoughts, upon the ceremony it selfe, or that to which that ceremony mis-leads them; as in particular, (for the time will not admit many examples) when they *kneel at the Sacrament*, they are not told, that they kneel because they are then in the act of receiving an inestimable benefit at the hands of God, (which was the first reason of kneeling then) And because the *Priest* is then in the act of *prayer* in their behalfe, that that may preserve them, in body and soule, unto eternall life. But they are suffered to go on, in kneeling in adoration of that *bread*, which they take to be God. We deny not that there are *Traditions*, nor that there must be *ceremonies*, but that maters of *faith* should depend of these, or be made of these, that we deny; and that they should be made equall to *Scriptures*; for with that especially doth *Tertullian* reproch the Heretiques, that being pressed with Scriptures, they fled to Traditions, as things equall or superiour to the word of God. I am loth to depart from *Tertullian*, both because he is every where a Patheticall expresser of himselfe, and in this point above himselfe. *Nobis curiositate opus non est, post Jesum Christum, nec Inquisitione, post Evangelium.* Have we seen that face of Christ Jesus here upon earth, which Angels desired to see, and would we see a better face? Traditions perfecter than the word? Have we read the four *Evangelists*, and would we have a better Library? Traditions fuller than the word? *Cum credimus, nihil desideramus ultra credere*; when I beleeve God in Christ, dead, and risen againe according to the Scriptures, I have nothing else to beleeve; *Hoc enim prius credimus, non esse quod ultra credere debeamus*; This is the first Article of my Faith, that I am bound to beleeve nothing but articles of faith in an equall necessity to them. Will we be content to be well, and thank God, when we are well? *Hilary* tells us, when we are well; *Bene habet quod iis, quæ scripta sunt, contentus sis*; then thou art well, when thou satisfiest thy self with those things, which God hath vouchsafed to manifest in the *Scriptures. Si aliquis aliis verbis, quam quibus a Deo dictum est, demonstrare velit*, if any man will speake a new language, otherwise than God hath spoken, and present new Scriptures, (as he does that makes traditions equall to them) *Aut ipse non intelligit, aut legentibus non intelligendum relinquit*, either he understands not himself, or I may very well be content not to understand him, if I understand God without him. The *Fathers* abound in this opposing of Traditions, when out of those traditions, our adversaries argue an insufficiency in the Scriptures. *Solus Christus audiendus*, says Saint *Cyprian*, we hearken to none but Christ; *nec debemus attendere quid aliquis ante nos faciendum putarit*, neither are we to consider what any man *before us* thought fit to be done, *sed quid qui ante omnes est, fecerit*; but what he, who is *before all* them, did; *Christ Jesus* and his *Apostles*, who were not onely the primitive but the *pre-primitive Church*, did and appointed to be done. In this treading down of our grasse then in the *Roman* Church, first by their supine *Ignorance*, and barbarisme, and then by *traditions*, of which, some are pestilently infectious and *destroy* good words, some *cover* it so, as that not being declared to the people in their signification, they are uselesse to them, no *Babylon* could exceed the *Italian Babylon, Rome*, in treading down their grasse.

## 52. From a Sermon Preached at White-Hall[1]

Now, beloved, when our Adversaries cannot deny us this truth, that our Church was enwrapped, (though smothered) in theirs, that as that *Balsamum naturale*, which *Paracelsus* speaks of, that naturall *Balme* which is in every body, and would cure any wound, if that wound were kept clean, and recover any body, if that body were

---

[1] On the same text as No. 51.
See note to No. 49.

purged, as that naturall balme is in that body, how diseased soever that body be, so was our Church in theirs, they vexe us now, with that question, Why, if the case stood so, if your Fathers, when they eat our troden grasse, and drunk our troubled waters, were sound and in health, and continued sheep, and Gods sheep, and Gods flock, his Church with us, why went they from us? They ought us their residence, because they had received their Baptisme from us. And truly, it is not an impertinent, a frivolous reason, that of Baptisme, where there is nothing but conveniency, and no necessity in the case. But, if I be content to stay with my friend in an aguish aire, will he take it ill, if I go when the plague comes? Or if I stay in town till 20 die of the plague, shall it be lookd that I should stay when there die 1000? The infection grew hotter and hotter in *Rome*; and their *may*, came to a *must*, those things which were done before *de facto*, came at last to be articles of *Faith*, and *de jure*, must be beleeved and practised upon salvation. They chide us for going away, and they drove us away; If we abstained from communicating with their poysons, (being now growen to that height) they excommunicated us; They gave us no room amongst them but the fire, and they were so forward to burne Heretiques, that they called it heresie, not to stay to be burnt.

Yet we went not upon their driving, but upon *Gods calling*. As the whole prophecy of the deliverance of *Israel*, from *Babylon*, belongs to the Christian Church, both to the *Primitive* Church, at first, and to the *Reformed* since, so doth that voice, spoken to them, reach unto us, *Egredimini de Babylone, Goe ye out of Babylon with a voice of singing*, declare, show to the ends of the earth, that the Lord hath redeemed his servant *Jacob*. For, that *Rome* is not *Babylon*, they have but that one half-comfort, that one of their own authors hath ministred, that *Romæ regulariter male agitur*; that *Babylon* is Confusion, disorder, but at *Rome* all sinnes are committed in order, by the book, and they know the price, and therefore *Rome* is not *Babylon*. And since that many of their authors confesse, that *Rome* was *Babylon*, in the time of the persecuting Emperours, and that *Rome shall* be *Babylon* againe, in the time of *Antichrist*, how they will hedge in a *Jerusalem*, a holy City, between these two *Babylons*, is a cunning peece of Architecture. From this *Babylon* then were our

Fathers called by God; not onely by that *whispering* sibilation of the
holy Ghost, *sibilabo populum, I will hisse for my people*, and so gather
them, for I have redeemed them, and they shall increase, not onely
*by private inspirations*, but by generall acclamations; every where
principall writers, and preachers, and Princes too, (as much as could
stand with their safety) crying out against them *before Luther*, howsoever they will needs doe him that honour, to have been the first
mover, in this blessed revolution.

## 53. From a Sermon Preached at S. Dunstanes upon Trinity Sunday. 1627[1]

### (i)

*QUATUOR animalia sunt Ecclesiæ Doctores*, sayes S. *Ambrose*; These
foure Creatures are the Preachers of the Gospell; that we had established afore; But then, we adde with S. *Ambrose, Eandem significationem
habet primum animal, quodse cundum, quod tertium, quod quartum*; All these
foure Creatures make up but one Creature; all their qualities
concurre to the Qualification of a Minister; every Minister of God
is to have all, that all foure had; the courage of a *Lion*, the laborious-
ness of an *Oxe*, the perspicuity and cleare sight of the *Eagle*, and the
humanity, the discourse, the reason, the affability, the appliablenesse of a *Man*. S. *Dionys* the *Areopagite* had the same consideration
as S. *Ambrose* had, before him. He imprints it, he expresses it, and
extends it thus; *In Leone vis indomabilis*; In every Minister, I looke
for such an invincible courage, as should be of proofe, against
Persecution, (which is a great) and against Preferment, which is a
greater temptation; that neither Feares, nor Hopes shake his
constancy; neither his Christian constancy, to stagger him, nor his
Ministeriall constancy, to silence him; For this is *Vis indomabilis*,
the courage required in the Minister as he is a *Lion*. And then saies
that Father; *In Bove vis salutaris*, In every Minister, as he is said to
be an *Oxe*, I looke for labour; that he be not so over-growne, nor

---

[1] On the text: 'And the four beasts ha ‹ each of them six wings about him, and they were
full of eyes within; and they rest not day and night, saying, Holy, Holy, Holy, Lord God
Almighty, which was, and is, and is to come' (Rev. iv. 8).

See note to No. 26.

stall-fed, that he be thereby lazie; He must labour; And then, as
the labour of the Oxe is, his labour must be imployed upon usefull
and profitable things, things that conduce to the cleering, not the
perplexing of the understanding; and to the collecting, the uniting,
the fixing, and not the scattering, the dissolving, the pouring out
of a fluid, an unstable, an irresolved conscience; things of edification,
not speculation; For this is that *Vis salutaris*, which we require in
every Minister; that he labour at the Plough, and plough the right
ground; that he Preach for the saving of soules, and not for the
sharpning of wits. And then againe, *In Aquila vis speculatrix*; As
the Minister is presented in the notion and quality of an *Eagle*, we
require both an Open eye, and a Piercing eye; First, that he dare
looke upon other mens sins, and be not faine to winke at their
faults, because he is guilty of the same himselfe, and so, for feare of
a recrimination, incurre a prevarication; And then, that he be not
so dim-sighted, that he must be faine to see all through other mens
spectacles, and so preach the purposes of great men, in a factious
popularity, or the fancies of new men, in a Schismaticall singularity; but, with the Eagle, be able to looke to the Sun; to looke
upon the constant truth of God in his Scriptures, through his
Church; For this is *Vis speculatrix*, the open and the piercing eye of
the Eagle. And then lastly, *In homine vis ratiocinatrix*; As the Minister
is represented in the notion and quality of a *Man*, we require a
gentle, a supple, an appliable disposition, a reasoning, a perswasive
disposition; That he doe not alwaies, presse all things with Authority, with Censures, with Excommunications; That he put not all
points of Religion, alwaies upon that one issue, *Quicunque vult salvus
esse*, If you wil be saved, you must beleeve this, all this, and *Qui non
crediderit, damnabitur*, If you doubt of this, any of this, you are
infallibly, necessarily damned; But, that he be also content to
descend to mens reason, and to worke upon their understanding,
and their naturall faculties, as well as their faith, and to give them
satisfaction, and reason (as far as it may be had) in that which they
are to beleeve; that so as the Apostle, though he had authority to
command, yet did *Pray them in Christs stead to be reconciled to God*,
So the Minister of God, though (as he is bound to doe) he doe tell
them what they are bound to beleeve, yet he also tels them, why

they are to beleeve it; for this is *Vis ratiocinatrix*, The holy gentle-
nesse and appliablenesse, implied in that forme of a Man.

## (ii)

But have the Saints of God no Vacation? doe they never cease?
nay, as the word imports, *Requiem non habent*, They have no *Rest*.
Beloved, God himselfe rested not, till the seventh day; be thou
content to stay for thy Sabbath, till thou maist have an eternall
one. If we understand this, of rest meerly, of bodily rest, the Saints
of God are least likely to have it, in this life; For, this life, is (to
them especially, above others) a businesse, and a perplext businesse,
a warfare, and a bloody warfare, a voyage, and a tempestuous
voyage. If we understand this rest to be Cessation, Intermission,
the Saints in heaven have none of that, in this service. It is a labour
that never wearies, to serve God there. As the Sun is no wearier
now, than when he first set out, six thousand yeares since; As that
Angel, which God hath given to protect thee, is not weary of his
office, for all thy perversenesses, so, howsoever God deale with
thee, be not thou weary of bearing thy part, in his Quire here in
the Militant Church. God will have low voyces, as well as high;
God will be glorified *De profundis*, as well as *In excelsis*; God will
have his tribute of praise, out of our adversity, as well as out of our
prosperity. And that is it which is intimated, and especially intended in the phrase which followes, *Day and night*. For, it is not
onely that those Saints of God who have their Heaven upon earth,
doe praise him in the night; according to that of S. *Jerome, Sanctis
ipse somnus, oratio*; and that of S. *Basil, Etiam somnia Sanctorum preces
sunt*; That holy men doe praise God, and pray to God in their sleep,
and in their dreames; nor only that which *David* speaks of, of rising
in the night, and fixing stationary houres for prayer; But even in
the depth of any spirituall night, in the shadow of death, in the
midnight of afflictions and tribulations, God brings light out of
darknesse, and gives his Saints occasion of glorifying him, not only
in the dark, (though it be dark) but from the dark, (because it is
dark.) This is a way unconceiveable by any, unexpressible to any,
but those that have felt that manner of Gods proceeding in themselves, That be the night what night it will, be the oppression of

what Extention, or of what Duration it can, all this retards not
their zeal to Gods service; Nay, they see God better in the dark,
than they did in the light; Their tribulation hath brought them to
a nearer distance to God, and God to a clearer manifestation to
them.

### (iii)

And therefore, let us reverently embrace such provisions, and such
assistances as the Church of God hath ordained, for retaining and
celebrating the Trinity, in this particular contemplation, as they
are to come to Judgement. And let us at least provide so far, to
stand upright in that Judgement, as not to deny, nor to dispute the
Power, or the Persons of those Judges. A man may make a pety
larceny high treason so; If being called in question for that lesser
offence, he will deny that there is any such Power, any such
Soveraigne, any such King, as can call him in question for it, he
may turne his whipping into a quartering. At that last Judgement,
we shall be arraigned for not cloathing, not visiting, not harbouring
the poore; For, our not giving is a taking away; our withholding,
is a withdrawing; our keeping to our selves, is a stealing from them.
But yet, all this is but a pety larceny, in respect of that high treason,
of infidelity, of denying or doubting of the distinct Persons of the
holy, blessed, and glorious Trinity. To beleeve in God, one great,
one universall, one infinite power, does but distinguish us from
beasts; For there are no men that do not acknowledge such a
Power, or that do not believe in it, if they acknowledge it; Even
they that acknowledge the devill to be God, beleeve in the devill.
But that which distinguishes man from man, that which onely
makes his Immortality a blessing, (for, even Immortality is part of
their damnation that are damned, because it were an ease, it were
a kind of pardon to them to be mortall, to be capable of death,
though after millions of generations) is, to conceive aright of the
Power of the Father, of the Wisdome of the Son, of the Goodnesse of
the Holy Ghost; Of the Mercie of the Father, of the Merits of the
Son, of the Application of the Holy Ghost; Of the Creation of
the Father, of the Redemption of the Son, of the Sanctification of the

Holy Ghost. Without this, all notions of God are but confused, all worship of God is but Idolatry, all confession of God is but Atheisme; For so the Apostle argues, *When you were without Christ, you were without God.* Without this, all morall vertues are but diseases; Liberality is but a popular baite, and not a benefit, not an almes; Chastity is but a castration, and an impotency, not a temperance, not mortification; Active valour is but a fury, whatsoever we do, and passive valour is but a stupidity, whatsoever we suffer. Naturall apprehensions of God, though those naturall apprehensions may have much subtilty, Voluntary elections of a Religion, though those voluntary elections may have much singularity, Morall directions for life, though those morall directions may have much severity, are all frivolous and lost, if all determine not in Christianity, in the Notion of God, so as God hath manifested and conveyed himself to us; in God the Father, God the Son, and God the Holy Ghost, whom this day we celebrate, in the Ingenuity, and in the Assiduity, and in the Totality, recommended in this text, and in this acclamation of the text, *Holy, Holy, Holy, Lord God Almighty, which was, and is, and is to come.*

## 54. From a Sermon of Commemoration of the Lady Danvers, late Wife of Sir John Danvers. Preach'd at Chilsey, where she was lately buried. By John Donne Dean of St. Pauls, London. 1 July 1627[1]

### (i)

*IT is a fearefull thing to fall into the hands of the living God,* if I doe but fall into his hands, in a fever in my bed, or in a tempest at Sea, or in a discontent at home; But, *to fall into the hands of the living God,* so, as that, that *living God,* enters into *Judgement,* with mee, and passes a finall, and irrevocable Judgement upon mee, this is a

---

[1] On the text: 'Nevertheless, we, according to his promises, look for new heavens, and new earth, wherein dwelleth righteousness' (2 Pet. iii. 13).

Magdalen, daughter of Sir Richard Newport, reputed the largest landowner in Shropshire, was first married to Richard Herbert, by whom she had seven sons and three daughters. Her eldest son was Lord Herbert of Cherbury, and her youngest, George Herbert, the poet. She was left a widow in 1596, and in 1608 she married Sir John Danvers. Donne's friendship with her went back to 1607 and during the plague of 1625 he took refuge in her house at Chelsea.

Consternation of all my spirits, an Extermination of all my succours.
I consider, what *God* did with one word, with one *Fiat* he made all;
And, I know, he can doe as much with another word; With one
*Pereat*, he can destroy all; As hee *spake, and it was done, he commanded
and all stood fast*; so he can *speak*, and all shall bee *undone*; *command*,
and all shall *fall in peeces*. I consider, that I may bee surpriz'd by
*that day*, the *day of Judgement*. Here Saint *Peter* saies, *The day of the
Lord wil come as a Thiefe*. And Saint *Paul* saies, we cannot be ignorant
of it, *Your selves know perfectly, that the day of the Lord so commeth as a
Thiefe*. And, as the *Judgement* it selfe, so the *Judge* himselfe saies of
himselfe, *I will come upon thee as a Thiefe*. He saies, *he will*, and he
*does it*. For it is not, *Ecce veniam*, but *Ecce venio, Behold I doe come upon
thee as a Thiefe*; There, the *future*, which might imply a *dilatorinesse*,
is reduc't to an infallible *present*; It is so sure, that he *will* doe it,
that he is said, to *have* done it already. I consider, *hee will come as a
Thiefe*, and then, *as a Thiefe in the night*; And I doe not only not
know *when* that night shall be, (For, himselfe, as he is the Son of
man, knowes not that) but I doe not only not know *what* night,
that is, *which* night, but not *what* night, that is, *what kinde* of night
he meanes. It is said so often, so often repeated, that *he will come as a
Thiefe in the night*, as that hee may meane all kinde of *nights*. In my
night of *Ignorance* hee may come; and hee may come in my night of
*Wantonnesse*; In my night of inordinate and sinfull *melancholy*, and
*suspicion* of his *mercy*, hee may come; and he may come in the night
of so *stupid*, or so *raging* a *sicknesse*, as that he shall not *come* by *comming*; Not come so, as that I shall receive him in the *absolution* of
his *Minister*, or receive him in the participation of his *body* and
his *bloud* in the *Sacrament*. So hee may come upon mee, as *such a
Thiefe*, in *such a night*; nay, when all these nights of *Ignorance*, of
*Wantonnesse*, of *Desperation*, of *Sicknesse*, of *Stupiditie*, of *Rage*, may bee
upon mee all at once. I consider, that the *Holy Ghost* meant to make
a deepe impression of a great *terror* in me, when he came to that
expression, *That the Heavens should passe away*, Cum stridore, *with a
great noise, and the Elements melt with fervent heat, and the earth, and the
workes that are therein*, shall be burnt up; And when he adds in *Esay*,
*The Lord will come with fire, and with his Chariots, like a whirlewind, to
render his anger, with fury; for by fire, and by his sword will the Lord*

*plead with all flesh.* So when hee proceeds in *Joel, a day of darknesse, and gloominesse; and yet a fire devoureth before them, and a flame burneth behind them.* And so in *Daniel* also, *His Throne a fiery flame, and his wheeles a burning fire, and a fiery streame issuing from him.* I consider too, that with this *streame of fire,* from him, there shall bee a *streame,* a deluge, a floud of teares, from us; and all that *floud,* and *deluge* of teares, shall not put out one coale, nor quench one sparke of that fire. *Behold, hee commeth with clouds, and every eye shall see him;* And, *plangent omnes, All the kindreds of the earth shall waile and lament,* and weepe and howle *because of him.* I consider, that I shall *looke* upon him then, and see all my *Sinnes, Substance,* and *Circumstance* of sin, *Waight,* and *measure* of sinne, *hainousnesse* and *continuance* of sinne, all my sinnes imprinted in his wounds; and how shall I bee affected then, confounded then to see him so mangled with my sinnes? But then I consider againe, that I shall looke upon him againe, and not see all my sinnes in his wounds; My *forgotten* sinnes, mine *un-considered, unconfest, unrepented* sinnes, I shall not see there; And how shall I bee affected then, when I shall stand in *Judgement,* under the guiltinesse of some sins, not buried in the wounds, not drown'd in the bloud of my *Saviour? Many,* and *many,* and *very many, infinite,* and *infinitely infinite,* are the *terrours* of that day.

### (ii)

To this consideration of her *person* then, belongs this, that *God* gave her such a *comelinesse,* as, though shee were not *proud* of it, yet she was so content with it, as not to goe about to mend it, by any *Art.* And for her *Attire,* (which is another *personall circumstance*) it was never *sumptuous,* never *sordid;* But alwayes agreeable to her *quality,* and agreeable to her *company;* Such as shee might, and such, as others, such as shee was, did weare. For, in such things of *indifferency* in themselves, many times, a *singularity* may be a little worse, than a fellowship in that, which is not altogether so good. It may be *worse,* nay, it may be a *worse pride,* to weare worse things, than others doe. Her *rule* was *mediocrity.*

And, as to the consideration of the *house,* belongs the considera-tion of the *furniture* too, so, in these *personall circumstances,* we consider her *fortune,* her *estate.* Which was in a faire, and noble proportion, deriv'd from her *first husband*, and fairely, and nobly dispenc'd, by her selfe, with the allowance of her *second*. In which shee was one of *Gods* true *Stewards*, and *Almoners* too. There are dispositions, which had rather *give presents*, than *pay debts*; and rather doe good to *strangers*, than to those, that are *neerer* to them. But *shee* always thought the care of her family, a *debt*, and upon that, for the *provision*, for the *order*, for the *proportions*, in a good largenesse, shee plac't her first thoughts, of that kinde. For, for our *families*, we are *Gods Stewards*; For those without, we are his *Almoners*. In which office, shee gave not at some *great dayes*, or some solemne goings abroad, but, as *Gods true Almoners*, the *Sunne*, and *Moone*, that passe on, in a continuall doing of good, as shee receiv'd her *daily bread* from God, so, *daily*, she distributed, and imparted it, to others. In which office, though she never turn'd her face from those, who in a strict inquisition, might be call'd idle, and vagrant Beggers, yet shee ever look't first, upon them, who *labour'd*, and whose *labours* could not overcome the *difficulties*, nor bring in the *necessities* of this life; and to the *sweat of their browes*, shee contributed, even her *wine*, and her *oyle*, and any thing that was, and any thing, that might be, if it were not, prepar'd for her owne table. And as her house was a *Court*, in the conversation of the best, and an *Almeshouse*, in feeding the *poore*, so was it also an *Hospitall*, in ministring releefe to the *sicke*. And truly, the love of doing good in this kind, of *ministring to the sicke*, was the *hony*, that was spread over all her bread; the *Aire*, the *Perfume*, that breath'd over all her house; The disposition that dwelt in those her children, and those her kindred, which dwelt with her, so bending this way, that the *studies* and *knowledge* of *one*, the *hand* of another, and *purse* of all, and a *joynt-facility*, and *opennesse*, and *accessiblenesse* to persons of the meanest quality, concur'd in this blessed *Act* of *Charity*, to *minister releefe to the sicke*. Of which, my selfe, who, at that time, had the favour to bee admitted into the *family*, can, and must testifie this, that when the late heavy *visitation* fell hotly upon this *Towne*, when every doore was shut up, and, lest *Death* should enter into the house, every house was made a *Sepulchre* of them that were in it, then, then, in that time of *infection*, divers persons visited with that *infection*, had their releefe, and releefe *appliable to that very infection*, from this house.

Now when I have said thus much (rather thus little) of her *person*, as of a *house*, That the *ground* upon which it was built, was the *family* where she was *borne*, and then, where she was *married*, and then, the time of her *widowhood*, and lastly, her *last mariage*, And that the *house* it selfe, was those faire *bodily endowments*, which *God* had bestow'd upon her, And the *furniture* of that *house*, the *fortune*, and the *use* of that *fortune*, of which *God* had made her *Steward* and *Almoner*, when I shall also have said, that the *Inhabitants* of this *house*, (rather the *servants*, for they did but wait upon *Religion* in her) were those married couples, of *morall vertues*, *Conversation* married with a *Retirednesse*, *Facility* married with a *Reservednesse*, *Alacrity* married with a *Thoughtfulnesse*, and *Largenesse* married with a *Providence*, I may have leave to depart from this consideration of her *person*, and *personall circumstances*, lest by insisting longer upon them, I should seeme to pretend, to say all the good, that might bee said of her; But that's not in my *purpose*; yet, onely therefore, because it is not in my *power*; For I would doe her all *right*, and all you that good, if I could, to say all. But, I haste to an end, in consideration of some things, that appertaine more expresly to me, than these *personall*, or *civill*, or *morall* things doe.

In those, the next is, the *Secundum promissa*, That shee govern'd her selfe, *according to his promises*; his promises, laid downe in his *Scriptures*. For, as the *rule* of all her *civill Actions*, was *Religion*, so, the *rule* of her *Religion*, was the *Scripture*; And, her *rule*, for her particular understanding of the *Scripture*, was the *Church*. Shee never diverted towards the *Papist*, in undervaluing the *Scripture*; nor towards the *Separatist*, in undervaluing the *Church*. But in the *doctrine*, and *discipline* of that *Church*, in which, *God* seal'd her, to himselfe, in *Baptisme*, shee brought up her children, shee assisted her family, she dedicated her soule to *God* in her life, and surrendered it to him in her death; And, in that forme of *Common Prayer*, which is ordain'd by that *Church*, and to which she had accustom'd her selfe, with her family, twice every day, she joyn'd with that company, which was about her *death-bed*, in answering to every part thereof, which the Congregation is directed to answer to, with a *cleere understanding*, with a *constant memory*, with a *distinct voyce*, not two houres before she died.

*According to this promise*, that is, the will of *God* manifested in the *Scriptures*, She *expected*; Shee expected this, that she hath received; *Gods Physicke*, and *Gods Musicke*; a *Christianly death*. For, *death*, in the *old Testament* was a *Commination*; but in the *new Testament*, *death* is a *Promise*; When there was a *Super-dying*, a *death* upon the *death*, a *Morte* upon the *Morieris*, a *Spirituall* death after the *bodily*, then wee died *according to Gods threatning*; Now, when by the *Gospell* that *second death* is taken off, though wee die still, yet we die *according to his Promise*; That's a part of his *mercy*, and his *Promise*, which his *Apostle* gives us from him, That wee shall *all bee changed*; For, after that *promise*, that *change*, follow's that triumphant *Acclamation*, *O death where is thy sting, O grave where is thy victory*? Consider us fallen in *Adam*, and wee are miserable, that wee must die; But consider us restor'd and redintegrated in *Christ*, wee were more miserable if wee might not die; Wee lost the *earthly Paradise* by death then; but wee get not *Heaven*, but by *death*, now. This shee expected till it came, and embrac't it when it came. How may we thinke, shee was joy'd to see that face, that *Angels* delight to looke upon, the face of her *Saviour*, that did not abhor the face of his fearfullest *Messenger*, Death? Shee shew'd no feare of his face, in any change of her owne; but died without any change of *countenance*, or *posture*; without any *strugling*, any *disorder*; but her *Death-bed* was as quiet, as her *Grave*. To another *Magdalen*, *Christ* said upon earth, *Touch me not, for I am not ascended*. Being ascended now, to his glory, and she being gone up to him, after shee had awaited his leisure, so many yeeres, as that more, would soone have growne to bee *vexation*, and *sorrow*, as her last words here, were, *I submit my will to the will of God*; so wee doubt not, but the first word which she heard there, was that *Euge*, from her *Saviour*, *Well done good and faithfull servant; enter into thy masters joy*.

Shee expected that; dissolution of body, and soule; and rest in both, from the incumbrances, and tentations of this world. But yet, shee is in *expectation* still; Still a *Reversionarie*; And a *Reversionary* upon a long life; The whole world must die, before she come to a *possession* of this *Reversion*; which is a *Glorified body in the Resurrection*. In which *expectation*, she return's to her former *charity*; shee will not have that, till *all wee* shall have it, as well as shee; She eat not her morsels alone, in her life, (as *Job* speakes) Shee lookes not for the *glory* of the *Resurrection* alone, after her death. But when *all we*, shall have beene mellow'd in the earth, many yeeres, or chang'd in the *Aire*, in the twinkling of an eye, (*God* knowes which) That *body* upon which you tread now, That *body* which now, whilst I speake, is mouldring, and crumbling into lesse, and lesse dust, and so hath some *motion*, though no *life*, That *body*, which was the *Tabernacle* of a *holy Soule*, and a *Temple* of the *holy Ghost*, That *body* that was eyes to the blinde, and hands, and feet to the lame, whilst it liv'd, and being dead, is so still, by having beene so *lively* an example, to teach others, to be so, That *body* at last shall have her last expectation satisfied, and dwell *bodily*, with that *Righteousnesse*, in these *new Heavens*, and *new Earth*, for *ever*, and *ever*, and *ever* and *infinite*, and *super-infinite evers*. Wee end all, with the *valediction* of the *Spouse* to *Christ*: *His left hand is under my head, and his right embraces mee*, was the *Spouses valediction*, and *goodnight* to *Christ* then, when she laid her selfe downe to sleepe in the strength of his *Mandrakes*, and in the power of his *Spices*, as it is exprest there; that is, in the *influence* of his *mercies*. Beloved, every good *Soule* is the *Spouse* of *Christ*. And this good *Soule*, being thus laid downe to sleepe in his peace, *His left hand under her head*, gathering, and composing, and preserving her *dust*, for *future Glory*, *His right hand embracing her*, assuming, and establishing her *soule* in present *Glory*, in his *name*, and in her *behalfe*, I say that, to *all you*, which *Christ* sayes there, in the behalfe of that *Spouse*, *Adjuro vos*, *I adjure you*, *I charge you*, *O daughters of Jerusalem, that yee wake her not, till she please*. The words are directed to the *daughters*, rather than to the *sons of Jerusalem*, because for the most part, the aspersions that women receive, either in *Morall* or *Religious* actions, proceed from women themselves. Therfore, *Adjuro vos*, I charge you, O ye daughters of *Jerusalem*, wake her not. Wake her not, with any *halfe calumnies*, with any *whisperings*; But if you wil wake her, wake her, and keepe her awake with an active imitation, of her *Morall*, and her *Holy vertues*. That so her *example* working upon you, and the number of *Gods Saints*, being the sooner, by this blessed *example*, fulfil'd wee may all meet, and meet quickly in that *kingdome*, which *hers*, and *our* Saviour, hath purchac't for us all, with the inestimable price, of his incorruptible bloud.

## 55. From a Sermon Preached at the Earl of Bridgewaters house in London at the mariage of his daughter, the Lady Mary, to the eldest sonne of the Lord Herbert of Castle-iland, Novemb. 19. 1627[1]

### (i)

THERE are so many evidences of the immortality of the soule, even to a naturall mans *reason*, that it required not an Article of the Creed, to fix this notion of the Immortality of the soule. But the Resurrection of the *Body* is discernible by no other light, but that of *Faith*, nor could be fixed by any lesse assurance than an *Article* of the *Creed*. Where be all the splinters of that Bone, which a shot hath shivered and scattered in the Ayre? Where be all the Atoms of that flesh, which a *Corrasive* hath eat away, or a *Consumption* hath breath'd, and exhal'd away from our arms, and other Limbs? In what wrinkle, in what furrow, in what bowel of the earth, ly all the graines of the ashes of a body burnt a thousand years since? In what corner, in what ventricle of the sea, lies all the jelly of a Body drowned in the *generall flood*? What cohærence, what sympathy, what dependence maintaines any relation, any correspondence, between that arm that was lost in Europe, and that legge that was lost in Afrique or Asia, scores of yeers between? One humour of our dead body produces worms, and those worms suck and exhaust all other humour, and then all dies, and all dries, and molders into dust, and that dust is blowen into the River, and that puddled water tumbled into the sea, and that ebs and flows in infinite revolutions, and still, still God knows in what *Cabinet* every *seed-Pearle* lies, in what part of the world every graine of every mans dust lies; and, *sibilat populum suum*, (as his Prophet speaks in another case) he whispers, he hisses, he beckens for the bodies of his Saints, and in the twinckling of an eye, that body that was scattered over all the

---

[1] On the text: 'For, in the resurrection, they neither marry nor are given in marriage, but are as the angels of God in Heaven' (Matt. xxii. 30).

John, first Earl of Bridgewater, was the son of Donne's old employer, Sir Thomas Egerton, and, like Donne, went on the Cadiz expedition of 1596. Edward Herbert, eldest son of Magdalen Herbert, was given the Irish peerage of Castle Island in 1624 and created Lord Herbert of Cherbury in the English peerage in 1629.

elements, is sate down at the right hand of God, in a glorious resurrection. A Dropsie hath extended me to an enormous corpulency, and unwieldinesse; a Consumption hath attenuated me to a feeble macilency and leannesse, and God raises me a body, such as it should have been, if these infirmities had not interven'd and deformed it. *David* could goe no further in his book of Psalms, but to that, *Let every thing that hath breath praise the Lord*; ye, saies he, ye that have breath, praise ye the Lord, and that ends the book: But, that my *Dead body* should come to praise the Lord, this is that *New Song*, which I shall learne, and sing in heaven; when, not onely *my soule* shall *magnify the Lord, and my Spirit rejoyce in God my Saviour*; but I shall have mine old eies, and eares, and tongue, and knees, and receive such glory in my body my selfe, as that, in that body, so glorifyed by God, I also shall glorify him.

## (ii)

That there are distinct orders of *Angels*, assuredly I beleeve; but what they are, I cannot tell; *Dicant qui possunt; si tamen probare possunt quod dicunt*, saies that Father, Let them tell you that can, so they be able to prove, that they tell you true. They are Creatures, that have not so much of a Body as *flesh* is, as *froth* is, as a *vapor* is, as a *sigh* is, and yet with a touch they shall molder a rocke into lesse Atomes, than the sand that it stands upon; and a milstone into smaller flower, than it grinds. They are Creatures *made*, and yet not a minute elder now, than when they were first made, if they were made before all measure of time began; nor, if they were made in the beginning of Time, and be now six thousand yeares old, have they one wrinckle of Age in their face, or one sobbe of wearinesse in their lungs. They are *primogeniti Dei*, Gods eldest sonnes; They are super-elementary meteors, they hang between the nature of God, and the nature of man, and are of middle Condition; And, (if we may offencelessely expresse it so) they are *ænigmata Divina*, The Riddles of Heaven, and the perplexities of speculation.

## 56. From a Sermon Preached at White-hall, February 29. 1628[1]

### (i)

HE that will dy with Christ upon Good-Friday, must hear his own bell toll all Lent; he that will be partaker of his passion at last, must conform himself to his discipline of prayer and fasting before. Is there any man, that in his chamber hears a bell toll for another man, and does not kneel down to pray for that dying man? and then when his charity breaths out upon another man, does he not also reflect upon himself, and dispose himself as if he were in the state of that dying man? We begin to hear Christs bell toll now, and is not our bell in the chime? We must be in his grave, before we come to his resurrection, and we must be in his death-bed before we come to his grave: we must do as he did, fast and pray, before we can say as he said, that *In manus tuas*, Into thy hands O Lord I commend my Spirit. You would not go into a Medicinal Bath without some preparatives; presume not upon that Bath, the blood of Christ Jesus, in the Sacrament then, without preparatives neither. Neither say to your selves, we shall have preparatives enough, warnings enough, many more Sermons before it come to that, and so it is too soon yet; you are not sure you shall have more; not sure you shall have all this; not sure you shall be affected with any. If you be, when you are, remember that as in that good Custome in these Cities, you hear cheerful street musick in the winter mornings, but yet there was a sad and doleful bel-man, that wak'd you, and call'd upon you two or three hours before that musick came; so for all that blessed musick which the servants of God shall present to you in this place, it may be of use, that a poor bell-man wak'd you before, and though but by his noyse, prepared you for their musick.

### (ii)

For to suffer for God, man to suffer for God, I to suffer for my Maker, for my Redeemer, is such a thing, as no such thing, except-

---

[1] On the text: 'And when he had said this, he fell asleep' (Acts vii. 60).
29 February 1628 was the first Friday in Lent, Donne's usual day for preaching at Court.

ing only Gods sufferings for man can fall into the consideration of
man. Gods suffering for man was the Nadir, the lowest point of
Gods humiliation, mans suffering for God is the Zenith, the highest
point of mans exaltation: That as man needed God, and God would
suffer for man, so God should need man, and man should suffer for
God; that after Gods general Commission, *fac hoc & vives*, do this
and thou shalt live, I should receive and execute a new Commission,
*Patere hoc & vives abundantius*, suffer this and you shall have life, and
life more abundantly, as our Saviour speaks in the Gospel; that
when I shall ask my soul *Davids* question, *Quid retribuam*, what shall
I render to the Lord, I shall not rest in *Davids* answer, *Accipiam
Calicem*, I will take the cup of salvation, in applying his blood to
my soul, but proceed to an *Effundam Calicem*, I will give God a Cup,
a cup of my blood, that whereas to me the meanest of Gods servants
it is honor enough to be believed for Gods sake: God should be
believed for my sake, and his Gospel the better accepted, because
the seal of my blood is set to it; that that dew which should water
his plants, the plants of his Paradise, his Church, should drop from
my veines, and that sea, that red sea, which should carry up his
bark, his Ark, to the heavenly Jerusalem, should flow from me:
This is that that poures joy even into my gladness, and glory even
into mine honor, and peace even into my security; that exaltes
and improves every good thing, every blessing that was in me
before, and makes even my creation glorious, and my redemption
precious; and puts a farther value upon things inestimable before,
that I shall fulfil the sufferings of Christ in my flesh, and that I shall
be offerd up for his Church, though not for the purchasing of it,
yet for the fencing of it, though not by way of satisfaction as he
was, but by way of example and imitation as he was too. Whether
that be absolutely true or no, which an Author of much curiosity
in the Roman Church saies, that *Inter tot millia millium*, amongst so
many thousand thousands of Martyrs in the Primitive Church, it
cannot be said that ever one lack'd burial, (I know not whence he
raises that) certainly no Martyr ever lack'd a grave in the wounds of
his Saviour, no nor a tomb, a monument, a memorial in this life, in
that sense wherein our Saviour speaks in the Gospel, That no man
shall leave house, or Brother, or wife for him, but he shall receive

an hundred fold in this life; Christ does not mean he shall have a
hundred houses, or a hundred wives, or a hundred Brethren; but
that that comfort which he lost in losing those things shall be
multiplied to him in that proportion even in this life. In which
words of our Saviour, as we see the dignity and reward of Martyrdome, so we see the extent and latitude, and compass of Martyrdome too; that not only loss of life, but loss of that which we love
in this life; not only the suffering of death, but the suffering of
Crosses in our life, contracts the Name, and entitles us to the reward of Martyrdome. All Martyrdome is not a *Smithfeild* Martyrdome, to burn for religion. To suffer injuries, and upon advantages
offerd, not to revenge those injuries is a Court Martyrdome. To
resist outward tentations from power, and inward tentations from
affections, in matter of Judicature, between party and party, is a
*Westminster* Martyrdome. To seem no richer than they are, not to
make their states better, when they make their private bargains
with one another, and to seem so rich, as they are, and not to make
their states worse, when they are call'd upon to contribute to
publick services, this is an Exchange-Martyrdome. And there is a
Chamber-Martyrdome, a Bosome-Martyrdome too; *Habet pudicitia
servata Martyrium suum*, Chastity is a dayly Martyrdome; and so
all fighting of the Lords battails, all victory over the Lords Enemies,
in our own bowels, all chearful bearing of Gods Crosses, and all
watchful crossing of our own immoderate desires is a Martyrdome
acceptable to God, and a true copy of our pattern *Stephen*, so it be
inanimated with that which was even the life and soul and price of
all *Stephens* actions and passions, that is, fervent charity, which is
the last contemplation, in which we propose him for your Example;
that as he, you also may be just paymasters in discharging the
debt, which you owe the world in the signification of your Names;
and early Disciples and appliers of your selves to Christ Jesus, and
humble servants of his, without inordinate ambition of high
places; and constant Martyrs, in dying every day as the Apostle
speaks, and charitable intercessors, and Advocates and Mediators
to God, even for your heaviest Enemies.

## (iii)

Here I shall only present to you two Pictures, two pictures in little: two pictures of dying men; and every man is like one of these, and may know himself by it; he that dies in the Bath of a peaceable, and he that dies upon the wrack of a distracted conscience. When the devil imprints in a man, *a mortuum me esse non curo*, I care not though I were dead, it were but a candle blown out, and there were an end of all: where the Devil imprints that imagination, God will imprint an *Emori nolo*, a loathness to die, and fearful apprehension at his transmigration: As God expresses the bitterness of death, in an ingemination, *morte morietur*, in a conduplication of deaths, he shall die, and die, die twice over; So *ægrotando ægrotabit*, in sicknesse he shall be sick, twice sick, body-sick and soul-sick too, sense-sick and conscience-sick together; when, as the sinnes of his body have cast sicknesses and death upon his Soule, so the inordinate sadnesse of his Soule, shall aggravate and actuate the sicknesse of his body. His Physitian ministers, and wonders it works not; He imputes that to flegme, and ministers against that, and wonders again that it works not: He goes over all the humors, and all his Medicines, and nothing works, for there lies at his Patients heart a dampe that hinders the concurrence of all his faculties, to the intention of the Physitian, or the virtue of the Physick. Loose not, O blessed Apostle, thy question upon this Man, *O Death where is thy sting? O Grave where is thy victory?* for the sting of Death is in every limb of his body, and his very body is a victorious grave upon his Soule: And as his Carcas and his Coffin shall lie equally insensible in his grave, so his Soule, which is but a Carcas, and his body, which is but a Coffin of that Carcas, shall be equally miserable upon his Death-bed; And Satan's Commissions upon him shall not be signed by Succession, as upon *Job*, first against his goods, and then his Servants, and then his children, and then himselfe; but not at all upon his life; but he shall apprehend all at once, Ruine upon himselfe and all his, ruine upon himselfe and all him, even upon his life; both his lives, the life of this, and the life of the next world too. Yet a drop would redeeme a shoure, and a Sigh now a Storme then: Yet a teare from the eye, would

save the bleeding of the heart, and a word from the mouth now, a
roaring, or (which may be worse) a silence of consternation, of
stupefaction, of obduration at that last houre. Truly, if the death
of the wicked ended in Death, yet to scape that manner of death
were worthy a Religious life. To see the house fall, and yet be afraid
to goe out of it; To leave an injur'd world, and meet an incensed
God; To see oppression and wrong in all thy professions, and to
foresee ruine and wastefulnesse in all thy Posterity; and Lands
gotten by one sin in the Father, molder away by another in the
Sonne; To see true figures of horror, and ly, and fancy worse; To
begin to see thy sins but then, and finde every sin (at first sight)
in the proportion of a Gyant, able to crush thee into despair; To
see the Blood of Christ, imputed, not to thee, but to thy Sinnes;
To see Christ crucified, and not crucifyed for thee, but crucified
by thee; To heare this blood speake, not better things, than the
blood of *Abel*, but lowder for vengeance than the blood of *Abel* did;
This is his picture that hath been Nothing, that hath done nothing,
that hath proposed no *Stephen*, No Law to regulate, No example to
certifie his Conscience: But to him that hath done this, Death is but
a Sleepe.

   Many have wondred at that note of Saint *Chrysostom's*, That till
Christ's time death was called death, plainly, literally death, but
after Christ, death was called but sleepe; for, indeede, in the old-
Testament before Christ, I thinke there is no one metaphor so often
used, as Sleepe for Death, and that the Dead are said to Sleepe:
Therefore wee wonder sometimes, that Saint *Chrysostome* should say
so: But this may be that which that holy Father intended in that
Note, that they in the old-Testament, who are said to have slept in
Death, are such as then, by Faith, did apprehend, and were fixed
upon Christ; such as were all the good men of the old-Testament,
and so there will not bee many instances against Saint *Chrysostome's*
note, That to those that die in Christ, Death is but a Sleepe; to
all others, Death is Death, literally Death. Now of this dying Man,
that dies in Christ, that dies the Death of the Righteous, that
embraces Death as a Sleepe, must wee give you a Picture too.

   There is not a minute left to do it; not a minutes sand; Is there
a minutes patience? Bee pleased to remember that those Pictures

which are deliver'd in a minute, from a print upon a paper, had many dayes, weeks, Moneths time for the graving of those Pictures in the Copper; So this Picture of that dying Man, that dies in Christ, that dies the death of the Righteous, that embraces Death as a Sleepe, was graving all his life; All his publique actions were the lights, and all his private the shadowes of this Picture. And when this Picture comes to the Presse, this Man to the streights and agonies of Death, thus he lies, thus he looks, this he is. His understanding and his will is all one faculty; He understands Gods purpose upon him, and he would not have God's purpose turned any other way; hee sees God will dissolve him, and he would faine be dissolved, to be with Christ; His understanding and his will is all one faculty; His memory and his fore-sight are fixt, and concentred upon one object, upon goodnesse; Hee remembers that hee hath proceeded in the sinceritie of a good Conscience in all the wayes of his calling, and he foresees that his good name shall have the Testimony, and his Posterity the support of the good men of this world; His sicknesse shall be but a fomentation to supple and open his Body for the issuing of his Soule; and his Soule shall goe forth, not as one that gave over his house, but as one that travelled to see and learne better Architecture, and meant to returne and re-edifie that house, according to those better Rules: And as those thoughts which possesse us most awake, meete us againe when we are asleepe; So his holy thoughts, having been alwaies conversant upon the directing of his family, the education of his Children, the discharge of his place, the safety of the State, the happinesse of the King all his life; when he is faln a sleepe in Death, all his Dreames in that blessed Sleepe, all his devotions in heaven shall be upon the same Subjects, and he shal solicite him that sits upon the Throne, and the Lamb, God for Christ Jesus sake, to blesse all these with his particular blessings: for, so God giveth his beloved sleep, so as that they enjoy the next world and assist this.

So then, the Death of the Righteous is a sleepe; first, as it delivers them to a present rest. Now men sleepe not well fasting; Nor does a fasting Conscience, a Conscience that is not nourish'd with a Testimony of having done well, come to this Sleepe: but *dulcis somnis operanti*, The sleepe of a labouring man is sweete. To him that laboureth in his calling, even this sleepe of Death is welcome. *When thou lyest downe thou shalt not be afraid*, saith *Salomon*; when thy Physician sayes, Sir, you must keepe your bed, thou shalt not be afraid of that sick-bed; And then it followes, *And thy sleepe shall be sweet unto thee*; Thy sicknesse welcome, and thy death too; for, in those two *David* seems to involve all, *I will both lay me downe in Peace, and sleep*; imbrace patiently my death-bed and Death it selfe.

So then this death is a sleepe, as it delivers us to a present Rest; And then, lastly, it is so also as it promises a future waking in a glorious Resurrection. To the wicked it is far from both: Of them God sayes, *I will make them drunke, and they shall sleepe a perpetuall sleepe and not awake*; They shall have no part in the *Second Resurrection*. But for them that have slept in Christ, as Christ sayd of *Lazarus*, Lazarus *Sleepeth, but I goe that I may wake him out of sleep*, he shall say to his father; Let me goe that I may wake them who have slept so long in expectation of my coming: And *Those that sleep in Jesus Christ* (saith the Apostle) *will God bring with him*; not only fetch them out of the dust when he comes, but bring them with him, that is, declare that they have beene in his hands ever since they departed out of this world. They shall awake as *Jacob* did, and say as *Jacob* said, *Surely the Lord is in this place*, and *this is no other but the house of God, and the gate of heaven*, And into that gate they shall enter, and in that house they shall dwell, where there shall be no Cloud nor Sun, no darkenesse nor dazling, but one equall light, no noyse nor silence, but one equall musick, no fears nor hopes, but one equal possession, no foes nor friends, but one equall communion and Identity, no ends nor beginnings, but one equall eternity. Keepe us Lord so awake in the duties of our Callings, that we may thus sleepe in thy Peace, and wake in thy glory, and change that infallibility which thou affordest us here, to an Actuall and undeterminable possession of that Kingdome which thy Sonne our Saviour Christ Jesus hath purchased for us, with the inestimable price of his incorruptible Blood. *Amen.*

## 57. From a Sermon Preached at S. Pauls, for Easter-day. 1628[1]

### (i)

THE whole frame of the world is the Theatre, and every creature the stage, the *medium*, the glasse in which we may see God. *Moses made the Laver in the Tabernacle, of the looking glasses of women*: Scarce can you imagine a vainer thing (except you will except the vain lookers on, in that action) than the looking-glasses of women; and yet *Moses* brought the looking-glasses of women to a religious use, to shew them that came in, the spots of dirt, which they had taken by the way, that they might wash themselves cleane before they passed any farther.

There is not so poore a creature but may be thy glasse to see God in. The greatest flat glasse that can be made, cannot represent any thing greater than it is: If every gnat that flies were an Archangell, all that could but tell me, that there is a God; and the poorest worme that creeps, tells me that. If I should aske the Basilisk, how camest thou by those killing eyes, he would tell me, Thy God made me so; And if I should aske the Slow-worme, how camest thou to be without eyes, he would tell me, Thy God made me so. The Cedar is no better a glasse to see God in, than the Hyssope upon the wall; all things that are, are equally removed from being nothing; and whatsoever hath any beeing, is by that very beeing, a glasse in which we see God, who is the roote, and the fountaine of all beeing. The whole frame of nature is the Theatre, the whole Volume of creatures is the glasse, and the light of nature, reason, is our light, which is another Circumstance.

Of those words, *John* 1. 9. *That was the true light, that lighteth every man that commeth into the World*, the slackest sense that they can admit, gives light enough to see God by. If we spare S. *Chrysostomes* sense, That *that light*, is the light of the Gospel, and of Grace, and that *that light*, considered in it self, and without opposition in us, *does enlighten*, that is, would enlighten, *every man*, if that man

---

[1] On the text: 'For now we see through a glass darkly, but then face to face; now I know in part, but then I shall know, even as also I am known' (1 Cor. xiii. 12).

did not wink at that light; If we forbear S. *Augustines* sense, *That light enlightens every man,* that is, every man that is enlightned, is enlightned by that light; If we take but S. *Cyrils* sense, that this *light* is the light of naturall Reason, *which*, without all question, *enlightneth every man that comes into the world,* yet have we light enough to see God by that light, in the Theatre of Nature, and in the glasse of Creatures. God affords no man the comfort, the false comfort of Atheism: He will not allow a pretending Atheist the power to flatter himself, so far, as seriously to thinke there is no God. He must pull out his own eyes, and see no creature, before he can say, he sees no God; He must be no man, and quench his reasonable soule, before he can say to himselfe, there is no God. The difference betweene the Reason of man, and the Instinct of the beast is this, That the beast does but know, but the man knows that he knows. The bestiall Atheist will pretend that he knows there is no God; but he cannot say, that hee knows, that he knows it; for, his knowledge will not stand the battery of an argument from another, nor of a ratiocination from himselfe. He dares not aske himselfe, who is it that I pray to, in a sudden danger, if there be no God? Nay he dares not aske, who is it that I sweare by, in a sudden passion, if there be no God? Whom do I tremble at, and sweat under, at midnight, and whom do I curse by next morning, if there be no God? It is safely said in the Schoole, *Media perfecta ad quæ ordinantur,* How weak soever those meanes which are ordained by God, seeme to be, and be indeed in themselves, yet they are strong enough to those ends and purposes, for which God ordained them.

## (ii)

The light of glory is such a light, as that our School-men dare not say confidently, That every beam of it, is not all of it. When some of them say, That some soules see some things in God, and others, others, because all have not the same measure of the light of glory, the rest cry down that opinion, and say, that as the Essence of God is indivisible, and he that sees any of it, sees all of it, so is the light of glory communicated intirely to every blessed soul. God made light first, and three dayes after, that light became a Sun, a more glorious Light: God gave me the light of Nature, when I

quickned in my mothers wombe by receiving a reasonable soule;
and God gave me the light of faith, when I quickned in my second
mothers womb, the Church, by receiving my baptisme; but in my
third day, when my mortality shall put on immortality, he shall
give me the light of glory, by which I shall see himself. To this
light of glory, the light of honour is but a glow-worm; and majesty
it self but a twilight; The Cherubims and Seraphims are but
Candles; and that Gospel it self, which the Apostle calls the glorious
Gospel, but a Star of the least magnitude. And if I cannot tell, what
to call this light, by which I shall see it, what shall I call that which
I shall see by it, The Essence of God himself? and yet there is
something else than this sight of God, intended in that which
remaines, I shall not only *see God face to face*, but I shall *know* him,
(which, as you have seen all the way, is above sight) and *know
him, even as also I am knowne.*

# 58. From a Sermon Preached to the King at White-hall, April 15. 1628[1]

## (i)

THIS civill Liberality, which we have hitherto spoken of, is a Type,
but yet but a Type of our spirituall Liberality. For, here we doe not
onely change termes, the temporall, to spirituall, and to call that,
which we called Liberality in the former part, Charity in this part;
nor do we onely make the difference in the proportion and measure,
that that which was a Benefit in the other part, should be an Almes
in this. But we invest the whole consideration in a meere spirituall
nature; and so that Liberality, which was, in the former acceptation, but a relieving, but a refreshing, but a repairing of defects,
and dilapidations in the body or fortune, is now, in this second
part, in this spirituall acceptation, the raising of a dejected spirit,
the redintegration of a broken heart, the resuscitation of a buried
soule, the re-consolidation of a scattered conscience, not with the
glues, and cements of this world, mirth, and musique, and comedies,

---

[1] On the text: 'But the liberal deviseth liberal things, and by liberal things he shall stand'
(Isa. xxxii. 8).

and conversation, and wine, and women, (miserable comforters are they all) nor with that Meteor, that hangs betweene two worlds, that is, Philosophy, and morall constancy, (which is somewhat above the carnall man, but yet far below the man truly Christian and religious) But this is the Liberality, of which the Holy Ghost himselfe is content to be the Steward, of the holy, blessed, and glorious Trinity, and to be notified, and qualified by that distinctive notion, and specification, *The Comforter*.

## (ii)

For the most part, men are of one of these three sorts; Either inconsiderate men; (and they that consider not themselves, consider not us, they aske not, they expect not this liberality from us) or else they are over-confident, and presume too much upon God; or diffident, and distrust him too much. And with these two wee meet often; but truly, with seven diffident, and dejected, for one presuming soule. So that we have much exercise of this liberality, of raising dejected spirits: And by this liberality we stand. For, when I have given that man comfort, that man hath given me a Sacrament, hee hath given me a seale and evidence of Gods favour upon me; I have received from him, in his receiving from me; I leave him comforted in Christ Jesus, and I goe away comforted in my selfe, that Christ Jesus hath made me an instrument of the dispensation of his mercy; And I argue to my selfe, and say, Lord, when I went, I was sure, that thou who hadst received me to mercy, wouldst also receive him, who could not be so great a sinner as I; And now, when I come away, I am sure, that thou who art returned to him, and hast re-manifested thy selfe to him, who, in the diffidence of his sad soule, thought thee gone for ever, wilt never depart from mee, nor hide thy selfe from me, who desire to dwell in thy presence. And so, by this liberality I stand; by giving I receive comfort.

## 59. From a Sermon Preached in Saint Pauls in the Evening, November 23. 1628[1]

(i)

BUT who is this *poor man*, and how shall you know him? How shall you know, whether he that askes be truly poor or no? Truly, beloved, there is scarce any one thing, in which our ignorance is more excusable than in this, *To know whether he to whom we give, be truly poor, or no*: In no case is our inconsideration more pardonable, than in this. God will never examine me very strictly, why I was no stricter in examining that mans condition to whom I gave mine almes. If I give to one that is poor in my sight, I shall finde that almes upon Gods score, amongst them, who were poor in Gods sight: And my mistaking the man, shall never make God mistake my meaning. Where I finde undeniable, unresistible evidence to the contrary, when I see a man able in his *limbes* live in continuall *idlenesse*, when I see a man poore in his meanes, and oppressed with his charge, spend in continuall *drunkennesse*, in this case, I were the oppressor of the poor, if I should give to that man, for this were *to give the childrens bread to dogs.* And that is not a name too bad for them; for, *foris Canes*, they are dogs that are without, that is, *without the Church*: And how few of these, who make beggery an occupation from their infancy, were ever within Church, how few of them ever *Christned*, or ever *maried*? *Foris Canes*, they are dogs, that are without; and the *Childrens bread must not be given to Dogs*. But to pursue our first intention, and so to finde out these poor in the origination of the words chosen by the holy Ghost here, we have in this text *two words* for the poor. One is *Ebion*; and *Ebion* is a begger. It was the name given to one of those *first heretiques* who occasioned the writing of St. *Johns Gospell*; he was called *Ebion*. So that it may well be imagined, that those first Heretiques were *Mendicants*: Men that professed begging, and lived upon the labours, and sweat of other

---

men. For the *Ebionit* is a begger; not onely he that needs, but he *that declares his need*, that askes, that craves, that begs: for, the root of *Ebion* is *Ahab*; which is not onely to *desire*, but to *declare* that desire, to aske, to crave, to beg. Now, this poor man must be relieved. The charity that God required in *Israel*, was, that no man should be put to this necessity, but provided for otherwise; *There shall be no begger amongst you*; for, there is our very word, no *Ebionite*; that is, no poor man shall be put to beg. But yet in the Prophet *Jeremy*, that man is well spoken of, that *did good even to the Ebionit*, to the begger; he that is brought to a necessity of asking, must be relieved. Not that we are not bound to give, till another aske, or never to open our hand, till another open his mouth; for, as Saint *John* did, in the beginning of the Revelation, a *man may see a sound*, see a voice. A sad aspect, a pale look, a hollow cheek, a bloudlesse lip, a sonke eye, a trembling hand, speake so lowd, as that if I will not heare them from him, God will heare them against me. In many cases, and with many persons, it is a greater anguish to aske, than to want; and easier to starve, than to beg; therefore I must hearken after another voice, and with another organ; I must *hearken* with mine *eye*. Many times I may see *need* speake, when the *needy man* says nothing, and *his case* may cry aloud, when he is silent. Therefore I must lay mine eare to the ground, and hearken after them that lie in the dust, and enquire after the distresses of such men; for this is an imitation of Gods *preventing grace*, that grace, than which we can conceive no higher thing in God himselfe, (*that God should be found of them, that seek him not*) if I relieve that man, that was ashamed to tell me he wanted. The *Ebionit*, the begger, but not he onely, must be relieved: for our word, in this part of the text, is not *Ebion*, but a word derived from *Dalal*; and *Dalal*, in this word, signifies *Exhaustum, attenuatum*, a man whose *former estate* is exhausted, and gone, or whose *present labours* doe not prosper, but that God, for ends best known to himselfe, exercises him with continuall poverty; the word signifies also a man enfeebled, and *decrepit with age*; and more than that, the word signifies *sicknesse* too: for this very word we have in *Hezekiahs* mouth, *The Lord will cut me off with sicknesse*. So that now you have the specification of the person, who is the poor man, that is most properly the object of your charity, he whose *former estate* is wasted, and not by his *vices*, but by the hand of God, He whose *present industry* does not prosper, He who is overtaken with *Age*, and so the lesse able to repaire his wants, and in his age, afflicted with *sicknesse*, and so the lesse able to *indure* his wants. And this poor man, this *labouring* man, this *decayed* man, this *aged* man, this *sickly* man, this oppressor in our text pursues, and pursues with *violence*, with *deceit*, with *scorne*.

(ii)

First, The poor are immediately in Gods *protection*. Rich and poore are in Gods administration, in his government, in his providence; But the poor are immediately in his protection. *Tibi derelictus est pauper*, says *David*, The poor commits himself unto thee. They are *Orphans*, *Wards*, delivered over to his tuition, to his protection. Princes have a care of all their Allies, but a more especiall care of those that are in their protection. And the poor are such; And therefore God [is] more sensible in their behalfe. And so, hee that oppresses the poor, Reproaches God, God in his *Orphans*.

Again, rich and poor are Images, Pictures of God; but, (as *Clement of Alexandria* says wittily and strongly) The poor is *Nuda Imago*, a naked picture of God, a picture without any drapery, any clothes about it. And it is much a harder thing, and there is much more art showed in making a *naked picture*, than in all the rich attire that can be put upon it. And howsoever the rich man, that is invested in Power, and Greatnesse, may be a better picture of God, of God considered *in himself*, who is all Greatnes, all Power, yet, of God considered in *Christ*, (which is the contemplation that concerns us most) the poor man is the better picture, and most resembles Christ who liv'd in continual poverty. And so, he that oppresses the poor, reproaches God, God in his *Orphans*, God in his *Picture*.

Saint *Augustine* carries this consideration farther, than that the poore is more immediately Gods Orphan, and more perfectly his picture, That he is more properly a member of himself, of his body. For, contemplating that head, which was not so much crowned as hedged with thorns, that head, of which, he whose it was, sayes, *The Sonne of man hath not where to lay his head*, Saint *Augustine* sayes,

*Ecce caput Pauperum,* Behold that head, to which, the poore make up
the body, *Ob eam tantum causam venerabiles,* sayes that Father, Therefore venerable, therefore honourable, because they are members
sutable to that head. And so, all that place, where the Apostle
sayes, *That upon those members of the body, which we think to be lesse
honourable, we bestow most honour,* that Father applies to the poore,
that therefore most respect and honour should be given to them,
because the poore are more sutable members to their head Christ
Jesus, than the rich are. And so also, he that oppresses the poore,
reproaches God, God in his *Orphans,* God in his *Image,* God in the
*Members* of his owne body.

Saint *Chrysostome* carries this consideration farther than this of
Saint *Augustine.* That whereas every creature hath *filiationem
vestigii,* that because God hath imparted a being, an essence, from
himselfe, who is the roote, and the fountaine of all essence, and all
being, therefore every creature hath a filiation from God, and is the
Sonne of God so, as we read in *Job,* God is *the father of the raine;* and
whereas every man hath *filiationem imaginis,* as well *Pagan* as
*Christian,* hath the Image of God imprinted in his soule, and so hath
a filiation from God, and is the Sonne of God, as he is made in his
likenesse; and whereas every Christian hath *filiationem Pacti,* by
being taken into the Covenant made by God, with the Elect, and
with their seed, he hath a filiation from God, and is the Sonne of
God, as he is incorporated into his Sonne Christ Jesus, by the
*Seals of the Christian Church;* besides these filiations, of being in all
creatures, of the Image in all men, of the Covenant in all Christians,
The poore, sayes that Father, are not onely *filii,* but *Hæredes,* and
*Primogeniti,* Sonnes and eldest Sonnes, Sonnes, and Sonnes and
Heires. And to that purpose he makes use of those words in St.
*James, Hearken, my beloved brethren, hath not God chosen the poore of this
world, rich in faith, and Heirs of that Kingdome?* Heirs, for, *Ipsorum est,*
sayes Christ himself, *Theirs is the Kingdome of heaven;* And upon those
words of Christ, Saint *Chrysostome* comments thus, *Divites ejus regni
tantum habent, quantum a pauperibus, eleemosynis coemerunt,* The rich
have no more of that Kingdome of heaven, than they have purchased
of the poore, by their almes, and other erogations to pious uses.
And so he that oppresses the poore reproaches God, God in his

*Orphans*, God in his *Image*, God in the *Members* of his own Body, God in his Sonnes, and Heires of his Kingdome.

But then Christ himself carries this consideration, beyond all these resemblances, and conformities, not to a *proximity* onely, but to an *identity*, The poore are He. *In as much as you did it unto these, you did it unto me*; and, *In as much as you did it not unto these, you did it not unto me*. And after his ascension, and establishing in glory, still he avowed them, not onely to be his, but to be He, *Saul, Saul, why persecutest thou me*? The poore are He, He is the poore. And so, he that oppresseth the poore, reproaches God, God in his *Orphans*, God in his *Image*, God in the *Members* of his owne Body, God in the *Heirs* of his Kingdome, God in *himself*, in his own person.

## 60. From a Sermon Preached at S. Pauls in the Evening, Upon the day of S. Pauls Conversion. 1629[1]

POORE intricated soule! Riddling, perplexed, labyrinthicall soule! Thou couldest not say, that thou beleevest not in God, if there were no God; Thou couldest not beleeve in God, if there were no God; If there were no God, thou couldest not speake, thou couldest not thinke, not a word, not a thought, no not against God; Thou couldest not blaspheme the Name of God, thou couldest not sweare, if there were no God: For, all thy faculties, how ever depraved, and perverted by thee, are from him; and except thou canst seriously beleeve, that thou art nothing, thou canst not beleeve that there is no God. If I should aske thee at a Tragedy, where thou shouldest see him that had drawne blood, lie weltring, and surrounded in his owne blood, Is there a God now? If thou couldst answer me, No, These are but Inventions, and Representations of men, and I beleeve a God never the more for this; If I should ask thee at a Sermon, where thou shouldest heare the Judgements of God formerly denounced, and executed, re-denounced, and applied to present occasions, Is there a God now? If thou couldst answer me, No, These are but Inventions of State, to souple and regulate

---

[1] On the text: 'And they changed their minds, and said, that he was a God' (Acts xxviii. 6).

Congregations, and keep people in order, and I beleeve a God never the more for this; Bee as confident as thou canst, in company; for company is the Atheists Sanctuary; I respit thee not till the day of Judgement, when I may see thee upon thy knees, upon thy face, begging of the hills, that they would fall downe and cover thee from the fierce wrath of God, to aske thee then, Is there a God now? I respit thee not till the day of thine own death, when thou shalt have evidence enough, that there is a God, though no other evidence, but to finde a Devill, and evidence enough, that there is a Heaven, though no other evidence, but to feele Hell; To aske thee then, Is there a God now? I respit thee but a few houres, but six houres, but till midnight. Wake then; and then darke, and alone, Heare God aske thee then, remember that I asked thee now, Is there a God? and if thou darest, say No.

## 61. From a Sermon Preached upon Easter-day. 1629[1]

### (i)

TRULY to me, this consideration, That as his mercy is new every morning, so his grace is renewed to me every minute, That it is not by yesterdaies grace that I live now, but that I have *Panem quotidianum*, and *Panem horarium*, My daily bread, my hourely bread, in a continuall succession of his grace, That the eye of God is open upon me, though I winke at his light, and watches over me, though I sleep, That God makes these returnes to my soule, and so studies me in every change, this consideration, infuses a sweeter verdure, and imprints a more cheerefull tincture upon my soule, than any taste of any one Act, done at once, can minister unto me. God made the Angels all of one naturall condition, in nature all alike; and God gave them all such grace, as that thereby they might have stood; and to them that used that grace aright, he gave a farther, a continuall succession of grace, and that is their Confirmation; Not that they cannot, but that they shall not fall; not that they are

---

[1] On the text: 'Behold, he put no trust in his servants, and his angels he charged with folly' (Job iv. 18).

safe in themselves, but by Gods preservation safe; for, otherwise, *He puts no trust in those Servants, and those Angels he charges with folly.*

This is our case too; ours that are under the blessed Election, and good purpose of God upon us; if we do not fall from him, it is not of our selves; for left to our selves, we should: For, so S. *Augustine* interprets those words of our Saviour, *Pater operatur, My Father worketh still*; God hath not accomplished his worke upon us, in one Act, though an Election; but he works in our Vocation, and he works in our Justification, and in our Sanctification he works still. And, if God himselfe be not so come to his Sabbath, and his rest in us, but that he works upon us still for all that Election, shall any man thinke to have such a Sabbath, such a rest, in that Election, as shall slacken our endeavour, to make sure our Salvation, and not worke as God works, to his ends in us? Hence then we banish all self-subsistence, all attributing of any power, to any faculty of our own; either by pre-operation, in any naturall or morall disposing of our selves, before Gods preventing grace dispose us, or by such a cooperation, as should put God and man in Commission together, or make grace and nature Collegues in the worke, or that God should do one halfe, and man the other; or any such post-operation, That I should thinke to proceed in the waies of godlinesse, by vertue of Gods former grace, without imploring, and obtaining more, in a continuall succession of his concomitant grace, for every particular action: In Christ I can do all things; I need no more but him; without Christ, I can doe nothing; not onely not have him, but not know that I need him; for I am not better than those Angels, of whom it is said, *He put no trust in those Servants, and those Angels hee charged with folly.*

And as we banish from hence all self-subsistence, all opinion of standing by our selves, so doe we also all impeccability, and all impossibility of falling in our selves, or in any thing, that God hath already done for us, if he should discontinue his future grace, and leave us to our former stock. They that were raised from death to life againe, *Dorcas, Lazarus,* and the rest, were subject to sin, in that new life, which was given them. They that are quickned by the soule of the soule, Election it selfe, are subject to sin, for all that. God sees the sins of the Elect, and sees their sins to be sins;

and in his Ephemerides, his journals, he writes them downe, under that Title, sins, and he reads them every day, in that booke, as such; and they grow greater and greater in his sight, till our repentance have washed them out of his sight. Casuists will say, that though a dead man raised to life againe, be not bound to his former marriage, yet he is bound to that Religion, that he had invested in Baptisme, and bound to his former religious vowes, and the same obedience to Superiours as before. We were all dead in *Adam*; and he that is raised againe, even by Election, though he be not so married to the world, as others are, not so in love with sin, not so under the dominion of sin, yet he is as much bound to an obedience to the Will of God declared in his Law, and may no more presume of a liberty of sinning before, nor of an impunity of sin after, than he that pretends no such Election, to confide in. For, this is excellently said, to be the working of our election, by *Prosper*, the Disciple of S. *Augustines* Doctrines, and the Eccho of his words, *Ut fiat permanendi voluntaria, foelixque necessitas,* That our assurance of salvation by perseverance, is necessary, and yet voluntary; Consider it in Gods purpose, easily it cannot, consider it in our selves, it might be resisted. For we are no better than those Angels, and, *In those servants he put no trust, and those Angels he charged with folly.*

(ii)

Apply to thy selfe that which S. *Cyril* saies of the Angels, *Tristaris, quia aliqui vitam amiserunt?* Does it grieve thee, that any are fallen? *At plures meliorem statum apud Deum obtinent,* Let this comfort thee, even in the application thereof to thy selfe, that more stood than fell. As *Elisha* said to his servant, in a danger of surprisall, *Feare not, for they that be with us, are more than they that are with them,* so, if a suspition of the paucity of them that shall be saved, make thee afraid, looke up upon this overflowing mercy of thy God, this super-abundant merit of thy Saviour, this plenteous Redemption, and thou maist finde, finde in a faire credulity, and in a well regulated hope, more with thee, than with them that perish. Live so, in such a warfare with tentations, in such a colluctation with thy concupiscences, in such a jealousie, and suspition of thine indifferent, nay, of thy best actions, as though there were but one man to be saved, and thou wouldst be that one; But live and die in such a sense of this plenteous Redemption of thy God, as though neither thou, nor any could lose salvation, except he doubted of it. I doubt not of mine own salvation; and in whom can I have so much occasion of doubt, as in my self? When I come to heaven, shall I be able to say to any there, Lord! how got you hither? Was any man lesse likely to come thither than I? There is not only an Onely God in heaven; But a Father, a Son, a Holy Ghost in that God; which are names of a plurality, and sociable relations, conversable notions. There is not only one Angel, a *Gabriel*; But *to thee all Angels cry aloud*; and Cherubim, and Seraphim, are plurall terminations; many Cherubs, many Seraphs in heaven. There is not only one Monarchall Apostle, a *Peter*, but *The glorious company of the Apostles praise thee*. There is not onely a Proto-Martyr, a *Stephen*, but *The noble army of Martyrs praise thee*. Who ever amongst our Fathers, thought of any other way to the Moluccaes, or to China, than by the Promontory of *Good hope*? Yet another way opened it self to *Magellan*; a Straite; it is true; but yet a way thither; and who knows yet, whether there may not be a North-East, and a North-West way thither, besides? Go thou to heaven, in an humble thankfulnesse to God, and holy cheerfulnesse, in that way that God hath manifested to thee; and do not pronounce too bitterly, too desperately, that every man is in an errour, that thinkes not just as thou thinkest, or in no way, that is not in thy way. God found folly, weaknesse in his Angels, yet more stood than fell; God findes weaknesse, wickednesse in us, yet hee *came to call, not the righteous, but sinners to repentance*; and who, that comes in that capacity, a Repentant sinner, can be shut out, or denied his part in this Resurrection?

*The key of David opens, and no man shuts.* The Son of *David*, is the key of *David*, Christ Jesus; He hath opened heaven for us all; let no man shut out himself, by diffidence in Gods mercy, nor shut out any other man, by overvaluing his own purity, in respect of others. But forbearing all lacerations, and tearings, and woundings of one another, with bitter invectives, all exasperations by odious names of subdivision, let us all study, first the redintegration of that body, of which Christ Jesus hath declared himselfe to be the head, the whole Christian Church, and pray that he would, and hope that he will enlarge the means of salvation to those, who have not yet been made partakers of it. That so, he that called the *gates* of heaven *straite*, may say to those gates, *Elevamini portæ æternales*, *Be ye lifted up*, *ye eternall gates*, and be ye enlarged, that as the King of glory himself is entred into you, for the farther glory of the King of glory, not only *that hundred and foure and forty thousand of the Tribes of the children of Israel*, but *that multitude* which is spoken of in that place, *which no man can number, of all Nations, and Kindreds, and People, and tongues*, may enter with that acclamation, *Salvation to our God, which sitteth upon the Throne, and to the Lamb for ever*. And *unto this City of the living God, the heavenly Jerusalem, and to the innumerable company of Angels, to the generall assembly, and Church of the first born, which are written in heaven, and to God the Judge of all, and to the spirits of just men made perfect, and to Jesus the Mediator of the new covenant, and to the blood of sprinkling, that speaks better things than that of Abel*, Blessed God bring us all, for thy Sons sake, and by the operation of thy Spirit. *Amen*.


## 62. From a Sermon Preached to the King, at the Court in April. 1629[1]

### (i)

WE shall pursue our great examples; God in doing, *Moses* in saying; and so make hast in applying the parts. But first receive them. And since we have the whole world in contemplation, consider in these words, the foure quarters of the world, by application, by fair, and just accommodation of the words. First, in the first word, that God speaks here, *Faciamus*, Let us, us in the plurall, (a denotation of divers Persons in one Godhead) we consider our East where we must beginne, at the knowledge and confession of the Trinity. For, though in the way to heaven, we be travelled beyond the Gentiles, when we come to confess but one God, (The Gentiles could not do that) yet we are still among the *Jews*, if we thinke that one God to be but one Person. Christs name is *Oriens*, the *East*; if we will be named by him, (called Christians) we must look to this

---

[1] On the text: 'And God said, Let us make man in our image, after our likeness' (Gen. i. 26).

East, the confession of the Trinity. There's then our East, in the *Faciamus*; Let us, us make man: And then our West is in the next word, *Faciamus Hominem.* Though we be thus made, made by the counsell, made by the concurrence, made by the hand of the whole Trinity; yet we are made but men: And man, but in the appellation, in this text: and man there, is but *Adam*: and *Adam* is but earth, but red earth, earth dyed red in bloud, in Soul-bloud, the bloud of our own soules. To that west we must all come, to the earth. *The Sunne knoweth his going down*: Even the Sun for all his glory, and heighth, hath a going down, and he knowes it. The highest cannot devest mortality, nor the discomfort of mortality. *When you see a cloud rise out of the west, straightway you say there commeth a storm*, says Christ. When out of the region of your west, that is, your later days, there comes a cloud, a sicknesse, you feele a storme, even the best morall constancy is shaked. But this cloud, and this storme, and this west there must be; And that's our second consideration. But then the next words designe a North, a strong, and powerfull North, to scatter, and dissipate these clouds: *Ad imaginem, & similitudinem*; That we are made according to a pattern, to an image, to a like-nesse, which God proposed to himselfe for the making of man. This consideration, that God did not rest in that præexistent matter, out of which he made all other creatures, and produced their formes, out of their matter, for the making of man; but took a forme, a patterne, a modell for that work: This is the North winde, that is called upon to carry out the perfumes of the garden, to spread the goodnesse of God abroad. This is that which is intended in *Job*; *Fair weather commeth out of the North.* Our West, our declination is in this, that we are but earth; our North, our dissipation of that dark-nesse, is in this, that we are not all earth: though we be of that matter, we have another forme, another image, another likenesse. And then, whose image and likenesse it is, is our Meridionall height, our noon, our south point, our highest elevation; *In Imagine nostra, Let us make man in our Image.* Though our Sun set at noon, as the Prophet *Amos* speakes; though we die in our youth, or fall in our height: yet even in that Sunset, we shall have a Noon. For this Image of God shall never depart from our soule; no, not when that soule departs from our body. And that's our South, our Meridionall height and glory. And when we have thus seen this East, in the *faciamus*, That I am the workmanship and care of the whole Trinity; And this West in the *Hominem*, That for all that, my matter, my substance, is but earth: But then a North, a power of overcomming that low and miserable state, *In Imagine*; That though in my matter, the earth, I must die; yet in my forme, in that Image which I am made by, I cannot die: and after all, a South, a knowledge, That this Image is not the Image of Angels, to whom we shall be like, but it is by the same life, by which those Angels themselves were made; the Image of God himselfe. When I am gone over this east, and west, and north, and south, here in this world, I should be as sorry as *Alexander* was, if there were no more worlds. But there is another world, which these considerations will discover, and lead us to, in which our joy, and our glory shall be, to see that God essentially, and face to face, after whose Image, and likenesse we were made before.

## (ii)

Now God did not say of man, as of other creatures, Let the earth bring forth hearbs, and fruits, and trees, as upon the third day; nor let the earth bring forth cattell, and wormes, as upon the sixth day, the same day that he made man; *Non imperiali verbo, sed familiari manu*, sayes *Tertullian*, God calls not man out with an imperious Command, but he leads him out, with a familiar, with his own hand. And it is not *Fiat homo*, but *Faciamus*; not, *Let there be*, but *Let us make man*. Man is but an earthen vessell. 'Tis true, but when we are upon that consideration, God is the Potter: if God will be that, I am well content to be this: let me be any thing, so that that I am be from my God. I am as well content to be a sheep, as a Lion, so God will be my Shepheard: and the Lord is my shepheard: To be a Cottage, as a Castle, so God will be the builder; And the Lord builds, and watches the City, the house, this house, this City, mee: To be Rye, as Wheate, so God will be the husbandman; And the Lord plants me, and waters, and weeds, and gives the encrease: and to be clothed in leather, as well as in silke, so God will be the Merchant; and he cloathed me in *Adam*, and assures me of clothing, in clothing the Lillies of the field, and is fitting the robe of Christs righteousness to me now, this minute. *Adam* is as good to me as *Gheber*, a clod of earth, as a hill of earth; so God be the Potter.

## 63. From a Sermon Preached to the King, at the Court. [April or May 1629][1]

### (i)

IN this point, the North, we place our first comfort. The North is not always the comfortablest clime: nor is the North always a type of happines in the Scriptures. Many times God threatens stormes from the North. But even in those Northern stormes, we consider that action, that they scatter, they dissipate those clouds, which were gathered, and so induce a serenity: And so, fair weather comes from the North. And that's the use which we have of the North in this place. The consideration of our West, our low estate; that we are but earth, but red earth, dyed red by our selves: and that imaginary white, which appeares so to us, is but a white of leprosie: this West enwraps us in heavy clouds of murmuring, in this life, that we cannot live so freely as beasts doe; and in clouds of desperation for the next life, that we cannot dye so absolutely as beasts do; we dye all our lives, and yet we live after our deaths. These are our clouds; And then the North shakes these clouds. *The North Winde driveth away the rain*, says *Solomon*. There is a North in our text, that drives all those teares from our eyes. Christ calls upon the North, as well as the South, to blow upon his Garden, and to diffuse the perfumes thereof. Adversity, as well as prosperity, opens the bounty of God unto us; and oftentimes better. But that's not the benefit of the North in our present consideration. But this is it, that first our sunne sets in the West. The Eastern dignity, which we received in our first Creation, as we were the worke of the whole Trinity, falls under a Western cloud, that that Trinity made us but earth. And then blowes our North, and scatters this cloud; that this earth hath a nobler forme, than any other part or limbe

---

1 'The second Sermon on Gen. i. 26.'

This sermon, preached on the same text as the preceding one, must have been preached shortly after, since the two sermons form a carefully prepared whole.

of the world. For, we are made by a fairer pattern, by a nobler Image, by a higher likenesse. *Faciamus*; Though we make but a man, *Let us make* him, *in our Image, after our likenesse.*

## (ii)

The Sphear then of this intelligence, the Gallery for this Picture, the Arch for this Statue, the Table, and frame and shrine for this Image of God, is inwardly and immediately the soule of man. Not immediately so, as that the soule of man is a part of the Essence of God; for so essentially, Christ onely is the Image of God. Saint *Augustine* at first thought so: *Putabam te Deus, Corpus Lucidum, & me frustum de illo Corpore*; I tooke thee, ô God, (says that Father) to be a Globe of fire, and my soule a sparke of that fire; thee to be a body of light, and my soule to be a beame of that light. But Saint *Augustine* does not onely retract that in himselfe, but dispute against it, in the Manichees. But this Image is in our soule, as our soule is the wax, and this Image the seale. The Comparison is Saint *Cyrills*, and he addes well, that no seale but that, which printed the wax at first, can fit that wax, and fill that impression after. No Image, but the Image of God can fit our soule. Every other seale is too narrow, too shallow for it. The magistrate is sealed with the Lion; The woolfe will not fit that seale: the Magistrate hath a power in his hands, but not oppression. Princes are sealed with the Crown; The Miter will not fit that seale. Powerfully, and gratiously they protect the Church, and are supreame heads of the Church; But they minister not the Sacraments of the Church. They give preferments; but they give not the capacity of preferment. They give order who shall have; but they give not orders, by which they are enabled to have, that have. Men of inferiour and laborious callings in the world are sealed with the Crosse; a Rose, or a bunch of Grapes will not answer that seale. Ease, and plenty in age, must not be looked for without Crosses and labour and industry in youth. All men, Prince, and People; Clergy, and Magistrate, are sealed with the Image of God, with the profession of a conformity to him: and worldly seales will not answer that, nor fill up that seale. We should wonder to see a Mother in the midst of many sweet Children passing her time in making babies and puppets for her own delight. We should wonder to see a man, whose Chambers and Galleries were full of curious master-peeces, thrust in a Village Fair to looke upon sixpenny pictures, and three farthing prints. We have all the Image of God at home, and we all make babies, fancies of honour, in our ambitions. The master-peece is our own, in our own bosome; and we thrust in countrey Fairs, that is, we endure the distempers of any unseasonable weather, in night-journies, and watchings: we indure the oppositions, and scornes, and triumphs of a rivall, and competitor, that seeks with us, and shares with us: we indure the guiltinesse, and reproach of having deceived the trust, which a confident friend reposes in us, and solicit his wife, or daughter: we endure the decay of fortune, of body, of soule, of honour, to possesse lower Pictures; pictures that are not originalls, not made by that hand of God, nature; but Artificiall beauties. And for that body, we give a soule, and for that drugge, which might have been bought, where they bought it, for a shilling, we give an estate. The Image of God is more worth than all substances; and we give it, for colours, for dreames, for shadowes.

## 64. From a Sermon Preached at S. Pauls, upon Whitsunday. 1629[1]

### (i)

THE Action of the Spirit of God, the Holy Ghost, in this place, is expressed in a word, of a double, and very diverse signification; for it signifies *motion*, and it signifies *rest*. And therefore, as S. *Augustine* argues upon those words of *David, Thou knowest my downe sitting, and my uprising,* That God knew all that he did, betweene his downe sitting and his uprising; So in this word which signifies the Holy Ghosts first motion, and his last rest, we comprehend all that was done in the production, and creation of the Creatures. This word, we translate, *As the Eagle fluttereth over her young ones,* so it is a word of Motion; And S. *Hierom* upon our Text expresses it by *Incubabat, to sit upon her young ones, to hatch them, or to preserve them,* so it is a word of rest. And so, the Jews take this word to signifie,

[1] On the text: 'And the spirit of God moved upon the face of the waters' (Gen. i. 2).

properly the birds hatching of eggs. S. *Cyprian* unites the two significations well, *Spiritus sanctus dabat aquis motum, & limitem*; The Holy
Ghost enabled the waters to move, and appointed how, and how
far they should move. The beginnings, and the waies, and the ends,
must proceed from God, and from God the Holy Ghost: That is,
by those meanes, and those declarations, by which God doth
manifest himselfe to us, for that is the office of the holy Ghost,
to manifest and apply God to us. Now the word in our Text is
not truly *Ferebatur*, The Spirit *moved*, which denotes a thing past;
but the word is *Movens*, *Moving*, a Participle of the present; So
that we ascribe first Gods manifestation of himself in the creation,
and then the continuall manifestation of himself in his providence,
to the holy Ghost; for God had two purposes in the creation, *Ut
sint, ut maneant*, That the creature should be, and be still; That it
should exist at first, and subsist after; Be made, and made permanent.
God did not mean that Paradise should have been of so small use
when he made it; he made it for a perpetuall habitation for man.
God did not mean that man should be the subject of his wrath
when he made him; he made him to take pleasure in, and to shed
glory upon him. The holy Ghost moves, he is the first author; the
holy Ghost perpetuates, settles, establishes, he is our rest, and
acquiescence, and center; Beginning, Way, End, all is in this word,
*Recaph*; *The Spirit of God moved, and rested.* And upon what? *And the
Spirit of God moved upon the face of the waters.*

## (ii)

To end all with the end of all, Death comes to us in the name, and
notion of waters too, in the Scriptures. The Widow of Tekoah
said to *David* in the behalfe of *Absalon*, by the Counsaile of *Joab*,
The water of death overflowes all; *We must needs dye*, saies she, *and
are as water spilt upon the ground, which cannot be gathered up againe: yet
God devises meanes, that his banished, be not expelled from him.* So the
Spirit of God moves upon the face of these waters, the Spirit of life
upon the danger of death. Consider the love, more than love, the
study, more than study, the diligence of God, he devises meanes,
that his banished, those whom sins, or death had banished, be not
expelled from him. I sinned upon the strength of my youth, and

God devised a meanes to reclaime me, an enfeebling sicknesse. I relapsed after my recovery, and God devised a meanes, an irrecoverable, a helpless Consumption to reclaime me; That affliction grew heavy upon me, and weighed me down even to a diffidence in Gods mercy, and God devised a meanes, the comfort of the Angel of his Church, his Minister, The comfort of the Angel of the great Counsell, the body and blood of his Son Christ Jesus, at my transmigration. Yet he lets his correction proceed to death; I doe dye of that sicknesse, and God devises a meanes, that I, though banished, banished into the grave, shall not be expelled from him, a glorious Resurrection. *We must needs dye and be as water spilt upon the ground, but yet God devises meanes, that his banished shall not be expelled from him.*

And this is the motion, and this is the Rest of the Spirit of God upon those waters in this spirituall sense of these words, He brings us to a desire of Baptisme, he settles us in the sense of the obligation first, and then of the benefits of Baptisme. He suffers us to goe into the way of tentations, (for *Coluber in via*, and every calling hath particular tentations) and then he settles us, by his preventing, or his subsequent grace. He moves, in submitting us to tribulation, he settles us in finding, that our tribulations, do best of all conforme us to his Son Christ Jesus. He moves in removing us by the hand of Death, and he settles us in an assurance, That it is he that now lets his Servants depart in peace; And he, who as he doth presently lay our soules in that safe Cabinet, the Bosome of *Abraham*, so he keepes an eye upon every graine, and atome of our dust, whither soever it be blowne, and keepes a roome at his owne right hand for that body, when that shall be re-united in a blessed Resurrection; And so *The Spirit of God moved upon the face of the waters.*

# 65. From a Sermon Preached at St. Pauls Crosse, November 22. 1629[1]

## (i)

THAT, which mis-affected them towards Christ, was not that he induced a Religion too low, too sordid, too humble, but *not low enough*, not humble enough; and therefore they would out-bid Christ, and undertake more, than his Disciples practised, or himselfe prescribed. Their Master, *John Baptist*, discerned this distemper in them, then when they said to him, *Rabbi, He that was with thee beyond Jordan, baptizes as fast as thou, and all the world comes to him.* *John Baptist* deals plainly with them, and he tels them, that they must not be offended in that, for so it must be, *He must increase, and I must decrease.* This troubled them; and because it did so, *John* sends them personally to Christ, to receive farther satisfaction. When they come at first to him, they say, *Sir, we fast, and, even the Pharisees fast, why doe not you, and your Disciples fast too?* And then our blessed Saviour enlarges himselfe to them, in that point of *fasting*, and they goe home satisfied. Now they returne againe, and they continue their wonder, that Christ should continue his greatnesse, and his estimation in the world, they exceeding him so far in this *outward austerity* of life, which was so specious, and so winning a thing amongst the Jews. But *duo Discipuli fortasse duo populi*, These two Disciples of *John* may have their Disciples in the world to this day; And therefore forbearing their *persons*, we shall consider their *off-spring*; Those men, who in an over-valuation of their *own purity*, despise others, as men whom nothing can save; and those men, who in an over-valuation of their *own merits*, think to save themselves and others too, by their *supererogations*.

---

[1] On the text: 'And blessed is he, whosoever shall not be offended in me' (Matt. xi. 6).

This sermon, in a simple, direct style suited to a large open-air audience, should be read with the violent political and religious conflicts of 1628 and 1629 in mind. The year 1629 saw the beginning of the eleven years of Charles's personal rule, and Laud, who had become Bishop of London in 1628, was attempting to enforce strict order in the Church and silence controversial preaching. Donne, though a fervent royalist, preached no sermon on the Divine Right of Kings, and his defences of the doctrine and practice of the Church of England are, as here, incidental to his main pastoral concern: the preaching of the fundamentals of the Christian Faith as held by all Churches.

Begin we with the first, The over-pure despisers of others; Men that will abridge, and contract the large mercies of God in Christ, and elude, and frustrate, in a great part, the generall promises of God. Men that are loth, that God should speak so loud, as to say, *He would have all men saved*, And loth that Christ should spread his armes, or shed his bloud in such a compasse, as might fall upon *all*. Men that think no sinne can hurt them, because they are *elect*, and that every sin makes every other man a *Reprobate*. But with the Lord there is *Copiosa redemptio*, plentifull redemption, *and an overflowing cup of mercy*. *Aquæ quae non mentiuntur*, As the holy Ghost sayes more than once, more than many times, in the Prophets, *Waters that will not lye*, that will not dry, not deceive, not disappoint any man. *The wisdome that is from above, is first pure, and then peaceable.* Purity, Sincerity, Integrity, Holinesse, is a skirt of Christs garment; It is the very livery that he puts upon us; wee cannot serve him without it, (we must *serve him in holiness and purenesse*) we cannot see him without it, *without holinesse no man shall see God*. But then to be pure, and not *peaceable*, to determine this purity in our selves, and condemne others, this is but an imaginary, but an illusory purity. Not to have relieved that poor wretch, that lay wounded, and weltring in his bloud in the way to *Jericho*, was the uncharitablenesse of the *Levite*, and the *Priest*, in that parable. But that parable presents no man so uncharitable, as would have hindred the Samaritan, from *pouring his Oyle, and his Wine into the wounds* of that distressed wretch. To hinder the bloud of Christ Jesus, not to suffer that bloud to flow as far, as it will, to deny the mercy of God in Christ, to any sinner, whatsoever, upon any pretence, whatsoever, this is to be offended in Christ, to be scandalized with his Gospel; for, that's his own precept, *Have salt in your selves*, (bee it *purity*, the best preservative of the soul) And then, *Have peace with one another*, Deny no man the benefit of Christ; Blesse thou the Lord, praise him, and magnifie him, for that which hee hath done for thee, and beleeve, that he means as well to others, as to thee. And these are one Sect of the Disciples of *Johns* Disciples, That think there are men, whom *Christ cannot* save, And the other is of men that think they *can* save other men.

(ii)

So then there is a *Viatory*, a preparatory, an initiatory, an inchoative blessednesse in this life. What is that? All agree in this definition, that blessednesse is that *in quo quiescit animus*, in which the minde, the heart, the desire of man hath settled, and rested, in which it found a *Centricall* reposednesse, an acquiescence, a contentment. Not that which might satisfie any *particular* man; for, so the object would be infinitely various; but that, beyond which no man could propose any thing; And is there such a blessednesse in this life? There is. *Fecisti nos Domine ad te, & inquietum est Cor nostrum, donec quiescat in te*; Lord thou hast made us for thy selfe, and our heart cannot rest, till it get to thee. But can we come to God here? We cannot. Where's then our viatory, our preparatory, our initiatory, our inchoative blessednesse? Beloved, though we cannot come to God here, here *God comes to us*; Here, in the *prayers* of the Congregation God comes to us; here, in his Ordinance of *Preaching*, God delivers himselfe to us; here in the administration of his *Sacraments*, he seals, ratifies, confirmes all unto us; And to rest in these his seals and means of reconciliation to him, this is not to *be scandalised, not to be offended in him*; and, not to be offended in him, *not to suspect* him or these meanes which he hath ordained, this is our viatory, our preparatory, our initiatory and inchoative Blessednesse, beyond which, nothing can be proposed in this life. And therefore, as the *Needle* of a *Sea-compasse*, thought it shake long, yet will rest at last, and though it do not look directly, exactly to the North Pole, but have some *variation*, yet, for all that variation, will rest, so, though thy heart have some variations, some deviations, some aberrations from that direct point, upon which it should be bent, which is an absolute conformity of thy will to the will of God, yet, though thou lack something of that, afford thy soul rest: settle thy soule in such an *infallibility*, as this present condition can admit, and beleeve, that God receives glory as well in thy *Repentance*, as in thine *Innocence*, and that the mercy of God in Christ, is as good a pillow to rest thy soule upon *after* a sinne, as the *grace* of God in Christ is a shield, and protection for thy soule, before. In a word, this is our viatory, our preparatory, our initiatory, and inchoative blessedness, beyond which there can bee no blessedness proposed here, first to receive a satisfaction, an acquiescence, that there are certaine and constant meanes ordained by Christ, for our reconciliation to God in him, in all cases, in which a Christian soule can bee distressed, that such a treasure there is deposited by him, in the Church, And then, the testimony of a rectified Conscience, that thou hast sincerely applied those generall helpes to thy particular soule. Come so farre, and then, as the *Suburbs* touch the City, and *the Porch* the Church, and deliver thee into it, so shall this Viatory, this preparatory, this initiatory and inchoative blessednesse deliver thee over to the everlasting blessednesse of the Kingdome of heaven.

## 66. From a Sermon Preached upon Christmas Day. [?1629]¹

### (i)

GOD, who vouchsafed to be made Man for man, for man vouchsafes also to doe all the offices of man towards man. He is our Father, for he made us: Of what? Of clay; So God is *Figulus*, so in the Prophet; so in the Apostle, God is our Potter. God stamped his Image upon us, and so God is *Statuarius*, our Minter, our Statuary. God clothed us, and so is *vestiarius*; he hath opened his wardrobe unto us. God gave us all the fruits of the earth to eate, and so is *œconomus*, our Steward. God poures his oyle, and his wine into our wounds, and so is *Medicus*, and *Vicinus*, that Physitian, that Neighbour, that Samaritan intended in the Parable. God plants us, and waters, and weeds us, and gives the increase; and so God is *Hortulanus*, our Gardiner. God builds us up into a Church, and so God is *Architectus*, our Architect, our Builder; God watches the City when it is built; and so God is *Speculator*, our Sentinell. God fishes for men, (for all his *Johns*, and his *Andrews*, and his *Peters*, are but the nets that he fishes withall) God is the fisher of men; And here, in this Chapter, God in Christ is our Shepheard. The book of *Job* is a

---

¹ On the text: 'I am come that they might have life, and that they might have it more abundantly' (John x. 10).

representation of God, in a Tragique-Comedy, lamentable beginnings comfortably ended: The book of the Canticles is a representation of God in Christ, as a Bridegroom in a Marriage-song,
in an Epithalamion: God in Christ is represented to us, in divers
formes, in divers places, and this Chapter is his Pastorall. The
Lord is our Shepheard, and so called, in more places, than by any
other name; and in this Chapter, exhibits some of the offices of a
good Shepheard. Be pleased to taste a few of them. First, he sayes,
*The good Shepheard comes in at the doore*, the right way. If he come in at
the window, that is, always clamber after preferment; If he come
in at vaults, and cellars, that is, by clandestin, and secret contracts
with his Patron, he comes not the right way: When he is in the
right way, *His sheep heare his voyce*: first there is a voyce, He is heard;
Ignorance doth not silence him, nor lazinesse, nor abundance
of preferment; nor indiscreet, and distempered zeale does not
silence him; (for to induce, or occasion a silencing upon our selves,
is as ill as the ignorant, or the lazie silence) There is a voyce, and
(sayes that Text) it is his voyce, not alwayes another in his roome;
for (as it is added in the next verse) *The sheep know his voyce*, which
they could not doe, if they heard it not often, if they were not used
to it. And then, for the best testimony, and consummation of all,
he sayes, *The good Shepheard gives his life for his sheep*. Every good
Shepheard gives his life, that is, spends his life, weares out his life
for his sheep; of which this may be one good argument, That there
are not so many crazie, so many sickly men, men that so soon grow
old in any profession, as in ours.

## (ii)

What eye can fixe it self upon East and West at once? And he
must see more than East and West, that sees God, for God spreads
infinitely beyond both: God alone is all; not onely all that is, but
all that is not, all that might be, if he would have it be. God is too
large, too immense, and then man is too narrow, too little to be
considered; for, who can fixe his eye upon an Atome? and he must
see a lesse thing than an Atome, that sees man, for man is nothing.
First, for the incomprehensiblenesse of God, the understanding of
man, hath a limited, a determined latitude; it is an intelligence

able to move that Spheare which it is fixed to, but could not move a greater: I can comprehend *naturam naturatam*, created nature, but for that *natura naturans*, God himselfe, the understanding of man cannot comprehend. I can see the Sun in a looking-glasse, but the nature, and the whole working of the Sun I cannot see in that glasse. I can see God in the creature, but the nature, the essence, the secret purposes of God, I cannot see there. There is *defatigatio in intellectualibus*, sayes the saddest and soundest of the Hebrew Rabbins, the soule may be tired, as well as the body, and the understanding dazeled, as well as the eye.

(iii)

Let man be something; how poore, and inconsiderable a ragge of this world, is man? Man, whom *Paracelsus* would have undertaken to have made, in a Limbeck, in a Furnace: Man, who, if they were altogether, all the men, that ever were, and are, and shall be, would not have the power of one Angel in them all, whereas all the Angels, (who, in the Schoole are conceived to be more in number, than, not onely all the Species, but all the individualls of this lower world) have not in them all, the power of one finger of Gods hand: Man, of whom when *David* had said, (as the lowest diminution that he could put upon him) *I am a worme and no man*, He might have gone lower, and said, I am a man and no worm; for man is so much lesse than a worm, as that wormes of his own production, shall feed upon his dead body in the grave, and an immortall worm gnaw his conscience in the torments of hell.

(iv)

There is Ayre enough in the world, to give breath to every thing, though every thing doe not breath. If a tree, or a stone doe not breathe, it is not because it wants ayre, but because it wants meanes to receive it, or to returne it. All egges are not hatched that the hen sits upon; neither could Christ himselfe get all the chickens that were hatched, to come, and to stay under his wings. That man that is blinde, or that will winke, shall see no more sunne upon S. *Barnabies* day, than upon S. *Lucies*; no more in the summer, than in the winter solstice. And therefore as there is *copiosa redemptio*, a plentifull redemption brought into the world by the death of Christ, so (as S. *Paul* found it in his particular conversion) there is *copiosa lux*, a great and a powerfull light exhibited to us, that we might see, and lay hold of this life, in the Ordinances of the Church, in the Confessions, and Absolutions, and Services, and Sermons, and Sacraments of the Church: Christ came *ut daret*, that he might bring life into the world, by his death, and then he instituted his Church, *ut haberent*, that by the meanes thereof this life might be infused into us, and infused so, as the last word of our Text delivers it, *Abundantius, I came, that they might have life more abundantly.*

## (v)

Humiliation is the beginning of sanctification; and as without this, without holinesse, no man shall see God, though he pore whole nights upon the Bible; so without that, without humility, no man shall heare God speake to his soule, though hee heare three two-houres Sermons every day. But if God bring thee to that humiliation of soule and body here, hee will emprove, and advance thy sanctification *abundantius*, more abundantly, and when he hath brought it to the best perfection, that this life is capable of, he will provide another *abundantius*, another maner of abundance in the life to come; which is the last beating of the pulse of this text, the last panting of the breath thereof, our anhelation, and panting after the joyes, and glory, and eternity of the kingdome of Heaven; of which, though, for the most part, I use to dismisse you, with saying something, yet it is alwaies little that I can say thereof; at this time, but this, that if all the joyes of all the Martyrs, from *Abel* to him that groanes now in the Inquisition, were condensed into one body of joy, (and certainly the joyes that the Martyrs felt at their deaths, would make up a far greater body, than their sorrowes would doe,) (for though it bee said of our great Martyr, or great Witnesse, (as S. *John* calls Christ Jesus) to whom, all other Martyrs are but sub-martyrs, witnesses that testifie his testimony, *Non dolor sicut dolor ejus*, there was never sorrow like unto his sorrow, it is also true, *Non gaudium sicut gaudium ejus*, There was never joy like unto that joy which was set before him, when he endured the crosse;) If I had all this joy of all these Martyrs, (which would, no

doubt, be such a joy, as would worke a liquefaction, a melting of
my bowels) yet I shall have it *abundantius*, a joy more abundant,
than even this superlative joy, in the world to come. What a
dimme vespers of a glorious festivall, what a poore halfe-holyday, is
*Methusalems* nine hundred yeares, to eternity? what a poore account
hath that man made, that saies, this land hath beene in my name,
and in my Ancestors from the Conquest? what a yesterday is that?
not six hundred yeares. If I could beleeve the transmigration of
soules, and thinke that my soule had beene successively in some
creature or other, since the Creation, what a yesterday is that? not
six thousand yeares. What a yesterday for the past, what a tomorrow for the future, is any terme, that can be comprehended in
Cyphar or Counters? But as, how abundant a life soever any man
hath in this world for temporall abundances, I have life more
abundantly than hee, if I have the spirituall life of grace, so what
measure soever I have of this spirituall life of grace, in this world,
I shall have that more abundantly in Heaven, for there, my terme
shall bee a terme for three lives; for those three, that as long as the
Father, and the Son, and the holy Ghost live, I shall not dye.

# 67. From a Sermon Preached on the Conversion of S. Paul. 1630[1]

## (i)

FIRST then, for the competency of his Judges, Whether a man be
examined before a competent Judge or no, he may not lye: we can
put no case, in which it may be lawfull for any man to lye to any
man; not to a midnight, nor to a noone thiefe, that breaks my
house, or assaults my person, I may not lye. And though many have
put names of disguise, as Equivocations, and Reservations, yet
they are all children of the same father, the father of lies, the devill,
and of the same brood of vipers, they are lyes. To an Incompetent

---

[1] On the text: 'But when Paul perceived that one part were Sadducees and the other
Pharisees, he cried out in the Council, Men and Brethren, I am a Pharisee, and the son of a
Pharisee; of the hope and resurrection of the dead I am called in question.

And when he had said so, there arose a dissention between the Pharisees and the Sadducees,
and the multitude was divided' (Acts xxiii. 6, 7).

Judge, if I be interrogated, I must speake truth, if I speake; but to a Competent Judge, I must speak: With the Incompetent I may not be false, but with the Competent, I may not be silent. Certainely, that standing mute at the Bar, which, of late times hath prevailed upon many distempered wretches, is, in it selfe, so particularly a sin, as that I should not venture to absolve any such person, nor to administer the Sacrament to him, how earnestly soever he desired it at his death, how penitently soever he confessed all his other sins, except he repented in particular, that sin, of having stood mute and refused a just triall, and would be then content to submit himselfe to it, if that favour might possibly at that time be afforded him. To an incompetent Judge I must not lie, but I may be silent, to a competent I must answer.

### (ii)

Beloved, there are some things in which all Religions agree; The worship of God, The holinesse of life; And therefore, if when I study this holinesse of life, and fast, and pray, and submit my selfe to discreet, and medicinall mortifications, for the subduing of my body, any man will say, this is Papisticall, Papists doe this, it is a blessed Protestation, and no man is the lesse a Protestant, nor the worse a Protestant for making it, Men and brethren, I am a Papist, that is, I will fast and pray as much as any Papist, and enable my selfe for the service of my God, as seriously, as sedulously, as laboriously as any Papist. So, if when I startle and am affected at a blasphemous oath, as at a wound upon my Saviour, if when I avoyd the conversation of those men, that prophane the Lords day, any other will say to me, This is Puritanicall, Puritans do this, It is a blessed Protestation, and no man is the lesse a Protestant, nor the worse a Protestant for making it, Men and Brethren, I am a Puritan, that is, I wil endeavour to be pure, as my Father in heaven is pure, as far as any Puritan.

### (iii)

Bring every single sin, as soon as thou committest it, into the presence of thy God, upon those two legs, Confession, and Detestation, and thou shalt see, that as, though an intire Iland stand firme in the Sea, yet a single clod of earth cast into the Sea, is quickly washt into nothing; so, howsoever thine habituall, and customary, and concatenated sins, sin enwrapped and complicated in sin, sin entrenched and barricadoed in sin, sin screwed up, and riveted with sin, may stand out, and wrastle even with the mercies of God, in the blood of Christ Jesus; yet if thou bring every single sin into the sight of God, it will be but as a clod of earth, but as a graine of dust in the Ocean. Keep thy sins then from mutuall intelligence, that they doe not second one another, induce occasion, and then support and disguise one another; and then, neither shall the body of sin ever oppresse thee, nor the exhalations, and damps, and vapors of thy sad soule, hang between thee, and the mercies of thy God; But thou shalt live in the light and serenity of a peaceable conscience here, and die in a faire possibility of a present melioration and improvement of that light. All thy life thou shalt be preserved, in an Orientall light, an Easterne light, a rising and a growing light, the light of grace; and at thy death thou shalt be super-illustrated, with a Meridionall light, a South light, the light of glory.

## 68. A Lent-Sermon Preached to the King, at White-hall, February 12. 1630[1]

### (i)

I HAVE seen Minute-glasses; Glasses so short-liv'd. If I were to preach upon this Text, to such a glass, it were enough for half the Sermon; enough to show the worldly man his Treasure, and the Object of his heart (*for, where your Treasure is, there will your Heart be also*) to call his eye to that Minute-glass, and to tell him, There flows, there flies your Treasure, and your Heart with it. But if I had a Secular Glass, a Glass that would run an age; if the two Hemispheres of the World were composed in the form of such a Glass, and all the World calcin'd and burnt to ashes, and all the ashes, and sands, and atoms of the World put into that Glass, it would not be enough to tell the godly man what his Treasure, and

---

[1] On the text: 'For, where your treasure is, there will your heart be also' (Matt. vi. 21).

the Object of his Heart is. A Parrot, or a Stare, docile Birds, and of pregnant imitation, will sooner be brought to relate to us the wisdom of a Council Table, than any *Ambrose*, or any *Chrysostome*, Men that have Gold and Honey in their Names, shall tell us what the Sweetness, what the Treasure of Heaven is, and what that mans peace, that hath set his Heart upon that Treasure.

## (ii)

When God sayes, *Fili, da mihi Cor; My Son, give me thy heart*; God means, the whole man. Though the Apostle say, *The eye is not the man, nor the ear is not the man*; he does not say, The heart is not the man: the heart is the man; the heart is all: and, as *Moses* was not satisfied with that Commission that *Pharaoh* offered him, That all the men might go to offer sacrifice; but *Moses* would have all their young, and all their old; all their sons, and all their daughters; all their flocks, and all their herds; he would have all: So, when God sayes, *Fili, da mihi Cor, My Son, give me thy heart*, God will not be satisfied with the eye, if I contemplate him in his Works: (for that's but the godliness of the natural man) nor satisfied with the ear, with hearing many Sermons: (for that's but a new invention, a new way of making Beads, if, as the Papist thinks all done, if he have said so many *Aves*, I think all done, if I have heard so many Sermons.) But God requires the heart, the whole man, all the faculties of that man. ...

There is a good nullification of the heart, a good bringing of the heart to nothing. For the fire of Gods Spirit may take hold of me, and (as the Disciples that went with Christ to *Emmaus*, were affected) *my heart may burn within me*, when the Scriptures are opened, that is, when Gods Judgements are denounced against my Sin; and this heat may overcome my former frigidity and coldness, and overcome my succeeding tepidity and lukewarmness, and may bring my heart to a mollification, to a tenderness, as *Job* found it; *The Almighty hath troubled me, and made my heart soft*: for there are hearts of clay, as well as hearts of wax; hearts, whom these fires of God, his Corrections, harden. But if these fires of his, these denunciations of his judgements, have overcome first my coldness, and then my lukewarmness, and made my heart soft for better impressions; the work is well advanc'd, but it is not all done: for Metal may be soft, and yet not fusil; Iron may be red hot, and yet not apt to run into another mold. Therefore there is a liquefaction, a melting, a pouring out of the heart, such as *Rahab* speaks of, to *Joshua's* Spies; (*As soon as we heard how miraculously God had proceeded in your behalf, in drying up Jordan, all our hearts melted within us, and no man had any spirit left in him.*) And when upon the consideration of Gods miraculous Judgements or Mercies, I come to such a melting and pouring out of my heart, that there be no spirit, that is, none of mine own spirit left in me; when I have so exhausted, so evacuated my self, that is, all confidence in my self, that I come into the hands of my God, as pliably, as ductily, as that first clod of earth, of which he made me in *Adam*, was in his hands, in which clod of earth, there was no kinde of reluctation against Gods purpose; this is a blessed nullification of the heart. When I say to my self, as the Apostle professed of him-self, *I am nothing*; and then say to God, Lord, though I be nothing, yet behold, I present thee as much as thou hadst to make the whole world of; O Thou that mad'st the whole world of nothing, make me, that am nothing in mine own eyes, a new Creature in Christ Jesus: This is a blessed nullification, a glorious annihilation of the heart. So is there also a blessed nullification thereof, in the con-trition of heart, in the sense of my sins; when, as a sharp winde may have worn out a Marble Statue, or a continual spout worn out a Marble Pavement, so, my holy tears, made holy in his Blood that gives them a tincture, and my holy sighs, made holy in that Spirit that breathes them in me, have worn out my Marble Heart, that is, the Marbleness of my heart, and emptied the room of that former heart, and so given God a *Vacuity*, a new place to create a new heart in.

## (iii)

But yet, a Treasure every man hath: *An evil man, out of the evil Treasure of his Heart, bringeth forth that which is evil*, says our Saviour: Every man hath some sin upon which his heart is set; and, *Where your Heart is, there is your Treasure also. The treasures of wickedness profit nothing*, says *Job*; 'Tis true: But yet, Treasures of wickedness there are. *Are there not yet Treasures of wickedness in the house of the wicked?* consider the force of that word, *yet; yet*, though you have the power

of a vigilant Prince executed by just Magistrates; *yet*, though you
have the Piety of a Religious Prince, seconded by the assiduity of a
laborious Clergy; *yet*, though you have many helps, which your
Fathers did, and your Neighbours do want, and have (by Gods
grace) some fruits of those many helps; *yet*, for all this, *Are there
not yet Treasures of wickedness in the house of the wicked?* No? *Are there
not scant measures? which are an abomination to God*, says the Prophet
there; which are not onely false measures of Merchandize, but false
measures of Men: for, when God sayes that, he intends all this; Is
there not yet supplantation in Court, and mis-representations of
men? When *Solomon*, who understood sub-ordination of places
which flowed from him, as well as the highest, which himself
possest, says, and says experimentally for his own, and prophetically
for future times, *If a Ruler* (a man in great place) *hearken to lyes, all his
servants are wicked*: Are there not yet misrepresentations of men in
Courts? Is there not yet Oppression in the Country? A starving
of men, and pampering of dogs? *A swallowing of the needy? A buying
of the poor for a pair of shooes, and a selling to the hungry refuse corn?* Is
there not yet Oppression in the Country? Is there not yet Extortion
in *Westminster? A justifying of the wicked for a reward, and a taking away
of the righteousness of the righteous from him?* Is there not yet Extortion
in *Westminster*? Is there not yet Collusion and Circumvention in the
City? Would they not seem richer than they are, when they deal in
private Bargains with one another? And would they not seem poorer
than they are, when they are call'd to contribute for the Publique?
Have they not increased their riches by Trade, and lifted up their
hearts upon the encrease of their riches? Have they not slackened
their trade, and layn down upon clothes laid to pledge, and ennobled
themselves by an ignoble and lazie way of gain? Is there not yet
Collusion and Circumvention in the City? Is there not yet Hypocrisie in the Church? In all parts thereof? Half preachings, and half
hearings? Hearings and preachings without practise? Have we not
national sins of our own, and yet exercise the nature of Islanders, in
importing the Sins of forreign Parts? And though we better no
forreign Commodity, nor Manufacture that we bring in, we
improve the sins of other Nations; and, as a weaker Grape growing
upon the *Rhene*, contracts a stronger nature in the *Canaries*; so do the

sins of other Nations transplanted amongst us. Have we not
secular sins, sins of our own age, our own time, and yet sin by
precedent of former, as well as create precedents for future? And,
not onely *Silver and Gold*, but *Vessels of Iron and Brass*, were brought
into the Treasury of the Lord; not onely the glorious sins of high
places, and National sins, and secular sins; But the wretchedest
Begger in the street, contributes to this Treasure, the Treasure
of sin; and to this mischievous use, to encrease this Treasure, the
Treasure of sin, is a Subsidy man. He begs in Jesus Name, and for
Gods sake; and in the same Name, curses him that does not give.
He counterfeits a lameness, or he loves his lameness, and would
not be cur'd; for, his lameness is his Stock, it is his Demean, it is (as
they call their Occupations in the City) his Mystery. *Are there not
yet Treasures of wickedness in the house of the wicked*, when even they,
who have no Houses, but lie in the Streets, have these Treasures?

## 69. From a Sermon Preached at S. Pauls, upon Easter-day. 1630

### (i)

OUR first consideration is upon the persons; and those we finde
to be Angelicall women, and Evangelicall Angels: Angels made
Evangelists, to preach the Gospell of the Resurrection, and Women
made Angels, (so as *John Baptist* is called an *Angel*, and so as the
seven Bishops are called *Angels*) that is, Instructers of the Church;
And to recompence that observation, that never good Angel
appeared in the likenesse of woman, here are good women made
Angels, that is, Messengers, publishers of the greatest mysteries of
our Religion. For, howsoever some men out of a petulancy and
wantonnesse of wit, and out of the extravagancy of Paradoxes, and
such singularities, have called the faculties, and abilities of women
in question, even in the roote thereof, in the reasonable and immortall soul, yet that one thing alone hath been enough to create
a doubt, (almost an assurance in the negative) whether S. *Ambroses*

---

1 On the text: 'He is not here, for he is risen, as he said; come, see the place where the
Lord lay' (Matt. xxviii. 6).

Commentaries upon the Epistles of S. *Paul,* be truly his or no, that in that book there is a doubt made, whether the woman were created according to Gods Image; Therefore, because that doubt is made in that book, the book it self is suspected not to have had so great, so grave, so constant an author as S. *Ambrose* was; No author of gravity, of piety, of conversation in the Scriptures could admit that doubt, whether woman were created in the Image of God, that is, in possession of a reasonable and an immortall soul.

The faculties and abilities of the soul appeare best in affaires of State, and in Ecclesiasticall affaires; in matter of government, and in matter of religion; and in neither of these are we without examples of able women. For, for State affaires, and matter of government, our age hath given us such a Queen, as scarce any former King hath equalled; And in the Venetian Story, I remember, that certain Matrons of that City were sent by Commission, in quality of Ambassadours, to an Empresse with whom that State had occasion to treate; And in the Stories of the Eastern parts of the World, it is said to be in ordinary practise to send women for Ambassadours. And then, in matters of Religion, women have evermore had a great hand, though sometimes on the left, as well as on the right hand. Sometimes their abundant wealth, sometimes their personall affections to some Church-men, sometimes their irregular and indiscreet zeale hath made them great assistants of great Heretiques; as S. *Hierome* tels us of *Helena* to *Simon Magus,* and so was *Lucilia* to *Donatus,* so another to *Mahomet,* and others to others. But so have they been also great instruments for the advancing of true Religion, as S. *Paul* testifies in their behalf, at *Thessalonica, Of the chiefe women, not a few*; Great, and Many. For, many times women have the proxies of greater persons than themselves, in their bosomes; many times women have voices, where they should have none; many times the voices of great men, in the greatest of Civill, or Ecclesiasticall Assemblies, have been in the power and disposition of women.

Hence is it, that in the old Epistles of the Bishops of Rome, when they needed the Court, (as, at first they needed Courts as much, as they brought Courts to need them at last) we finde as many letters of those Popes to the Emperours Wives, and the Emperours

Mothers, and Sisters, and women of other names, and interests in
the Emperours favours and affections, as to the Emperours themselves. S. *Hierome* writ many letters to divers holy Ladies; for the
most part, all of one stocke and kindred; and a stock and kindred so
religious, as that I remember, the good old man saies, That if
*Jupiter* were their Cousin, of their kindred, he beleeves *Jupiter*
would be a Christian; he would leave being such a God as he was,
to be their fellow-servant to the true God.

Now if women were brought up according to S. *Hieromes* instructions in those letters, that by seaven yeares of age, they should be
able to say the Psalmes without book; That as they grew in yeares,
they should proceed in the knowledge of Scriptures, That they
should love the Service of God at Church, but not *sine Matre*, not
goe to Church when they would, but when their Mother could
goe with them, *Nec quærerent celebritatem Ecclesiarum*, They should
not alwaies goe to the greatest Churches, and where the most
famous Preachers drew most company; If women have submitted
themselves to as good an education as men, God forbid their sexe
should prejudice them, for being examples to others. Their sexe?
no, nor their sins neither: for, it is S. *Hieromes* note, That of all those
women, that are named in Christs pedegree in the Gospell, there
is not one, (his onely Blessed Virgin Mother excepted) upon whom
there is not some suspitious note of incontinency. Of such women
did Christ vouchsafe to come; He came of woman so, as that he
came of nothing but woman; of woman, and not of man. Neither
doe we reade of any woman in the Gospel, that assisted the persecutors of Christ, or furthered his afflictions; Even *Pilats* wife
disswaded it. Woman, as well as man, was made after the Image of
God, in the Creation; and in the Resurrection, when we shall rise
such as we were here, her sexe shall not diminish her glory: Of
which, she receives one faire beame, and inchoation in this Text,
that the purpose of God is, even by the ministery of Angels,
communicated to women.

(ii)

We know that God is alike in all places, but he does not worke
in all places alike; God works otherwise in the Church, than in an

Army; and diversly in his divers Ordinances in the Church; God works otherwise in Prayer than in Preaching, and otherwise in the Sacraments than in either; and otherwise in the later, than in the first Sacrament. The power is the same, and the end is the same, but the way is not so. *Athanasius*, scarce three hundred yeares after Christ, found the Church in possession of that Custome (and he takes knowledge of it, as of a precept from the Apostles themselves) That the Congregation should pray towards the East, to testifie (saies that Father) their desire of returning to the Country, which they had lost, Paradise. Places of prophane and secular use should not be made equall with holy places; nor should holy actions, and motions, and gestures, and positions of the body in divine service, be submitted to scorne and derision. They have their use; either in a reall exaltation of Devotion, or for a peaceable conservation of uniformity, and decency, or for a reverentiall obedience to lawfull Authority; and any of these is enough, to authorize things in their use, which in themselves and in their owne nature are indifferent. And though the principall purpose of the Angell, in shewing these women the place, were to assure them, that Christ was risen, yet may there also be an intimation of the helpe and assistance that we receive from holy places, in this their *Ecce locus, Come, and see the place.*

## 70. From a Sermon Preached in Lent, to the King, April 20. 1630 [?][1]

IF they knew, (may *Job* have said) how it stood between God and my soule, how earnestly I have repented, how fully he hath forgiven, they would never say, these afflictions proceeded from those sins.

And truly, so may I, so may every soule say, that is rectified, refreshed, restored, re-established by the seales of Gods pardon, and his mercy, so the world would take knowledge of the conse-

---

[1] On the text: 'Not for any injustice in my hands: also my prayer is pure. O earth cover not thou my blood; and let my cry have no place. Also now behold, my witness is in heaven, and my record is on high' (Job xvi. 17, 18, 19).

The date in the Folio cannot be correct since in 1630 Easter fell on 28 March. It seems likely that the words 'in Lent' are an error, since the sermon, unlike Donne's other Lenten sermons, contains no reference to the season.

quences of my sins, as well as of the sins themselves, and read my
leafes on both sides, and heare the second part of my story, as well
as the first; so the world would look upon my temporall calamities,
the bodily sicknesses, and the penuriousnesse of my fortune contracted by my sins, and upon my spirituall calamities, dejections of
spirit, sadnesse of heart, declinations towards a diffidence and distrust in the mercy of God, and then, when the world sees me in
this agony and bloody sweat, in this agony and bloody sweat would
also see the Angels of heaven ministring comforts unto me; so they
would consider me in my *Peccavi*, and God in his *Transtulit*, Me in
my earnest Confessions, God in his powerful Absolutions, Me
drawne out of one Sea of blood, the blood of mine owne soule, and
cast into another Sea, the bottomelesse Sea of the blood of Christ
Jesus; so they would know as well what God hath done for my
soule, as what my soule and body have done against my God;
so they would reade me throughout, and look upon me altogether,
I would joyne with *Job*, in his confident adjuration, *O Earth
cover not thou my blood*; Let all the world know all the sins of my
youth, and of mine age too, and I would not doubt, but God should
receive more glory, and the world more benefit, than if I had never
sinned.

71. *Deaths Duell, or, a Consolation to the Soule,
against the dying Life, and living Death of the Body.
Delivered in a Sermon at White Hall, before the Kings
Majesty, in the beginning of Lent,* 1631[1]

### To the Reader

*This Sermon was, by Sacred Authoritie, stiled the Authors owne funeral
Sermon. Most fitly: whether wee respect the time, or the matter. It was preached
not many dayes before his death; as if, having done this, there remained nothing*

1  Donne fell ill in the autumn of 1630 and was too unwell to obey the King's command to
preach the Gunpowder Plot sermon on 5 November. He had to excuse himself from preaching
the Christmas sermon at St. Paul's, but wrote that he would preach on Candlemas day
(2 February). He was still unable to preach then; but he determined that he would preach at
Court on his 'old constant day' the first Friday in Lent. In spite of the efforts of his friends to
dissuade him, he insisted and as Walton writes 'When to the amazement of some beholders
he appeared in the Pulpit, many of them thought he presented himself not to preach mortification by a living voice: but mortality by a decayed body and a dying face . . . And yet, after
some faint pauses in his zealous prayer, his strong desires enabled his weak body to discharge

*for him to doe, but to die: And the matter is, of Death; the occasion and subject of all funerall Sermons. It hath beene observed of this Reverend Man, That his Faculty in Preaching continually encreased: and, That as hee exceeded others at first; so, at last hee exceeded himselfe. This is his last Sermon; I will not say, it is therefore his best; because, all his were excellent. Yet thus much: A dying Mans words, if they concerne our selves; doe usually make the deepest impression, as being spoken most feelingly, and with least affectation. Now, whom doth it not concerne to learn, both the danger, and benefit of death? Death is every mans enemy, and intends hurt to all; though to many, hee be occasion of greatest goods. This enemy wee must all combate dying; whom hee living did almost conquer; having discovered the utmost of his power, the utmost of his crueltie. May wee make such use of this and other the like preparatives, That neither death, whensoever it shall come, may seeme terrible; nor life tedious; how long soever it shall last.*

Psa. 68. vers. 20. In fine. And unto God the Lord belong the issues of death. i.e. from death.

Buildings stand by the benefit of their *foundations* that susteine and *support* them, and of their *butteresses* that comprehend and *embrace* them, and of their *contignations* that knit and *unite* them: The *foundations* suffer them not to *sinke*, the *butteresses* suffer them not to *swerve*, and the *contignation* and knitting suffers them not to *cleave*. The body of our building is in the former part of this verse: It is this, hee that *is our God* is the *God of salvation; ad salutes*, of salvations in the plurall, so it is in the originall; the *God* that gives us spirituall and temporall salvation too. But of this *building*, the *foundation*, the *butteresses*, the *contignations* are in this part of the *verse*, which constitutes *our text*, and in the three divers *acceptations* of the words amongst our expositors, *Unto God the Lord belong the issues of death*. For *first* the *foundation* of this *building*, (that our *God* is the *God of all salvations*) is laid in this; That *unto* this *God the Lord belong the issues of death*, that is, it is in his power to give us an *issue* and deliverance, even then when wee are brought to the jawes and teeth of death, and to the lippes of that whirlepoole, the

his memory of his preconceived meditations, which were of dying: the Text being, *To God the Lord belong the issues from death*. Many that then saw his tears, and heard his faint and hollow voice, professing they thought the Text prophetically chosen, and that Dr. Donne had *preach't his own Funeral Sermon*.'

The Sermon was printed immediately after Donne's death with the portrait of Donne in his shroud prefixed.

grave. And so in this acceptation, this *exitus mortis*, this *issue of death* is *liberatio a morte, a deliverance from death*, and this is the most obvious and most ordinary acceptation of these words, and that upon which our *translation* laies hold, the *issues from death*. And then *secondly*, the butteresses that comprehend and settle this building, That hee that is *our God*, is the *God of* all *salvation*, are thus raised; unto *God the Lord belong the issues of death*, that is, the disposition and *manner of our death*: what kinde of *issue*, and *transmigration* wee shall have out of this world, whether prepared or sudden, whether violent or naturall, whether in our perfect senses or shaken and disordered by sicknes, there is no condemnation to bee argued out of that, no Judgement to bee made upon that, for howsoever they dye, *precious in his sight is the death of his saints*, and with him are *the issues of death*, the *wayes* of our *departing* out of this *life* are in his *hands*. And so in this *sense* of the *words*, this *exitus mortis*, the *issue of death*, is *liberatio in morte, A deliverance in death*; Not that *God* will *deliver* us *from dying*, but that hee will *have a care* of us in the *houre of death*, of what kinde soever our passage be. And this *sense* and acceptation of the *words*, the naturall frame and contexture doth well and pregnantly administer unto us. And then *lastly* the *contignation* and knitting of this building, that hee that is *our God* is the *God of all salvations*, consists in this, *Unto this God the Lord belong the issues of death*, that is, that this *God* the *Lord* having *united* and knit *both natures in one*, and being *God*, having also *come* into this *world*, in our *flesh*, he could have no other meanes to save us, he could have no other *issue* out of this world, nor *returne* to his former *glory*, but by *death*; And so in this sense, this *exitus mortis*, this *issue of death*, is *liberatio per mortem*, a *deliverance by death*, by the death of this *God* our *Lord Christ Jesus*. And this is Saint *Augustines* acceptation of the words, and those many and great persons that have adhered to him. In all these three lines then, we shall looke upon these words; *First*, as the *God* of *power*, the *Almighty Father* rescues his servants from the jawes of death: *And then*, as the *God* of *mercy*, the glorious *Sonne* rescued us, by taking upon himselfe this *issue of death*: *And then* betweene these two, as the *God* of *comfort*, the *Holy Ghost* rescues us from all discomfort by his blessed impressions before hand, that what manner of death soever be ordeined for us, yet this *exitus mortis* shall bee *introitus in vitam,* our *issue in death,* shall be an *entrance into everlasting life.* And these three considerations, our deliverance *a morte, in morte, per mortem, from death, in death,* and *by death,* will abundantly doe all the offices of the *foundations,* of the *butteresses,* of the *contignation* of this our *building;* That he that is our *God,* is the *God of all salvation,* because *unto* this *God the Lord belong the issues of death.*

*First,* then, we consider this *exitus mortis,* to bee *liberatio a morte,* that with *God,* the *Lord* are the *issues of death,* and therefore in all our deaths, and deadly calamities of this life, wee may justly *hope* of a good *issue* from him; and all our *periods* and *transitions* in this life, are so many passages *from death* to *death.* Our very *birth* and entrance into this life, is *exitus a morte,* an *issue from death,* for in our mothers *wombe* wee are *dead so,* as that wee doe *not know* wee *live,* not so much as wee doe in our *sleepe,* neither is there any *grave* so close, or so *putrid* a *prison,* as the *wombe* would be unto us, if we stayed in it *beyond* our time, or dyed there *before* our time. In the *grave* the *wormes* doe not kill us, wee *breed* and *feed,* and then *kill* those wormes which wee our selves produc'd. In the wombe the dead *child* kills the *Mother* that conceived it, and is a murtherer, nay a *parricide,* even after it is dead. And if wee bee not dead so in the *wombe,* so as that being dead, wee kill her that gave us our first life, our life of *vegetation,* yet wee are dead so, as *Davids Idols* are dead. In the *wombe* wee have *eyes and see not, eares and heare not;* There in the wombe wee are fitted for *workes of darkenes,* all the while deprived of light: And there in the *wombe* wee are taught *cruelty,* by being *fed with blood,* and may be *damned,* though we be *never borne.* Of our very making in the *wombe, David* says, *I am wonderfully and fearefully made, and, Such knowledge is too excellent for me,* for even that *is the Lords doing, and it is wonderfull in our eyes. Ipse fecit nos, it is hee that hath made us, and not wee our selves,* no, nor our parents neither; *Thy hands have made me and fashioned me round about,* saith *Job,* and, (as the *originall word* is) *thou hast taken paines about me,* and *yet,* sayes he, *thou doest destroy me.* Though I bee the *Master peece* of the greatest *Master* (*man* is so,) yet if thou doe no more for me, if thou leave me where thou madest mee, destruction will follow. The *wombe* which should be the *house of life,* becomes *death* it selfe, if *God* leave us there. That which God threatens so often, the *shutting of the womb,* is not so *heavy,* nor so discomfortable a *curse* in the *first,* as in the *latter* shutting, nor in the shutting of *barrennes,* as in the shutting of *weakenes,* when *children are come to the birth,* and there is not *strength to bring forth.*

It is the *exaltation* of *misery,* to *fall* from a *neare hope* of *happines.* And in that vehement imprecation, the *Prophet* expresses the highth of *Gods* anger, *Give them o Lord, what will thou give them? give them a mis-carying wombe.* Therefore as soone as wee are men, (that is, inanimated, quickned in the womb) thogh we cannot our selves, our parents have reason to say in our behalf, *wretched man that he is, who shall deliver* him *from this body of death?* for even the *wombe* is a *body of death,* if there bee no deliverer. It must be he that said to *Jeremy, Before I formed thee I knew thee, and before thou camest out of the wombe I sanctified thee.* Wee are not sure that there was no kinde of shippe nor boate to fish in, nor to passe by, till *God* prescribed *Noah* that absolute *form* of *the Arke.* That word which the *holy Ghost* by *Moses* useth for the *Arke,* is common to all kinde of *boates, Thebah,* and is the same word that *Moses* useth for the *boate* that he was *exposed* in, that *his mother layed him in an arke* of *bulrushes.* But we are sure that *Eve* had no *Midwife* when she was *delivered* of *Cain,* therefore shee might well say, *possedi virum a Domino, I have gotten a man from the Lord,* wholly, entirely from the Lord; It is the *Lord* that *enabled* me to *conceive,* The *Lord* that *infus'd* a *quickning soule* into that conception, the *Lord* that *brought into the world* that which himselfe *had quickened;* without all this might *Eve* say, *My body had bene* but *the house of death,* and *Domini Domini sunt exitus mortis,* to *God the Lord belong the issues of death.*

But then this *exitus a morte,* is but *introitus in mortem,* this *issue,* this deliverance *from* that *death,* the death of the *wombe,* is an *entrance,* a delivering over to *another death,* the manifold deathes of this *world.* Wee have a winding sheete in our Mothers wombe, which growes with us from our conception, and wee come into the world, wound up in that *winding sheet,* for wee come to *seeke a grave;* And as prisoners discharg'd of actions may lye for fees; so when the *wombe* hath discharg'd us, yet we are bound to it by *cordes* of flesh, by such a *string,* as that wee cannot goeth thence, nor stay there. We celebrate our owne funeralls with cryes, even at our birth; as though our *three-score and ten years of life* were spent in our mothers labour, and our circle made up in the first point thereof. We begge one Baptism with another, a sacrament of tears; And we come into a world that lasts many ages, but wee last not. *In domo Patris*, says our blessed *Saviour*, speaking of *heaven, multae mansiones*, there *are many mansions*, divers and durable, so that if a man cannot possesse a *martyrs* house, (he hath shed no blood for *Christ*) yet hee may have a *Confessors*, he hath bene ready to glorifie *God* in the *shedding of his blood*. And if a woman cannot possesse a *virgins* house (she hath embrac'd the *holy state* of *mariage*) yet she may have a *matrons* house, she hath brought forth and brought up *children in the feare of God. In domo patris, in my fathers house*, in heaven there *are many mansions*; but here upon earth *The Son of man hath not where to lay his head*, sayes he himselfe. *Nonne terram dedit filiis hominum*? how then hath *God given this earth* to the *sonnes of men*? hee hath *given* them *earth* for their *materialls* to bee made of earth, and he hath given them *earth* for their *grave* and sepulture, to *returne* and resolve to *earth*, but not for their *possession: Here wee have no continuing citty*, nay no *cottage* that continues, nay no persons, no bodies that continue. Whatsoever moved Saint *Jerome* to call the journies of the *Israelites*, in the wildernes, Mansions, the *word* (the word is *Nasang*) signifies but a *journey*, but a peregrination. Even the *Israel of God* hath no mansions; but journies, pilgrimages in this life. By that measure did *Jacob* measure his life to *Pharaoh, The daies of the years of my pilgrimage*. And though the *Apostle* would not say *morimur*, that, whilest *wee are in the body* wee *are dead*, yet hee sayes, *Peregrinamur*, whilest wee are *in the body*, wee are but in *a pilgrimage*, and wee are *absent from the Lord*; hee might have sayd *dead*, for this whole *world* is but an *universall church-yard*, but our *common grave*; and the life and motion that the greatest persons have in it, is but as the shaking of buried bodies in their graves by an *earth-quake*. That which we call life, is but *Hebdomada mortium, a week of deaths*, seaven dayes, seaven periods of our life spent in dying, *a dying seaven times over*; and there is an end. *Our birth dyes* in *infancy*, and our *infancy* dyes in *youth*, and *youth* and the rest dye in *age*, and *age* also dyes, and *determines all*. Nor doe all these, youth out of infancy, or age out of youth arise so, as a *Phoenix* out of the *ashes* of another *Phoenix* formerly *dead*, but as a *waspe* or a *serpent* out of a *caryon*, or as a *Snake* out of *dung*. Our *youth* is *worse* than our *infancy*, and our *age worse* than our *youth*. Our *youth* is *hungry and thirsty*, after those *sinnes*, which our *infancy knew not*; And our *age* is *sory* and *angry*, that it *cannot pursue* those *sinnes* which our *youth* did. And besides, al the way, so many deaths, that is, so many deadly calamities accompany every condition, and every period of this life, as that death it selfe would bee an ease to them that suffer them. Upon this sense doth *Job* wish that *God had not given him* an *issue* from the *first death*, from the *wombe, Wherefore hast thou brought me forth out of the wombe? O that I had given up the Ghost, and no eye had seen me; I should have been, as though I had not been.*

And not only the impatient *Israelites* in their murmuring (*would to God wee had dyed by the hand of the Lord in the land of Egypt*) but *Eliah* himselfe, when he *fled* from *Jesabell*, and went for his life, as that text sayes, under the juniper tree, requested that *hee might dye*, and sayd, *It is enough, now O Lord, take away my life.* So *Jonah* justifies his impatience, nay his anger towards *God* himselfe. *Now o Lord take, I beseech thee, my life from mee, for it is better for me to dye than to live.* And when *God* asked him, *doest thou well to be angry for this*, and after, (about the Gourd) *dost thou well to be angry for that*, he replies, *I doe well to be angry, even unto death.* How much worse a death than death, is this life, which so good men would so often change for death? But if my case bee as Saint *Paules* case, *quotidie morior*, that *I dye dayly*, that something heavier than death fall upon me every day; If my case be *Davids* case, *tota die mortificamur, all the day long wee are killed*, that not onely every day, but every houre of the day some thing heavier than death fall upon me, though that bee true of me, *Conceptus in peccatis, I was shapen in iniquity, and in sinne did my mother conceive me*, (there I dyed one death,) though that be true of me (*Natus filius iræ*) *I was borne* not onely the child of sinne, but *the child of wrath*, of the wrath of *God* for sinne, which is a heavier death; Yet *Domini Domini sunt exitus mortis*, with *God the Lord are the issues of death*, and after a *Job*, and a *Joseph*, and a *Jeremie*, and a *Daniel*, I cannot doubt of a deliverance. And if no other deliverance conduce more to his glory and my good, yet he hath the *keys of death*, and hee can let me out at that dore, that is, deliver me from the manifold deaths of this world, the *omni die* and the *tota die*, the *every dayes death* and *every houres death*, by that *one death*, the *final dissolution* of body and soule, the end of all.

But then is that the end of all? Is that dissolution of body and soule, the last death that the body shall suffer? (for of spirituall death wee speake not now) It is not. Though this be *exitus a morte*, it is *introitus in mortem*: though it bee an *issue from* the manifold *deaths* of this *world*, yet it is an *entrance* into the *death of corruption* and *putrefaction* and *vermiculation* and *incineration*, and dispersion in and from the *grave*, in which every dead man dyes over againe. It was a *prerogative* peculiar to *Christ*, not to dy this death, *not to see corruption*. What gave him this priviledge? Not *Josephs* great proportion of *gummes* and *spices*, that might have preserved his body from corruption and *incineration* longer than he needed it, longer than *three dayes*, but it would not have done it for ever. What preserved him then? did his exemption and *freedome from originall sinne* preserve him from this corruption and *incineration*? 'Tis true that original sinne hath induced this corruption and *incineration* upon us; If wee had not sinned in *Adam*, *mortality had not put on immortality*, (as the *Apostle* speakes) nor *corruption had not put on incorruption*, but we had had our *transmigration* from this to the other world, without any *mortality*, any *corruption at all*. But yet since *Christ* tooke *sinne* upon him, so farre as made him *mortall*, he had it so farre too, as might have made him see this corruption and *incineration*, though he had no *originall sinne* in himself. What preserv'd him then? Did the *hypostaticall union* of both natures, *God* and *Man*, preserve him from this corruption and *incineration*? 'tis true that this was a most powerfull *embalming*, to be embalmd with the *divine nature* it selfe, to bee embalmd with *eternity*, was able to preserve him from corruption and *incineration* for ever. And he was embalm'd so, embalmd with the *divine nature* it selfe, even in his *body* as well as in his *soule*; for the *Godhead*, the *divine nature* did not depart, but remained still *united* to his *dead body* in the *grave*; But yet for al this powerful *embalming*, this *hypostaticall union* of both natures, we see *Christ* did *dye*; and for all this *union* which made him *God* and *Man*, hee became no man (for the *union* of the *body* and *soule* makes the man, and hee whose *soule* and body are separated by death, (as long as that state lasts) is properly no man.) And therefore as in him the dissolution of *body* and *soule* was no *dissolution* of the *hypostaticall union*; so is there nothing that constraines us to say, that though the *flesh* of *Christ* had *seene corruption* and *incineration* in the grave, this had bene any *dissolution* of the *hypostaticall union*, for the *divine nature*, the Godhead might have remained with all the *Elements* and *principles* of *Christs* body, as well as it did with the two *constitutive* parts of his *person*, his *body* and his *soul*. This *incorruption* then was not in *Josephs gummes* and *spices*, nor was it in *Christs* innocency, and *exemption* from *originall sin*, nor was it (that is, it is not necessary to say it was) in the *hypostaticall union*. But this *incorruptiblenes* of his *flesh* is most conveniently plac'd in that, *Non dabis, thou wilt not suffer thy holy one to see corruption*. We looke no further for *causes* or *reasons* in the *mysteries of religion*, but to the *will* and pleasure of *God*: *Christ* himselfe limited his *inquisition* in that *ita est, even so Father, for so it seemed good in thy sight. Christs* body did *not see corruption*, therefore, because *God* had *decreed* it shold not. The humble soule (and onely the humble soule is the religious soule) rests himselfe upon *Gods* purposes, and his decrees; but then, it is upon those purposes, and decrees of *God*, which he hath declared and manifested; not such as are *conceived* and imagined in our selves, though upon some probability, some *verisimilitude*. So, in our present case, *Peter* proceeded in his *Sermon* at *Jerusalem*, and so *Paul* in *his* at *Antioch*. They preached *Christ* to have *bene risen* without seeing *corruption*, not onely because *God* had *decreed* it, but because he had *manifested* that *decree* in his *Prophet*. Therefore doth Saint *Paul* cite by special number the *second Psalme* for that *decree*; And therefore both Saint *Peter* and S. *Paul* cite for it that place in the 16. *Psalme*, for when *God* declares his *decree* and purpose in the expresse words of his *Prophet*, or when he declares it in the reall execution of the decree, then he makes it ours, then he manifests it to us. And therfore as the *Mysteries* of our *Religion*, are *not* the *objects* of *our reason*, but *by faith we rest* on *Gods decree* and purpose, (It is so, O *God*, because it is *thy will*, it should be so) so *Gods decrees* are ever to be considered in the *manifestation* thereof. All *manifestation* is either in the *word* of *God*, or in the *execution* of the *decree*; And when these two concur and meete, it is the strongest *demonstration* that can be: when therefore I finde those *markes* of *adoption* and *spirituall filiation*, which are delivered in the *word* of *God*, to be upon me, when I finde that reall *execution* of his *good purpose* upon me, as that *actually* I doe *live* under the *obedience*, and under the *conditions* which are *evidences* of *adoption* and *spirituall filiation*; then, and so long as I see these *markes* and live so, I may safely comfort my selfe in a *holy certitude* and a *modest infallibility* of my *adoption*. *Christ* determines himself in that, the purpose of *God*; because the purpose of *God* was manifest to him: S. *Peter* and S. *Paul* determine themselves in those two wayes of knowing the *purpose* of *God*, the *word* of *God* before, the *execution* of the *decree* in the *fulnes of time*. It was *prophecyed before*, say they, and it *is performed now*, *Christ is risen* without seeing corruption.

Now this which is so singularly peculiar to him, that *his flesh should not see corruption*, at his *second* coming, his coming to *Judgement*, shall extend to all that are then alive, their *flesh* shall not *see corruption*, because (as the Apostle saies, and saies as a secret, as a mystery, *behold I shew you a mystery*) *wee shall not all sleepe*, (that is, not continue in the state of the dead in the grave,) *but wee shall all be changed*. In an instant we shall have a *dissolution*, and in the *same* instant a *redintegration*, a *recompacting* of *body* and *soule*, and that shall be truely a death and truely a resurrection, but no sleeping, no corruption. But for us that dye now and sleepe in the state of the dead, we must al passe this *posthume* death, this *death* after *death*, nay this death after buriall, this *dissolution* after *dissolution*, this *death* of *corruption* and *putrifaction*, of *vermiculation* and *incineration*, of *dissolution* and *dispersion* in and *from* the grave. When those bodies that have beene the *children* of *royall parents*, and the *parents* of *royall children*, must say with *Job*, *to corruption thou art my father*, and *to the Worme thou art my mother and my sister*. *Miserable riddle*, when the *same worme* must bee *my mother*, and *my sister*, and *my selfe*. *Miserable incest*, when I must bee *maried* to my *mother* and my *sister*, and bee both *father* and *mother* to my *owne mother* and *sister*, *beget*, and *beare* that *worme* which is all that *miserable penury*; when my *mouth* shall be *filled* with *dust*, and the *worme* shall *feed*, and *feed sweetely* upon me, when the *ambitious* man shall have *no satisfaction*, if the *poorest alive* tread upon him, nor the *poorest* receive any *contentment* in being made *equall* to *Princes*, for they *shall bee equall* but *in dust*. One dyeth at his full strength, being wholly at ease and in quiet, and another dyes in the *bitternes of his soul*, and never *eates* with *pleasure*, but they lye downe *alike* in *the dust*, and the *worme covers them*; The worm covers them in *Job*, and in *Esay*, it *covers them and is spred under them*, the worme is spred *under thee*, and the worme *covers thee*; There's the *Mats* and the *Carpets* that *lye under*, and there's the *State* and the *Canapye*, that *hangs over* the greatest of the sons of men. Even those bodies that were *the temples of the holy Ghost*, come to this *dilapidation*, to ruine, to rubbidge, to dust: even the *Israel of the Lord*, and *Jacob* himselfe hath no other specification, no other denomination, but that *vermis Jacob*, thou *worme of Jacob*. Truely the consideration of this *posthume death*, this death after buriall, that after *God*, (with whom are the *issues of death*) hath delivered me from the *death* of the *wombe*, by bringing mee into the *world*, and from the manifold *deaths* of the *world*, by laying me in the *grave*, I must dye againe in an *Incineration* of this *flesh*, and in a dispersion of that dust: That that *Monarch*, who spred over many nations alive, must in his dust lye in a corner of that *sheete of lead*, and there, but so long as that lead will laste, and that privat and *retir'd man*, that thought himselfe his owne for ever, and never came forth, must in his dust of the grave bee published, and (such are the *revolutions* of the *graves*) bee mingled in his dust, with the dust of every high way, and of every dunghill, and swallowed in every puddle and pond: This is the most inglorious and contemptible *vilification*, the most deadly and peremptory *nullification* of man, that wee can consider. *God* seemes to have caried the declaration of his *power* to a great height, when hee sets the *Prophet Ezechiel* in the *valley of drye bones*, and sayes, *Sonne of man can these bones live*? as though it had bene impossible, and yet they did; The *Lord* layed *Sinewes upon them, and flesh*, and breathed into them, and *they did live*: But in that case there were *bones* to bee *seene*, something visible, of which it might be sayd, can this thing live? But in this death of *incineration*, and dispersion of dust, wee see *nothing* that wee can call *that mans*; If we say, can this dust live? perchance it *cannot*, it may bee the meere *dust* of the *earth*, which never did live, nor never shall. It may be the dust of that mans worms which did live, but shall no more. It may bee the dust of *another* man, that concernes not him of whom it is askt. This death of *incineration* and dispersion, is, to naturall *reason*, the most *irrecoverable death* of all, and yet *Domini Domini sunt exitus mortis, unto God the Lord belong the issues of death*, and by *recompacting* this *dust* into the *same body*, and *reanimating* the *same body* with the *same soule*, hee shall in a blessed and glorious *resurrection* give mee such an *issue from* this *death*, as shal never passe into any other death, but establish me into a life that shall last as long as the *Lord of life* himselfe. And so have you that that belongs to the *first acceptation* of these words, (*unto God the Lord belong the issues of death*) That though from the *wombe* to the *grave* and in the grave it selfe wee passe from *death* to *death*, yet, as *Daniel* speakes, *The Lord our God is able to deliver us, and hee will deliver us.*

And so wee passe unto our *second accommodation* of *these words* (*unto God the Lord belong the issues of death*) That it *belongs* to *God*, and *not* to *man* to *passe a judgement* upon us at our death, or to conclude a dereliction on *Gods* part upon the manner thereof.

Those *indications* which the *Physitians* receive, and those *presagitions* which they give for *death* or *recovery* in the *patient*, they receive and they give out of the grounds and the *rules of their art*: But we have no such rule or art to give a *presagition* of *spirituall death* and damnation upon any such *indication* as wee see in any *dying man*; wee see often enough to be sory, but not to despaire; for the *mercies* of *God* worke *momentarily* in minutes, and many times *insensibly* to *bystanders* or any other than the party departing, and wee may bee deceived both wayes: wee use to comfort our selves in the death of *a friend*, if it be testified that he went away like a *Lambe*, that is, without any *reluctation*. But, *God* knowes, that may bee accompanied with a *dangerous damp* and *stupefaction*, and *insensibility* of his *present state*. Our blessed *Saviour* suffered *colluctations* with *death*, and a *sadnes even in his soule to death*, and an *agony* even to a *bloody sweate* in his *body*, and *expostulations* with *God*, and *exclamations* upon the crosse. He was a *devout man*, who said upon his death bed, or death-turfe (for hee was an *Heremit*) *septuaginta annos Domino servivisti, & mori times? hast thou served a good Master three-score and ten yeares, and now art thou loath to goe into his presence?* yet *Hilarion* was loath. He was a *devout* man (an *Heremit* too) that sayd that day hee died, *Cogita te hodie cœpisse servire Domino, & hodie finiturum. Consider this to be the first days service that ever thou didst thy Master*, to glorifie him in a Christianly and a constant death, *and if thy first day be thy last day too, how soone dost thou come to receive thy wages*? yet *Barlaam* could have beene content to have stayd longer for it: Make no *ill conclusions* upon any mans *loathnes* to *dye*. And then, upon *violent deaths* inflicted, as upon malefactors, *Christ* himselfe hath forbidden us by his owne death to make any *ill conclusion*; for his owne *death* had those impressions in it; He was *reputed*, he was *executed* as a *malefactor*, and no doubt many of them who concurred to his death, did beleeve him to bee so. Of *sudden death* there are scarce examples to be found in the *scriptures* upon *good men*, for *death* in *battaile* cannot be called *sudden death*; But *God* governes not by *examples*, but by *rules*, and therefore make no *ill conclusion* upon *sudden death* nor upon distempers neyther, though perchance accompanied with some *words of diffidence* and distrust in the *mercies of God*. The *tree lyes as it falles*; 'Tis true, but yet it is *not* the *last stroake* that *fells* the *tree*, nor the *last word* nor *gaspe* that *qualifies* the *soule*. Stil *pray* wee for a *peaceable life* against *violent death*, and for *time* of *repentance* against *sudden death*, and for *sober* and *modest assurance* against *distemperd* and *diffident death*, but never make *ill conclusions* upon persons overtaken with such deaths; *Domini Domini sunt exitus mortis, to God the Lord belong the issues of death*. And *he* received *Sampson*, who went out of this world in *such a manner* (consider it *actively*, consider it *passively*, in his *owne death*, and in those whom he *slew* with himselfe) as was subject to interpretation hard enough. Yet the *holy Ghost* hath moved S. *Paul* to celebrate *Sampson* in his *great Catalogue*, and so doth all the *Church*. Our *criticall* day is *not* the *very day* of our *death*: but the whole course of our life. I thanke him that *prayes* for me when my bell tolles, but I thank him much more that *Catechises* mee, or *preaches* to mee, or *instructs mee how to live*. *Fac hoc & vives*, there's my securitie, the mouth of the *Lord hath sayd it, doe this and thou shalt live*: But *though I doe it, yet I shall dye too*, dye a bodily, a naturall death. But *God* never mentions, never seems to consider that death, the bodily, the naturall death. *God* doth not say, Live well and thou shalt dye well, that is, an easie, a quiet death; But *live well here*, and thou shalt *live well for ever*. As the first part of a sentence peeces wel with the last, and never respects, never hearkens after the *parenthesis* that comes betweene, so doth a *good life* here flowe into an *eternall life*, without any consideration, what *manner* of *death* wee dye: But whether the *gate* of *my prison* be *opened* with an *oyld key* (by a gentle and *preparing sicknes*) or the gate bee *hewen downe* by a *violent death*, or the gate bee *burnt downe* by a *raging* and *frantique feaver*, *a gate into heaven I shall have*, for *from the Lord* is the *cause* of *my life*, and *with God the Lord are the issues of death*. And further wee cary not this *second acceptation* of the *words*, as this *issue of death* is *liberatio in morte*, *Gods care* that the *soule* be *safe*, what *agonies* soever the *body suffers* in the *houre* of death; but passe to our *third part* and last part; as this *issue of death* is *liberatio per mortem*, a *deliverance by the death* of another, by the *death* of Christ.

*Sufferentiam Job audiistis, & vidistis finem Domini*, sayes Saint *James* 5. 11. *You have heard of the patience of Job*, says he, All this while you have done that, for in every man, calamitous, miserable man, a *Job* speakes; Now *see the end of the Lord*, sayth that *Apostle*, which is not that end that the *Lord* propos'd to himselfe (*salvation to us*) nor the end which he proposes to us (*conformitie to him*) but *see the end of the Lord*, sayes he, The end, *that the Lord* himselfe came to, *death*, and a painefull and a shamefull death. But why did he dye? and why dye so? *Quia Domini Domini sunt exitus mortis* (as Saint *Augustine* interpreting this *text* answeres that question) because *to* this *God our Lord belong'd the issues of death*. *Quid apertius diceretur?* sayes hee there, what can bee more obvious, more manifest than this sense of these words? In the former part of this verse, it is sayd, *He that is our God, is the God of salvation, Deus salvos faciendi*, So hee reads it, the *God* that must save us: Who can that be, sayes he, but *Jesus?* for *therefore* that *name* was *given him*, because he was to *save us*. And to this *Jesus*, sayes he, this *Saviour, belongs the issues of death; Nec oportuit eum de hac vita alios exitus habere quam mortis*. Being come into this life in our mortal nature, he could not goe out of it any other way than by Death. *Ideo dictum*, sayes he, *therefore it is sayd, To God the Lord belong the issues of death; ut ostenderetur moriendo nos salvos facturum*, to shew that his way to save us was to dye. And from this *text* doth Saint *Isiodore* prove, that Christ was *truely Man*, (which as many *sects* of *heretiques denyed*, as that he was *truely God*) because to him, though he were *Dominus Dominus* (as the *text* doubles it) *God* the *Lord*, yet to *him*, to *God the Lord belong'd the issues of death*. *Oportuit eum pati*, more can not be sayd, than *Christ* himselfe sayes of himself, *These things Christ ought to suffer*; hee had no other way but by death. So then *this part* of our *Sermon* must needes be a *passion Sermon*; since all his *life* was a *continuall passion*, all *our Lent* may well bee a *continuall good Fryday*. *Christs* painefull life tooke off none of the paines of his death, hee felt not the lesse then for having felt so much before. Nor will any thing that shall be sayd before, lessen, but rather inlarge your devotion, to that which shall be sayd of his passion at the time of the due *solemnization* thereof. *Christ* bled not a droppe the lesse at the last, for having bled at his *Circumcision* before, nor wil you shed a teare the lesse then, if you shed some now. And therefore bee now content to consider with mee how to *this God the Lord belong'd the issues of death*.

That *God*, this *Lord*, the *Lord* of *life could dye*, is a strange contemplation; That the *red Sea* could bee *drie*, That the *Sun* could *stand still*, That an *Oven* could be *seaven times heat* and *not burne*, That *Lions* could be *hungry* and *not bite*, is strange, *miraculously strange*, but *supermiraculous* that *God could dye*; but that *God would dye* is an *exaltation* of that. But even of that also it is a *super-exaltation*, that *God shold dye, must dye*, and *non exitus* (said S. *Augustin*) *God the Lord had no issue but by death*, and *oportuit pati* (says *Christ* himself) all this *Christ ought to suffer*, was bound to suffer. *Deus ultionum Deus* says *David*, *God* is the *God of revenges*, he wold *not passe* over the sin of man unrevenged, unpunished. But then *Deus ultionum libere egit* (sayes *that place*) The *God of revenges workes freely*, he *punishes*, he *spares whome he will*. And wold he *not spare himselfe*? he would not: *Dilectio fortis ut mors, love is strong as death*, stronger, it drew in death that naturally is not welcom. *Si possibile*, says Christ, *If it be possible, let this Cup passe*, when his *love expressed in a former decree* with his *Father*, had *made* it *impossible*. *Many waters quench not love*, Christ tryed many; He was *Baptized* out of his *love*, and his love determined not there; He wept over *Jerusalem* out of his love, and his love determined not there; He *mingled blood* with *water* in his *agony* and that determined not his love; hee *wept pure blood*, all his blood at all his eyes, at all his pores, in his *flagellation* and *thornes* (*to the Lord our God belong'd the issues of blood*) and these *expressed*, but these did *not quench his love*.

Hee *would not* spare, nay he *could not spare himselfe*. There was
nothing more free, more voluntary, more spontaneous than the
death of *Christ*. 'Tis true, *libere egit*, he *dyed voluntarily*, but yet
when we consider the *contract* that had passed betweene his *Father*
and *him*, there was an *oportuit*, a kind of *necessity* upon him. All
this *Christ ought to suffer*. And when whall we *date* this *obligation*, this
*oportuit*, this *necessity*? when shall wee say *that* begun? Certainly this
*decree* by which *Christ was to suffer* all this, was an *eternall decree*, and
was there any thing before that, that was eternall? *Infinite love,*
*eternall love*, he pleased to follow this home, and to consider it
seriously, that what liberty soever wee can *conceive* in *Christ*, to dye
or not to dye; this *necessity of dying*, this *decree* is as *eternall* as that
*liberty*; and yet how small a matter made hee of this *necessity* and
this *dying*? His *Father* cals it but *a bruise*, and but a *bruising of his*
*heele* (*the serpent shall bruise his heele*) and yet that was, that the *serpent*
should *practise* and *compasse* his *death*. Himselfe calls it but a *Baptisme*,
as though he were to bee the better for it. *I have a Baptisme to be*
*Baptized with*, and he was in paine till it was accomplished, and yet
this *Baptisme* was *his death*. The *holy Ghost* calls it *Joy* (*for the Joy*
*which was set before him hee indured the Crosse*) which was not a *joy* of
his reward after his passion, but a joy that filled him even in the
middest of those torments, and arose from them. When *Christ* calls
his passion *Calicem, a Cuppe*, and no worse, (*Can ye drink of my Cuppe?*)
he speakes not odiously, not with detestation of it: Indeed it was a
*Cup, salus mundo, a health to all the world*. And *quid retribuam*, says
*David, what shall I render to the Lord*? answere you with *David,*
*accipiam Calicem, I will take the Cup of salvation*; take it, that *Cup of*
*salvation*, his *passion*, if not into your *present imitation*, yet into your
*present contemplation*. And behold how that *Lord* that was *God*, yet
could *dye, would dye, must dye*, for your *salvation*.

That *Moses* and *Elias talkt with Christ* in the *transfiguration*, both
Saint *Mathew* and Saint *Marke* tel us, but what they talkt of, onely
S. *Luke, Dicebant excessum eius*, says he, *they talkt of his decease, of his*
*death* which *was to be accomplished* at *Jerusalem*. The *word* is of his
*Exodus*, the very word of our Text, *exitus*, his *issue by death*. *Moses*
who in his *Exodus* had *prefigured* this *issue of our Lord*, and in passing
*Israel* out of *Egypt* through the *red Sea*, had foretold in that actual

*prophesie, Christs passing* of *mankind through* the *sea* of his *blood,* and *Elias,* whose *Exodus* and *issue out of* this *world* was a *figure* of *Christs ascension,* had no doubt a great satisfaction in *talking* with our *blessed Lord de excessu eius,* of the *full consummation* of *all this* in *his death,* which was to bee *accomplished* at *Jerusalem.* Our *meditation* of his *death* should be more *viscerall* and affect us more because it is of a thing already done. The ancient *Romanes* had a certain tenderness, and detestation of the name of death, they cold not name death, no, not in their wills. There they could not say *Si mori contigerit,* but *si quid humanitus contingat,* not if, or when I dye, but when the course of nature is accomplished upon me. To us that speake dayly of the *death* of *Christ,* (he was *crucified, dead and buried*) can the memory or the mention of our owne *death* bee yrkesome or bitter? There are in these latter times amongst us, that name death freely enogh, and the death of *God,* but in *blasphemous oathes* and *execrations.* Miserable men, who shall therefore bee sayd never to have named *Jesus,* because they have named him *too often;* and therfore heare *Jesus* say, *Nescivi vos, I never knew you,* because they made themselves *too familiar* with him. *Moses* and *Elias* talkt with *Christ* of his *death,* only in *a holy* and *joyfull sense* of the *benefit* which *they* and *all* the world were to *receive by that. Discourses* of *Religion* should not be *out* of *curiosity,* but to *edification.* And then they talkt with *Christ* of his *death* at that time, when he was in the greatest *height* of *glory* that ever he admitted in this world, that is, his *transfiguration.* And wee are afraid to speake to the *great men* of this world of their *death,* but nourish in them a *vaine imagination* of *immortality,* and *immutability.* But *bonum est nobis esse hic* (as Saint *Peter* said there) *It is good to dwell here,* in this *consideration* of his *death,* and therefore *transferre* wee our *tabernacle* (our *devotions*) through some of those *steps* which *God* the *Lord* made to his *issue of death* that *day.*

Take in the *whole day* from the *houre* that *Christ* received the *passeover* upon *Thursday, unto* the *houre* in which hee *dyed* the *next day.* Make *this* present *day* that *day* in thy *devotion,* and consider what *hee did,* and remember what *you have done.* Before hee *instituted* and *celebrated* the *Sacrament,* (which was *after* the *eating of the passeover*) hee proceeded to that *act* of *humility,* to *wash his disciples feete,* even *Peters, who* for a while *resisted* him; In thy *preparation* to the holy and blessed *Sacrament*, hast thou with a sincere *humility* sought a *reconciliation* with all the *world*, even with those that have beene *averse* from it, and *refused* that *reconciliation* from thee? If so (and not else) thou hast spent that *first part* of this his *last day*, in a *conformity* with him. After the *Sacrament* hee spent the time till night in *prayer*, in *preaching*, in *Psalmes*; Hast thou considered that a *worthy receaving* of the *Sacrament* consists in a *continuation* of *holinesse after*, as well as in a *preparation* before? If so, thou hast therein also *conformed* thy selfe to him, so *Christ* spent his time till night. *At night* hee *went into the garden* to *pray* and he prayed *prolixius*; he spent *much time* in prayer. How much? Because it is literally expressed, that he *prayed there three severall times*, and that *returning to his Disciples* after his *first prayer*, and *finding them a sleepe* sayd, *could ye not watch with me one houre*, it is collected that he *spent three houres* in *prayer*. I dare scarce aske thee *whither* thou *wentest*, or *how* thou *disposedst* of *thy self*, when it *grew darke* and after *last night*: If that time were spent in a *holy recommendation* of thy selfe to *God*, and a *submission* of *thy will* to his, it was spent in a *conformity* to him. In that *time* and in those *prayers* was his *agony* and *bloody sweat*. I will *hope* that thou didst *pray*; but not *every ordinary* and *customary prayer*, but *prayer actually* accompanied with *shedding of teares*, and *dispositively* in a readines to *shed blood* for his *glory* in *necessary cases*, puts thee into a *conformity* with him. About midnight he was *taken* and *bound with a kisse*, art thou not *too conformable* to him in that? Is not that *too literally*, too exactly *thy case*? at *midnight* to have *bene taken* and *bound with a kisse*? From thence he was *caried back* to *Jerusalem*, first to *Annas*, then to *Caiphas*, and (as late as it was) then hee was *examined* and *buffeted*, and *delivered over* to the custody of those *officers*, from whome he received all those *irrisions*, and *violences*, the *covering of his face*, the *spitting upon his face*, the *blasphemies of words*, and the *smartnes of blowes* which that *Gospell* mentions. In which compasse fell that *Gallicinium*, that *crowing of the Cock* which *called up Peter* to his *repentance*. How thou passedst all that time last night, thou knowest. If thou didst any thing then that needed *Peters teares*, and hast *not shed them*, let me be thy *Cock*, doe it now, Now thy *Master* (in the unworthiest of his servants) *lookes back upon thee*, doe it now. *Betimes*, in the morning, so soone as it was day, the *Jewes* held *a counsell* in the *high Priests hall*, and *agreed upon their evidence* against him, and then caried him to *Pilate*, who was to be his *Judge*. Diddest thou *accuse* thy selfe when thou *wakedst this morning*, and wast thou content to admit even *false accusations* (that is) rather to *suspect actions* to have beene sin, which were not, than to *smother* and *justify* such as were *truly sins*? then thou spentst that *houre* in *conformity* to him. *Pilate* found *no evidence against him*, and therefore to ease himselfe, and to passe a *complement* upon *Herod*, *Tetrarch* of *Galilee*, who was at that time at *Jerusalem* (because *Christ* being a *Galilean* was of *Herods jurisdiction*) *Pilat sent him* to *Herod*, and rather as a *madman* than a *malefactor*, *Herod* remaunded him (*with scornes*) to *Pilat* to proceed against him; And this was about *eight* of the *clock*. Hast thou been content to come to this *Inquisition*, this examination, this agitation, this cribration, this pursuit of thy *conscience*, to *sift* it, to follow it from the *sinnes* of thy *youth* to thy *present sinnes*, from the *sinnes* of thy *bed*, to the *sinnes* of thy *boorde*, and from the *substance* to the *circumstance* of thy *sinnes*? That's *time spent* like thy *Saviours*. *Pilat* wold have *saved Christ*, by using the *priviledge* of the *day* in his behalfe, because that *day* one *prisoner was to be delivered*, but they chose *Barrabas*; hee would have *saved* him *from death*, by *satisfying their fury*, with *inflicting* other *torments* upon him, *scourging* and *crowning with thornes*, and *loading* him with many *scornefull* and *ignominious contumelies*; But this redeem'd him not, they pressed a *crucifying*. Hast thou gone about to *redeeme thy sinne*, by *fasting*, by *Almes*, by *disciplines* and *mortifications*, in the way of *satisfaction* to the *Justice* of *God*? that will not serve, that's not the right way, *wee presse* an utter *Crucifying* of that *sinne* that governes thee; and that *conformes* thee to *Christ*. Towards *noone Pilat* gave *judgement*, and they made such *hast* to execution, as that *by noone* hee was *upon the Crosse*. There now hangs that *sacred Body* upon the *Crosse*, *rebaptized* in his owne *teares* and *sweat*, and *embalmed* in his *owne blood alive*. There are those *bowells of compassion*, which are so conspicuous, so manifested, as that you may *see them through his wounds*. There those *glorious eyes* grew faint in their light: so as the *Sun ashamed* to survive them, *departed with his light too*. And then that *Sonne of God*, who was *never from us*, and yet had now come a *new way unto* us in *assuming our nature*, delivers that *soule* (which was *never out* of his *Fathers hands*) by a *new way*, a *voluntary emission* of it into his Fathers hands; For though to this *God our Lord,* *belong'd these issues of death,* so that considered in his owne contract, he *must* necessarily *dye,* yet at *no breach* or *battery,* which they had made upon his *sacred Body,* issued his soule, but *emisit,* hee *gave up the Ghost,* and as *God breathed a soule into* the *first Adam,* so this *second Adam breathed his soule into God, into the hands of God.* There wee leave you in that *blessed dependancy,* to *hang* upon *him* that *hangs* upon the *Crosse,* there *bath* in his *teares,* there *suck* at his *woundes,* and *lye downe in peace* in his *grave,* till hee vouchsafe you a *resurrection,* and an ascension into that *Kingdome,* which hee *hath purchas'd for you,* with the *inestimable price* of his *incorruptible blood.* AMEN.

# LIST OF REFERENCES

## PARADOXES AND PROBLEMS

References are to the edition published by the Nonesuch Press, 1923.

### Paradoxes

1. Pp. 1–5.
2. Pp. 6–8.
3. Pp. 9–11.
4. Pp. 12–14.
5. Pp. 15–16.
6. Pp. 17–18.
7. Pp. 19–20.
8. Pp. 21–23.
9. Pp. 24–25.
10. Pp. 26–29.
11. Pp. 30–33.

### Problems

1. P. 42.
2. P. 44.
3. Pp. 47–48.
4. P. 61.
5. P. 62.
6. Pp. 64–65.
7. P. 68.

## BIATHANATOS

References are to *ΒΙΑΘΑΝΑΤΟΣ* [1646]

1. *2v.
2. Pp. 17–24.
3. Pp. 47–48.
4. Pp. 62–63.
5. Pp. ⟨9–11.
6. Pp. 147–9.
7. Pp. 153–6.
8. Pp. 206–7.
9. Pp. 213–15.

## PSEUDO-MARTYR

References are to *Pseudo-Martyr*, 1610

1. A2–A3v.
2. q–q2
3. (i) B1v–B3v.
   (ii) C3–C4.
   (iii) E1–E2.
4. Pp. 1–2.
5. Pp. 92–95.
6. P. 357.

## IGNATIUS HIS CONCLAVE

References are to *Ignatius His Conclave*, 1611.

1. Pp. 30–38.
2. Pp. 48–95.
3. G6–G7v.

## ESSAYS IN DIVINITY

References are to the edition by Evelyn M. Simpson, 1952.

1. Pp. 20–21.
2. Pp. 36–38.
3. Pp. 39–41.
4. Pp. 43–44.
5. Pp. 48–52.
6. Pp. 63–64.
7. P. 66.
8. Pp. 74–76.
9. Pp. 79–81.
10. Pp. 81–82.
11. Pp. 96–97.
12. Pp. 97–98.
13. Pp. 98–99.
14. Pp. 99–100.

## DEVOTIONS UPON EMERGENT OCCASIONS

References are to the edition by John Sparrow, 1923.

1. Pp. 1–5.
2. Pp. 7–8.
3. Pp. 18–20.
4. Pp. 22–24.
5. Pp. 54–55.
6. Pp. 69–70.
7. Pp. 96–98.
8. Pp. 113–14.

## LETTERS

References are to *Letters to Several Persons of Honour*, 1651 (*Letters*); *A Collection of Letters made by Sir Tobie Mathews*, 1660 (*T.M. Coll.*); *The Losely Manuscripts*, edited by A. Kempe, 1835 (*Losely MSS.*); Burley MS. transcripts in E. M. Simpson, *A Study of the Prose Works of John Donne*, second edition, 1948 (*Burley MS., P.W.*).

1. *Burley MS., P.W.*, pp. 303–4.
2. *Burley MS., P.W.*, pp. 313–14.
3. *Burley MS., P.W.*, pp. 316–17.
4. *Losely MSS.*, pp. 328–30.
5. *Losely MSS.*, pp. 330–2.
6. *Losely MSS.*, pp. 332–3.
7. *Losely MSS.*, pp. 334–5.
8. *Losely MSS.*, pp. 339–40.
9. *Losely MSS.*, pp. 341–3.
10. *Losely MSS.*, pp. 343–4.
11. *Letters*, pp. 105–8.
12. *Letters*, pp. 212–13.
13. *Letters*, pp. 146–7.
14. Walton, *Life of Herbert*, 1670, p. 17.
15. *Letters*, pp. 85–88.
16. *Letters*, pp. 137–9.
17. *Letters*, pp. 48–52.
18. *Letters*, pp. 31–37.
19. *Letters*, pp. 61–64.
20. *Letters*, pp. 67–68.
21. *Letters*, pp. 160–4.
22. *Letters*, pp. 26–31.
23. *Letters*, pp. 20–21.
24. *T.M. Coll.*, pp. 67–69.
25. *Letters*, pp. 237–9.
26. *Losely MSS.*, pp. 344–5.
27. *Letters*, pp. 194–8.
28. Herbert MSS., first printed by John Hayward, *John Donne: Complete Poetry and Selected Prose*, 1929, p. 465.

29. *Letters*, pp. 100–5.
30. *T.M. Coll.*, pp. 323–7.
31. *Letters*, pp. 24–26.
32. *Letters*, pp. 21–22.
33. *T.M. Coll.*, pp. 336–7.
34. *Letters*, pp. 134–7.
35. *T.M. Coll.*, pp. 305–7.
36. *Letters*, pp. 249–50.
37. *T.M. Coll.*, pp. 296–7.

38. *Letters*, pp. 7–10; also in *T.M. Coll.*, pp. 106–8.
39. *Letters*, pp. 305–6.
40. *Letters*, pp. 306–7.
41. *Letters*, pp. 307–10.
42. *T.M. Coll.*, pp. 349–56.
43. *T.M. Coll.*, pp. 341–4.
44. *T.M. Coll.*, pp. 344–9.
45. *Letters*, pp. 241–4.
46. *Letters*, pp. 316–18.

## SERMONS

References are to volume and page of the edition of *The Sermons of John Donne*, edited by G. R. Potter and Evelyn M. Simpson, University of California Press, 1953–62.

1. (i) i. 236–7.
   (ii) i. 244–5.
   (iii) i. 248–9.
2. ii. 107–8.
3. ii. 170–1.
4. (i) ii. 197–8.
   (ii) ii. 210–11.
5. ii. 235–49.
6. (i) iii. 58–59.
   (ii) iii. 65–66.
7. (i) iii. 97.
   (ii) iii. 111–12.
8. iii. 202.
9. iii. 302–3.
10. iii. 339–40.
11. iii. 359–62.
12. (i) iv. 45.
   (ii) iv. 48–49.
   (iii) iv. 53–54.
   (iv) iv. 55–56.
13. (i) iv. 69–70.
   (ii) iv. 87.

14. (i) iv. 95–96.
   (ii) iv. 127–8.
15. iv. 162.
16. iv. 176–7.
17. v. 266–7.
18. iv. 280–1.
19. iv. 301–2.
20. (i) iv. 310.
   (ii) iv. 321–2.
21. (i) iv. 328.
   (ii) iv. 330–1.
22. v. 232–3.
23. x. 56–58.
24. (i) vi. 62–63.
   (ii) vi. 76.
   (iii) vi. 79–80.
25. vi. 161.
26. x. 189–90.
27. (i) ix. 301–2.
   (ii) ix. 310–11.
   (iii) ix. 312–13.

28. (i) ix. 401–2.
    (ii) ix. 410–11.

29. (i) vi. 170–2.
    (ii) vi. 173–5.
    (iii) vi. 184–5.

30. vi. 212–13.

31. vi. 223–4.

32. vi. 257–61.

33. vi. 265–7.

34. vi. 286–91.

35. vi. 297–8.

36. (i) vi. 316.
    (ii) vi. 323–4.

37. (i) vii. 56–57.
    (ii) vii. 68–69.

38. (i) vii. 133–5.
    (ii) vii. 137–9.

39. (i) vii. 152–3.
    (ii) vii. 156–7.

40. vii. 232–3.

41. vii. 244–5.

42. (i) vii. 257–8.
    (ii) vii. 260–1.
    (iii) vii. 264–5.
    (iv) vii. 271–8.

43. (i) vii. 279.
    (ii) vii. 282–3.
    (iii) vii. 298–9.

44. vii. 317–18.

45. (i) vii. 325–6.
    (ii) vii. 329–30.
    (iii) vii. 340.

46. (i) vii. 355–7.
    (ii) vii. 366–9.

47. (i) vii. 373–4.
    (ii) vii. 383–4.
    (iii) vii. 389–90.

48. vii. 417–18.

49. (i) x. 105–7.
    (ii) x. 110–11.

50. (i) x. 128–9.
    (ii) x. 137–8.

51. x. 149–52.

52. x. 170–2.

53. (i) viii. 41–43.
    (ii) viii. 52–53.
    (iii) viii. 59–60.

54. (i) viii. 67–69.
    (ii) viii. 88–93.

55. (i) viii. 97–98.
    (ii) viii. 106.

56. (i) viii. 174–5.
    (ii) viii. 185–7.
    (iii) viii. 188–91.

57. (i) viii. 224–5.
    (ii) viii. 232–3.

58. (i) viii. 245–6.
    (ii) viii. 249.

59. (i) viii. 277–9.
    (ii) viii. 285–7.

60. viii. 332–3.

61. (i) viii. 368–70.
    (ii) viii. 371–2.

62. (i) ix. 49–50.
    (ii) ix. 62–63.

63. (i) ix. 70.
    (ii) ix. 79–81.

64. (i) ix. 98–99.
    (ii) ix. 107–8.

65. (i) ix. 118–20.
    (ii) ix. 126–7.

66. (i) ix. 131–3.
    (ii) ix. 134.
    (iii) ix. 136–7.
    (iv) ix. 148.
    (v) ix. 153–4.

67.  (i) ix. 162–3.
     (ii) ix. 166.
     (iii) ix. 172.

68.  (i) ix. 173.
     (ii) ix. 175–7.

(iii) ix. 182–3.

69.  (i) ix. 190–2.
     (ii) ix. 208–9.

70. ix. 224.

71. x. 229–48.

PRINTED IN GREAT BRITAIN
AT THE UNIVERSITY PRESS, OXFORD
BY VIVIAN RIDLER
PRINTER TO THE UNIVERSITY